Network+ Certification Exam Guide

Network+ Certification Exam Guide

Michael Meyers
Brian Schwarz

McGraw-Hill
New York San Francisco Washington, D.C.
Auckland Bogotá Caracas Lisbon London
Madrid Mexico City Milan Montreal New Delhi
San Juan Singapore Sydney Tokyo Toronto

McGraw-Hill

A Division of The McGraw-Hill Companies

1 2 3 4 5 6 7 8 9 0 DOC/DOC 9 0 4 3 2 1 0 9

PN 0-07-134564-7

Part of 0-07-134563-9

The sponsoring editor for this book was Michael Sprague and the production supervisor was Clare Stanley. It was set in Berkeley by Patricia Wallenburg.

Printed and bound by R. R. Donnelly & Sons.

This book is printed on recycled, acid-free paper containing a minimum of 50% recycled, de-inked fiber.

Dedications

Mike's Dedication

Here's to Brian and all the good times we've had at Total. Remember listening to the '95 NBA finals driving from Dallas? Knocking down THE WALL? Debating the Law of Testosterone? Playing the Highland Games, complete with kilts? Has it really been six years?

The good bottle of port, as well as the 26 bucks, will be arriving shortly.

Brian's Dedication

Here's to Mike and all the good times we've had at Total: New Orleans casinos ($100 on red!), bloody knuckles, too much cold pizza and warm Diet Dr. Pepper, not to mention the odd crossbow, BFG, and snark. Thanks for giving me the opportunity to grow within the active culture Petri dish that is Total Seminars, and for teaching me that a good argument and a little chaos can be an opportunity, not a crisis.

And as always, I dedicate this book to my wife, Libby Ingrassia Schwarz, who supports me on every level.

Acknowledgments

Brain and I would like to make a special acknowledgment to our Editors. First is our own in-house editor, Scott Jernigan. Once again, you take our lumps of literary clay and turn them into statuesque tomes of quality work. (How does that sound Scott?) Thank you, Scott.

Next we salute Libby Ingrassia Schwarz, who once again came through in crunch time and made valuable contributions to both the writing and editing of this work. We especially want to thank Libby for writing Chapter 11, sharing her expertise in network troubleshooting.

And last but not least, we thank our editor at McGraw-Hill, Michael Sprague. Michael's job is to ensure we got the book out and by golly he did! Michael is a man of many names at Total Seminars. When this book was being written, most of the names we used for him weren't exactly printable. It's not until we proudly stare at the completed manuscript that we realize he is a really great editor. Thanks Michael—heat and pressure do make diamonds.

Contents

Introduction

Are you ready to take the plunge into the wild and woolly (and well-paid) world of network technicians? Do you already work in the field but need some credentials to prove your skill levels to potential employers? This is the book—and the certification—for you. Network+ provides a vendor-neutral certification for network technicians. Getting Network+ certified shows that you have knowledge in the Information Technology (IT) industry equivalent to the skills of techs with 18 to 24 months of experience in the field. Network+ certified technicians also prove that they know their way around TCP/IP, the protocol of the Internet. Network+ certification is the most popular new certification in the industry and this book provides an essential tool for getting Network+ certified. Are you ready?

Read This First!

There are many reasons to read this book. Maybe you have never even heard of Network+ and are curious. Perhaps you have heard about Network+ but are fishing for more information. Maybe you just want to see what skills are tested. Then again, maybe you are ready to sign up for the exam and start studying. Regardless of your motivation, you have managed to pick up the right book. You have chosen the best, most concise, and most complete Network+ certification study guide available. This book contains every piece of information you need:

- To determine if you should take the Network+ exam
- To know what you need to study
- To learn how to study for the exam
- To sign up for the exam
- To get Network+ Certified.

If you are convinced that you want to take the Network+ exam and are ready to get to work, skip to the section in this Introduction called "Network+." If you are still on the fence about the Network+ exam—here is information that you will certainly find exciting.

There has never been a more exciting time to be a computer person. The demand for those possessing any type of IT skills has grown every year for over a decade—without any sign of letting up. Money is good at every level, from application specialists to ZIP drive manufacturers. Finding a job these days seems more a matter of many companies vying for single individuals than many individuals fighting for a single job. Economy up or economy down, the demand just keeps growing and growing. It is good to be a computer person.

So what is a "computer person?" What process takes place that turns the typical person-on-the-street into one with sufficient skills to qualify for the title Computer Person? The answer starts with a question. "What kind of computer person does he or she want to be?" Does she want to be a programmer, creating applications or games? Does he want to provide application technical support, helping people who don't know how to make margins in Microsoft Word? How about being a hardware technician, replacing hard drives and installing sound cards? Maybe a network installer, configuring servers and setting up networks? Then there are always network administrators, providing the day-to-day support for those networks. This list could continue forever.

There is no one process to become a computer person. The vast span of this industry requires a conscious decision on the part of the person to select a career path, then to find the training and experience that takes him to where he wants to be. These paths are very different and not well defined. For example, most employers prefer their programmers to have a bachelor's degree in Computer Science. But a CS degree does not prove to the employer that the person knows how to write real-world programs in Visual Basic. A person who supports other users with Microsoft Word usually needs nothing more than a little practice using Word, but that does not guarantee he or she knows how to embed an Excel table in a Word document. It is difficult to define precisely what skills are needed for any particular IT job.

Traditionally, people learn enough skills for a profession by either going to school or through on-the-job training. Both of these methods are used in the IT industry, but don't give employers the one thing they need—a person who can walk up to a new position and hit the ground running. Schools provide the necessary basic, conceptual training, and jobs give good practical experience, but how can an employer know that a candidate can do a certain job? How can the candidate show the employer in no uncertain terms that he or she can do the job?

The IT industry has long appreciated this problem. The best way to prove a particular skill, regardless of how the skills were derived, is to pass a test that directly challenges those skills. If you pass the exam, you are then "certified" in that particular IT skill. Certifications first came to prominence in the 1980s when Novell created the Certified Novell Engineer (CNE) certification for Novell NetWare. Following Novell's lead, Microsoft created the Microsoft Certified Systems Engineer (MCSE) for Microsoft NT. Today, almost every software package and PC manufacturer sponsors some type of certification for hardware or software products.

All these certifications have common points. Very few require official class work. If the candidate knows the material, he or she takes the exam(s). Passing means certification. The majority of the exams are computer based. Sylvan Prometric has a near monopoly with their thousands of testing centers across the United States and overseas. A person wanting to take an exam calls Sylvan Prometric to schedule an exam and a location, pays some money and sits in front of a computer for some amount of time taking the test. The test tells the candidate immediately whether he or she has passed or failed.

Some of the more common software certifications include:

Lotus

- Certified Lotus Specialist (CLS)
- Certified Lotus Professional (CLP)

Microsoft

- Microsoft Office User Specialist (MOUS)
- Microsoft Certified Professional (CLP)
- Microsoft Certified Systems Engineer (MCSE)
- Microsoft Certified Systems Developer (MCSD)

Novell

- Certified Novell Administrator (CNA)
- Certified Novell Engineer (CNE)

Some of the more common hardware certifications* include:

Cisco

- Cisco Certified Network Associate (CCNA)
- Cisco Certified Network Professional (CCNP)
- Cisco Certified Internetwork Expert (CCIE)

Compaq

- Accredited System Engineer (ASE)

IBM

- IBM Certified Specialist
- IBM Certified Professional Server Specialist

All these certifications are vendor specific. They definitely prove the skills for their respective products and are highly sought after. If you decide to work on a specific hardware or software, you will find employers' doors opened with one or more of these certifications. These vendor-specific certifications, however, do not address one very important group of people—those who have basic skills that are not specific to any one hardware type or software package; the people, in other words, who have taken the time to understand conceptually how computers and networks operate.

These people, the "general practitioners," form the cornerstone of the IT industry. They carry screwdrivers and bootable disks in their pockets. They understand how to format hard drives. General practitioners know how to set up a Windows system to link into an NT network. They know how to set the TCP/IP information to access the Internet. They know a network cable from a telephone cable. General practitioners (GPs) define the term "computer people."

The vendor-specific certifications fail comprehensively to test these more generic skills. You cannot blame the vendors. General network skills do not enhance their bottom lines. The vendor certifications *assume* this more basic knowledge, but are only interested in how this

*Hardware certifications often have strict qualification requirements and may require hands-on demonstrations of skills.

knowledge applies to their product, not to a more general concept of computers or networks. Until recently, there were no certifications to address general skills.

By the mid '90s, IT employers began to notice this discrepancy. It was not an easy lesson to learn. Highly paid CNEs could not install a network card and MCSEs did not really understand how to install a hard drive. They did not have to know these things to pass the exams. Their lack of knowledge showed up in a very painful manner when they were put in front of real, working computers and networks. The big certification folks made the money, but it always seemed that every installed base of PCs, networked or not, had one or two GPs to help the certified folks.

The IT industry realized that it needed a general, non-vendor-specific certification desperately. Yet no single vendor had the momentum to be able to forward a standardized certification. A new body, an association with strong IT vendor support was needed to sponsor such a large undertaking. The answer was CompTIA.

Enter CompTIA

The Computing Technology Industry Association (CompTIA) is, according to their brochures, "a vendor-neutral association of over 7500 computer hardware and software manufacturers, distributors, retailers, resellers, VARs, system integrators, training, service, telecommunications and Internet companies." That's nice, but before the mid '90s, CompTIA was a small, virtually unknown association of mainly computer value added resellers (VARs) and a few original equipment manufacturers (computer makers, called OEMs), including Apple. If anybody needed qualified GPs, it was the VARs. These are the companies that installed 1500 Gateway 2000 computers for corporate accounts. They acted as the warranty centers for most brands of PCs. Working for a VAR was, and still is, a wonderful way for a computer person to see a broad cross-section of the IT industry.

Why CompTIA?

CompTIA has not yet provided an official history, but it does not take a stretch of imagination to go back to around 1993. Visualize a group of

VAR and OEM representatives sitting around a smoky bar after a particularly dull warranty meeting, drinking beers and complaining about the low quality of basic technical skills. No doubt, a CompTIA person simultaneously picking up the tab and the conversation, had the idea that put CompTIA on the map: "What if CompTIA sponsors a general, vendor-neutral certification?"

In 1993, CompTIA first offered the A+ Certification exams. After a rocky start, A+ has now become the only significant certification that tests basic PC technical skills. As of this writing, CompTIA has given over 100,000 GPs the A+ Certification. Most IT people feel that A+ is the logical first certification for the majority of people wanting an IT career.

A+ does a great job at testing the basic skills of a standalone PC, but barely touches any network issues. CompTIA knew that network skills also needed testing, but the general consensus is that CompTIA felt a serious attack on networking would be too much to fit into the "6 months' experience" goal of the A+. They were right. Another test, and a separate certification were needed.

Network+

In April 1999, CompTIA unveiled the new Network+ certification. Network+, like A+, does not support any particular vendor, hardware or software. Network+ concentrates on the skills that any good network General Practitioner (GP) with 18 to 24 months of experience should know and use almost every day. Network+ is, for the most part, a highly practical exam that is not afraid to dive into some of the more conceptual aspects of networking.

Network+ is a computer-based exam composed of 65 multiple-choice questions. You need to score a grade of 68% or better in order to pass. There are no required courses for Network+; neither are there any continuing education requirements. Once a person has passed the Network+ exam, he or she holds the certification for life.

Network+ rides on the coattails of the success of the A+ Certification program and has strong support from the networking industry, as well as from the IT industry as a whole. Some of the major players who helped in the development of Network+ include:

- 3Com Corporation

- Banyan
- Compaq Computers
- IBM
- Lotus
- Microsoft
- Novell
- US West

The demand for this certification, combined with the strong support of CompTIA, assures that Network+ will become the de facto first certification for those who wish to pursue a career in the networking field. Does Network+ guarantee a job? Of course not. But it does provide a recognized certification that will catch the eye of an employer. Get Network+ certified, you'll be glad you did.

How to Become Network+ Certified

The logistics of Network+ certification are simple. You take the test and you are Network+ certified. There are no required courses, no "CompTIA Authorized Training Centers" (although CompTIA requires a technical review on training materials that want to use the Network+ logo), and no required networking experience. CompTIA does recommend 18 to 24 months of experience (that's what the test is geared to) and taking the A+ exam before taking the Network+.

Read the word "recommend." You do not have to have experience or the A+, but take it from personal experience—they both help. The A+ Certification comes in very handy on the I/O address and IRQ type of questions. Some of the Network+ questions relating to "which type of connector is used for what device" sound as though they were taken directly from the A+ exams. Those who have experience with the A+ SCSI questions will be very happy when they see Network+. As for experience, remember that Network+ is mostly a practical exam. Those who have been "out there," supporting real networks, will find many of the questions indicative of the types of problems that actually take place on Local Area Networks (LANs). While you do not have to have experience or A+ to take the exams, you will probably have a much easier time with that experience under your belt.

The secret to becoming Network+ certified is to make a plan. Here is a 5-point plan, used by the authors and thousands of our students all over the world, which has proven to be extremely successful in getting to the big goal, certification.

1. Read the book.
2. Determine study time needed.
3. Sign up for the exam.
4. Study.
5. Take the test.

Let's look at each step in the plan.

Read This Book

The first step is to read this book, cover to cover. This is not a reference book. Each chapter is carefully designed to refer to the previous chapters. It does not matter how much network experience you have—every chapter will teach you something. Start at the beginning and read it through to the end. Don't bother with the questions at the end of the chapters or the CD-ROM. Just read. The goal here is to get a feel for how much you do not know so that you can judge how long it is going to take you to study.

Determine How Much Study Time You Need

Take a quick look at the next step. You are about to call Sylvan Prometric to schedule the exam. "Heat and pressure makes diamonds," so you need to put on a little heat here, especially if you have not taken any kind of test for a while. By scheduling the exams, you will be less tempted to play solitaire and more motivated to study.

But you will not pass the test if you're not ready. You need to be able to make a good "guesstimate" as to how long it will take you to study. Use the following chart to give yourself a feel for the number of hours of study you should put into this course.

If you don't know what a particular topic means, select None.

Start with 10 hours.

If you are not A+ certified, add 20 hours.

If you are not an MCSE (any type) or a CNE (NetWare 4 or 5), add 30 hours.

For every Core MCSE exam passed, subtract 5 hours. (If you already are an MCSE, don't add or subtract anything.)

Add hours based on the following experience:

Amount of experience	**None**	**Once or Twice**	**Every Now and Then**	**Quite a bit**
Installing structured network cabling	10	8	6	1
Installing network cards	8	7	2	1
Installing RAID devices	4	2	1	1
Building PCs from scratch	4	4	1	0
Installing NetWare 4 or 5 using IP	8	8	6	1
Installing NT Server using IP	8	8	5	1
Configuring a DHCP server	1	1	0	0
Configuring a WINS server	1	1	0	0
Configuring Internet dial-ups	5	4	2	1
Supporting an NT network	6	5	3	2
Supporting a NetWare 4 or 5 network	6	5	3	1
Supporting a UNIX network	4	4	1	1
Supporting a Windows 95/98 network	3	3	2	2
Installing/troubleshooting routers	3	3	1	1
Installing/troubleshooting hubs	2	2	1	1
Creating tape backups	1	1	0	0

A complete neophyte will need over 120 hours of study minimum.

An experienced network technician with A+ and MCSE or CNE will only need around 24 hours of study time.

Keep in mind that these are estimates. Study habits also come into play. A person with solid study habits (you know who you are) can reduce the number by 15%. People with poor study habits should increase that number by 20%.

Now you know how long you need to study for the Network+ exam. It's time to schedule your exam date.

Sign Up For the Exam

To schedule an exam, call the Sylvan Prometric registration number at 888-895-6116. Tell the appointment people your location and they will tell you the location of the closest testing center and what times are available. Location, date, and time are negotiable, so if you don't like the when or where, tell them. They are nice people and will be glad to accommodate you. They will need your social security number and some form of payment, preferably a credit card. Sylvan will accept checks, but will not schedule the exam until the payment has been received.

Let's talk about money for a moment. Here are the fees as posted by CompTIA as of the writing of the book. All prices are subject to change without notice. If CompTIA does as they did with A+, these prices will rise as Network+ gains momentum. Check with CompTIA's website (**www.comptia.org**) or call Sylvan's registration number for the latest pricing.

U.S. and Canada Pricing

Quantity	Member Price	Non-Member Price
1-50 tests	$135.00	$185.00
51-250 tests	$120.00	$170.00
251-1000	$105.00	$155.00
1000 + tests	$100.00	$150.00

Network+ is an international exam. International prices are slightly higher. For international registration, contact the local Sylvan Prometric office in the following countries:

Australia: 61-2-9414-3663
France: 33-1-4289-3122
Germany: 31-320-239-800
Japan: 813-3269-9620
Latin America/Caribbean: 410-843-4300
The Netherlands: 31-320-239-894 or 0800-55-69-66

You need not pay the full price for the exams. Most people use vouchers. You buy a voucher, and when the Sylvan Prometric appointment person asks how you will pay, you give the voucher number. Vouchers are convenient and you can usually save a few dollars. You can get discount vouchers from Sylvan Prometric by ordering in quantity at the prices shown above. Most Network+ training companies provide individual discount vouchers. Total Seminars (the authors' employer), for example, has discount vouchers for sale. Call 800-446-6004 for pricing.

Study For the Exam

The exam is scheduled. The clock is ticking and you had better be ready. Don't worry, Network+ is a (relatively) easy exam and you have the best study guide available. Time to lay down a study plan to make sure you are ready when that day comes. Here's the process.

Read the book again. This time you are not just trying to determine what you don't know, you are reading to learn. Again, read front to back, just like a novel. Don't let any terms get by you. Use the glossary in the back to make sure all new terms are clear. Use a highlighter to mark important terms and concepts. When you finish a chapter, skim back through it, mentally quizzing yourself on the highlighted terms.

Having a network available really helps. With the exception of the first few chapters, everything in the book is designed to reflect the practical, real-world nature of the Network+ exams. Even if you don't have a network, just installing a network card into a standalone PC allows you to try many aspects of networking, at least in terms of setting up drivers, protocols, etc. There is no doubt that the test skews a little bit—not a lot—towards the Microsoft world, so access to Windows 95/98 and an NT system can really help. Don't ignore NetWare. Having a NetWare server is also quite helpful. Try unplugging cables and seeing what happens to the systems and the network cards; visualize error situations, maybe even intentionally create a few, and create a method for diagnosis and repair. Don't make anything too complicated—Network+ keeps things simple. Install TCP/IP and use the many diagnostic programs on your systems. For a Windows 95/98 system, try NBTSTAT, WINIPCFG, and PING, including any special switches. Try to locate the HOSTS and LMHOSTS files. Practice makes perfect.

Once you complete a chapter, try the questions at the end of that chapter. Don't just read through them and guess. If you don't know the answer, you need to pull out the highlighter one more time and find the answer. Remember, each question builds on information from previous chapters so you may have to look in more than one place to get the answer. After you answer all the questions, then refer to the answer page. Make mental arguments for the wrong answers to confirm each correct answer. Then take each question and rephrase it to make a new question. This is a powerful strategy that really reinforces the concept—and it is fun to do with someone else studying for the exam.

After you have gone through the book and worked the questions at the end of each chapter, it is time to do the free questions on the CD-ROM. Take the exams in Final Mode first. That way, you can get your first measure of how well you are doing. If you don't like the score, take the test in Practice Mode. Use the information window to help you through the tough questions.

If you really like questions, the CD-ROM comes with extra practice exams that can be purchased over the Internet. These are not required but might be very helpful for those who like to have some extra practice.

Once you begin to score in the 90% or better range, you are ready to take the exams. How close are you to your test date? If you used the study guide to determine your hours, you are probably pretty close. Time to take the exam.

Take the Test

The most important item to remember on the day of the exam is that you are ready. The practice exams on the CD-ROM are designed closely to approximate the real exams, so you will not see anything you have not seen before. Be confident. Too many times people—especially those who have not taken a test in a while—tend to freeze up and get frazzled. There is no reason for this to happen; you have what it takes to pass this exam.

Be sure to bring two forms of ID to the testing center. You are not allowed to bring calculators, cell phones, laptops, books, or notebooks into the test. Although the testing center is supposed to provide a pencil and paper, they sometimes run out, so bring 4-5 sheets of paper and a couple of pencils for notes. CompTIA says you do not need a pen or paper—don't believe that. They are handy tools for taking any multiple-choice exam, including the Network+.

Here are some important tips on taking the Network+ exam:

1. You have an hour and a half. Most people finish in less than half that. You have plenty of time to do this exam.
2. Go through and get all the easy questions first. You can go back and forth on the test to any question, so get the easy ones out of the way first. Return to the beginning of the exam to take on the tougher questions.
3. Don't make stupid mistakes. Read the question carefully. Questions are often worded ambiguously. Watch out for "Which of the following is not" type of question.
4. There have been complaints to CompTIA that say the test is rife with poor grammar and even a few typos. Fortunately, they do not seem to detract from the questions or answers too much, but they can slow you down. While CompTIA will fix these eventually, it probably won't be very soon. Live with it.
5. The second pass will take the longest. First, many of the questions that seemed difficult will seem easier since other questions have already answered them. Check the time remaining; you should have plenty left. Your goal here is to answer *all* of the questions. Use the Mark feature to mark the questions you are not sure about. Then write down the question number and all the possible answers on the paper and move on.
6. All multiple-choice questions usually have at least one answer, sometimes two that are just flat wrong. You don't lose marks for wrong answers, so it is best to complete every question, even if you are just guessing. Remember, you have a 25% chance of getting a four-answer question right.
7. Time for the third and last pass. Don't look at the questions that are not marked. You will start second guessing—turning more right answers wrong than wrong answers right. Stick to the marked questions. Look at the other possible answers that you wrote down on the sheet. If you have the time, go slowly and really study them. Close your eyes and dream about reading the book for the answer, trying to remember the graphic that accompanied the text. This really works.

8. When you are done, you are done. Don't dally around staring at the END TEST button. You will instantly get your score.
9. Enjoy your new certification. Go get your beverage of choice and celebrate!

This certification process has helped thousands of students get certified. Use it. And remember, the goal is to pass the Network+ exam.

Objectives

CompTIA has published a set of 12 test objectives for the exam. While these objectives are tested in detail, two words define the Network+ exam: Clients and TCP/IP. A qualified candidate for the Network+ will be able to install and configure a PC to connect to a network. This includes installing and testing a network card, configuring drivers, and loading all network software. Network+ wants the candidate to know about servers, but not to be able to do anything with them. That is the job of the CNE and MCSE certifications. As for TCP/IP, Network+ tests on the ability to configure a network client PC properly with TCP/IP, especially understanding the many TCP/IP terms like "DHCP" and "subnet mask." People should also be able to configure a Windows 95/98 client to use a TCP/IP network—and understand why they are doing what they are doing.

Network+ loves troubleshooting. Many of the test objectives deal with direct, real-world troubleshooting. Be prepared for hardware and software failures, both from a "what do you do next" to a "what is probably the problem" standpoint.

The one place where the test gets conceptual is the popular OSI seven-layer model. While this model rarely comes into play during the daily grind of supporting a network, it does give a solid conceptual feel for the many hardware and software components that make up a network. Understanding OSI alone does not fix networks, but understanding OSI makes it easier for the network technician to zero in on problems to fix networks faster. Know the OSI seven-layer model.

CompTIA breaks down the Network+ objectives as follows:

Objectives in Brief

I. Knowledge of Networking Technology	77%
1. Basic Knowledge	18
2. Physical Layer	6
3. Data-link Layer	5
4. Network Layer	5
5. Transport Layer	5
6. TCP/IP Fundamentals	16
7. TCP/IP Suite: Utilities	11
8. Remote Connectivity	5
9. Security	6
II. Knowledge of Networking Practices	23%
1. Implementing the Installation of the Network	6
2. Maintaining and Supporting the Network	6
3. Troubleshooting the Network	11

Objectives in Detail

I. Knowledge of Networking Technology (77%)

I.1 Basic Knowledge (18%)

I.1.1 Demonstrate understanding of basic network structure, including:

- The characteristics of star, bus, mesh, and ring topologies, their advantages and disadvantages
- The characteristics of segments and backbones.

I.1.2 Identify the following:

- The major network operating systems, including Microsoft Windows NT, Novell NetWare, and UNIX
- The clients that best serve specific network operating systems and their resources
- The directory services of the major network operating systems.

I.1.3 Associate IPX, IP, and NetBEUI with their functions.

I.1.4 Define the following terms and explain how each relates to fault tolerance or high availability:

- Mirroring

- Duplexing
- Striping
- Volumes
- Tape backup

I.1.5 Define the layers of the OSI model and identify the protocols, services, and functions that pertain to each layer.

I.1.6 Recognize and describe the following characteristics of networking media and connectors:

- The advantages and disadvantages of coax, CAT 3, CAT 5, fiber optic, UTP, and STP, and the conditions under which they are appropriate
- The length and speed of 10Base2, 10BaseT, and 100BaseT
- The length and speed of 10Base5, 100BaseVGAnyLAN, 100BaseTX
- The visual appearance of RJ 24 (sic) and BNC and how they are crimped.

NOTE

While CompTIA uses the term RJ 24, everyone else uses RJ-45. CompTIA is incorrect on this one—just watch out for any question that refers to RJ 24.

I.1.7 Identify the basic attributes, purpose, and function of the following network elements:

- Full- and half-duplexing
- WAN and LAN
- Server, workstation, and host
- Server-based networking and peer-to-peer networking
- Cable, NIC, and router
- Broadband and baseband
- Gateway, as both a default IP router and as a method to connect dissimilar systems or protocols.

I.2 Physical Layer (6%)

I.2.1 Given an installation, configuration, or troubleshooting scenario, select an appropriate course of action if a client workstation does not connect to the network after installing or replacing a network interface card. Explain why a given action is warranted. The following issues may be covered:

- Knowledge of how the network card is usually configured, including EPROM, jumpers, and plug-and-play software
- Use of network card diagnostics, including the loopback test and vendor-supplied diagnostics
- The ability to resolve hardware resource conflicts, including IRQ, DMA, and I/O Base Address.

I.2.2 Identify the use of the following network components and the differences between them:

- Hubs
- MAUs
- Switching hubs
- Repeaters
- Transceivers

I.3 Data-Link Layer (5%)

I.3.1 Describe the following data-link layer concepts:

- Bridges, what they are and why they are used
- The 802 specs, including the topics covered in 802.2, 802.3, and 802.5
- The function and characteristics of MAC addresses.

I.4 Network Layer (5%)

I.4.1 Explain the following routing and network layer concepts, including:

- The fact that routing occurs at the network layer
- The difference between a router and a brouter
- The difference between routable and nonroutable protocols
- The concept of default gateways and subnetworks
- The reason for employing unique network IDs
- The difference between static and dynamic routing.

I.5 Transport Layer (5%)

I.5.1 Explain the following transport layer concepts:

- The distinction between connectionless and connection transport
- The purpose of name resolution, either to an IP/IPX address or a network protocol.

I.6 TCP/IP Fundamentals (16%)

I.6.1 Demonstrate knowledge of the following TCP/IP fundamentals:

- The concept of IP default gateways
- The purpose and use of DHCP, DNS, WINS, and HOSTS files
- The identity of the main protocols that make up TCP/IP suite, including TCP, UDP, POP3, SMTP, SNMP, FTP, HTTP, and IP
- The idea that TCP/IP is supported by every operating system and millions of hosts worldwide
- The purpose and function of Internet domain name server hierarchies (how e-mail arrives in another country).

I.6.2 Demonstrate knowledge of the fundamental concepts of TCP/IP addressing, including:

- The A, B, and C classes of IP addresses and their default subnet mask numbers
- The use of port number (HTTP, FTP, SMTP) and port numbers commonly assigned to a given service.

I.6.3 Demonstrate knowledge of TCP/IP configuration concepts including:

- The definition of IP proxy and why it is used
- The identity of the normal configuration parameters for a workstation, including IP address, DNS, default gateway, IP proxy configuration, WINS, DHCP, host name, and Internet domain name.

I.7 TCP/IP Suite: Utilities (11%)

I.7.1 Explain how and when to use the following TCP/IP utilities to test, validate, and troubleshoot IP connectivity:

- ARP
- Telnet
- NBTSTAT
- TRACERT
- NETSTAT
- Ipconfig/winipcfg
- FTP
- PING

I.8 Remote connectivity (5%)

I.8.1 Explain the following remote connectivity concepts:

- The distinction between PPP and SLIP
- The purpose and function of PPTP and the conditions under which it is useful
- The attributes, advantages, and disadvantages of ISDN and PSTN (POTS).

I.8.2 Specify the following elements of dial-up networking:

- The modem configuration parameters that must be set, including serial port IRQ, I/O address and maximum port speed
- The requirements for a remote connection.

I.9 Security (6%)

I.9.1 Identify good practices to ensure network security, including:

- Selection of a security model (user and share level)
- Standard password practices and procedures
- The need to employ data encryption to protect network data
- The use of a firewall.

II. Knowledge of Networking Practices (23%)

II.1 Implementing the Installation of the Network (6%)

II.1.1 Demonstrate awareness that administrative and test accounts, passwords, IP addresses, IP configurations, relevant SOPs, etc., must be obtained prior to network implementation.

II.1.2 Explain the impact of environmental factors on computer networks. Given a network installation scenario, identify unexpected or atypical conditions that could either cause problems for the network or signify that a problem condition already exists, including:

- Room conditions (e.g., humidity, heat, etc.)
- The placement of building contents and personal effects (e.g., space heaters, TVs, radios, etc.)
- Computer equipment
- Error messages.

II.1.3 Recognize visually, or by description, common peripheral ports, external SCSI (especially DB-25 connectors), and common network components, including:

- Print servers
- Peripherals
- Hubs
- Routers
- Brouters
- Bridges
- Patch panels
- UPSs
- Token Ring media filters.

II.1.4 Given an installation scenario, demonstrate awareness of the following compatibility and cabling issues:

- NICs
- The consequences of trying to install an analog modem in a digital jack
- That the uses of RJ-45 connectors may differ greatly depending on the cabling
- That patch cables contribute to the overall length of the cabling segment.

II.2 Maintaining and Supporting the Network (6%)

II.2.1 Identify the kinds of test documentation that are usually available regarding a vendor's patches, fixes, upgrades, etc.

II.2.2 Given a network maintenance scenario, demonstrate awareness of the following issues:

- Standard backup procedures and backup media storage practices
- The need for periodic application of software patches and other fixes to the network
- The need to install anti-virus software on the server and workstations
- The need of frequent updating of virus signatures.

II.3 Troubleshooting the Network (11%)

II.3.1 Identify the following steps as a systematic approach to identifying the extent of a network problem, and, given a problem scenario, select the appropriate next step based on this approach:

1. Determine whether the problem exists across the network

2. Determine whether the problem is workstation, workgroup, LAN, or WAN
3. Determine whether the problem is consistent and replicable and
4. Use standard troubleshooting methods.

II.3.2 Identify the following steps as a systematic approach to determining whether a problem is attributable to the operator or the system, and, given a problem scenario, select the appropriate next step based on this approach:

1. Identify the exact issue
2. Recreate the problem
3. Isolate the cause
4. Formulate a correction
5. Implement the correction
6. Test
7. Document the problem and the solution
8. Give feedback.

II.3.3 Identify the following steps as a systematic approach to determining whether a problem is attributable to the operator or the system, and, given a problem scenario, select the appropriate next step based on this approach:

1. Have a second operator perform the same task on an equivalent workstation
2. Have a second operator perform the same task on the original operator's workstation
3. See whether operators are following standard operating procedure.

II.3.4 Given a network troubleshooting scenario, demonstrate awareness of the need to check for physical and logical indicators of trouble, including:

- Link lights
- Power lights
- Error displays
- Error logs and displays
- Performance monitors.

II.3.5 Given a network problem scenario, including symptoms, determine the most likely cause or causes of the problem based on the available information. Select the most appropriate course of action based on this inference. Issues that may be covered include:

- Recognizing abnormal physical conditions
- Isolating and correcting problems in cases where there is fault in the physical media (patch cable)
- Checking the status of servers
- Checking for configuration problems with DNS, WINS, HOSTS file
- Checking for viruses
- Checking the validity of the account name and password
- Rechecking operator logon procedures
- Selecting and running appropriate diagnostics.

II.3.6 Specify the tools that are commonly used to resolve network equipment problems. Identify the purpose and function of common network tools, including:

- Crossover cable
- Hardware loopback
- Tone generator
- Tone locator (fox and hound).

Seems like a tall order? Don't let this big list fool you. CompTIA almost gives the test away with such a detailed objective list. The book covers all these items in great detail.

Critical Contact Information

For non-technical information about Network+:

Tancy Stanbery— Network+ Certification
CompTIA
450 East 22nd St., Suite 230
Lombard, IL 60148-6158

(Be aware that CompTIA people tend to come and go—the names may change.)

http://www.comptia.org
e-mail: **tstanbery@comptia.org**
telephone: (630) 268-1818 ext. 354

For more technical questions about the Network+ exam access the CompTIA website or e-mail **questions@comptia.org**.

To register for the exams:

Sylvan Prometric: (888) 895-6116

Or register online:

http://www.2test.com

A Closing Note

Before you get started on the book, the authors, Mike Meyers and Brian Schwarz, want to thank you for getting the *Network+ Exam Guide*. We are very interested in your success in passing the Network+ exam and would love to hear from you. Should you have any questions, please e-mail us directly at **total23@totalsem.com**. We love to talk tech and we usually reply that same day.

Good luck!

Network+ Certification Exam Guide

Chapter 1

Bus Topologies and Ethernet

Why do we build networks? What benefits do they provide? The simple answer is access to resources. A *resource* is anything that exists on another computer that a person wants to use without getting up and going to that computer. The most common network resources are files and printers.

Network designers and administrators strive to create an ideal world, where users (the people who actually sit at computers and try to get real work done) can sit at their terminals and access any information or device without getting up. Need to print to the printer on the other side of the hallway? No problem, just print and it will be there. Need to look up information in a company database stored on a machine sitting in the basement of your building? No problem, just double-click on the shortcut sitting on your desktop, and the database magically opens. In the ideal networked environment, users rise from their chairs for only two reasons: to get coffee and to answer the call of nature.

Our job as network techs is to bring the networks we build, support, and maintain as close to that ideal as possible. Using a variety of tools with arcane names such as Ethernet, Token Ring, routers, 10BaseT, etc., techs strive to build networks where end users can concentrate on doing whatever it is they do best: let Bob the accountant be the best accountant he can be!

In the ideal world, the network would function so smoothly that Bob would not even notice it was there. Fortunately for those of us who work as network techs, this utopia does not exist. Otherwise, we would be unemployed.

As you delve into the details of computer networking, keep the goal in mind—enabling users to access resources and get work done. Before they can get work done across the network, you have to build the network. To accomplish this goal you must first decide what network topology to use.

What Does "Topology" Mean?

Topology is a general description of how computers connect to each other without regard to how they actually communicate. The most common network topologies are bus, ring, star, and mesh. Figure 1.1 shows a *bus topology*, where all computers connect to the network via a central bus cable. In a *ring topology*, all the computers on the network attach to a central ring of cable, as shown in Figure 1.2. In a *star topology*, the computers on the network connect to a central wiring point, as shown in Figure 1.3. Finally, Figure 1.4 shows a *mesh topology*, where each computer has a dedicated line to every other computer. Mesh topologies rarely appear in the real world because of the excessive number of cables involved. All these topologies will rear their ugly heads again during the course of your Network+ studies, but for the remainder of Chapter 1, we will concentrate on the bus topology and its most common implementation—Ethernet.

FIGURE 1.1
A bus topology: computers attached to a single bus wire.

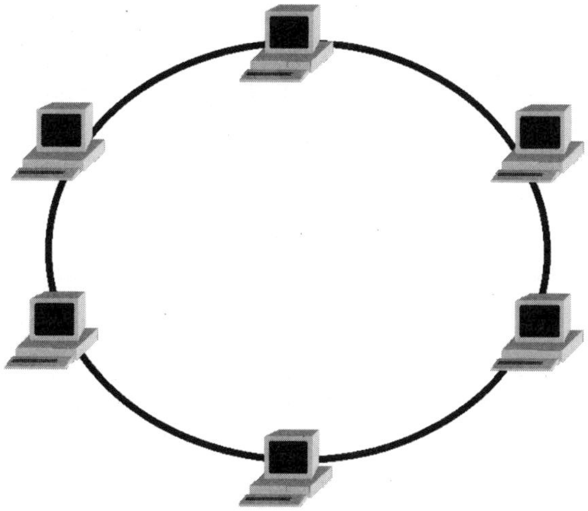

FIGURE 1.2
A ring topology: computers attached to a ring of wire.

Bus Topology

The term *bus topology* describes a network that consists of some number of machines connected by a single piece of cable that has ends (as opposed to looping around to form a ring). In a bus topology, each machine connects to the network via the same piece of cable. Notice that this definition of a bus topology leaves a lot of questions unanswered. What is the cable made of? How long can it be? How do the machines decide which machine should send data at a specific moment? A network based on a bus topology can answer these questions in a number of different ways. For answers to these questions, you have to look to a specific technology such as *Ethernet*, the most common technology based on a bus topology.

FIGURE 1.3

A star topology: computers arranged like points on a star around a central point.

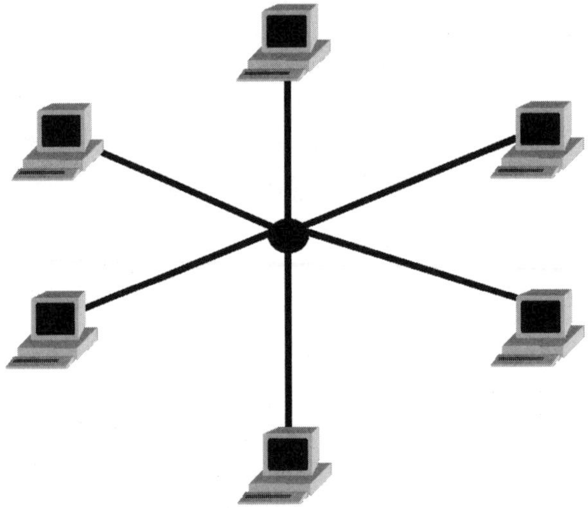

FIGURE 1.4

A mesh topology: computers with dedicated connections to every other.

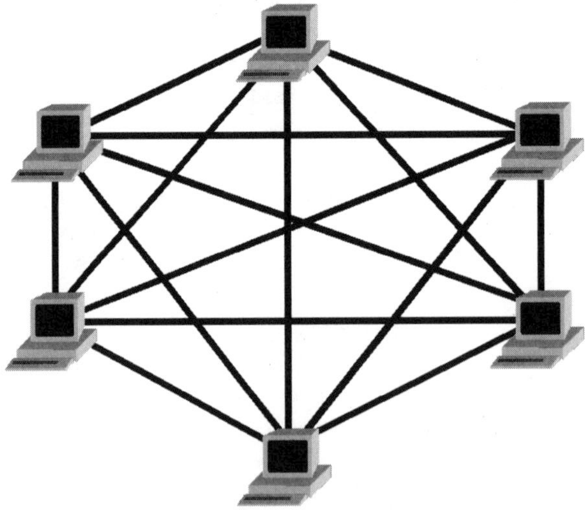

NOTE

A *bus topology* refers to any network that connects all machines on the network to a single piece of cable.

Ethernet refers to a particular set of technologies and standards for networking that uses a bus topology.

What Is Ethernet?

In the beginning, there were no networks. Life was bad. To move a file from one machine to another, we had to use *sneakernet*. In other words, we put the data on a floppy disk, laced up our tennis shoes and walked it across the floor. Despite the health benefits of all that walking, the increasing need to transfer data between computers created the need for a replacement for sneakernet. In 1973, Xerox answered this challenge with Ethernet, a networking technology based on a bus topology.

The original Ethernet used a single piece of coaxial cable to connect several computers, allowing them to transfer data at up to 3 megabits per second. While slow by today's standards, this early version of Ethernet provided the foundation for all later versions of Ethernet.

Ethernet remained a largely in-house technology within Xerox until 1979, when Xerox decided to look for partners to help promote Ethernet as an industry standard. Working with Digital Equipment Corporation (DEC) and Intel, they published what became the DIX (Digital-Intel-Xerox) standard. Running on coaxial cable, the DIX standard allowed multiple computers to communicate with each other at 10 megabits/second. While 10 Mb/s represents the low end of standard network speeds today, at the time it was revolutionary.

IEEE and the 802 Standards

By the early 1980s, the IEEE 802.3 standard for Ethernet supplanted the DIX standard for Ethernet. The *Institute of Electrical and Electronics Engineers (IEEE)* defines industry-wide standards that promote the use and implementation of technology. Rather than keeping the Ethernet standard as a proprietary standard, Xerox ceded control of the standard to the IEEE.

IEEE committees define standards for a wide variety of electronics. The names of these committees are often used to refer to the standards that they publish. The IEEE 1284-committee, for example, sets standards for parallel communication. Have you ever seen a printer cable marked "IEEE 1284 compliant," as in Figure 1.5? That means the manufacturer followed the rules set by the IEEE 1284 committee. Another committee you may have heard of is the IEEE 1394 committee, which controls the FireWire standard.

FIGURE 1.5
An IEEE 1284-compliant printer cable.

The IEEE 802 committee sets the standards for networking. Although the committee was originally created to define a single, universal standard for networking, it quickly became apparent that no single solution would work for all needs. The 802 committee was split up into smaller subcommittees, with names such as IEEE 802.3 and IEEE 802.5. Table 1.1 shows the currently recognized IEEE 802 subcommittees.

TABLE 1.1
IEEE 802 subcommittees

IEEE 802.1	Higher Layer LAN Protocols
IEEE 802.2	Logical Link Control
IEEE 802.3	CSMA/CD (a.k.a. Ethernet)
IEEE 802.4	Token Bus
IEEE 802.5	Token Ring
IEEE 802.6	MAN (Metropolitan Area Network)
IEEE 802.7	Broadband
IEEE 802.8	Fiber Optic
IEEE 802.9	Isochronous LAN
IEEE 802.10	Security
IEEE 802.11	Wireless
IEEE 802.12	Demand Priority/100baseVG
IEEE 802.13	*Not used*
IEEE 802.14	Cable Modems

Some of these committees deal with technologies that were not entirely successful, and the committees associated with those standards—such as IEEE 802.4 Token Bus—have become dormant. When preparing for the Network+ exam, concentrate on the IEEE 802.2, IEEE 802.3, and IEEE 802.5 standards. The others rarely have direct impact on the life of a network tech. (Chapters 1 and 2 will cover IEEE 802.3, Chapter 3 will cover IEEE 802.5 Token Ring, and Chapter 5 will discuss the IEEE 802.2 Logical Link Control standard.)

Ethernet or IEEE 802.3?

Today the IEEE 802.3 standard has completely supplanted the original Ethernet standard, and the term Ethernet refers to any network based on the IEEE 802.3 standard. Occasionally, there will be references that imply that IEEE 802.3 and Ethernet are not the same thing. Technically, that might be true. For many years, Ethernet referred specifically to the original Xerox Ethernet standard, whereas IEEE 802.3 referred to the standard set forth by the IEEE some years later. The IEEE 802.3 standard differed in a few relatively minor details from the original Xerox standard, and early on it was important for the designers of certain pieces of software and hardware to make a distinction about which standard they were following. Someone who corrects you when you use the term Ethernet to refer to the IEEE 802.3 standard, is technically correct. Those who do it often, will prove Grandma Erna's golden rule: "You might be right, but you won't have any friends." The remainder of this book follows common parlance and uses the terms Ethernet and IEEE 802.3 interchangeably.

How Ethernet Works

The designers of Ethernet faced the same challenges that face the designers of any network. They had to decide how to send data across the wire, how to identify the sending and receiving computers, and how to determine which computer should use the shared cable next. The engineers resolved these issues by using packets for data that contain MAC addresses to identify computers on the network, and utilizing a process called CSMA/CD to determine which machine should access the wire at any given time. What follows is an overview of each of these solutions.

Organizing the Data: Packets

All computer networks break data transmitted between computers into smaller pieces called *packets*. Using packets addresses two issues for Ethernet networks. First, it prevents any single machine from monopolizing the shared bus cable. Second, packets make the process of retransmitting lost data more efficient.

The process of transferring a large word processing document between two computers illustrates these two issues. First, if the sending computer sends the document as a single piece, it will monopolize the cable and prevent other machines from using it. Using packets allows computers to share the cable, each computer sending a few pieces of data whenever it has access to the cable. Second, in the real world bad things can happen to good data. When errors occur during transmission, only the damaged packets need to be retransmitted. If the large word processing document had been transmitted as a single piece, the entire file would need to be retransmitted. Breaking the file up into smaller packets allows a computer to retransmit only the damaged portion. Because of the benefits of allowing shared access and reducing the retransmission of data, virtually all networking technologies use packets.

An Ethernet packet contains four basic pieces of information: the actual data to be sent, the MAC (Media Access Control) address of the packet's source, the MAC address of the intended recipient, and a Cyclic Redundancy Check (CRC) code. Figure 1.6 shows a simplified data packet.

NOTE

For a more detailed look at the actual structure of an Ethernet packet, see Chapter 5 and the discussion of the relationship between IEEE 802.3 and IEEE 802.2.

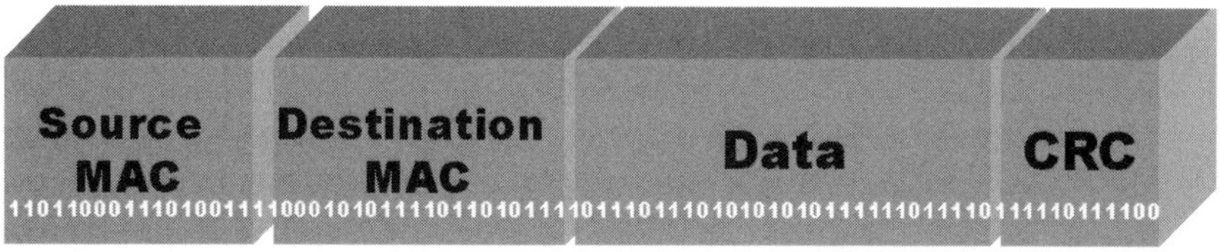

FIGURE 1.6
A simplified look at an Ethernet packet.

MAC Addresses

Ethernet requires that each computer, called a *node*, have a unique identifying address. While human beings tend to refer to machines by names ("the server," ACCOUNTING7, etc.), computers communicate using strings of ones and zeroes known as binary code. Ethernet uses special 48-bit addresses known as *MAC addresses* to identify all machines on the network. Every network card has a unique MAC address.

A 48-bit address provides for 2^{48} (281,474,976,710,656) possible MAC addresses, which means that an Ethernet network can conceivably have more than 281 trillion machines! (Other factors limit Ethernet networks to a much smaller size.) The machine used to write this paragraph has a Linksys PCMCIA Ethernet card in it whose MAC address is 0000000011100000100110000000000010000100100001110. Just try saying that three times fast! To make it easier for network technicians to talk about MAC addresses, the addresses are usually written in hexadecimal notation. Instead of writing

000000001110000010011000000000001000010010000111 0, simply write 00 E0 98 01 09 0E. While not the easiest thing to say out loud or write down, the hexadecimal number is certainly easier to deal with than its binary equivalent.

NOTE

Every device that has a MAC address is called a *node*.

MAC addresses serve a function on an Ethernet network very similar to the function provided by I/O addresses within an individual PC. I/O addresses provide a way for the CPU to identify each device in the computer, and every device (sound card, network card, hard drive controller, etc.) must have a unique I/O address. If two devices share the same I/O address, neither can function properly. Whenever the CPU attempts to send a command to one of the devices, both devices would respond, causing a conflict. The two devices would "talk over" each other, making both of their responses to the CPU unintelligible, just as two people trying to talk at the same time can fail to communicate. See Figure 1.7. In the same way, two devices on a network that share the same MAC address would prevent communication from taking place, as shown in Figure 1.8.

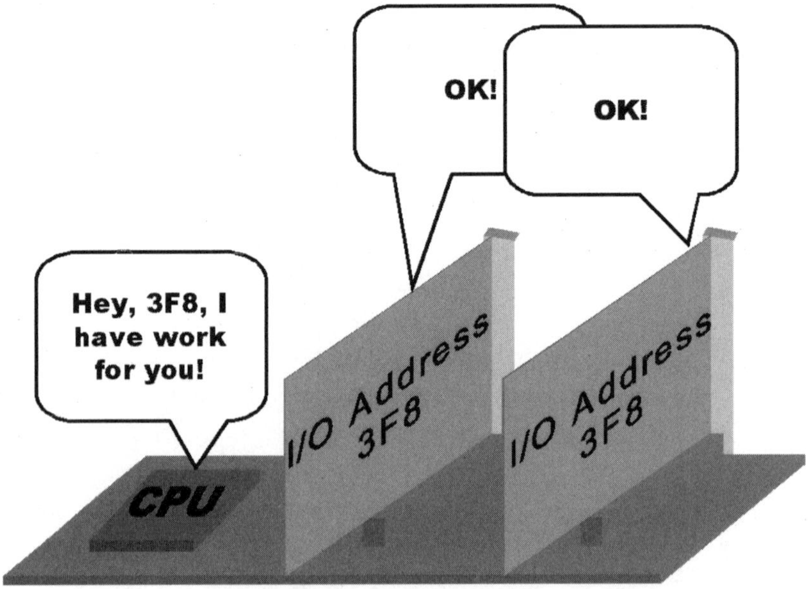

FIGURE 1.7
Two devices that share the same I/O address in a PC cause a conflict, preventing effective communication from taking place.

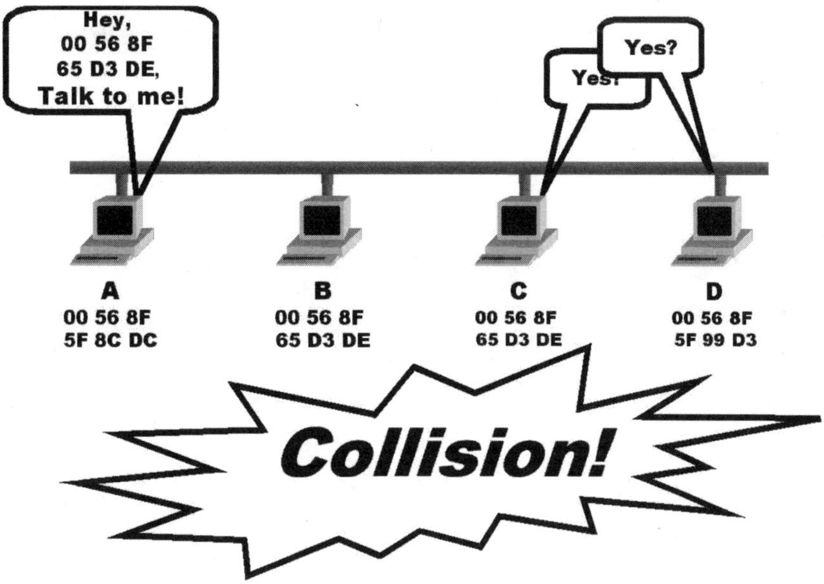

FIGURE 1.8
Two devices sharing the same MAC address would prevent either from communicating effectively.

Because the pool of possible MAC addresses is so large, the IEEE has taken on the job of ensuring that no two network interface cards (NICs) ever share the same MAC address. Network interface card manufacturers must apply to the IEEE for a block of MAC addresses. Before manufacturing the Ethernet card used in the previous example, Linksys applied to the IEEE for a block of addresses and was assigned all addresses that match the form 00 E0 98 *xx xx xx*. The IEEE assigned Linksys the first 24 bits, and made it their responsibility to ensure that every NIC they manufactured had a unique address between 00 E0 98 00 00 01 and 00 E0 98 FF FF FE. If Linksys ever exhausts this pool of 2^{24} addresses (approximately 16 million), they can apply to the IEEE for more.

To determine the MAC address of a specific NIC, use the diagnostic utility that came with the card, as shown in Figure 1.9. On Windows 95 or Windows 98 systems running the TCP/IP protocol, you can also run the WINIPCFG program to determine a card's MAC address, as shown in Figure 1.10. On Windows NT systems, the IPCONFIG command line utility, shown in Figure 1.11, displays the same information. As a last resort, look at the NIC itself. Many manufacturers will place a MAC address label on the card as shown in Figure 1.12.

FIGURE 1.9

Most NIC setup disks include a diagnostic utility that will display the MAC address of the NIC.

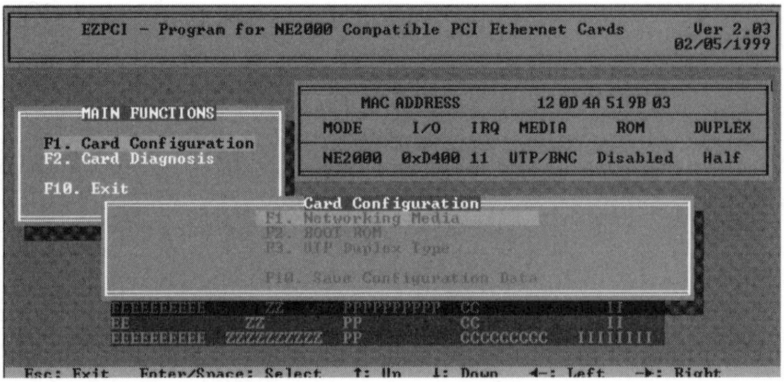

FIGURE 1.10

The WINIPCFG program displays the MAC address of the NIC.

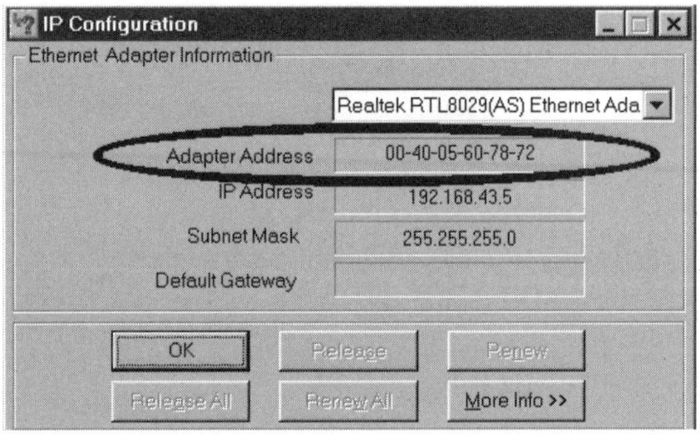

FIGURE 1.11

The Windows NT command line utility IPCONFIG also displays the MAC address of the card.

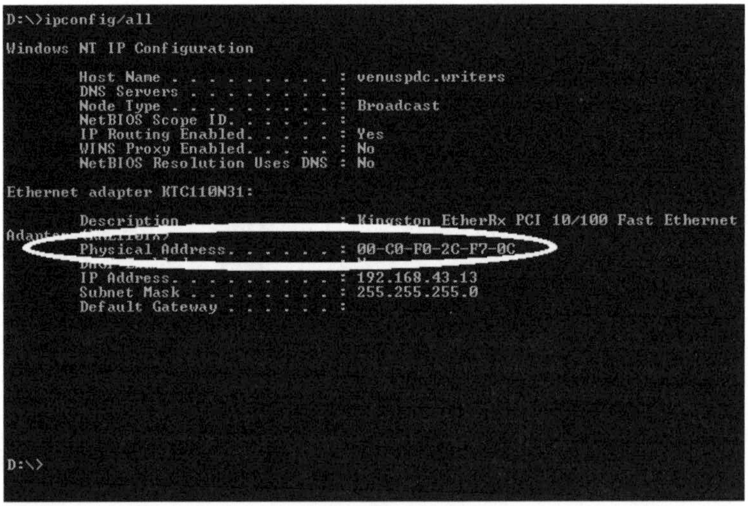

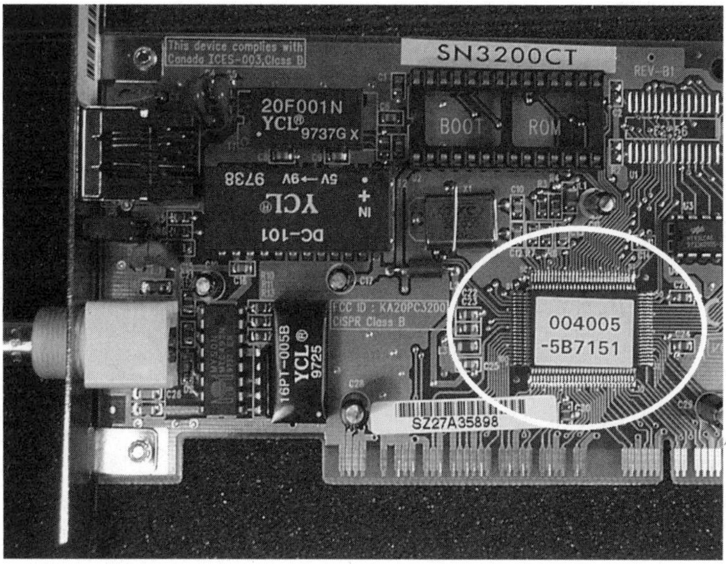

FIGURE 1.12
Most NICs will have the MAC address labeled on the card itself.

Using MAC Addresses

MAC addresses allow each machine on the network to determine which data packets to process. When a computer sends out a data packet, it transmits it across the wire in both directions, as shown Figure 1.13. All the other computers on the network listen to the wire and examine the packet to see if it contains their MAC address. If it does not, they ignore the packet. If a machine sees a packet with its MAC address, it opens the packet and begins processing the data.

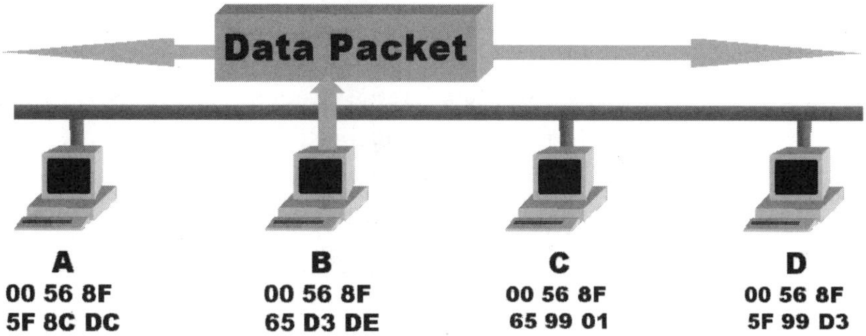

FIGURE 1.13
A computer on the network sends out a packet.

This system of allowing each machine to decide which packets to process does not provide any security. Keep in mind that any device that can connect to the network cable can conceivably capture any data packet transmitted across the wire. Many network diagnostic programs, commonly referred to as *packet sniffers*, can tell a NIC to run in *promiscuous mode*. Running in promiscuous mode, the computer will process all packets it sees on the cable, regardless of the specified MAC addresses. Packet sniffers can be valuable troubleshooting tools in the right hands, but Ethernet provides no protections against unscrupulous use. If security of the data is important, consider installing some type of additional encryption software to safeguard the data.

NOTE

MAC stands for Media Access Control, which simply means that the MAC address has something to do with how machines on the network control access to the network cable (the "media"). Don't worry about what MAC stands for. Just remember that the MAC address is a unique identifier for each machine on the network.

NOTE

Don't confuse MAC addresses with IP addresses, which serve a different purpose. See Chapter 7 for more detail about the relationship between MAC addresses and IP.

CRC (Cyclic Redundancy Check) Error Correction

The CRC code in a data packet enables Ethernet nodes to deal with the fact that sometimes bad things happen to good data. Machines on the network must be able to detect when data packets have been damaged in transit. In order to detect errors, the computers on an Ethernet network attach a special code to each packet. When creating an Ethernet packet, the sending machine runs the data through a special mathematical formula and attaches the result, called the *Cyclic Redundancy Check (CRC)*, to the packet. The receiving machine opens up the packet, performs the same calculation, and compares its answer with the one included with the packet. If the CRC codes do not match, the receiving machine will ask the sending machine to retransmit that packet. Keeping packets small reduces the time required to retransmit data following an error.

At this point, those crafty network engineers have solved two of the problems they faced. Data packets organize the data to be sent and MAC addresses identify machines on the network. But the challenge of determining which machine should send data at which time required another solution: CSMA/CD.

CSMA/CD or Who Gets to Send the Next Packet?

Ethernet networks use a system called *Carrier Sense, Multiple Access/ Collision Detection (CSMA/CD)* to determine which computer should use the shared cable at a given moment. "Carrier sense" means that each machine on the network, referred to as a *node*, examines the cable before sending a data packet. See Figure 1.14. If another machine is using the network, the node will detect traffic and wait until the cable is free. If it detects no traffic, the node will send out its data packet. Carrier sense is analogous to the process of trying to get an outside phone line in a large office building. To make a call, pick up the phone, press a button, and listen. If there is a dial tone (i.e. the line is free), make the call. If you hear a busy signal (i.e. someone else is already using the line), wait your turn.

FIGURE 1.14
A node on an Ethernet network listens for traffic before it sends out a data packet.

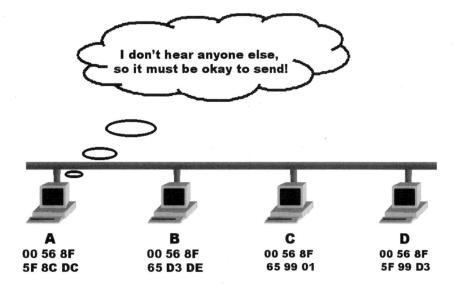

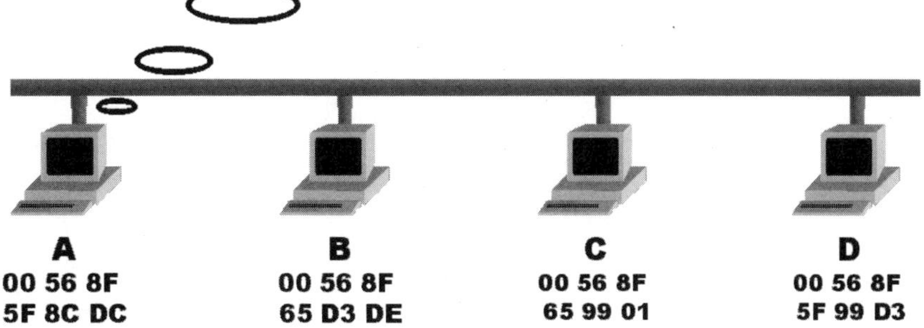

NOTE

A *node* is any device on the network that has its own MAC address. If it has a MAC address, it can be a source or destination for data packets.

"Multiple Access" means that all machines have equal access to the wire. If the line is free, an Ethernet node does not have to get approval to use the wire—it just uses it. From the point of view of Ethernet, it does not matter what function the node is performing. It could be a desktop system running Windows 95 or a high-end file server running Windows NT 4.0 or Novell NetWare. As far as Ethernet is concerned, a node is just a node, and access to the cable is assigned on a strictly first-come, first-served basis. But what happens if two machines listen to the cable and simultaneously determine that it is currently free? They both try to send.

When two computers try to use the cable simultaneously, a *collision* occurs. Both of their transmissions are lost. See Figure 1.15. A collision resembles the effect of two people talking simultaneously—a listener who hears the mixture of the two voices cannot understand either one.

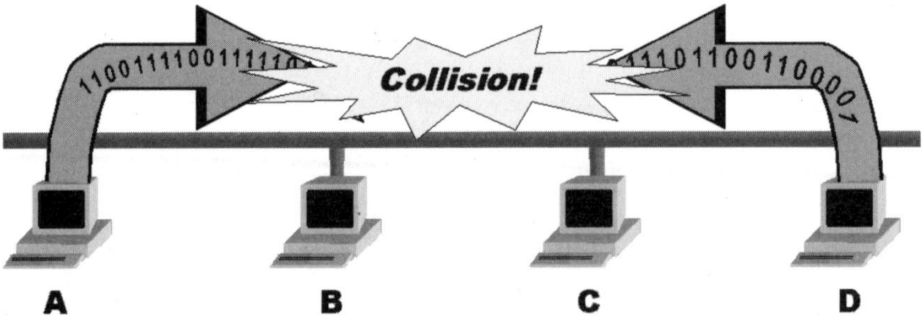

FIGURE 1.15 *If two machines transmit at the same time, their data packets are hopelessly mangled.*

In the event of a collision, both machines will detect that a collision has occurred by listening to their own transmissions. A person uses a similar technique to know whether or not he is the only one speaking at a particular moment. By comparing the words they speak with the sounds they hear, people know whether or not other people are talking. If a person speaks and hears words other than his own, he knows that someone else is also talking, as shown in Figure 1.16.

FIGURE 1.16

Two people talking at the same time can tell that they are not the only ones talking.

Ethernet nodes do the same thing. They compare their own transmissions with the transmission they are receiving over the cable and can detect if another node has transmitted at the same time, as shown in Figure 1.17. If they detect a collision, both nodes immediately stop transmitting. They then each generate a random number and wait for a random period of time. If you imagine that each machine rolls its magic electronic dice and waits for that number of seconds, you would not be too far from the truth, except that the amount of time an Ethernet node waits to retransmit is much shorter than one second. See Figure 1.18. Whichever node generates the lowest random number would begin its retransmission first, "winning" the collision. The "losing" station would see traffic on the wire and wait for another moment of silence on the wire before attempting to transmit.

CSMA/CD has the benefit of being very simple to program into Ethernet devices such as NIC cards. The Token Ring method of determining access to a shared cable, discussed in Chapter 3, requires much more sophisticated programming algorithms. For this reason, Ethernet devices tend to be less expensive than those with competing technologies.

That simplicity comes at a price: an Ethernet node will waste some amount of its time dealing with collisions instead of sending data. To illustrate this waste, and the chaos inherent to CSMA/CD, imagine a five-node network, as shown in Figure 1.19. Machines A and C both have outgoing data packets and begin the CSMA/CD process for sending traffic. They examine the cable and determine that no other node is currently sending out data (Carrier Sense). Because the cable is available, both A and C assume that they are free to use it (Multiple Access). When they begin sending their respective data packets, they detect that another station is also sending data (Collision Detection). Nodes A and C both generate a random number and begin counting down. Sticking with the dice analogy, assume node A rolls a 5 and node C rolls a 6. They begin counting down. 1, 2, 3, WAIT! Node E just started sending! Node E had no involvement in the original collision, and has no idea that nodes A and C are contending for the right to use the cable. All E knows is that no device is using the cable at this moment. According to the CSMA/CD rules, E can begin sending. Nodes A and C have both lost out, and now must wait again for the cable to be free.

FIGURE 1.17
An Ethernet node detects a collision.

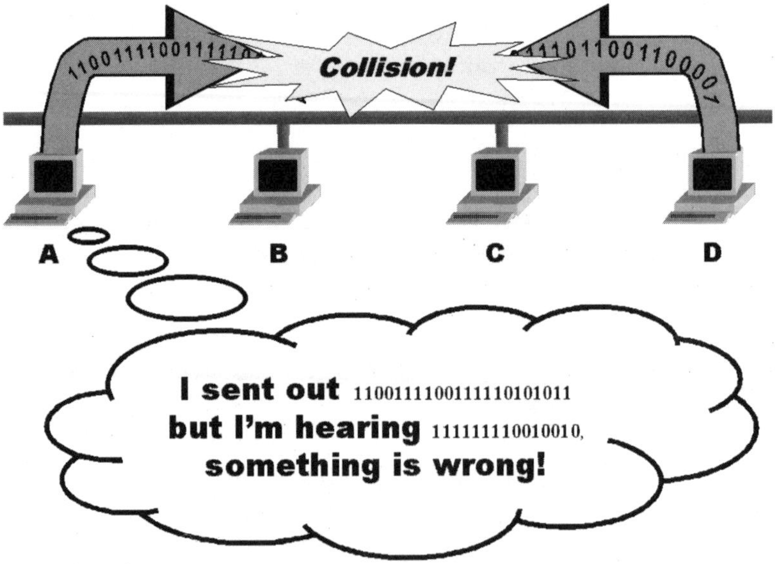

FIGURE 1.18
Following a collision, each node generates a random number and waits to try again.

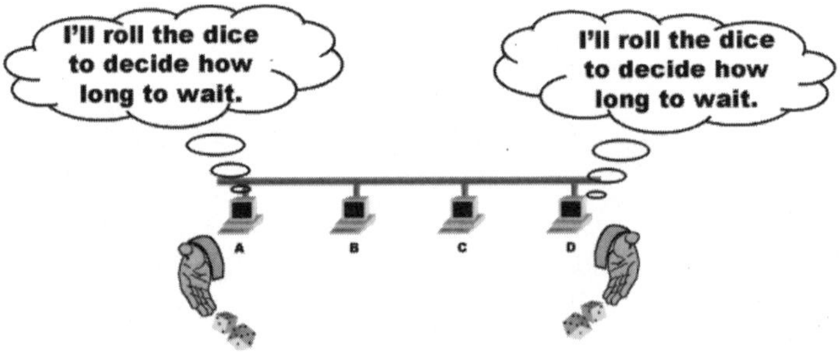

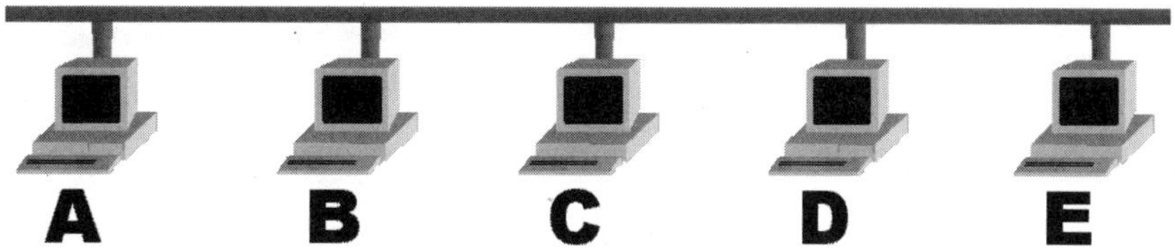

FIGURE 1.19
A five-node Ethernet network

The chaotic CSMA/CD method of determining access to the cable explains experiences common to users of Ethernet networks. At 9:00 a.m. on a Monday morning, 100 users sit down at approximately the same time and type in their names and passwords to log in to their Ethernet network. Virtually every station on the network contends for the use of the cable at the same time, causing massive collisions and attempted retransmissions. Only rarely will the end-users receive any kind of error message caused by high levels of traffic. Instead, they will perceive that the network is running slowly. The Ethernet NICs will continue to retry transmission and will eventually send the data packets successfully. Only in the event that the collisions get so severe that a packet cannot be sent after 16 retries will the sending station give up, resulting in an error of some kind being reported to the user.

Every Ethernet network wastes some amount of its available bandwidth dealing with these collisions. The typical Ethernet network is advertised to run at either 10 Mb/s or 100 Mb/s, but that advertised speed assumes that no collisions ever take place! In reality, collisions are a normal part of the operation of an Ethernet network.

Termination

The use of CSMA/CD in the real world has physical consequences for Ethernet networks. Most Ethernet networks use some type of copper cabling. For a CSMA/CD network using copper cabling to function properly, both ends of the network bus cable must be terminated with *terminating resistors*. Ethernet networks using copper cabling transmit their data packets as electrical signals. When an electrical signal travels down a copper wire, several things happen when the signal reaches the end of the wire. Some of the energy radiates out as radio waves, the cable functioning like the antennae on a radio transmitter. But some of the energy reflects off the end of the wire and travels back up the wire, as shown in Figure 1.20.

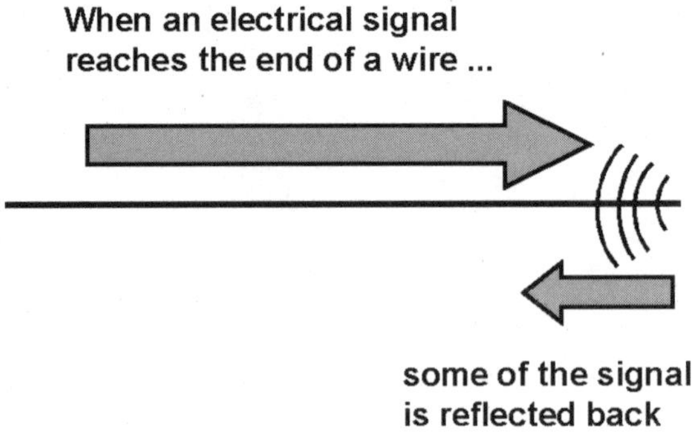
When an electrical signal
reaches the end of a wire ...
some of the signal
is reflected back

FIGURE 1.20 *When electricity hits the end of the wire, some of the electricity comes back up the wire as a reflection.*

When the other Ethernet nodes on the network attempt to send, they check the cable and misinterpret that reflection as another node sending out data packets. They wait for the reflection to dissipate before sending. Unfortunately, the reflections quickly build up to a point that the network looks permanently busy to all the nodes attached to it. See Figure 1.21. In order to prevent these reflections, a terminating resistor must be connected at each end of the segment. This resistor absorbs the reflections and allows the segment to function properly. See Figure 1.22.

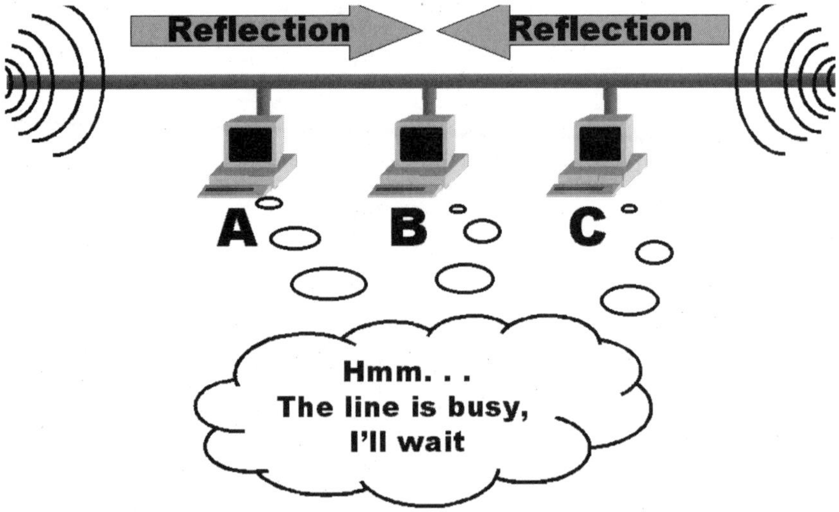
Reflection
Reflection
A
B
C
Hmm. . .
The line is busy,
I'll wait

FIGURE 1.21 *Reflections look like busy signals to the computers attached to the network.*

FIGURE 1.22
Two 50Ω terminating resistors of the type used in 10Base2, a common cabling system used for Ethernet.

Cable Breaks

The use of CSMA/CD in Ethernet networks causes some interesting behavior when the cable breaks. Figure 1.23 shows a 5-node network connected to a single segment of cable. If the piece of cable between computer A and computer B breaks, obviously computer A will not be able to communicate with the rest of the machines. See Figure 1.24. Worse, the break in the cable between computers A and B will shut down the entire network. The break in the cable causes reflections in both directions, so that all stations on the network to go into perpetual "waiting mode." See Figure 1.25. A break anywhere in the bus cable causes a loss of termination and shuts down the network.

NOTE

The bus cable to which the computers on an Ethernet network connect is called a *segment*.

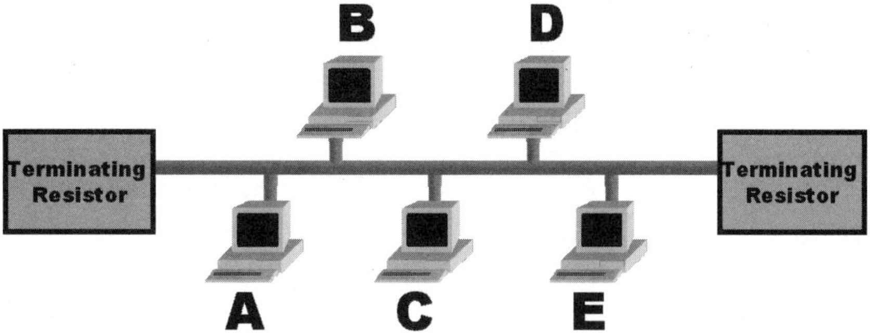

FIGURE 1.23
An Ethernet network with 5 computers.

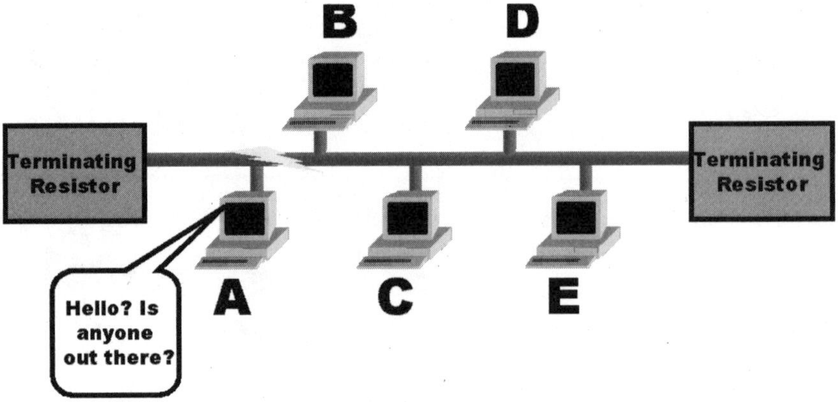

FIGURE 1.24
A cable break cuts computer A off from the rest of the network.

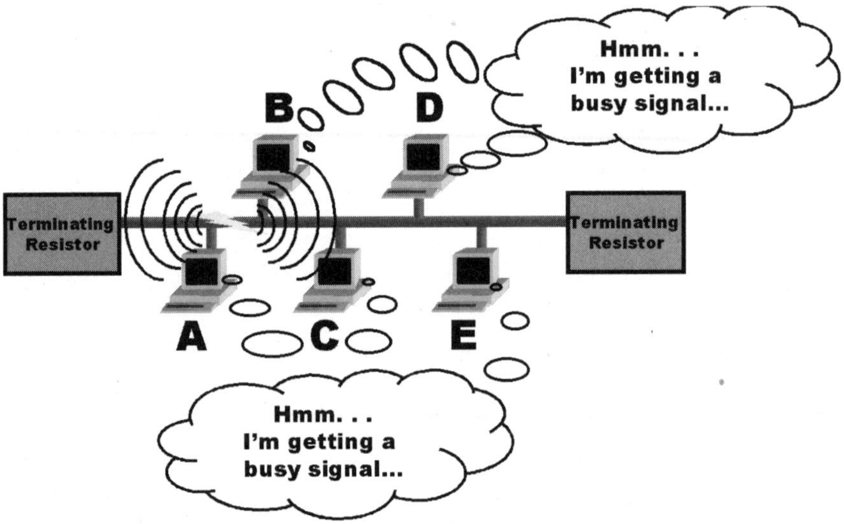

FIGURE 1.25
Reflections caused by the cable break bring the whole network down.

Now we have the answers to many of the questions that faced those early Ethernet designers. MAC addresses identify each machine on the network. CSMA/CD determines which machine should have access to the cable next. But we still need to build the thing. What kind of cables should we use? What should they be made of? How long can they be? The IEEE 802.3 standard provides the answers to these questions.

Ethernet Cabling Systems

The IEEE 802.3 committee recognizes that no single cabling solution can work in all situations and provides a variety of cabling standards with bizarre names, including 10Base5, 10Base2, 10BaseT, and 100BaseTX. This chapter will concentrate on Ethernet cabling systems based on coaxial cabling (10Base5 and 10Base2), while Chapter 2 will discuss Ethernet cabling based on other cable types such as twisted pair (10BaseT and 100baseTX) and fiber optic (100BaseFX). After defining coaxial cable, we will look at the two common Ethernet coaxial cabling systems, 10Base5 and 10Base2. Finally, we will discuss Ethernet repeaters, which allow network designers to link multiple Ethernet segments together.

Coaxial Cable

Coaxial cable contains a central conductor wire, surrounded by an insulating material, which in turn is surrounded by a braided metal shield, as shown in Figure 1.26. The cable is referred to as coaxial (or simply coax) because both the center wire and the braided metal shield share a common axis or centerline. See Figure 1.27.

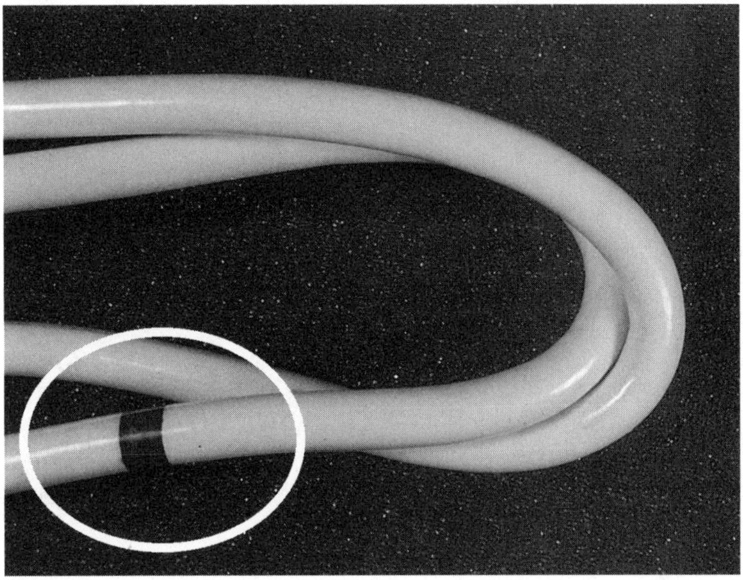

FIGURE 1.26

Thick coaxial cable (RG-8), with a black band marked every 2.5 meters.

FIGURE 1.27

A cutaway view of a coaxial cable.

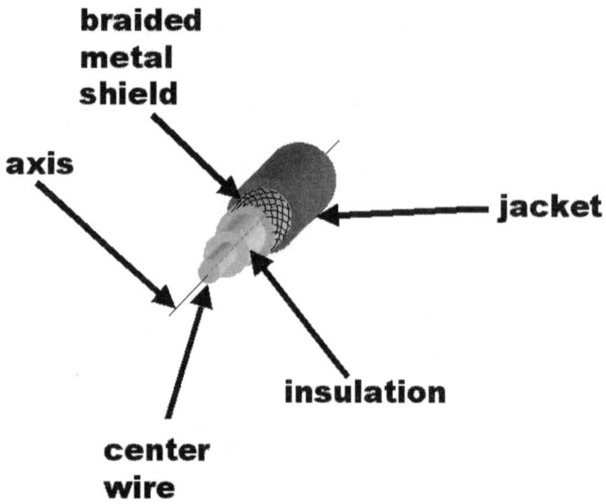

Coaxial cable is designed to shield data transmissions from *electrical interference*. Many devices in the typical office environment generate magnetic fields, including lights, copy machines, and refrigerators. When a piece of metal wire, such as an Ethernet network cable, encounters these magnetic fields, electrical current is generated on the wire. This extra current can shut down a network because it is easily misinterpreted as a signal by devices such as Ethernet NICs. To prevent this interference from affecting the network, the outer mesh shield of a coaxial cable shields the center wire (on which data are actually transmitted) from any interference in the vicinity. See Figure 1.28.

FIGURE 1.28

The braided metal shield prevents interference from reaching the center wire.

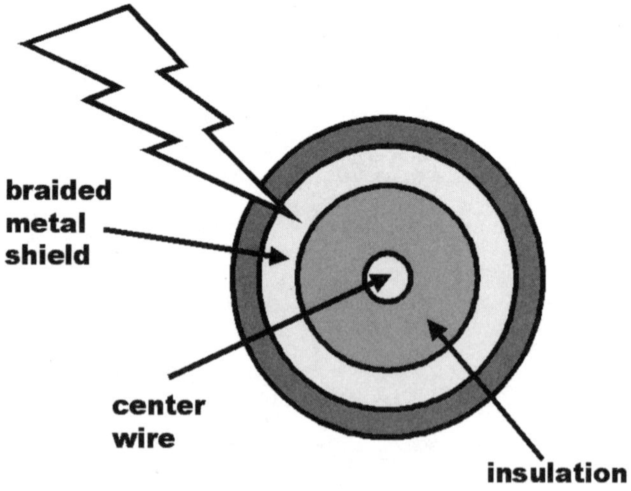

10Base5

In the beginning, Ethernet referred specifically to a CSMA/CD network running over a thick RG-8 coaxial cable like the one shown in Figure 1.26. Although not required by any standard, the cable was almost always yellow. Network techs refer to the original thick yellow cable used for Ethernet as Thick Ethernet, or Thicknet. Thicknet has the heaviest shielding of any cabling commonly used for 10 megabit per second Ethernet, making it an excellent choice for high interference environments. Because of its rigidity and the typical color of the RG-8 cable used, the less formal among us occasionally refer to it as "yellow cable" or "frozen yellow garden hose."

When the IEEE took charge of the Ethernet standard, it created a more structured way to refer to the various Ethernet cabling systems, and began referring to Thick Ethernet as 10Base5, a term that specifies the speed of the cabling system, its signaling type, and its distance limitations. The term 10Base5 breaks down as follows (See Figure 1.29):

- **Speed:** The "10" signifies an Ethernet network that runs at 10 megabits/second.
- **Signal type:** "Base" signifies that 10Base5 uses baseband signaling, meaning that there is a single signal on the cable.
- **Distance:** The "5" indicates that 10Base5 segments may not be longer than 500 meters.

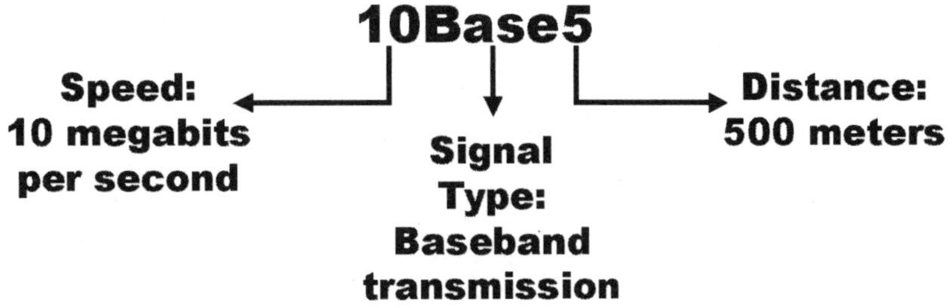

FIGURE 1.29 *The term 10Base5 provides three key pieces of information.*

Baseband vs. Broadband

Data signals can be sent over a network cable in two ways: broadband and baseband. Cable television serves as the obvious example of broadband transmission. A single piece of coaxial cable comes into a home. That cable carries multiple signals, and a small box allows the viewer to tune to different channels. Baseband signaling sends a single signal over the cable. With the exception of the rarely used 10Broad36 standard, Ethernet networks use baseband signaling, in which a single signal is sent over the cable. Baseband signaling uses very simple *transceivers*, the devices that send and receive signals on the cable, because they only need to distinguish between three states on the cable: one, zero, and idle. Broadband transceivers must be more complex because they have to be able to determine those same three states on multiple channels within the same cable. Because of its relative simplicity, most computer networks use baseband signaling. See Figure 1.30.

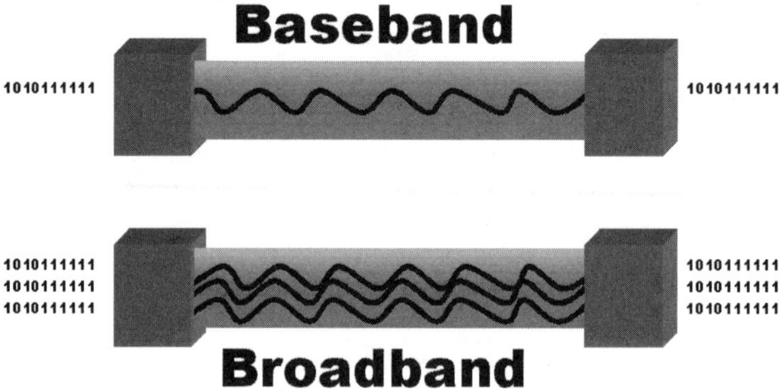

FIGURE 1.30
Baseband signaling sends a single signal at any given instant, whereas broadband signaling sends multiple signals on separate frequencies, a.k.a. channels.

NOTE

The dominance of baseband signaling may not last forever. Cable modems, which connect computers to the Internet using the same cable used for cable television, use broadband signaling. As cable modems become more popular, the networking industry may reexamine the use of broadband signaling in other types of networks.

500 Meters Per Segment

10Base5 segments may not be longer than 500 meters. A *segment* is the single length of cable, the "bus," to which the computers on an Ethernet network connect. The terminating resistors at each end of the segment define the ends of the segment. See Figure 1.31. The 500-meter segment limitation applies to the entire segment, and has nothing to do with the length of the piece of cable between two machines.

FIGURE 1.31
A 10Base5 Ethernet segment.

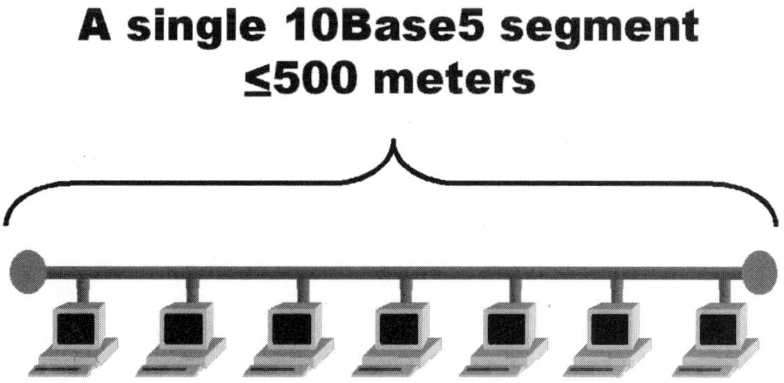

Connecting to the Cable

The 10Base5 cabling standard strictly defines how nodes connect to the segment. Unlike nodes in many other cabling systems, 10Base5 nodes do not connect directly to the bus cable. Instead, 10Base5 NICs use an AUI connector—a 15-pin female DB connector, as shown in Figure 1.32—to connect to an external transceiver. This connector looks physically identical to the MIDI and joystick connectors found on most soundcards. Reversing these cables drops the node off the network and makes those flight-simulator games much more challenging! The cable between the NIC and the transceiver can be up to 50 meters long, but the external transceivers must be placed exactly at 2.5-meter intervals, as shown in Figure 1.33. Remember that black band in Figure 1.26? Those black bands, spaced every 2.5 meters, help technicians space the connections properly when installing the cable. Figure 1.34 shows the connection between a 10Base5 transceiver and a NIC. Because 10Base5 uses an extremely stiff cable, cables are often run through the ceiling, with *drop cables* used to connect the cable to the individual NICs. See Figure 1.35. Finally, 10Base5 allows for up to 100 nodes per segment.

FIGURE 1.32
An AUI connector on a 10Base5 NIC.

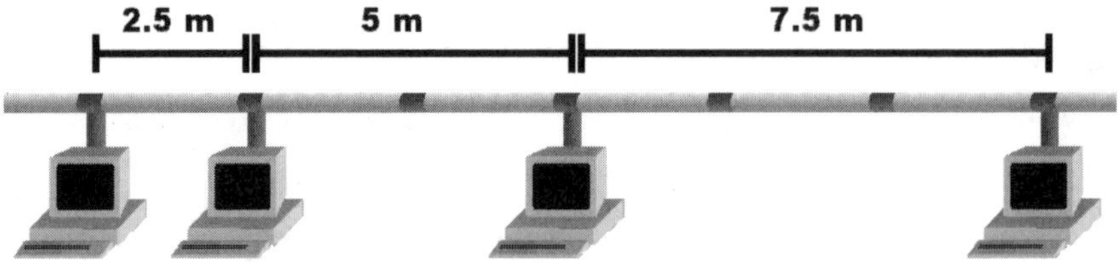

FIGURE 1.33
10Base5 requires that nodes be spaced at 2.5-meter intervals.

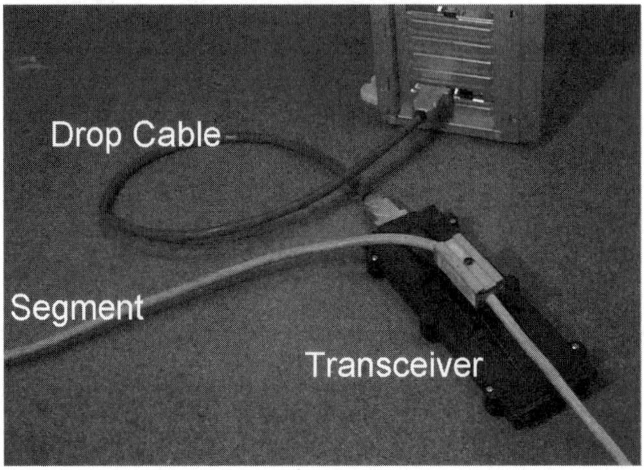

FIGURE 1.34
A 10Base5 transceiver connected to a NIC via a drop cable.

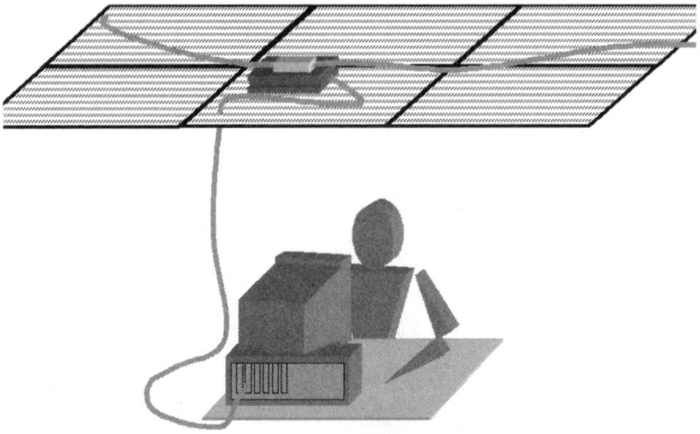

FIGURE 1.35
10Base5 uses drop cables to connect individual NICs to the segment, typically installed in the ceiling.

Why Not 10Base5 ?

Although some organizations continue to use 10Base5 cabling, most new 10 megabit per second installations will use either 10Base2 (discussed below) or 10BaseT (discussed in Chapter 2). Although all three systems run at 10 megabits per second, 10Base5 costs far more than either 10Base2 or 10BaseT. The RG-8 cable used in 10Base5 networks costs more both for material and installation. Organizations continue to use 10Base5 where it is already installed or in high-interference environments that require RG-8's heavy shielding.

10Base5 Summary

- **Speed:** 10 megabits/second
- **Signal type:** Baseband
- **Distance:** 500 meters/segment
- No more than 100 nodes per segment
- Nodes must be spaced at 2.5 meter intervals
- Cables marked with a black band every 2.5 meters to ease installation
- The thick coaxial cable used for 10Base5 is almost always yellow, although nothing in the standard requires that color.
- Expensive cost per foot compared to other cabling systems
- Known as Thick Ethernet, Thicknet, "Yellow Cable," or "Frozen Yellow Garden Hose"

While 10Base5 represented a revolutionary cabling system when originally introduced, its high cost and difficult installation limit its use today. New installations incorporate 10Base5 only in situations that require heavy shielding or generous distance limitation. Cheaper alternatives were needed.

NOTE

10Base5 will become even less common as fiber optic cabling, which is immune to electrical interference and has even more generous distance limitations, becomes less expensive.

10Base2

10Base2 can be used in many of the same instances as 10Base5, but is much easier to install and much less expensive. 10Base2 uses RG-58 coaxial cable with BNC connectors, as shown in Figure 1.36. Although RG-58 cabling has less shielding than the more expensive RG-8 cabling used in 10Base5, its shielding is adequate for most installations.

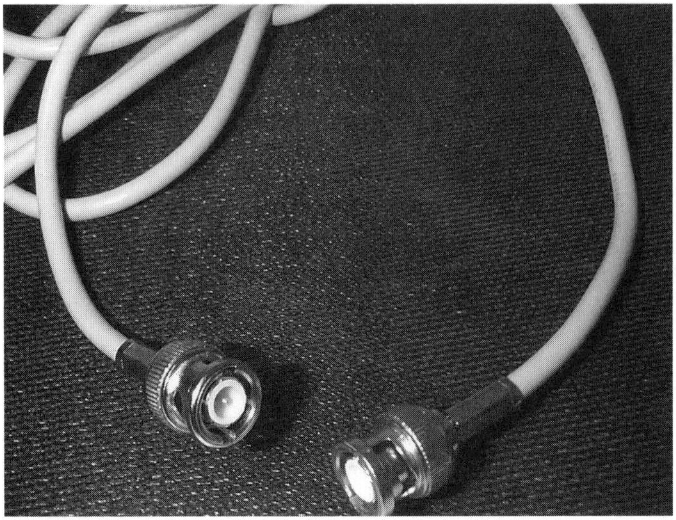

FIGURE 1.36

A piece of RG-58 coaxial cabling with BNC connectors.

The IEEE 802.3 committee tried to stay consistent with their *name-signal type-distance* scheme for naming Ethernet. The term 10Base2 breaks down like this:

- **Speed:** The "10" signifies an Ethernet network that runs at 10 megabits/second.
- **Signal type:** "Base" signifies that 10Base2 uses baseband signaling, meaning that there is a single signal on the cable.
- **Distance:** The "2" indicates that 10Base2 cables may not be longer than 185 meters.

What? How does the 2 in 10Base2 translate into "185 meters?" Don't try to argue, just live with it. Maybe at some point in the process, the distance limitation really was 200 meters and the IEEE later decided that it had to be shortened. Maybe they thought that 10Base1.85 looked funny. Who cares? Just be sure to remember that the distance limitation for 10Base2 is 185 meters.

10Base2 possesses several advantages that make it the preferred choice for running Ethernet over coaxial cable (Chapter 2 will discuss running Ethernet over twisted pair cabling, an even more popular choice), even though it allows only 30 computers per segment, far fewer than 10Base5. 10Base2 costs much less to install than 10Base5. RG-58 cabling costs significantly less per foot than 10Base5's RG-8 cabling. 10Base2's spacing requirements are also much less strict: computers must be spaced at least .5 meters apart, but do not have to be spaced at a specific interval as required by 10Base5. RG-58's greater flexibility makes modifying and extending 10Base2 segments relatively painless. Except for instances that require the longer distance or greater shielding of 10Base5, network technicians today choose 10Base2 for running Ethernet over coaxial cabling.

Connectors

The connectors used in 10Base2 networks make 10Base2 much easier to install and support than 10Base5. Unlike 10Base5's awkward requirement for external transceivers, 10Base2 NICs have a built-in transceiver and connect to the bus cable using a BNC connector. See Figure 1.37. The BNC connector provides an easy way to separate the center wire, which transmits data, from the outer shield, which protects the center wire from interference. See Figure 1.38.

FIGURE 1.37
Male and female BNC connectors.

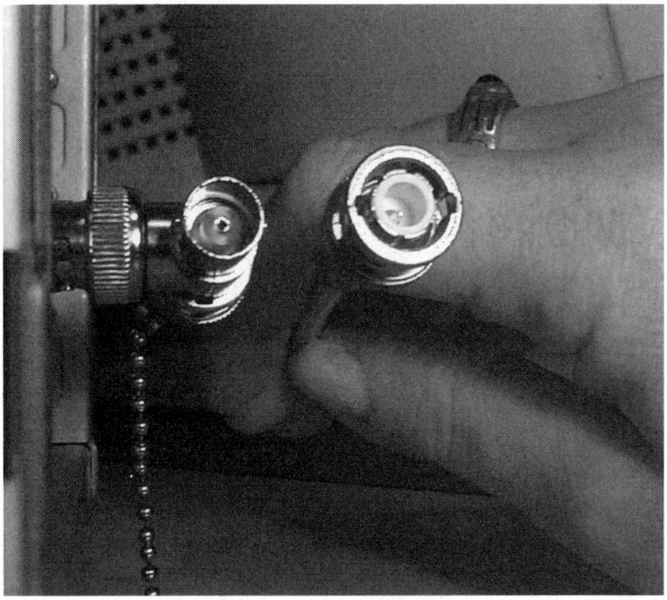

BNC connectors are crimped onto the wire using a crimping tool like the one shown in Figure 1.39. *Crimping* means to bend the metal of the connector around the cable to secure it to the cable. A properly crimped BNC connector keeps the center wire electrically insulated from the shield. An improperly crimped BNC connector allows the shield and the center wire to make electrical contact, creating a short in the cable as in Figure 1.40. A *short*, or short circuit, allows electricity to pass between the center wire and the shield. Because any current on the shield caused by interference will be conducted to the center strand, machines on the network will assume the network is busy and will not transmit data. The effect of a short circuit is the same as a break in the cable: the entire network goes down.

FIGURE 1.38
The BNC connector keeps the center wire and the shield from touching.

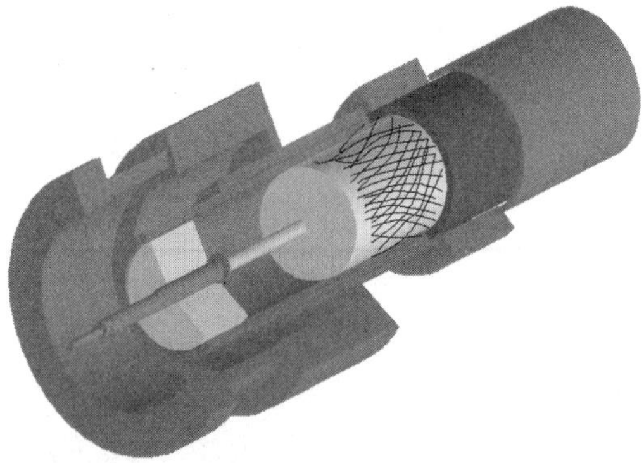

FIGURE 1.39
A typical crimping tool used for putting BNC connectors on a piece of RG-58 coaxial cable.

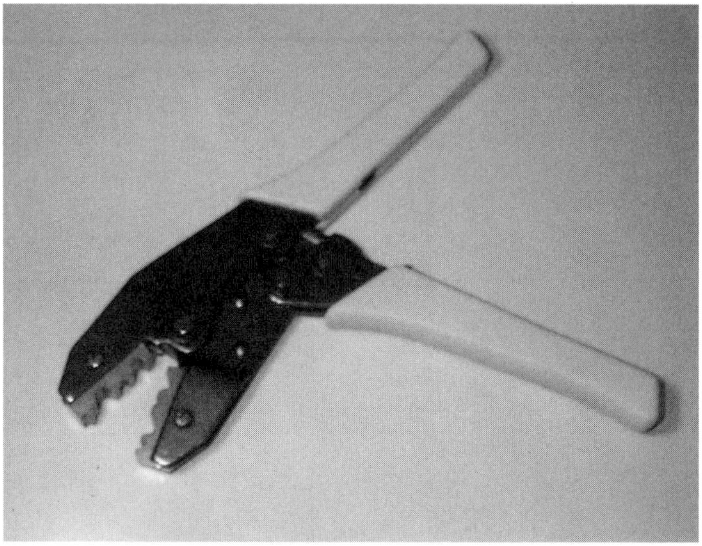

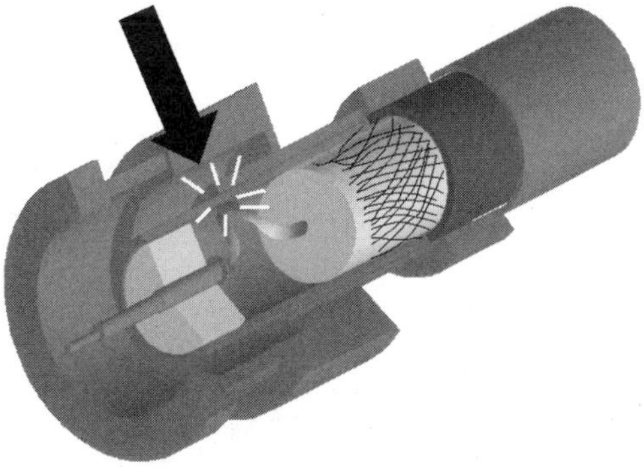

FIGURE 1.40
A poorly crimped cable allows electricity to pass between the shield and the center wire, creating a short.

NOTE

The origins of the acronym BNC have been lost. Various translations call it a Bayonet Connector, Bayonet Navy Connector, British Naval Connector, Bayonet Neill Concelman, Bayonet Nut Connector, etc. Don't worry about it! If you can look at a BNC connector and know what it is for and how to use it, don't worry about what the acronym stands for!

10Base2 requires the use of a T-connector, shown in Figure 1.41, when connecting devices to the cable. The T-connector plugs into the female connector on the Ethernet NIC and the coaxial cable is attached to either side of the T-connector. See Figure 1.42. In the event that the Ethernet node sits at the end of the cable, a terminating resistor takes the place of one of the cables. See Figure 1.43. All BNC connectors, including terminators and T-connectors, should be locked into place by turning their locking ring. See Figure 1.44. Although the connectors are easy to use, mistakes can happen. Novices frequently connect BNC connectors directly to the female connection on the NIC, as shown in Figure 1.45. While the connector locks in place just fine, the network will not function because there is no place to attach the terminating resistor.

FIGURE 1.41
A T-connector.

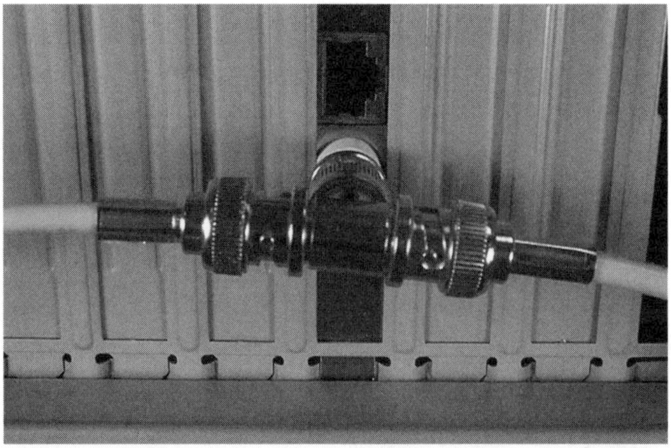

FIGURE 1.42
A T-connector with an RG-58 cable attached to either side.

FIGURE 1.43
A T-connector with a terminating resistor attached.

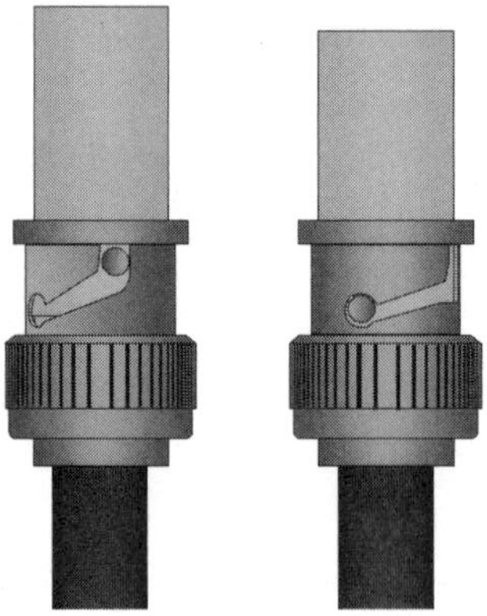

FIGURE 1.44
The BNC connector on the right is locked into place, whereas the one on the left is not.

FIGURE 1.45
BNC connectors should never be attached directly to the NIC.

10Base2 Summary

- **Speed:** 10 megabits/second
- **Signal type:** Baseband
- **Distance:** 185 meters/segment
- No more than 30 nodes per segment
- Nodes must be spaced at least .5 meters apart.
- Inexpensive cost per foot compared to 10Base5
- Known as Thin Ethernet, Thinnet, "Cheapernet"

10Base2 offers a cheap and quick way to network a small number of computers using coaxial cable and Ethernet. As Chapter 2 will discuss, larger networks typically use twisted pair wiring for Ethernet, but 10Base2 retains a strong installed base in smaller networks. 10Base2 retains the basic mechanisms of Ethernet: CSMA/CD, MAC addresses, the Ethernet packet format. Rather than designing a new networking technology from scratch, 10Base2's designers built on proven, existing technology.

Repeaters

Some networks function perfectly well within the segment limits of 10Base2 and 10Base5. For some organizations, however, the limitations of these cabling systems are unacceptable. Organizations that need longer distances, more computers, more fault tolerance, or the ability to combine different cabling systems can add repeaters their networks.

A *repeater* is any device that takes all of the data packets it receives from one Ethernet segment and repeats it on another segment. Figure 1.46 shows a typical Ethernet repeater. An Ethernet repeater does exactly what it advertises: it takes packets from one Ethernet segment and repeats them on another. A repeater takes the incoming electrical signals, translates them into binary code, and then retransmits the electrical signals. A repeater does not function as an amplifier. Amplifiers boost signals, flaws and all, like a copy machine making a copy of a bad original. A repeater, in contrast, recreates these signals from scratch. Repeaters address the need for more computers, greater distances, improved fault tolerance, and integration of different cabling systems, but cannot do anything to deal with the downside of these larger networks: increased traffic.

FIGURE 1.46
A typical Ethernet repeater.

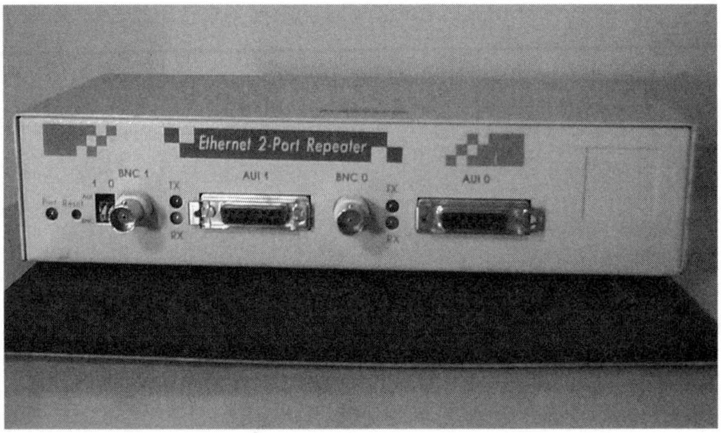

The words "all data packets" in the definition of a repeater are important. Chapter 2 discusses other types of devices (switches, bridges, and routers) that forward only some of the packets received from one segment to another.

NOTE

Repeater Benefits

Repeaters have four key benefits. First, they extend the distance that a network can cover. Second, they increase the number of machines that can connect to the network. Third, they provide a measure of fault tolerance, limiting the impact of breaks in the cable to the segment on which the break occurs. Fourth, they can link different types of cabling segments together.

A repeater increases the maximum possible distance between machines by linking together two segments. Each segment retains its own distance limitation. If a repeater connects two 10Base2 segments, for example, the maximum distance that can separate two machines on different segments is 370 meters (2 x 185 meters). See Figure 1.47. Two 10Base5 segments connected by a repeater can cover 1000 meters (2 x 500 meters).

FIGURE 1.47
Two 10Base2 segments connected by a repeater can cover 370 meters.

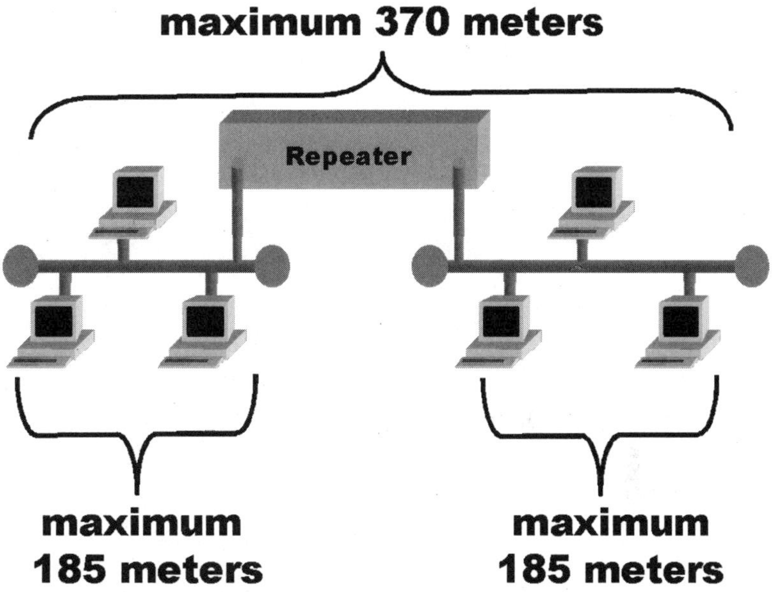

In addition to increasing the distance covered by a single Ethernet network, repeaters also increase the number of machines that can connect to the network. If a repeater connects two 10Base2 segments, then the network can have 60 computers attached to it (2 segments x 30 nodes per segment). See Figure 1.48.

NOTE

See Chapter 2's discussion of the 5-4-3 rule for information about limits to the number of repeaters that can exist on the network.

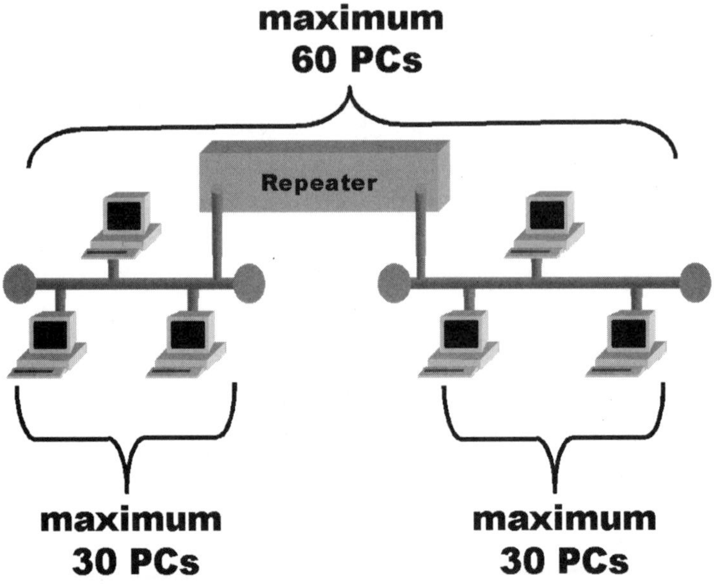

FIGURE 1.48
Repeaters increase the number of machines that can be connected to the network.

Repeaters also add a degree of *fault tolerance* to a network. If one of the segments breaks, only that segment will fail. Computers on the remaining segment will continue to function, unaffected when communicating within their own segment. The segment with the cable break fails because of reflections, but the segment on the far side of the repeater remains properly terminated and functions normally. See Figure 1.49.

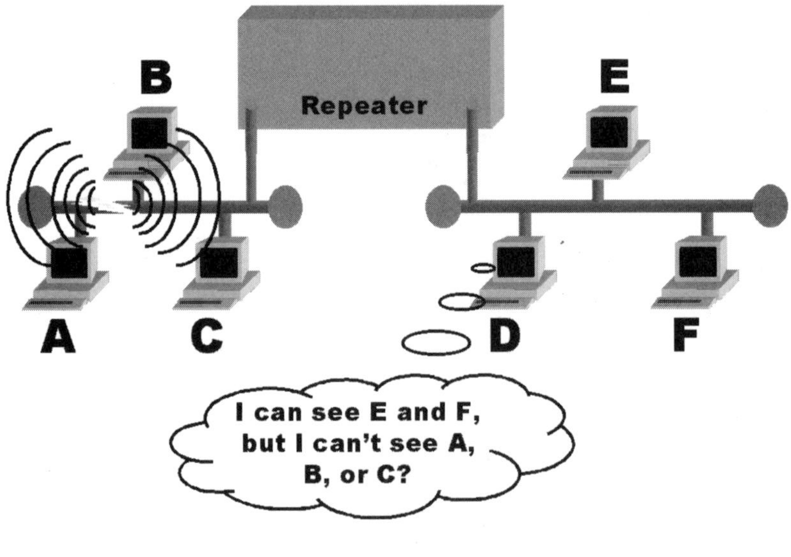

FIGURE 1.49
Cable breaks affect only the segment on which the break occurs.

NOTE

Fault tolerance is the ability of a system to continue functioning even after some part of the system has failed.

As an added benefit, repeaters can give network designers the flexibility to combine different cabling types on the same network. Both 10Base5 and 10Base2 use exactly the same packet structure—the actual ones and zeroes used are identical. A repeater can connect a 10Base5 and a 10Base2 segment without difficulty. See Figure 1.50. Many repeaters come with both AUI and BNC connectors for that purpose. See Figure 1.51.

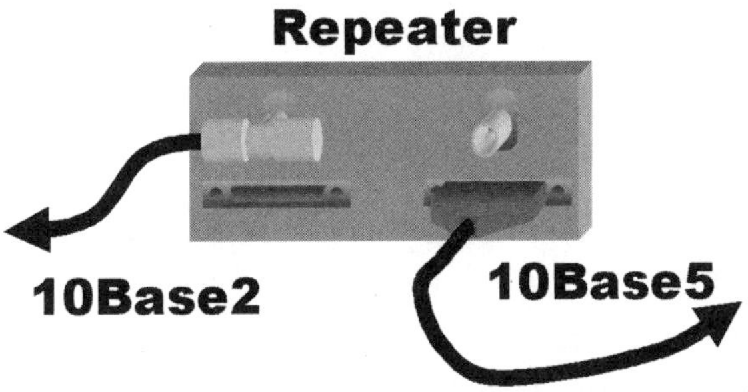

FIGURE 1.50
A repeater can connect Ethernet segments that use different types of cabling.

FIGURE 1.51
A typical Ethernet repeater with both AUI connections for 10Base5 and BNC connectors for 10Base2.

Repeaters Repeat Traffic, They Don't Manage It

Using repeaters to build larger networks can lead to traffic jams, because they repeat all packets that hit the wire. This results in more traffic and slower overall performance. Because the repeater repeats all packets without regard to the source or destination, the rules of CSMA/CD apply to the entire network as a whole. If two computers on two different segments connected by a repeater both transmit a packet at the same time, a collision will result. Repeaters are not smart devices—they repeat every data packet they "hear," regardless of its origin. In Figure 1.52, computers A, B, and C connect to segment 1, and computers D, E, and F connect to segment 2. Computer A transmits a packet to computer C, which sits on the same side of the repeater. Computers D, E, and F, sitting on the far side of the repeater, do not need to "hear" the packets sent between computers A and C, but the repeater sends the packets to their network segment anyway. Machines on network 1 cannot transmit while machines on network 2 are using the network and vice versa. Because all the machines, regardless of the network segment to which they attach, can potentially have collisions with all the other machines, segments 1 and 2 are both considered part of the same *collision domain*. See Figure 1.53. Even when using repeaters, an Ethernet network functions like a single CB radio channel: only one user can talk and be understood at any given time.

NOTE

A set of Ethernet segments that receive all traffic generated by any node within those segments is a *collision domain*. Chapter 2 discusses devices (bridges, routers, and switches) that can break a network into multiple collision domains.

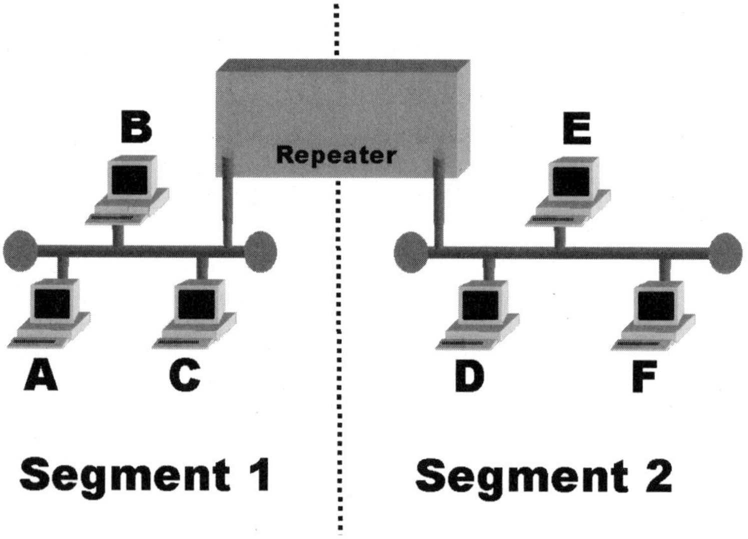

FIGURE 1.52
Two Ethernet segments connected by a repeater.

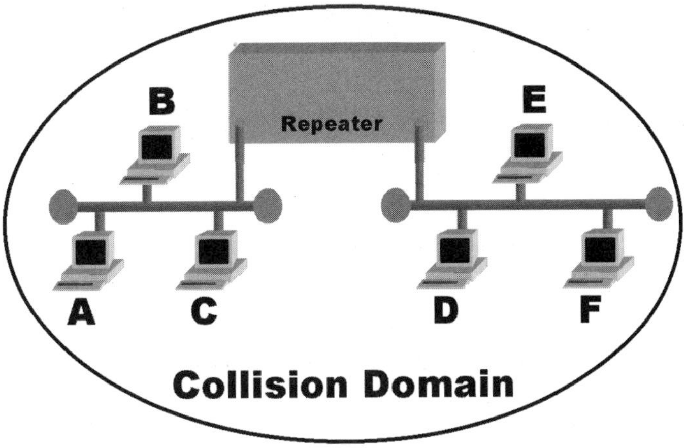

FIGURE 1.53
A single collision domain.

Repeater Summary

Repeaters provide four key benefits:

- Increased distance
- More computers
- Fault tolerance
- Interoperability between different Ethernet cabling systems.

Repeaters do not help reduce or manage traffic on networks that experience too much traffic, but they remain important tools for network technicians and architects.

Conclusion

The IEEE 802.3 standard, commonly referred to as Ethernet, must deal with the same issues as any networking system. The defining characteristics of Ethernet include:

- The use of MAC addresses assigned by the IEEE to identify each node on the network
- A standard packet structure that includes a source and destination MAC address, the actual data being transmitted, and a CRC code for error correction
- The use of CSMA/CD (Carrier Sense, Multiple Access/Collision Detection) as a means for sharing the network cable.

These defining features of Ethernet leave out any mention of what the cables actually look like. The IEEE 802.3 standard for Ethernet provides for two distinct systems of copper coaxial cable: 10Base2 and 10Base5. As Chapter 2 illustrates, the IEEE does not limit Ethernet to 10 megabit per second speeds running over coaxial cable. The Ethernet standard is flexible enough to allow for a wide variety of cabling systems and speeds.

Review Questions

1) The DIX standard for networking computers was an early version of the ______________ standard.

a) Token Ring
b) FDDI
c) TCP/IP
d) Ethernet

2) 10Base2 uses a ______________ topology.

a) Bus
b) Ring
c) Mesh
d) Star

3) How long can a segment be in 10Base5?

a) 485 meters
b) 485 feet
c) 500 meters
d) 500 feet

4) What kind of cable does 10Base2 use?

a) RJ-45
b) RJ-58
c) RG-45
d) RG-58

5) How long can a 10Base2 segment be?

a) 200 meters
b) 200 feet
c) 185 meters
d) 500 meters

6) Which of the following requires an external transceiver?

a) 10Base2
b) 10Base5
c) Ethernet
d) Bus Topology

7) Which of the following are other names for 10Base5?

a) Thinnet
b) Thicknet
c) Thin coax
d) Twisted pair

8) An Ethernet repeater:

a) Connects multiple segments, forwarding all traffic received from one segment to the segment on which the destination machine resides.
b) Connects multiple segments, forwarding all traffic received from one segment to all other segments to which it is attached.
c) Connects multiple segments, determining which machines on the network can access machines on the other segment.

9) The connector used in 10Base2 is called a(n):

a) AUI
b) RJ-45
c) BNC
d) DB-9

10) Computers in 10Base2 networks must be a minimum of _____ meters apart.

a) 2.5
b) 3
c) .5
d) 1

Review Answers

1) **D.** The DIX (Digital-Intel-Xerox) standard is an early version of the Ethernet standard.

2) **A.** 10Base2 Ethernet uses a bus topology.

3) **C.** 10Base5 Ethernet has a maximum segment length of 500 meters. (Remember that distance limitations are normally discussed in terms of meters, not feet.)

4) **D.** 10Base2 uses RG-58 coaxial cable. RJ-45 is a type of connector used with unshielded twisted pair wiring (see Chapter 2 for more information). RJ-58 and RG-45 are not common network terms.

5) **C.** A 10Base2 segment can be 185 meters in length.

6) **B.** 10Base5 requires an external transceiver. 10Base2 transceivers are built in to the NIC. 10Base5 is a type of Ethernet technology, and is based on a bus topology, but neither Ethernet nor bus topologies in general require an external transceiver.

7) **B.** Thicknet. 10Base5 can be referred to as Thick Ethernet, Thick Coax, Thicknet, "yellow cable," or "frozen yellow garden hose." Thinnet and Thin Coax refer to 10Base2, and twisted pair is a type of cabling not used in 10Base2 or 10Base5.

8) **B.** Repeaters forward all traffic received from one segment to all other segments. Repeaters do not discriminate based on the destination address and have no role in determining access to the wire. Access to the Ethernet network continues to be controlled by CSMA/CD.

9) **C.** 10Base2 uses a BNC connector. 10Base5 uses AUI connectors. RJ-45 connectors are used for a variety of purposes with unshielded twisted pair cabling (see Chapters 2 and 3). DB-9 connectors are 9-pin serial ports commonly used on PCs.

10) **C.** Computers in 10Base2 networks must be a minimum of .5 meters apart. 10Base5 networks require the computers to be spaced precisely at 2.5-meter intervals.

CHAPTER 2

Ethernet: Bigger, Faster, Stronger than Before

The 10Base5 and 10Base2 networks described in Chapter 1 can meet the needs of some organizations, but have significant disadvantages for network architects in larger organizations. First, a single break in the cable shuts down an entire 10Base2 or 10Base5 segment. In larger networks of hundreds of machines, finding a break in the cable can be a time-consuming and expensive endeavor. Second, both 10Base5 and 10Base2 impose limits on the number of machines that can connect to the network. Large organizations require more room for growth. Third, networks running over a shared cable at 10 megabits per second cannot provide enough bandwidth to support some of today's more demanding network applications.

NOTE

Bandwidth is the capacity of the network to transmit a given amount of data during a given period of time.

Fortunately, as Steve Austin might say: "We have the technology. We can rebuild it—bigger, faster, stronger than before." To solve the problem of a single break in the cable bringing down an entire network segment, Ethernet designers have shifted away from the pure bus topology used in 10Base5 and 10Base2. They base newer Ethernet standards such as 10BaseT, on a *star bus*, a hybrid of the bus and star topologies. To create larger networks, network technicians have begun to link together distinct Ethernet networks (a.k.a. collision domains) with devices such as bridges and routers. To create higher-speed networks, the IEEE has introduced newer cabling standards such as Switched Ethernet, Fast Ethernet, and Gigabit Ethernet.

What Is a Star Bus Topology?

Newer Ethernet standards discard the pure bus topology of 10Base2 and 10Base5, employing instead a star bus topology. A *star bus topology* is a hybrid of the star and bus topologies discussed in Chapter 1. Star bus networks use a physical star that provides improved stability and a logical bus that maintains compatibility with existing Ethernet standards.

In a star topology, all nodes connect to a central wiring point, as shown in Figure 2.1. The key advantage of the star topology is that a break in the cable affects only the machine connected to that cable. In Figure 2.2, machine C cannot communicate with any other node, but machines A, B, D, E, and F communicate with each other just fine. While the star topology boasts a more robust, fault-tolerant cabling system, pure star topologies do not exist in modern computer networks.

NOTE

When bad things happen, a *robust* system continues to operate, at least to some degree. *Fault tolerance* means the ability of a system to continue functioning even when some part of the system has failed. In other words, the more robust the system, the more fault tolerant it is.

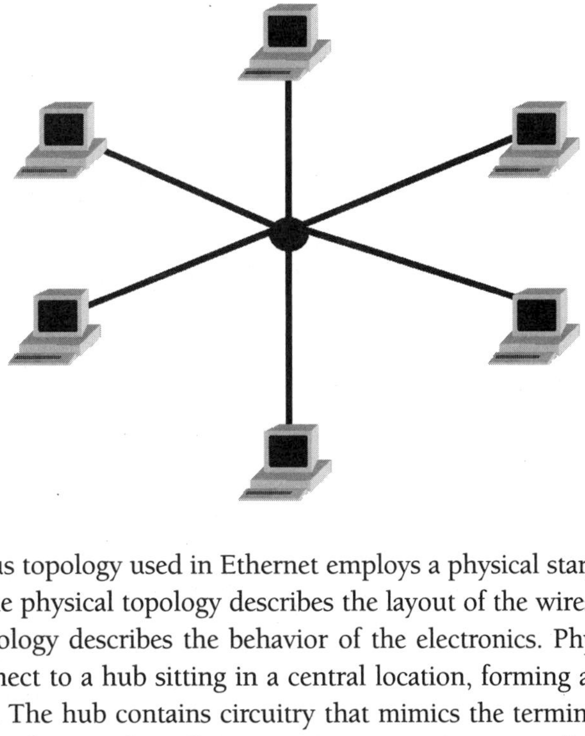

FIGURE 2.1
A star topology.

The star bus topology used in Ethernet employs a physical star and a logical bus. The physical topology describes the layout of the wires, while the logical topology describes the behavior of the electronics. Physically, the nodes connect to a hub sitting in a central location, forming a "star." See Figure 2.3. The hub contains circuitry that mimics the terminated Ethernet segment discussed in Chapter 1. See Figure 2.4. Logically, the nodes behave as though attached directly to the segment. The nodes share the segment according to the same CSMA/CD rules used for 10Base2 and 10Base5. Using the star bus topology maintains consistency with previous Ethernet standards such as CSMA/CD, but provides the stability of a star topology: if a cable gets cut, only one node drops off the network.

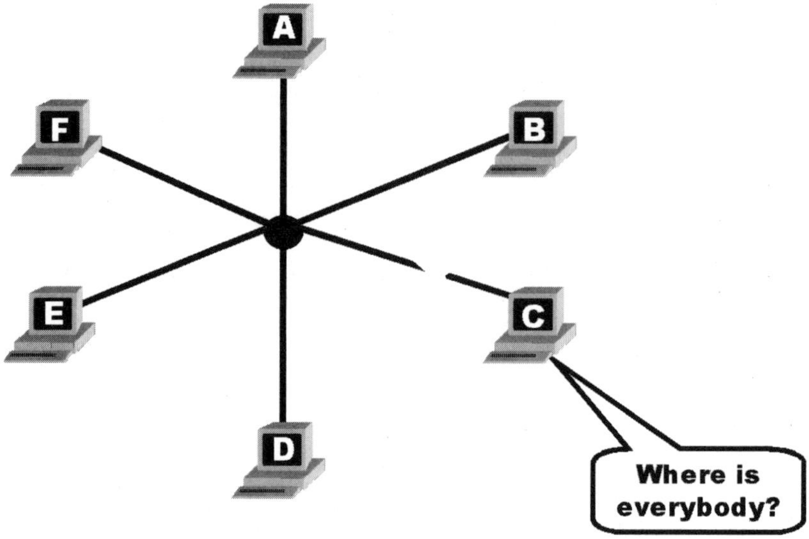

FIGURE 2.2
In a star topology, a broken cable affects only the machine connected to it.

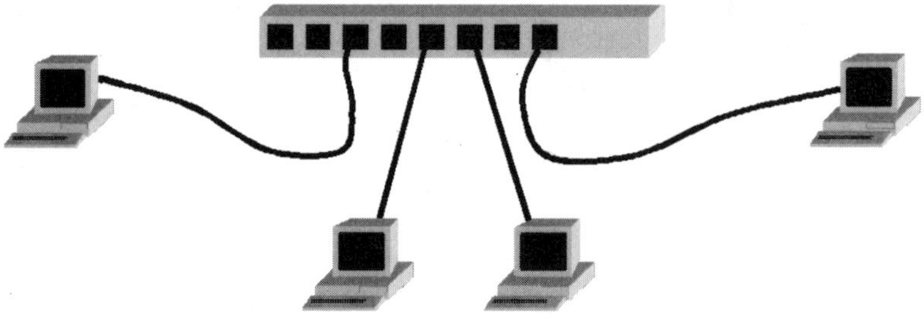

FIGURE 2.3
A 10BaseT network, with each node connected to the hub.

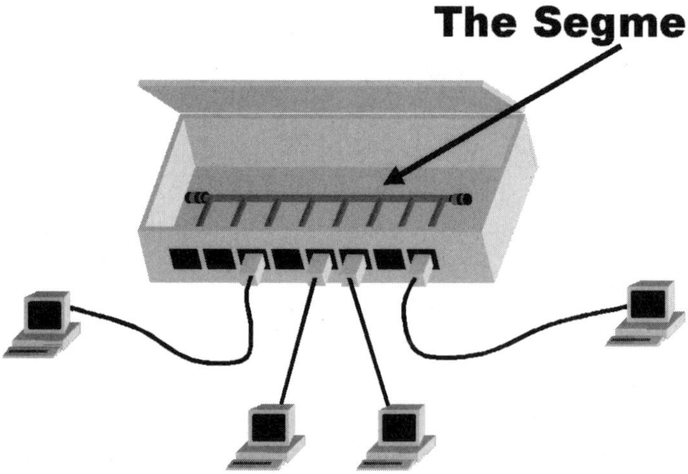

FIGURE 2.4
A 10BaseT hub contains the electronic equivalent of a properly terminated Ethernet segment.

10BaseT

The term *10BaseT* describes an Ethernet cabling system that uses a star bus topology. Except for the cable used, 10BaseT NICs behave much the same way as 10Base2 or 10Base5 NICs. They use precisely the same packet structure. Machines still identify other machines by their MAC addresses and use CSMA/CD to determine when to use the shared segment. They operate at the same speed, 10 megabits per second. The key difference between 10BaseT and its pure bus topology predecessors is the location of the Ethernet segment. In 10Base2 or 10Base5, the segment winds its way around the network. In 10BaseT, the segment lies protected inside the hub. While 10BaseT shares the same logical bus structure as 10Base2 and 10Base5, it brings its own cabling system and limitations to the table.

AB CD TERMINOLOGY

TERMINOLOGY ALERT!

Various sources will call 10BaseT a star topology, a bus topology, or a star bus topology. Which term is used to describe 10BaseT's topology often depends on the job description of the person generating the term. For someone whose main job involves installing cable, 10BaseT is a star. Those who crawl through ceiling tiles and punch holes in walls, could not care less how the electronics that will use the cable actually function. Similarly, a software engineer writing a device driver for an Ethernet NIC could not care less where the cables go. He needs to think about all those rules associated with a bus topology: CSMA/CD, MAC addresses, etc. Many techs split the difference. Rather than saying that 10BaseT uses a physical star topology and a logical bus topology, they say that 10BaseT uses a *star bus topology*.

Using this hybrid star bus topology, 10BaseT enjoys the key benefit of a star topology: fault tolerance. If a cable running to a specific node breaks, the break affects only that computer because the Ethernet segment itself is unbroken. See Figure 2.5. If the segment itself breaks inside the hub, as shown in Figure 2.6, then the entire network goes down.

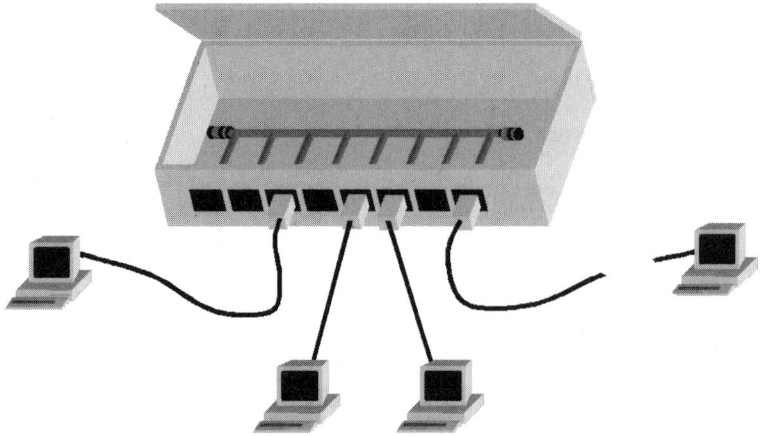

FIGURE 2.5
Because the Ethernet segment is protected inside the hub and remains unbroken, the break in the cable affects only one machine.

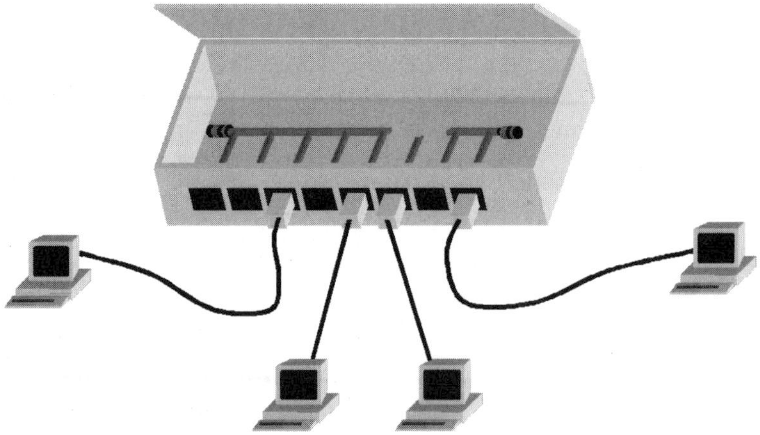

FIGURE 2.6
If the segment inside the hub "breaks," then the entire segment fails.

NOTE

Do not crack open your Ethernet hubs looking for a piece of coaxial cable—it won't be there. The interior of an Ethernet hub contains a circuit board that serves the same function as coaxial segments used in 10Base5 and 10Base2. When a hub fails, there is no cable inside it to break. Instead, some part of the circuit board fails. The effect remains the same—if the hub fails, the entire segment fails.

The name "10BaseT" tries to follow the naming convention used for earlier Ethernet cabling systems. The "10" refers to the speed: 10 megabits per second. The "base" refers to the signaling type: baseband. The "T," however, does not refer to a distance limitation as do the "2" in 10Base2 or the "5" in 10Base5. Instead, it refers to the type of cable used: twisted pair. 10BaseT uses unshielded twisted pair (UTP) cabling.

UTP

10BaseT uses four-pair UTP wiring like that shown in Figure 2.7 to connect devices to the hub. Although more sensitive to interference than coaxial cable, UTP cabling provides an inexpensive and flexible means to cable physical star networks. Take care when installing UTP—many other technologies employ the same cabling and connectors. Because of the wide array of uses, UTP cabling has strict standards for the proper crimping of the connectors and comes in a variety of grades, not all of which can support 10BaseT.

FIGURE 2.7
A typical 4-pair unshielded twisted pair cable.

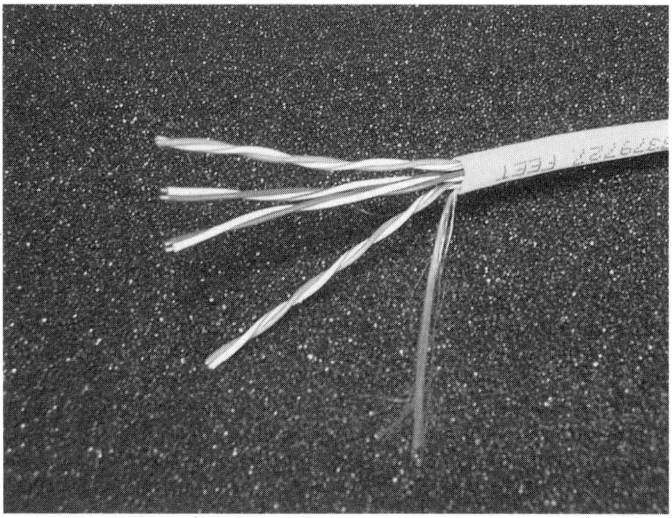

Unlike the coaxial cable discussed in Chapter 1, UTP has no shield—which is what "unshielded" means. As a result, the wise network tech does not install UTP cabling in high-interference environments. Fortunately, most office environments do not generate that much interference. (See Chapter 10 for a discussion of environmental factors such as electrical interference.) Because UTP lacks the heavy metal shield used in coaxial cabling, it costs significantly less per foot than coaxial cable.

UTP cabling uses an RJ-45 connector, shown in Figure 2.8, that enables devices to put voltage on the individual wires within the cable.

Each pin on the RJ-45 connects to a single wire inside the cable. The pins on the RJ-45 are numbered from 1 to 8, as shown in Figure 2.9. The 10BaseT standard designates some of these numbered wires for specific purposes.

Although the cable has 4 pairs, 10BaseT uses only 2 of the pairs. Instead of using a single wire both to receive and to transmit data, 10BaseT devices use pins 1 and 2 to send data and pins 3 and 6 to receive data. Even though one pair of wires sends data and another receives data, a 10BaseT device cannot send and receive simultaneously. The rules of CSMA/CD still apply. Only one device can use the segment contained in the hub without causing a collision.

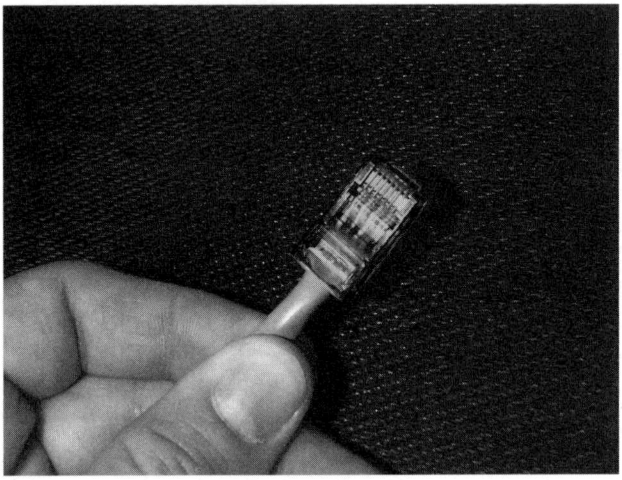

FIGURE 2.8
An RJ-45 connector

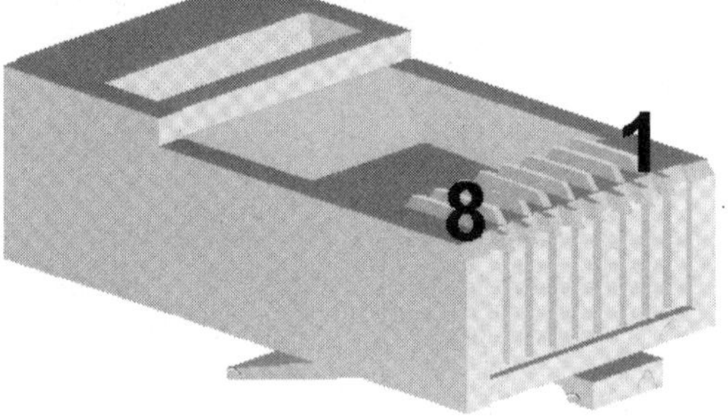

FIGURE 2.9
The pins on an RJ-45 connector are numbered 1 through 8.

While 10BaseT Ethernet uses only four wires, cable manufacturers included the remaining four wires for compatibility with other standards. Other technologies, including Token Ring and PBX phone systems, employ the same UTP cabling as Ethernet. Even some other Ethernet standards, such as the 100BaseT4 standard discussed below, require all eight wires. Don't give in to the temptation to connect only the wires needed by 10BaseT. When installing UTP cabling, connect all the wires so that they can be used for other applications in the future.

NOTE

PBX phone systems are private phone systems used within an organization. *PBX* stands for Private Branch eXchange.

Each wire inside a UTP cable must connect to the proper pin on the RJ-45 connector at each end of the cable. Manufacturers color code each wire within a piece of 4-pair UTP to assist in properly matching the ends. Each pair of wires has a solid colored wire and a striped wire: blue/blue-white, orange/orange-white, brown/brown-white, and green/green white. Because signals sent down pin 1 on one end of a cable must be received on pin 1 on the other end, the same wire must connect to pin 1 on both ends. Industry organizations have developed a variety of standard "color codes" to facilitate installation. Figure 2.10 shows the EIA/TIA 568A standard. Note that the pairs used by Ethernet (1-2 and 3-6) come from the same color pairs (green/green-white and orange/orange-white). Using the RJ-45 connector to match the twisted pairs from the cable with the pairs used by 10BaseT helps to minimize interference between the wires. Following an established color code scheme such as EIA/TIA 568A ensures that the wires match up correctly at each end of the cable.

FIGURE 2.10
The EIA/TIA 568A standard

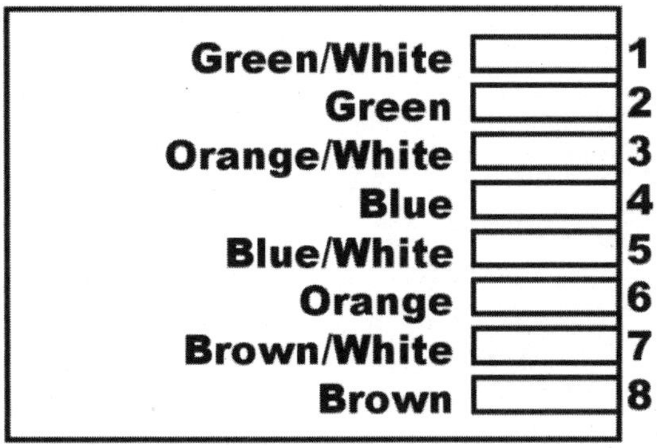

NOTE

EIA/TIA is the Electronics Industry Association/Telecommunications Industry Association.

NOTE

The precise electronic benefits gained by using the twists are well beyond the scope of the Network+ exams and this book.

The EIA/TIA 568A standard is not the only game—or color-code—in town. Theoretically, as long as each end of each cable uses the same color code, many color codes could be used within the same building and everything would still work. 10BaseT devices do not care what color the wires are—they just need to have the pins on the RJ-45 connector match up at each end. Despite the fact that multiple color codes can work, the wise network tech will use a single color code throughout an organization. Consistency makes troubleshooting and repair easier, allowing network techs to assume the proper color code. If an end-user trips over a cable and breaks the connector (of course, wise network techs such as ourselves would never do such a thing), putting a new connector on the cable takes little time if the tech knows the color code being used. If no standard color code exists, then the poor network tech has to find the other end of the cable and figure out the color code used for that specific cable. Save wear and tear on the tennis shoes—pick a standard color code and stick with it.

TIP

EXAM TIP

For the Network+ exam, do not worry about memorizing the EIA/TIA 568A color code. Just know that it is an industry standard color code for UTP cabling.

Further, don't just install any old UTP cabling off the street. UTP comes in a variety of grades, called *categories*, numbered Category 1 through Category 5. These categories define the maximum supported speed of the cable. See Table 2.1. When selecting cable for use with 10BaseT, choose a cable that can support at least 10 megabits per second (i.e. Category 3 or higher).

TABLE 2.1

Category 1	Regular analog phone lines—not used for data communications
Category 2	Supports speeds up to 4 megabits per second
Category 3	Supports speeds up to 16 megabits per second
Category 4	Supports speeds up to 20 megabits per second
Category 5	Supports speeds up to 100 megabits per second

Most new cabling installations use Category 5 (Cat 5) cabling. Cat 5 cabling costs only a few pennies per foot more than Category 3 cabling and provides for future upgrades. Installing CAT 5 cabling from the beginning makes sense even if the network will initially use 10BaseT. Labor, not materials, constitutes the major expense when cabling a new network. Why pay a cable installer once to wire the network for Cat 3 today and again to wire it for Cat 5 in two years when you need to upgrade to a higher speed network? Because so few cable installers use Category 3 cabling anymore, the higher-grade Cat 5 cabling can sometimes be cheaper than Cat 3 cabling. The category level of a piece of cable will normally be written on the cable itself, as shown in Figure 2.11.

FIGURE 2.11 *Markings on the cable will show its category level.*

10BaseT Limits and Specifications

Like any other Ethernet cabling system, 10BaseT has limitations for distance and the number of computers that can be connected. The key distance limitation for 10BaseT is the distance between the hub and the computer. The twisted pair cable connecting a computer to the hub may not exceed 100 meters in length. See Figure 2.12. A 10BaseT hub can connect no more than 1024 computers, although that limitation rarely comes into play. It makes no sense for vendors to build such large hubs and, more to the point, such expensive hubs, because Ethernet performance typically bogs down due to excessive collisions with far fewer than 1024 computers.

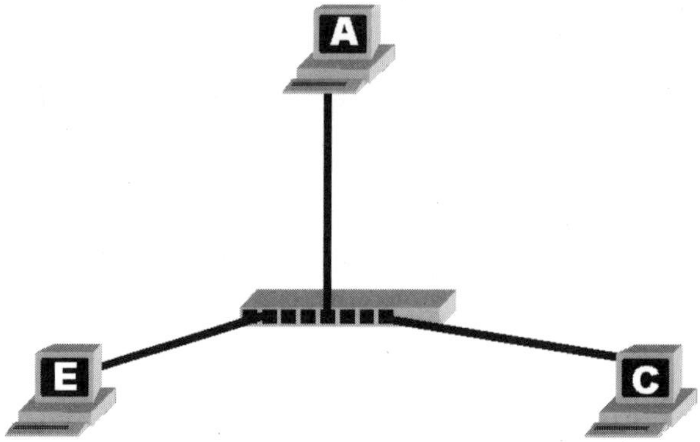

FIGURE 2.12
The cable between any node and the hub may not exceed 100 meters in length.

Connecting the Segments

Sometimes, one hub is just not enough. Once an organization uses every port on its existing hub, adding additional nodes requires additional hubs. In addition, fault tolerance can motivate an organization to add more hubs. If every node on the network connects to the same hub, that hub becomes a "single point of failure"—if it fails, everybody drops off the network. The 10BaseT standard provides two methods of connecting multiple hubs—coax cable and crossover cables.

Coaxial cabling, either 10Base2 or 10Base5, can link together multiple 10BaseT hubs. By definition, a 10BaseT hub is a repeater. It brings in signals from one port and repeats them on all other ports, as shown in Figure 2.13. With the addition of an AUI or BNC port, it can repeat packets onto a coaxial segment just as easily as it can repeat them on UTP cabling. The coax segment can simply connect two 10BaseT hubs, as shown in Figure 2.14, or can have nodes directly attached to it, as shown in Figure 2.15.

NOTE

A *port* is the female plug on the hub.

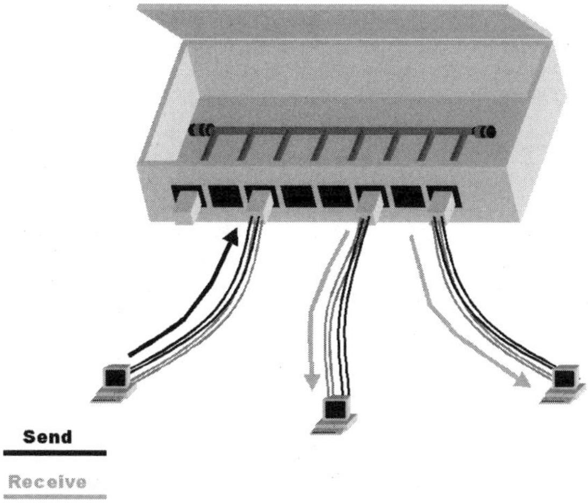

FIGURE 2.13
A hub acts as a repeater.

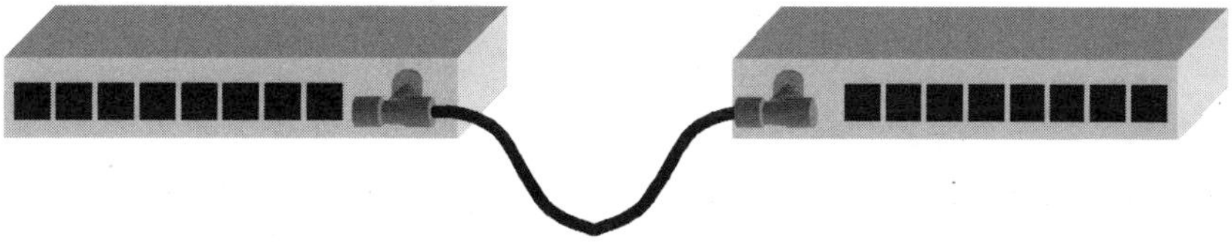

FIGURE 2.14
Hubs can connect to each other via either 10Base2 or 10Base5.

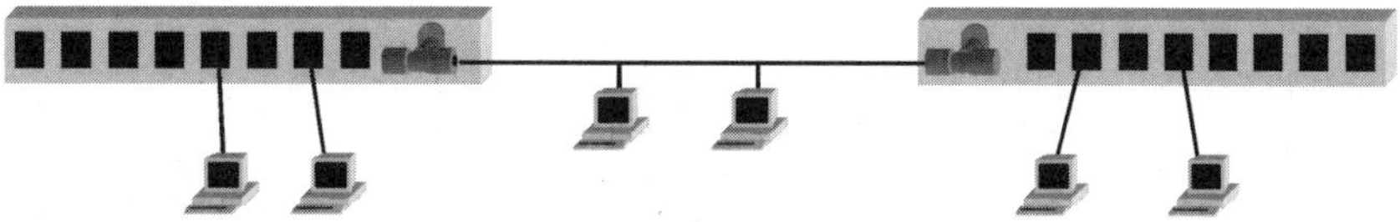

FIGURE 2.15
The segment connecting two hubs can be populated with machines.

> **NOTE** A *populated segment* has one or more nodes directly attached to it.

Hubs can also connect to each other via special twisted pair cables called *crossover cables*. A standard cable cannot connect two hubs because both hubs will attempt to send on the first pair of wires (1 and 2) and will listen on the second pair (3 and 6). The hubs cannot "hear" each other. A crossover cable reverses the sending and receiving pairs on one end of the cable, as shown in Figure 2.16. One end of the cable is wired according to the EIA/TIA 568A standard, while the other end is wired according to the EIA/TIA 568B standard. With the pairs reversed, the hubs can "hear" each other. To spare network techs the trouble of making special crossover cables, most hubs have a special crossover port that crosses the wires inside the hub, as shown in Figure 2.17. Unfortunately, manufacturers label these special crossover ports in more than one way. When describing and labeling their crossover ports, hub manufacturers use a wide variety of terms, including "crossover," "uplink," "in port," and "out port."

FIGURE 2.16
A crossover cable reverses the sending and receiving pair.

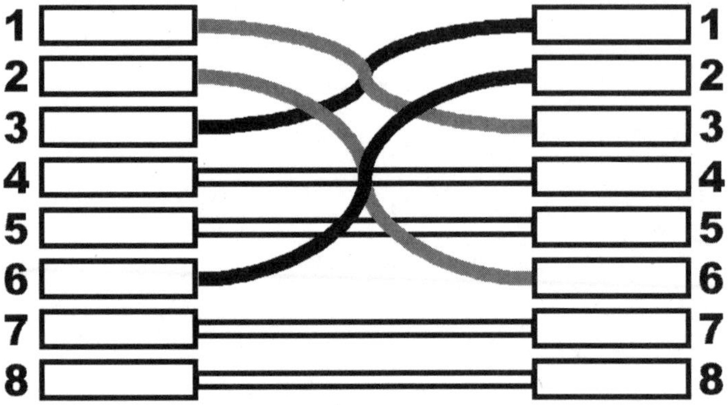

FIGURE 2.17
Special crossover ports cross the pairs internally.

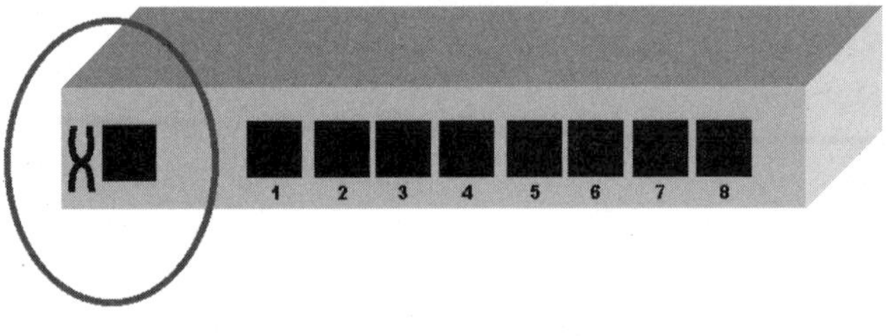

Be careful when using crossover ports. Connecting two crossover ports with a regular piece of twisted pair cabling ranks among the most common Ethernet misconfigurations. The first crossover port crosses the pairs, while the second uncrosses them, resulting in a standard, straight through cable that will not work.

Multiple segments in a network provide greater fault tolerance than a single segment. Each segment functions or fails on its own. Figure 2.18 shows three segments: A, B, and C. Segments A and B are 10BaseT hubs; segment C is a 10Base2 segment. A failure of one segment does not cause other segments to fail. The failure affects only transmissions that rely on the failed segment. If Cindy's pet hamster Gidget escapes and chews through segment C, for example, computers on segments A and B cannot communicate with each other, but computers on segment A can continue to communicate with each other and computers on segment B can continue to communicate with each other. See Figure 2.19. Of course, the poor computers on segment C must sit idle and twiddle their thumbs until some kind network tech repairs the damage wrought by the evil hamster.

FIGURE 2.18

Two hubs connected by a 10Base2 segment.

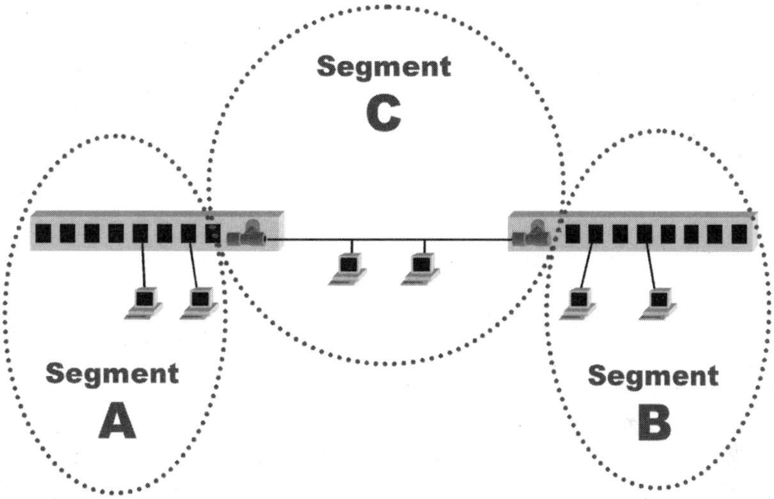

FIGURE 2.19

Segment C's failure prevents communication between segments A and B, but does not affect communication within segments A and B.

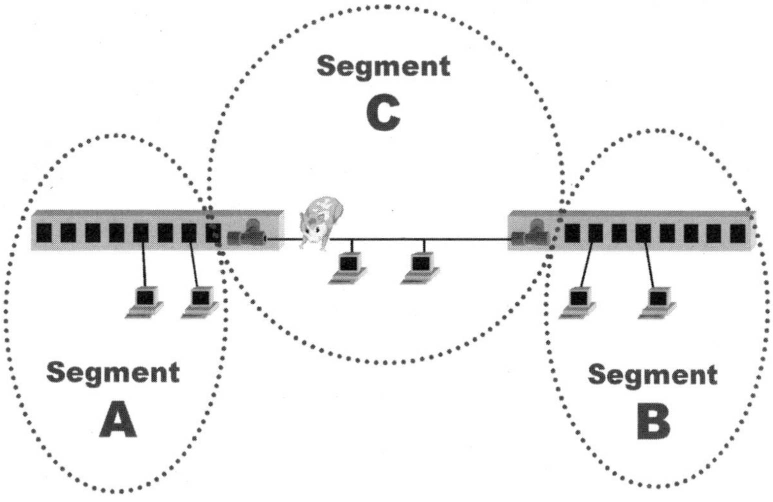

10BaseT Summary

- **Speed:** 10 megabits/second
- **Signal type:** Baseband
- **Distance:** 100 meters between the hub and the node
- No more than 1024 nodes per hub
- Star bus topology—physical star, logical bus
- Uses UTP cabling with RJ-45 connectors

How Big Can an Ethernet Network Be? The 5-4-3 Rule

When multiple Ethernet segments connect to each other with hubs and repeaters, they remain part of the same collision domain. See Figure 2.20. As discussed in Chapter 1, a collision domain is a set of Ethernet segments that receive all traffic generated by any node within those segments. A set of restrictions known as the 5-4-3 rule limits the size of an Ethernet collision domain.

FIGURE 2.20 *An Ethernet collision domain.*

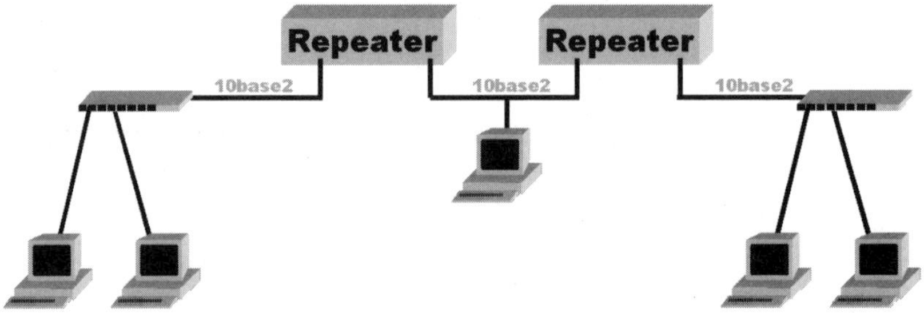

The 5-4-3 Rule Is Only an Approximation

For Ethernet networks to function properly, each node must detect when its own transmissions "collide" with those of another node. When a node detects a collision, it waits a random period of time and then resends the packet. (See Chapter 1 for a more detailed discussion of CSMA/CD.) If the sending node fails to detect a collision, the node does not know to resend the packet and the packet is lost. The most common reason for a machine to fail to detect a collision is if the network is too large.

Ethernet nodes cease checking for collisions once they send the last byte of each data packet. If the network is large enough that the last byte leaves the sending node before the first byte reaches every other node on the network, undetected collision can occur. In the event of a collision between two machines on the extreme edges of the network, neither node retransmits its data packet and the data packets are lost.

To arrive at a precise answer to the question "how big is too big?" requires a series of arcane calculations that determine variables with names like "round trip signal propagation delay" and "inter-packet gap." Fortunately, the average network tech does not need to do these difficult calculations. To allow network technicians to build networks that keep within the limits without requiring them to earn advanced math degrees, the networking industry has developed a rule of thumb: the 5-4-3 rule.

The 5-4-3 Rule

The 5-4-3 rule approximates the more precise and complex calculations that determine the maximize size of an Ethernet collision domain. In a collision domain, no two nodes may be separated by more than:

- 5 repeaters
- 4 segments
- 3 populated segments

A *populated segment* is an Ethernet segment with at least one machine directly connected to it.

To calculate a network's compliance with the 5-4-3 rule, trace the "worst case" path between two machines—i.e. the path between the two machines that will yield the highest number of segments, repeaters, and populated segments. Figure 2.21 shows a network with 5 segments, 4 repeaters, and 3 populated segments. The path between machines A and C represents the worst case path because the packets must pass through all the segments and repeaters on the network. The paths between A and B or B and C are irrelevant for calculating compliance with the 5-4-3 rule because a longer path exists between two other machines. The path between machine A and machine C uses all 5 segments, all four repeaters, and all three populated segments.

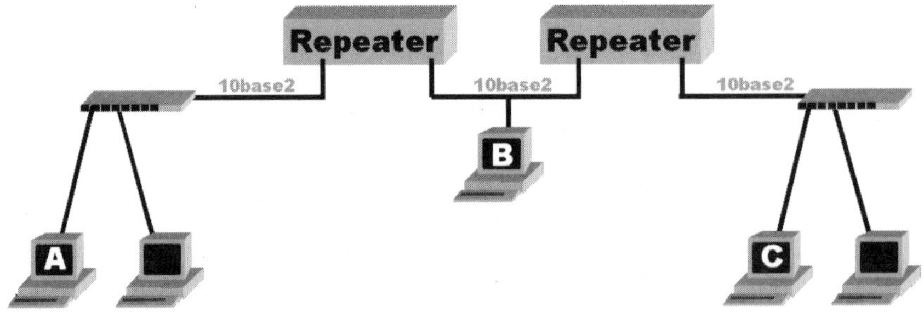

FIGURE 2.21
A network with 5 segments, 4 repeaters, and 3 populated segments.

NOTE

When the 5-4-3 rule is calculated, a hub counts as both a repeater and a segment.

The 5-4-3 rules limitations do not apply to the entire network, but rather to the paths within the network. Figure 2.22 shows a network that complies with the 5-4-3 rule but has 6 segments, 6 repeaters, and 5 populated segments within the entire network. Hub 1 counts as both a segment and a repeater, but not as a populated segment because no computers attach directly to it. Segments that link other segments together but have no computers directly attached to them are called *link segments*. This network follows the 5-4-3 rule because no path between two machines ever traverses more than 5 segments, 4 repeaters, or 3 populated segments. The path between computers A and C, for example, runs through 3 segments (hubs 2, 1, and 4), three repeaters (hubs 2, 1, and 4) and two populated segments (hubs 2 and 4).

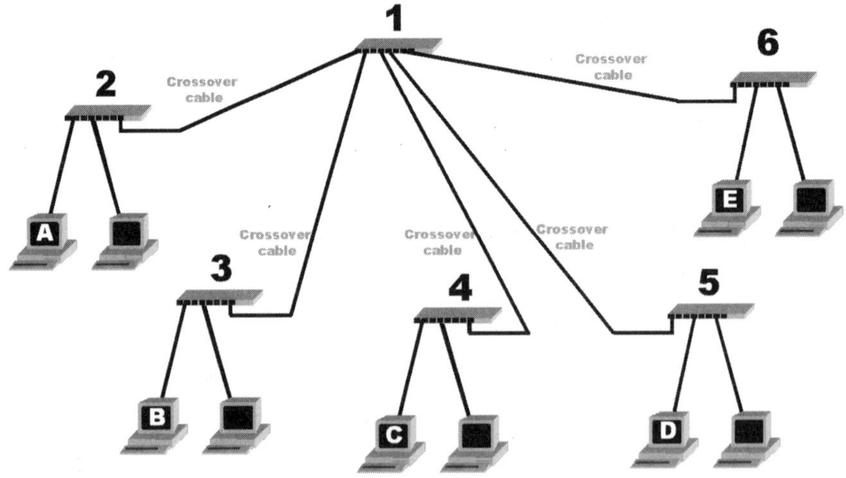

FIGURE 2.22
A network with 6 segments that complies with the 5-4-3 rule.

The 5-4-3 rule imposes limits on the size of an individual Ethernet collision domain, but the limits are generous. The network shown in Figure 2.22 above can contain thousands of individual machines. Remember that each hub can support up to 1024 PCs. With the demands of modern operating systems and applications, however, 10 megabit-per-second Ethernet networks with far fewer machines can become too busy and congested to function well. Two tools exist to relieve this congestion and allow larger networks: traffic management and high speed Ethernet.

NOTE

"STACKABLE" HUBS

Rather than make 1024 port hubs that would have a limited market and be expensive to replace in the event of failure, manufacturers make stackable hubs. *Stackable hubs* are hubs with a special proprietary connection that enables them to combine and function as a single device. For the purposes of the 5-4-3 rule, all the hubs in a stack are a single segment, repeater, and populated segment.

Traffic Management—Bridges and Routers

As the demands placed on network bandwidth grow, the number of machines that can peacefully coexist within an Ethernet collision domain shrinks. In the days of DOS-based network clients accessing a few small word processing and spreadsheet files from a file server, several hundred machines could sit on the same collision domain and expect reasonable performance. Today, many networks demand more bandwidth. A typical network might consist of Windows 9x and NT Workstation clients accessing Windows NT database servers, NetWare file servers, and UNIX-based Web servers. Instead of occasionally accessing a few files on a server, users constantly demand a wide variety of services from their servers. Depending on the specific demands placed on the network's bandwidth, the number of machines that can peacefully coexist on a single Ethernet collision domain can vary from as many as 100 to as few as 2. Fortunately, devices exist that can link together multiple Ethernet collision domains to form larger networks:

bridges and routers. These devices do not simply connect networks. They also filter traffic between the networks, preserving precious bandwidth.

Bridges

Bridges filter and forward traffic between two or more networks based on the MAC addresses contained in the data packets. To *filter* traffic means to stop it from crossing from one network to the next; to *forward* traffic means to pass traffic originating on one side of the bridge to the other. Figure 2.23 shows two Ethernet collision domains connected by a bridge. The bridge is represented as a simple box because the physical appearance of a bridge can vary a great deal. The bridge can be a standalone device that looks similar to an Ethernet repeater or hub, or it might be a PC with two NICs running special bridging software. The bridge might even be built into a multifunction device that provides other functions in addition to acting as a bridge.

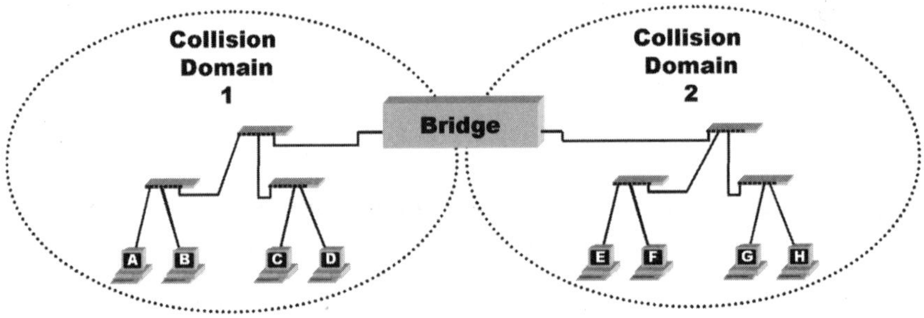

FIGURE 2.23 *Two Ethernet collision domains connected by a bridge.*

How Bridges Function

Ethernet bridges behave just like repeaters when first plugged in. In the network shown in Figure 2.23 above, machine A sends a data packet to machine D. Because machines A, B, C, and D all lie on the same collision domain, they will all receive that data packet. When the data packet destined for machine D hits the bridge, the bridge does not know the location of machine D, and forwards the packet to collision domain 2. At this point the bridge begins building a list of machines, and makes a note that it received a data packet from machine A's MAC address from collision domain 1. Now that the bridge knows the location of at least one machine, it can begin filtering. When machine D responds to machine A, the bridge will not forward the packet to collision domain 2 because it knows that the destination of the data packet lies on the same collision domain in which it originated.

Eventually, each machine will have sent out at least one data packet and the bridge will have a full list of each machine's MAC address and location. For the example used here, the table would look something like Table 2.2, but without the letters for each machine. Bridges care about MAC addresses—they could not care less what designations (like letters or names) we mortals assign to our machines.

TABLE 2.2

Collision Domain 1	
Machine	MAC address
A	00 45 5D 32 5E 72
B	9F 16 C6 55 4D EE
C	9F 16 C6 99 DF F1
D	00 45 5D 75 D3 95
Collision Domain 2	
E	9F 16 C6 85 E5 55
F	9F 16 C6 DD 41 11
G	00 45 5D 00 25 19
H	9F 16 C6 88 58 F5

With a complete table listing each machine's MAC address and the side of the bridge on which it sits, the bridge can look at every incoming packet and decide whether or not to forward it to the other side. If machine C sends a packet to machine D, machines A and B will receive that packet as well because the hubs between them and machine C lack the ability to decide what to forward. The hubs are repeaters, and they repeat everything. The more sophisticated bridge recognizes that no machine on collision domain 2 needs to see the packet destined for machine D on collision domain 1 and filters the packet accordingly.

NOTE

Bridges operate at layer 2 of the OSI model, also known as the data-link layer. Chapter 4 discusses the OSI model in detail.

Bridges provide two key benefits: relief from the 5-4-3 rule and the ability to segment traffic. The purpose of the 5-4-3 rule is to prevent undetected collisions. With a bridge, machines do not need to be within 5 segments, 4 repeaters, and 3 populated segments of machines on the far side of the bridge—they simply must be within 5-4-3 of the bridge. Once the packet reaches the bridge, the bridge takes over the responsibility of sending it to its final destination. If the bridge forwards the packet that collides with another packet, the bridge, not the original source machine, detects the collision and re-transmits the packet. Bridges also provide a performance benefit by breaking the network up into independent pieces. In the example above, machine A can send a packet to machine D at exactly the same instant that machine G sends a packet to machine H without causing a collision. When no traffic crosses the bridge, the bridge effectively doubles the bandwidth of the network as a whole.

Bridges always forward broadcast traffic. Most network traffic is *unicast* traffic, destined for a single machine, and bridges can easily make decisions about whether to filter or forward these packets. A *broadcast* is a packet directed to all machines. Network devices use broadcast addresses to "discover" information about the network. Human beings like to call machines by names, like Titan or Sales20. In order for a machine on the network to find out the MAC address of the machine named Titan, it sends out a special broadcast packet that says, "If your name is Titan, please send me a response with your MAC address." Every machine on the network must examine that broadcast and determine whether or not its name is Titan. Most machines think, "hmm … that's not me" and ignore the broadcast. The machine named Titan, however, will respond back with a unicast packet that tells the machine that sent the broadcast Titan's MAC address. Because the bridge does not know the MAC address of the intended recipient of the broadcast, it plays it safe and forwards all broadcast traffic. This increases traffic on both sides of the bridge, but allows all functions that rely on broadcasts to work correctly.

Machines on either side of the bridge can remain blissfully unaware of the bridge's presence. When bridges retransmit a packet, they copy it precisely, even using the originating machine's MAC address as the source MAC address in the packet. Adding a bridge to a network does not require any reconfiguration of any of the other nodes on the network. Rewire the cabling and the bridge takes care of the rest. The "invisible" nature of bridges makes them the easiest way to break an Ethernet network into multiple collision domains.

Because bridges forward data packets without changing the packets themselves, the packet format used on each side of the bridge must be the same. The examples above discuss bridges that connect two Ethernet networks. Bridges also exist for other technologies, such as Token Ring (see Chapter 3 for a discussion of Token Ring). Bridges cannot, however, connect an Ethernet network to a Token Ring network because of differences in the structure of the packets.

TERMINOLOGY ALERT!

To be absolutely precise, the type of bridging described here is *transparent bridging*. Some documentation, especially documentation that deals with networking theory, will refer to *translational bridges*, which can translate between different packet formats. Translational bridges rarely, if ever, appear in Ethernet or Token Ring networks. If you see the term "bridge," assume it refers to the transparent bridge discussed here unless specifically told otherwise.

Bridges also lack the ability to handle multiple routes between machines. Figure 2.24 shows a network with multiple bridges that create a bridging loop. When machine A transmits a packet, bridges 2 and 3 will both forward the packet to bridge 1, making it appear to bridge 1 that machine A lies on both sides of bridge 1. The bridging loop confuses each of the other bridges in the same way. According to the simplified routing rules discussed above, the bridges would forward a packet bound for machine A endlessly. To prevent this excess traffic, bridges should not be allowed to form loops. Most bridges use a technique called the *spanning tree algorithm* to detect bridging loops and automatically disable bridges that form loops. Do not use bridges to provide multiple routes between nodes.

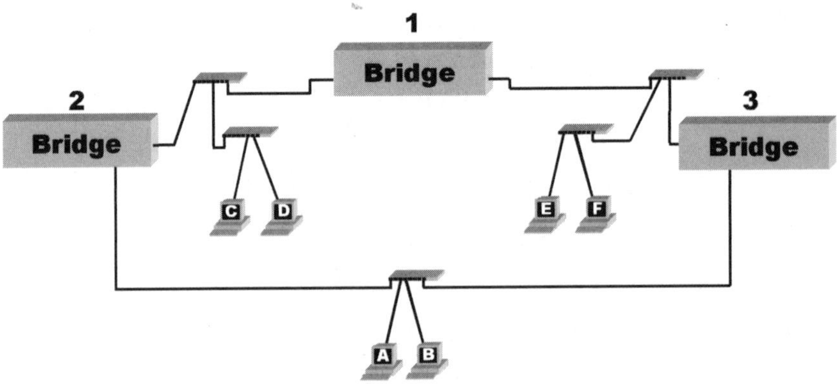

FIGURE 2.24
Loops can confuse bridges and should be avoided.

EXAM TIP

TIP

The Network+ exam does not cover the spanning tree algorithm and the term is mentioned here only for completeness.

Bridge Summary

- Bridges filter or forward traffic based on the MAC addresses contained in each data packet.
- Bridges always forward broadcast packets.
- Bridges operate at the data-link layer, layer 2 of the OSI model (see Chapter 4).
- Bridges can only connect two networks if they use the same type of data packets (i.e. Ethernet to Ethernet, Token Ring to Token Ring).
- Bridges learn the MAC addresses of machines on each network by listening to the cable.
- Bridges cannot be used to provide multiple routes between machines.

Bridges filter some unnecessary traffic, preserving precious network bandwidth. They free Ethernet networks from the limitations imposed by the 5-4-3 rule and increase the available bandwidth on a network by filtering traffic. Bridges do have limitations, however. They cannot connect dissimilar networks and cannot take advantage of multiple routes between nodes. Overcoming these challenges requires another type of device, a router.

Routers

Routers provide a more flexible and robust solution than bridges for connecting multiple networks. Routers, as the name implies, can filter and forward traffic between networks connected by multiple routes. These additional routes provide fault tolerance for the network, ensuring that a single cable break cannot shut down the network. In addition, the networks connected by the routers can be different types of networks (i.e. Ethernet and Token Ring).

Although routers support the use of multiple routes, simple routed networks do not necessarily have multiple routes and can appear very similar to bridged networks. Figure 2.25 shows a typical routed network with multiple routes between the machines A and C. Although most routed networks will use multiple routes to provide fault tolerance, multiple routes are not strictly required. See Figure 2.26.

FIGURE 2.25 *A typical routed network with multiple routes.*

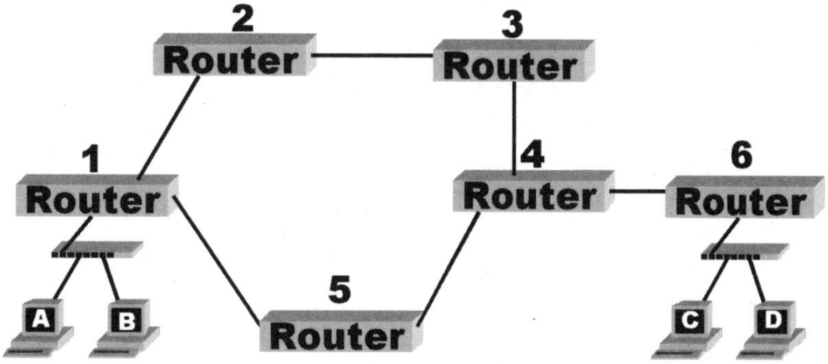

FIGURE 2.26 *A simple routed network without multiple routes.*

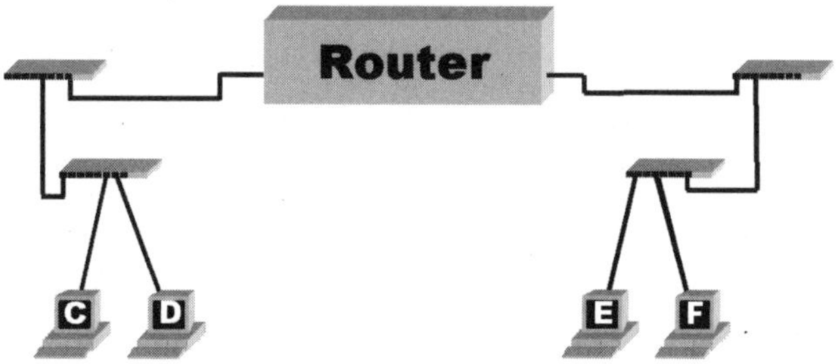

NOTE

Routers operate at layer 3 of the OSI model, also known as the network layer. Chapter 4 discusses the OSI model in detail.

How Routers Function

Routers forward traffic more selectively than bridges. Unlike bridges, routers discard all broadcast traffic by default. Routed networks tend to consist of some number of Local Area Networks (LANs) connected to form a Wide Area Network (WAN). While LANs typically run at speeds of 10 megabits per second or faster, the links between LANs that form a WAN tend to be much slower. Speeds between 56 kilobits per second and 1.5 megabits per second are common. If all broadcast traffic from each LAN were forwarded over those slower WAN links, the network would quickly bog down. In addition, in very large WANs such as the Internet, most broadcast traffic is irrelevant to most machines outside the local LAN. Does Microsoft's Web server in Seattle care that two machines in Total Seminars' Houston office are trying to find out each other's MAC addresses by broadcasting? I don't think so! See Figure 2.27. The discarding of broadcast traffic prevents packets that would be ignored anyway from eating up bandwidth.

TERMINOLOGY

TERMINOLOGY ALERT!

A *LAN* is one or more small networks in a single location. A *WAN* is a network of LANs, usually spread out over a larger area.

FIGURE 2.27

The router connecting the Total Seminars' Houston network to the Internet discards any broadcast packets that reach it.

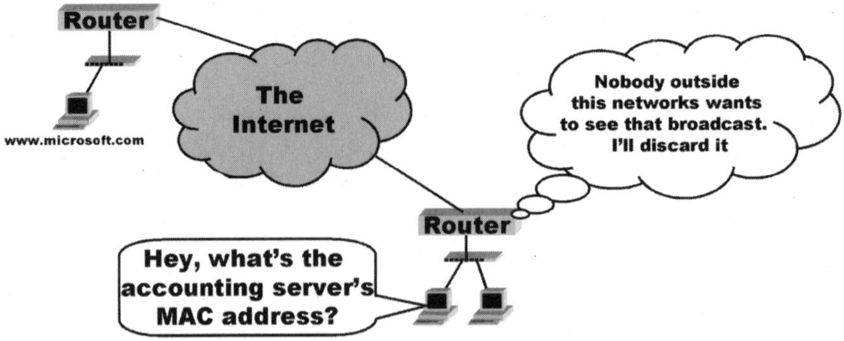

NOTE

When a network is too large to show in a single diagram, the majority of the network is often shown as a cloud. In Figure 2.27, the exact structure of the Internet between the Total Seminars' Houston office and the Microsoft network in Seattle is irrelevant (as long as it works).

Because routers discard broadcast packets, they cannot "learn" where all the machines on the network are by listening to their traffic the way a bridge would. Instead they rely on an additional level of addressing called *network addressing*. A network address tells the router two pieces of information: the specific machine that a packet should be delivered to, and the network on which that machine lies. The IP addresses used on the Internet are an example of network addresses (see Chapter 7 for a discussion of IP addressing).

Given the destination network address, a properly configured router can determine the best route to the destination machine. In Figure 2.28, router 1 needs to deliver a packet from machine A to machine D. Assuming that all the links between the routers operate at the same speed, the most efficient route for the packet should be: router 1 to 5 to 4 to 6. That route requires 4 hops. A *hop* is the process of passing through a router en route to the final destination. Alternative routes exist, but the router ignores them because they require more hops. In the event of a break in the link between routers 1 and 5, router 1 should automatically calculate the next best route (if one exists) and redirect traffic to the alternative route: router 1 to 2 to 3 to 4 to 6. See Figure 2.29.

FIGURE 2.28
Properly configured routers choose the best path between two nodes.

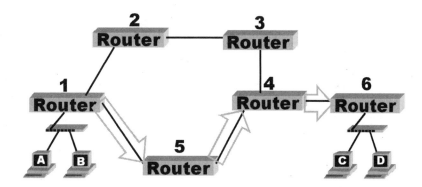

Routed networks require significantly more planning and configuration than bridged networks. In a bridged network, the bridge does all the work. Bridges listen to the data packets transmitted by machines on the network and determine the location of each machine without any intervention by a network tech. No configuration changes need be done to the nodes on either side of the bridge—they need not even know that the bridge exists. In a routed network, each node requires configuration changes to communicate with machines on the far side of the router. First, the network tech must assign the correct network address to every device on the network. Second, he must configure the routers so that they can find each of the networks within the WAN. While the example above relied on hop counts to determine the best route, other factors can be considered as well, including the speed of the links between routers and the financial cost of using the link. In return for the additional configuration required, routed networks grant the network tech greater control over the movement of packets than bridged networks do.

FIGURE 2.29
In the event of a break in the cable, properly configured routers automatically switch to an alternate route if one is available.

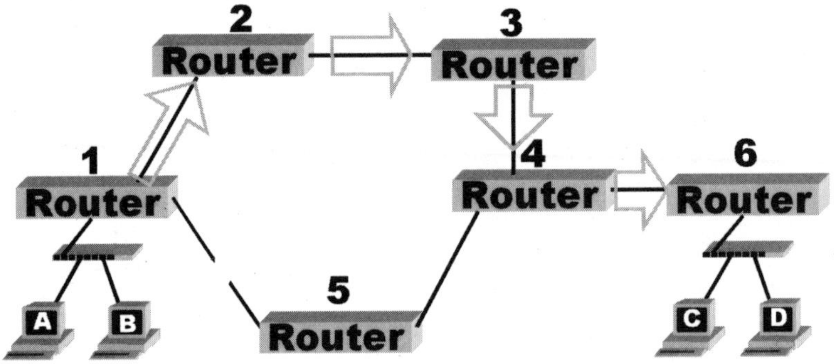

EXAM TIP

TIP

The Network+ exam requires only a general knowledge of how routers function and does not cover router configuration in detail. For the exam, understand the role of routers in a network and the TCP/IP specific information covered in Chapter 6.

Router Summary

- Routers filter and forward traffic based on network addresses (such as IP addresses), not based on MAC addresses.
- Routers can choose among multiple paths between two nodes.
- Routers operate at layer 3 of the OSI model, known as the Network layer (see Chapter 4).

High Speed Ethernet

As any fighter pilot will tell you, sometimes you just "feel the need, the need for speed." While plain vanilla Ethernet performs well enough for basic file and print sharing, today's more demanding network applications (e.g. Lotus Notes, SAP, Microsoft Exchange, Half-Life, Quake Arena) can quickly saturate a network running at 10 megabits per second. Fortunately, the people at the IEEE keep expanding the standard, providing the network tech in the trenches with new tools that provide additional bandwidth: Fast Ethernet, Switched Ethernet, Full-duplex Ethernet, and Gigabit Ethernet.

Fast Ethernet

Fast Ethernet is not a single technology. The term *Fast Ethernet* refers to any of several Ethernet flavors that operate at 100 megabits per second. Rather than limiting Ethernet to a single high-speed solution, the IEEE endorsed multiple standards for Fast Ethernet and allowed the marketplace to choose among them. The major variations include 100BaseT and 100BaseFX.

100BaseT

The IEEE supports two variations of 100BaseT: 100BaseTX and 100BaseT4. Both look physically similar to 10BaseT, using a star bus topology and connecting to hubs with UTP cabling. The cable connecting a device to the hub may be no more than 100 meters long. The difference between 100BaseTX and 100BaseT4 lies in the quality of the cable used. 100BaseTX requires CAT 5 cabling to achieve 100 megabits per second speed using only 2 pairs of wires. Like 10BaseT, 100BaseTX ignores the remaining 2 pairs. 100BbaseT4 uses all 4 pairs to achieve 100 megabit per second performance using lower quality CAT 3 cabling. Think of the cable as a highway—100BaseTX increases capacity by raising the speed limit, 100BaseT4 increases capacity by adding additional lanes.

Both 100BaseTX and 100BaseT4 allow organizations to take advantage of their existing UTP cabling. If the properly installed UTP wiring exists, upgrading from 10BaseT consists of simply replacing hubs and network cards, with no recabling required. UTP cabling does not, however, meet the needs of all organizations for three key reasons. First, for networks covering large buildings or campuses, the 100-meter distance limitation allowed with UTP-based networks proves inadequate. Second, for networks functioning in locations with high levels of electrical interference, UTP's lack of electrical shielding makes it a poor choice. Finally, the Maxwell Smarts and James Bonds of the world find UTP cabling (and copper cabling in general) easy to tap, making it an inappropriate choice for high-security environments. To address these issues, the IEEE 802.3 standard provides for 100-megabit Ethernet using fiber optic cable: 100BaseFX.

100BaseFX

The 100BaseFX standard specifies 100-megabit Ethernet running over two optical fibers. Fiber optic cabling uses pulses of light instead of electrical current to transmit data packets. Using light instead of electricity addresses the three key weaknesses of copper cabling. First, optical signals can travel much further. The maximum length for a 100BaseFX cable is 400 meters. Second, fiber optic cable is immune to electrical interference, making it an ideal choice for high-interference environments. Third, the cable is much more difficult to tap into, making it a good choice for environments with security concerns. Despite its benefits, the use of fiber optic cable for Ethernet remains limited because of high cost.

NOTE

100Base VG, also known as 100BaseVGAnyLAN, is not a version of Ethernet. Designed to run over Cat 3 (Voice Grade) cabling, it does not use CSMA/CD to determine access to the cable. The IEEE 802.12 committee controls the standards for 100BaseVG. As the popularity of 100BaseTX has grown, the importance of competitors like 100BaseVG has diminished.

Migrating to Fast Ethernet

Upgrading an entire network to 100BaseTX can be a daunting task. 100BaseTX requires new hubs and NICs, and often requires upgrades to the existing wiring. For organizations with more than a few machines, upgrading every node can be the work of months or even years. Fortunately, the conversion can be done slowly. Organizations that want to migrate slowly can purchase 10/100BaseT devices. A 10/100BaseT device automatically functions as a 100BaseTX device when plugged into another 10/100BaseT or 100BaseTX device, but will function as a 10BaseT device when plugged into another 10BaseT device. The existence of these hybrid devices allows organizations to roll out 10BaseT in batches, providing high-speed access to the machines that need it.

Switched Ethernet

Feeling the need for even more speed? Then Switched Ethernet may be the solution. An *Ethernet switch* is a special hub that can place some devices into their own collision domains. In essence, an Ethernet switch is a hub with a bridge built in. Physically, an Ethernet switch looks much like any other Ethernet hub except for the addition of one or more bridged ports. See Figure 2.30. Logically, an Ethernet switch puts devices plugged into one of its switched ports into their own collision domain. See Figure 2.31. The switch provides two benefits. First, if both the sender and the receiver are on their own switched ports, the full bandwidth of that connection (10 or 100 megabits) is available to them—no other machine can cause a collision. Second, the switch can act as a buffer, allowing 10-megabit and 100-megabit devices to communicate with each other.

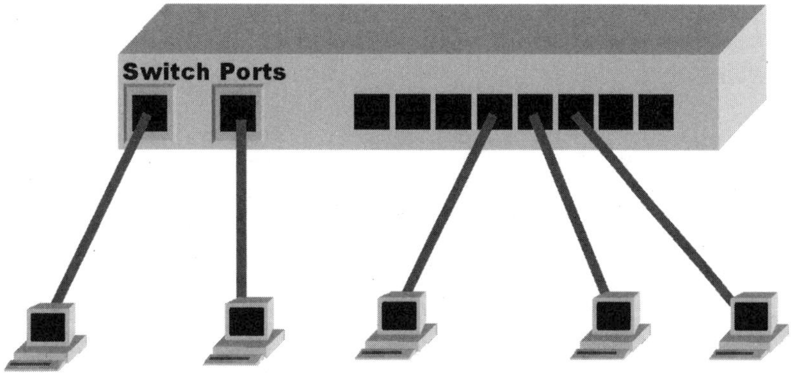

FIGURE 2.30
An eight-port switch with two switched ports.

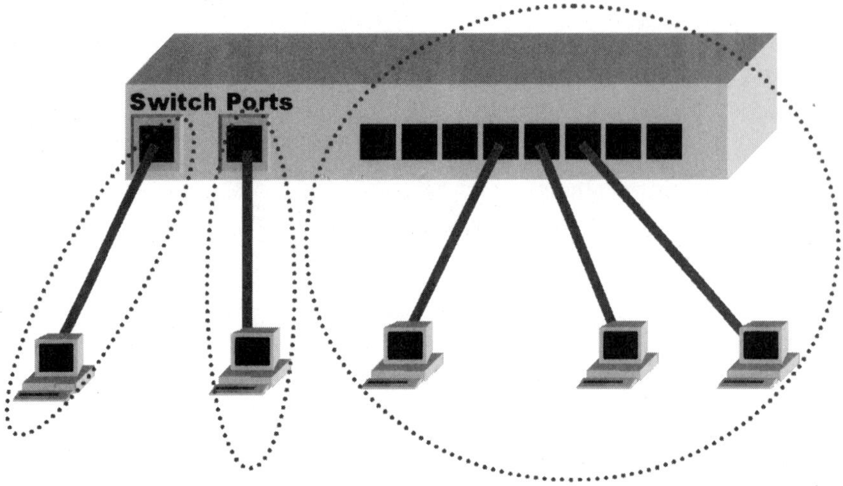

FIGURE 2.31
The devices plugged into the switched ports are isolated on their own collision domains.

Ethernet switches can also connect segments to a backbone. A *backbone* is a segment, usually a high speed one, that connects other segments. Figure 2.32 shows a network that supplies 10BaseT to the desktop, and connects the hubs to a 100BaseT backbone segment. In some cases, heavily accessed machines such as file servers plug directly into the backbone, as shown in Figure 2.33.

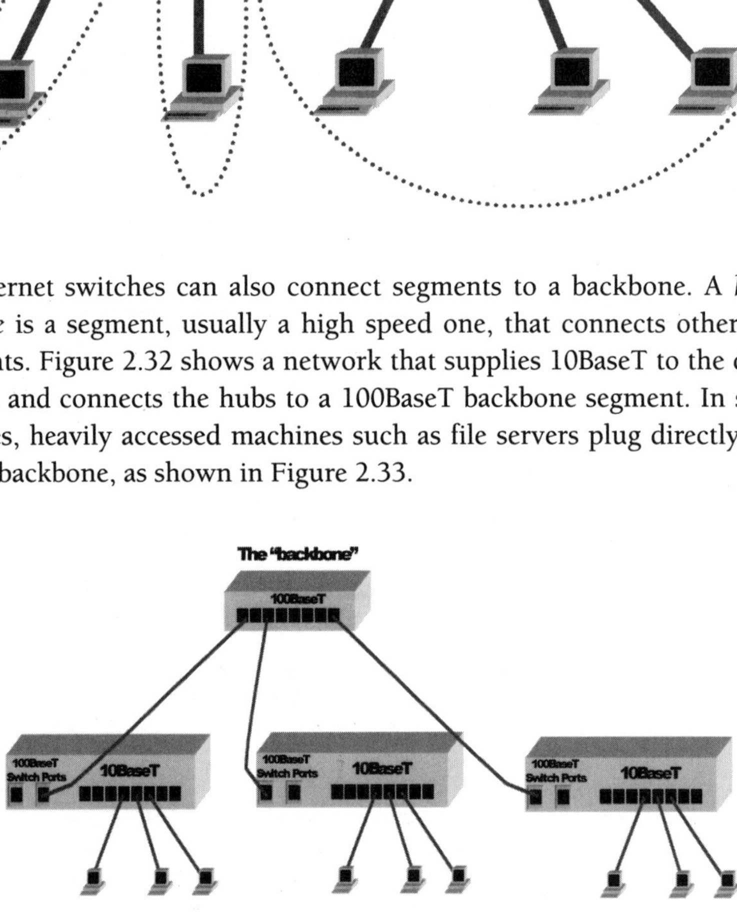

FIGURE 2.32
Desktop machines run at 10 megabits, but the backbone runs at 100 megabits.

Full-duplex Ethernet

Ethernet switching opens up another avenue for improving the performance of the network: full-duplex Ethernet. *Full-duplex* means that a device can send and receive data simultaneously. Normally, Ethernet transmissions are half-duplex, meaning that a machine can either send or receive data at any given moment. If a machine sends and receives simultaneously, a collision occurs. In the event of a collision, the rules of CSMA/CD kick in and the machine stops sending and waits a random period of time before trying again. CSMA/CD allows many machines to share the same segment, but requires all communication to be half-duplex.

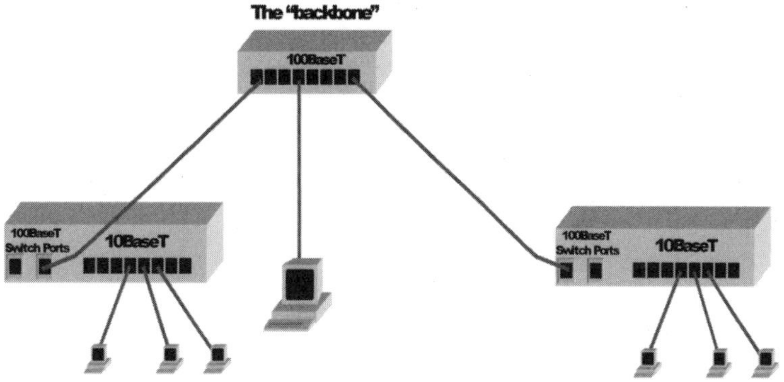

FIGURE 2.33 *Heavily accessed machines can be plugged directly into the backbone.*

In a Switched Ethernet connection running over UTP, however, not only are there only two machines on the segment, but there are separate sets of wires used for sending and receiving. Each pair of wires can act as a separate channel, allowing the devices at each end to communicate with each other in full-duplex mode. If the Ethernet NICs on each end of a switched connection support full-duplex mode, turn it on and enjoy the benefits. While not all Ethernet NICs support full-duplex operation, those that do will have an option to turn it on in their setup programs, as shown in Figure 2.34.

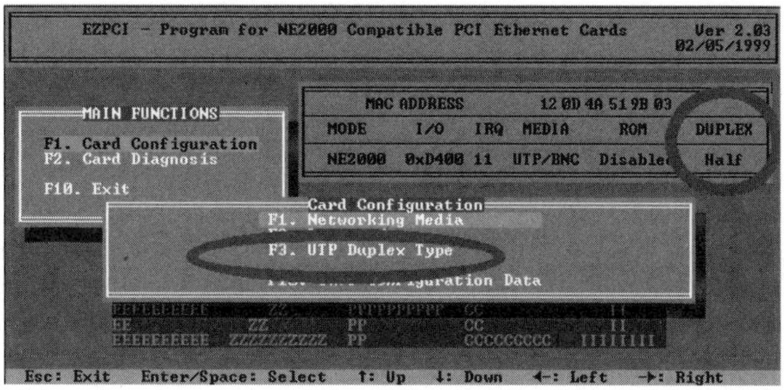

FIGURE 2.34 *If a card supports full-duplex, then its setup program will have an option to switch from half- to full-duplex.*

Full-duplex Ethernet offers impressive performance gains. A 10BaseT full-duplex connection has a theoretical bandwidth of 20 megabits per second (2 x 10 megabits per second). A 100BaseT full-duplex has a theoretical bandwidth of 200 megabits per second (2 x 100 megabits per second). Because there should never be collisions on a full-duplex connection, the real-world speeds of full-duplex Ethernet actually approach these theoretical maximums. Unfortunately, many Ethernet devices do not support full-duplex operation.

TIP

EXAM TIP

The Network+ exam does not delve into full-duplex Ethernet in detail. For the exam, know that in half-duplex communication a device cannot send when it is receiving and vice versa. In full-duplex communication, a device can send and receive at the same time.

Gigabit Ethernet

For the true speed junkie, an even more powerful version of Ethernet exists: Gigabit Ethernet. The IEEE approved the official standard for Gigabit Ethernet(1000BaseX) in 1998. Gigabit Ethernet is an important backbone technology, but only very high-end systems can generate enough traffic of their own to justify implementing it between individual PCs. A more likely scenario will have three layers of speed: 10BaseT to the desktop, 100BaseT between the first level of routers, and 1000BaseX between the second layer of routers.

NOTE

Gigabit Ethernet (1000BaseX) is not covered on the Network+ exam.

Conclusion

While 10Base2 and 10Base5 continue to fill valuable niches, the use of the star bus hybrid topology for UTP and fiber optic-based Ethernet networks enables network architects to build more robust and flexible networks. The proper use of high-speed segments, full-duplex operation, bridging, routing, and switching gives the network architect a full tool kit with which to build fast, stable networks.

Review Questions

(Select the best answer)

1) 100BaseTX uses a ______________ topology.
- a) Fast Ethernet
- b) bus
- c) star
- d) star bus

2) A bridge filters or forwards data packets based on:
- a) I/O addresses
- b) IP addresses
- c) MAC addresses
- d) Network addresses

3) The maximum distance that can separate a 10BaseT node from its hub is:
- a) 50 meters
- b) 100 meters
- c) 185 meters
- d) 200 meters

4) Within an Ethernet collision domain, the 5-4-3 rule limits 10 megabit Ethernet networks to______________ between any two machines.
- a) 5 populated segments, 4 repeaters, and 3 hubs
- b) 5 segments, 4 repeaters, and 3 populated segments
- c) 5 tokens, 4 packets, and 3 broadcasts
- d) 5 segments, 4 repeaters, and 3 hubs

5) Which of the following would be best described as a collision domain?
  a) A set of Ethernet segments connected by brouters
  b) A set of Ethernet segments connected by repeaters
  c) A set of Ethernet segments connected by routers
  d) A set of Ethernet segments connected by bridges

6) In the diagram below, what type of UTP cable does the arrow point to?
  a) Thinnet
  b) Thicknet
  c) Crossover
  d) Link

7) In the diagram below, which of the following cabling systems could be used for the segment indicated by the arrow? (Choose all that apply)
  a) 10BaseT
  b) 10Base2
  c) 10Base5

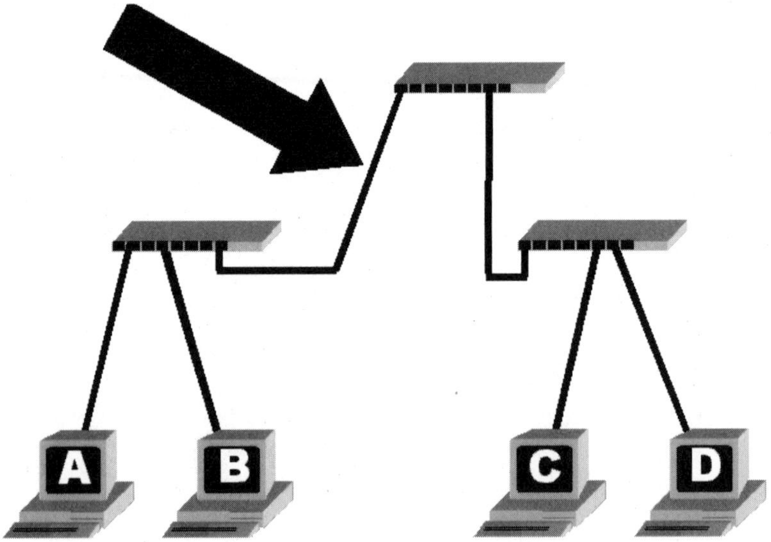

FIGURE 2.35
Diagram for Review Questions 6 and 7

8) When used for Ethernet, unshielded twisted pair uses ____________ connectors.

a) RG-58
b) RJ-45
c) RJ-11
d) RS-232

9) In the diagram shown below, the cable between computer B and its hub has been broken. What will the effect of the break be?

a) Machine A can send and receive with C and D, but not with B.
b) Machines C and D can still communicate, but machines A and B are off the network.
c) All network communication stops until the cable break is repaired.
d) Machine A can communicate with machines B and C, but not machine D.

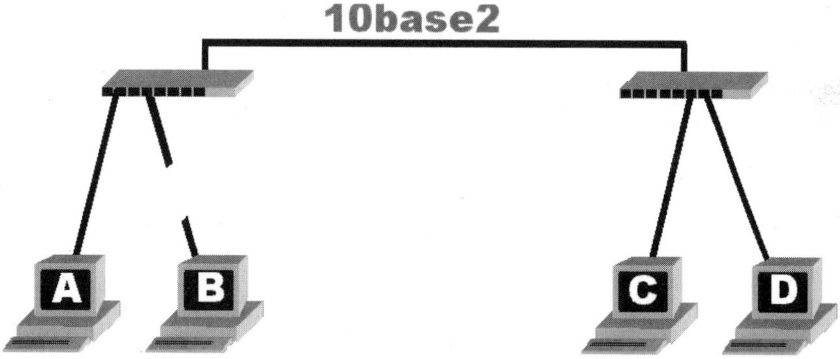

FIGURE 2.36
Diagram for Review Question 9

10) In the diagram shown below, the coaxial segment connecting the hubs has been broken. What will the effect of the break be?

a) Machine A can send and receive with C and D, but not with B.

b) Machines C and D can still communicate, but machines A and B are off the network.

c) All network communication stops until the cable break is repaired.

d) Machine A can communicate with machine B. Machine C can communicate with machine D. D cannot communicate with A or B, and B cannot communicate with C or D.

FIGURE 2.37

Diagram for Review Question 10

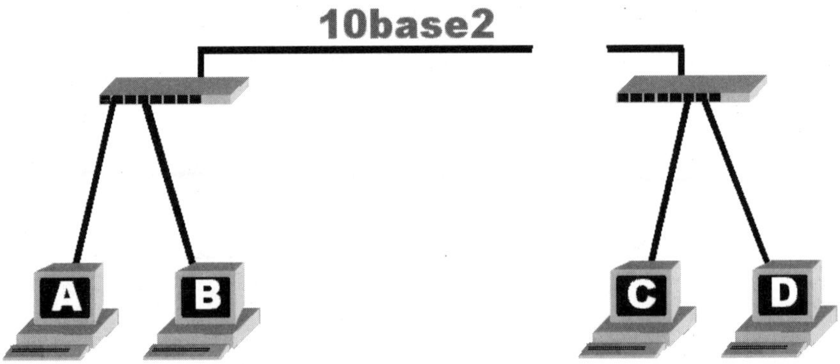

Review Answers

1) **D.** 100BaseTX uses a star bus topology. Fast Ethernet is another name for all versions of 100BaseT, including 100BaseTX. While 100BaseTX uses a physical bus topology and a logical star topology, calling it a star bus is a more complete answer.

2) **C.** Bridges make their decisions based on MAC addresses. IP addresses are a form of network address, which are used in routing, not bridging. I/O addresses are used to distinguish different devices within a PC, and have nothing to do with bridges.

3) **C.** The maximum distance between a 10BaseT node and its hub is 100 meters.

4) **B.** Within a collision domain, the 5-4-3 limits 10-megabit Ethernet networks to 5 segments, 4 repeaters, and 3 populated segments between any two machines.

5) **B.** A set of Ethernet segments connected by repeaters would be a collision domain.

6) **C.** Because the cable is UTP and connects two hubs, it must be a crossover cable. While Thinnet (10Base2) and Thicknet (10Base5) can be used to connect hubs, the question specified that the cable was UTP (Unshielded Twisted Pair), not coax. Link cable is not a commonly used Ethernet term.

7) **C.** 10Base5, with a maximum segment length of 500 meters, could easily cover the required 200 meters. Neither 10Base2, with a maximum segment length of 185 meters, nor 10BaseT, with a maximum cable length of 100 meters, can span the require 200 meters without adding a repeater.

8) **B.** UTP cable uses an RJ-45 connector when used with Ethernet. RG-58 is the type of coaxial cable used with 10Base2. RJ-11 is the standard 4-wire connector for regular phone lines. RS-232 is a standard for serial connectors.

9) **A.** Because the break occurred on the cable connecting B to the hub, only B should be affected.

10) **D.** The break in the coaxial cable shuts down the coax segment because the cable is no longer terminated properly (see Chapter 1). The two hubs continue to operate normally, but are no longer connected with each other.

CHAPTER 3

Ring Topologies and Token Ring

Token Ring, also known as 802.5, competes directly with Ethernet as an option for connecting desktop computers to a LAN. Although Token Ring possesses a much smaller share of the market than Ethernet, Token Ring's installed base has remained extremely loyal. Token Ring offers greater speed and efficiency than 10-megabit Ethernet, but at increased cost. Token Ring networks can look much like 10BaseT Ethernet networks, even using identical UTP cabling in some cases. Although the networks share the same physical star topology, Token Ring uses a logical ring topology rather than a logical bus topology.

NOTE

Although originally a proprietary IBM technology, today the IEEE 802.5 committee defines the standards for Token Ring. Just as there are minor differences between the original Xerox Ethernet standard and IEEE 802.3, there are minor differences between the original IBM standard for Token Ring and the IEEE 802.5 standard. These differences have little impact on the average network tech, and for all intents and purposes Token Ring and IEEE 802.5 should be considered synonymous.

Logical Ring Topology

A Token Ring network functions as a logical ring, as shown in Figure 3.1. Unlike Ethernet nodes, which broadcast their packets across a shared cable, Token Ring nodes only communicate directly with two other machines—their upstream and downstream neighbors. See Figure 3.2. Token Ring employs a token-passing system to control access to the ring. Token Ring nodes only transmit data when they receive a special packet called the token. By preventing all collisions, token passing operates more efficiently than Ethernet's CSMA/CD system, allowing Token Ring nodes full use of the network's bandwidth.

Token Passing

Token passing preserves network bandwidth by never allowing more than one node at a time to transmit data. Most Token Ring packets contain much the same information as an Ethernet packet: the source MAC address, the destination MAC address, the data to be transmitted, and a Frame Check Sequence (FCS) used to check the data for errors. See Figure 3.3. When receiving a packet, a Token Ring node checks the destination MAC address to determine whether to process the data it contains or send the packet to its downstream neighbor. When the intended recipient processes the data, it adds a special code to the packet that indicates the packet was received in good order. The receiving node then sends the packet back to the sending node. When the sending node receives its original data packet with the "received in good order" mark, the sending machine removes the packet from the wire. The original sending machine then generates a new packet with a special additional field, the *token*.

FIGURE 3.1
Token Ring networks use a logical ring topology.

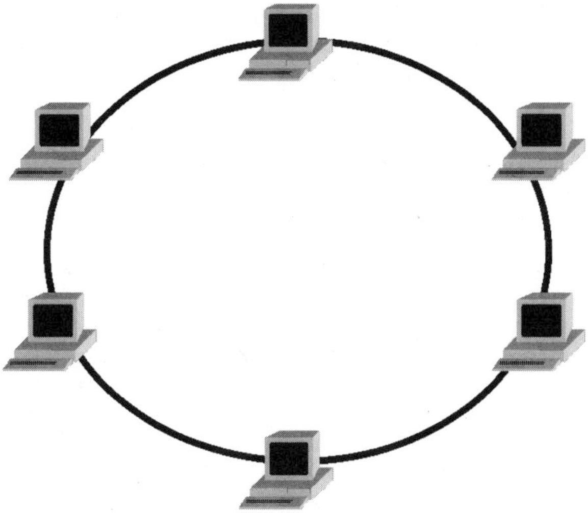

FIGURE 3.2
Node A is the downstream neighbor.

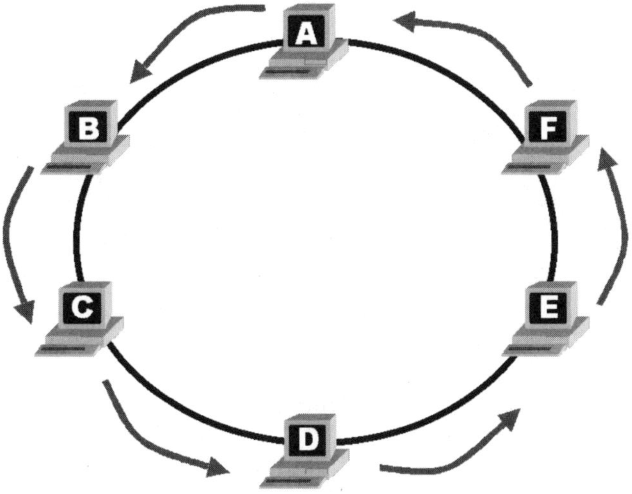

FIGURE 3.3
A Token Ring packet.

The token tells the next node that the ring is available. A node with data to send waits until it receives the token. After receiving the free token, the node creates a data packet and sends the new packet on to its downstream neighbor. See Figure 3.4. When the sending node receives confirmation that the intended recipient received the packet, it generates a new token, giving the next machine in line access to the ring.

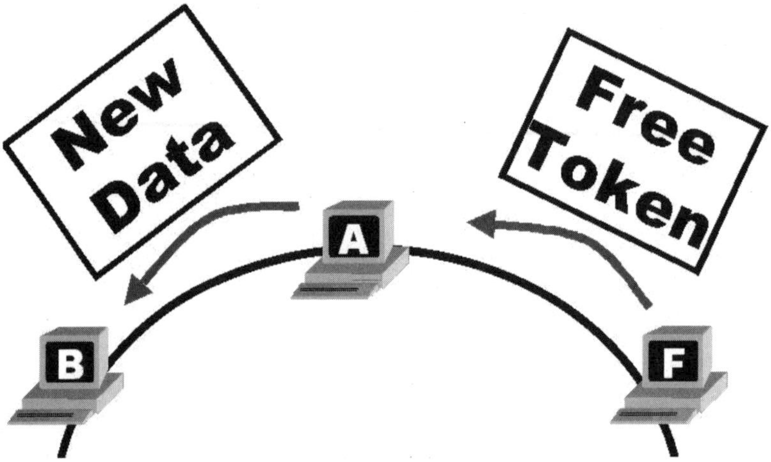

FIGURE 3.4
After receiving the token, a Token Ring node creates a new packet and sends it to its downstream neighbor.

A token passing network sends data packets more efficiently than one using CSMA/CD because no collisions occur. A station may have to wait for the token before it can send, but if it has the token it knows that no other station will try to send at the same time. In contrast, a CSMA/CD-based network, such as Ethernet, can waste significant bandwidth resolving collisions.

Token passing is a deterministic method to resolve which machine should have access to the wire at a given moment. *Deterministic* means that access to the wire is granted in a predictable way, rather than through a random process like CSMA/CD.

Token Ring Speed

Token Ring networks can run at either 4 or 16 megabits per second, speeds that sound slow compared to 10-megabit-per-second and 100-megabit-per-second Ethernet. With Token Ring, however, the raw numbers do not tell the full story. Token Ring networks use every bit of their bandwidth to send data. Ethernet networks, in contrast, waste significant amounts of bandwidth resolving collisions. Because of the wasted bandwidth inherent to Ethernet, many well-informed techs argue that 4-megabit-per-second Token Ring performs almost as fast as 10-megabit-per-second Ethernet and that 16-megabit-per-second Token Ring performs significantly faster.

The speed at which the ring operates, however, depends on the slowest device on the ring. A Token Ring network consisting of five 4/16-megabit Token Ring nodes and one 4-megabit Token Ring node will run at 4 megabits per second. See Figure 3.5.

FIGURE 3.5

The slowest device on the ring determines the speed of the ring.

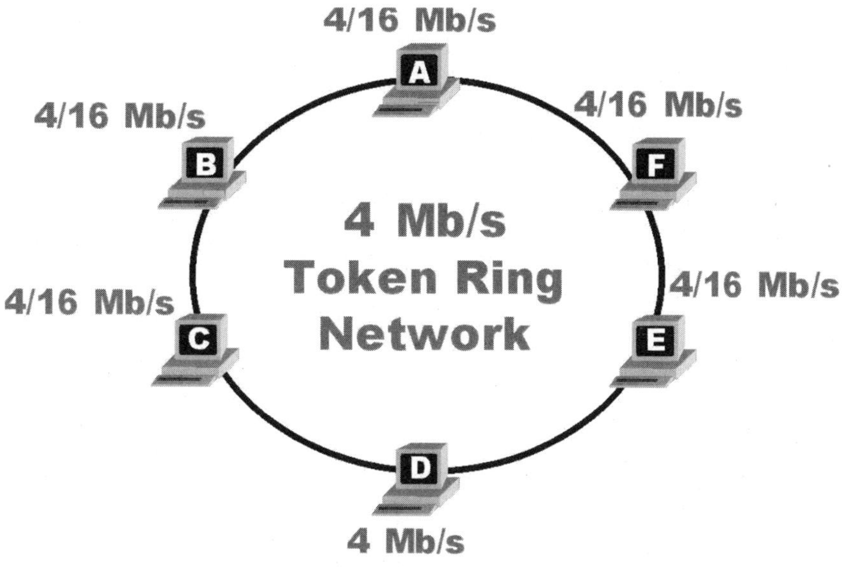

Token Ring networks also allow some stations to have a higher priority for the token. Conceivably a network architect could set a high priority for a particular node, ensuring that it would get access to the token more often than other stations. Token Ring networks rarely take advantage of the ability to prioritize traffic, making the feature less useful than it might seem.

Physical Star

A physical ring topology would share the same vulnerability to cable breaks that a physical bus topology possesses. When the cable used by a physical bus topology such as 10Base2 breaks, the entire network shuts down due to electrical reflections, as discussed in Chapter 1. A physical ring topology would also fail completely should the cable break, but for a different reason. In a ring topology, all traffic travels in one direction. If the ring breaks, traffic can never complete a round trip around the network and no node will generate a free token. See Figure 3.6. To avoid the problems inherent to a physical ring topology, Token Ring uses a physical star topology.

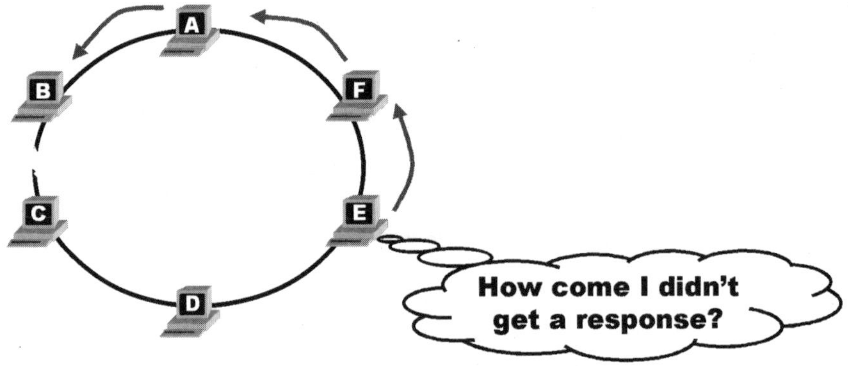

FIGURE 3.6
A physical ring topology cannot function if the ring breaks.

Token Ring hides the logical ring inside a hub, technically referred to as an *MAU (Multistation Access Unit)*. See Figure 3.7. Individual nodes connect to the hub via either Unshielded Twisted Pair (UTP) or Shielded Twisted Pair (STP) cabling. See Figure 3.8.

TERMINOLOGY

TERMINOLOGY ALERT

To make our lives difficult, Token Ring documentation can refer to Multistation Access Units by two different acronyms: MAU and MSAU. The terms Token Ring hub, MAU, and MSAU are synonymous.

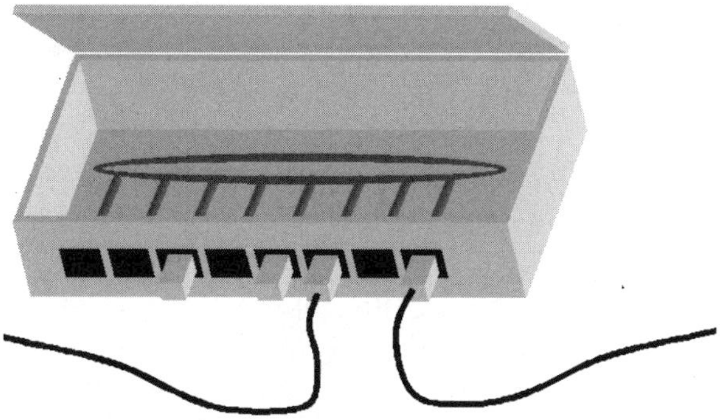

FIGURE 3.7
The MAU contains the ring.

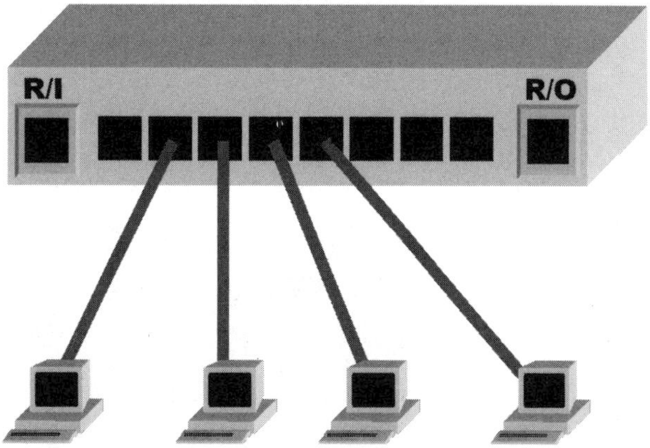

FIGURE 3.8
Token Ring nodes connect to the MAU.

Token Ring over STP

Originally, Token Ring networks used a heavily shielded version of twisted pair cabling referred to as Shielded Twisted Pair (STP). STP consists of two pairs of copper wires surrounded by a metal shield, as shown in Figure 3.9. Token Ring uses a special Type 1 connector for STP, as shown in Figure 3.10. STP's metal shield serves the same function as the shield used in coaxial cables, preventing electrical interference from affecting the wires used to send signals. When using STP, a single Token Ring MAU can support up to 260 computers. The STP cable connecting the computer to the hub may not be longer than 100 meters. While the heavy shielding of STP cabling makes it an ideal choice for environments with high levels of electrical interference, the high cost of that shielding makes it too expensive for most installations.

FIGURE 3.9
STP (Shielded Twisted Pair) cabling.

FIGURE 3.10
An IBM Type 1 connector.

Token Ring over UTP

Unshielded Twisted Pair (UTP) offers a cost-effective alternative to STP for normal business environments. As discussed in Chapter 2, UTP cabling has many other uses, including Ethernet and PBX phone systems. Because it lacks the heavy shielding of STP and works in a variety of other applications, UTP cabling costs relatively little.

Token Ring can run over UTP using the same cable and RJ-45 connectors as Ethernet. See Figure 3.11. Like 10BaseT, Token Ring uses only two of the four pairs in the typical UTP cable: the 3-6 pair and the 4-5 pair, as shown in Figure 3.12. Provided that the cable installer uses a proper wiring color code (such as the EIA/TIA 568A standard discussed in Chapter 2), the UTP cable and connectors used for Token Ring are identical to those used for Ethernet. Token Ring MAUs using UTP can support up to 72 nodes, and each node must be within 45 meters of the MAU.

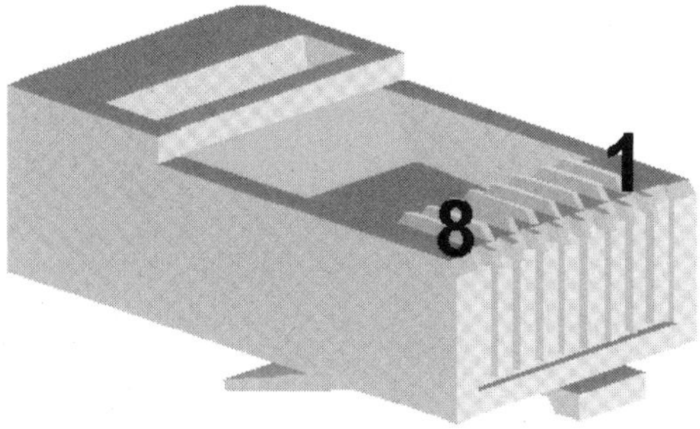

FIGURE 3.11 *The same UTP cable with RJ-45 connectors can be used for either Ethernet or Token Ring.*

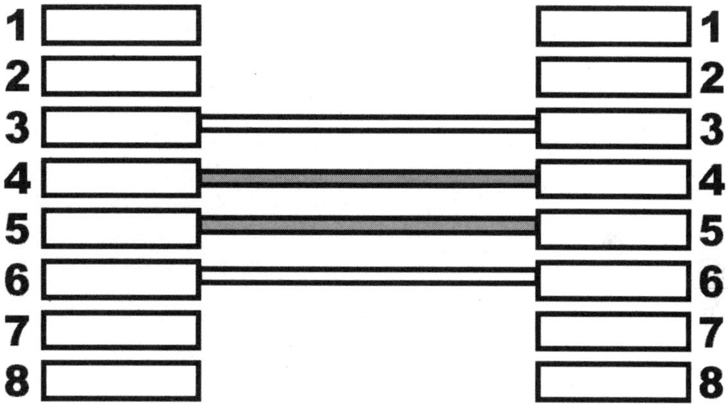

FIGURE 3.12 *Token Ring uses two of the four available wires.*

Connecting MAUs

To connect multiple Token Ring hubs to form a larger network requires the extension of the logical ring used by the Token Ring nodes. Token Ring MAUs, whether using UTP or STP, have two special ports on the MAU, labeled "Ring In" and "Ring Out." These special connections link multiple MAUs together to form a single ring. Both UTP and STP Token Ring MAUs use Ring In and Ring Out ports.

The Ring In port on the first MAU must connect to the Ring Out port on the second MAU, and vice versa, in order to form a single logical ring. Figure 3.13 shows two MAUs connected using the Ring In and

Ring Out ports. Logically, the two MAUs look like a single ring to the devices attached to them, as shown in Figure 3.14. Up to 33 MAUs can combine to form a single logical ring. Building a network with more than 33 MAUs requires the use of bridges or routers. Routers can also connect Token Ring LANs to other types of LANs, such as Ethernet.

FIGURE 3.13
Two MAUs connected via Ring In and Ring Out ports.

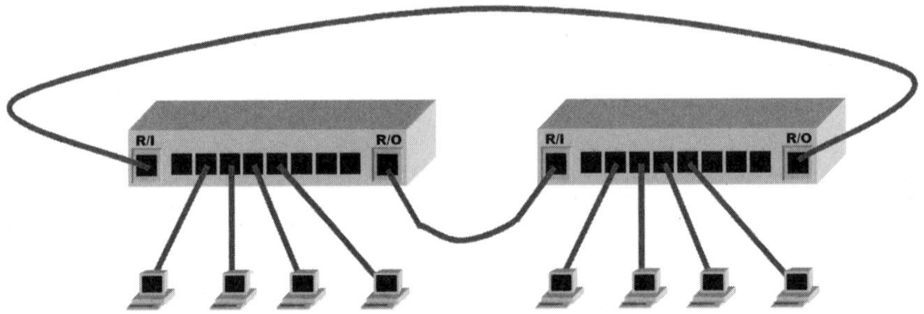

FIGURE 3.14
When linked together properly, the two MAUs form a single logical ring.

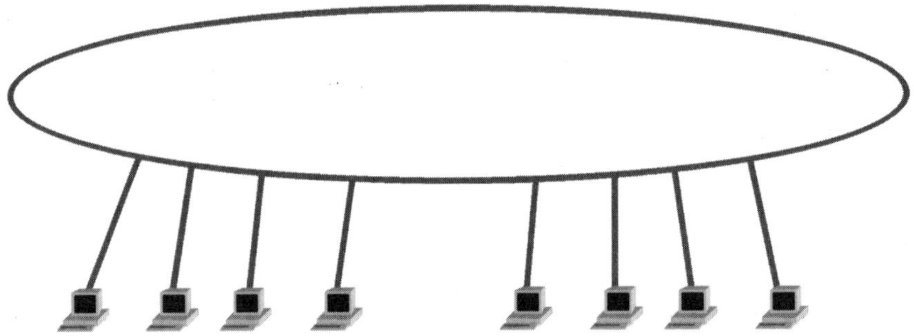

Token Ring vs. Ethernet

The Token Ring vs. Ethernet debate has been a fixture in computer networking journals for many years. Like many of the other technology debates that have raged through the IT industry (PC vs. Macintosh, Microsoft vs. Novell, paper vs. plastic), proponents of one side or the other invest an amazing amount of emotion into a technical debate.

Token Ring advocates argue that Token Ring's token-passing system utilizes available bandwidth more efficiently than Ethernet's random CSMA/CD process. In addition, the token-passing system guarantees that every node will get some amount of bandwidth. In an Ethernet network, the network can get so busy that some machines never get to send their data because of excessive collisions. The argument is that Token Ring is more *scalable*, meaning that it handles growth better.

Ethernet advocates argue that it does not matter if Token Ring has technical advantages if it costs too much to implement. Ethernet technology has always been cheaper than Token Ring for two reasons. First, Ethernet devices are simpler than Token Ring devices. CSMA/CD is a very simple algorithm to program into a device, whereas Token Ring devices must deal with more complex issues such as differing priority levels among the nodes on the ring. Second, economies of scale make Ethernet even less expensive. Because the market for Ethernet devices dwarfs the market for Token Ring devices, Ethernet manufacturers can make a smaller profit on each piece sold and still make money.

In addition, Ethernet overcomes the efficiency advantages of Token Ring by throwing bandwidth at the problem. While 16-megabit Token Ring may be faster than 10BaseT, it runs significantly slower than 100BaseT. Although high-speed Token Ring standards exist, Fast Ethernet and Gigabit Ethernet have achieved a far greater penetration of the market. Most industry pundits agree that Token Ring is a dying technology. While it will continue to exist in niche markets and in organizations with a large installed base of Token Ring equipment, Ethernet will retain its dominance in the marketplace for the foreseeable future.

NOTE Don't be surprised if you run into a few staunch Token Ring evangelists from time to time. In technical matters, as in life, people of good faith can disagree.

Review Questions

1) Which of the following standards defines Token Ring networks?

a) IEEE 802.3
b) IEEE 802.5
c) EIA/TIA 568A
d) IEEE 1284

2) Token Ring networks use a ________________ physical topology and a ______________ logical topology.
a) mesh, ring
b) ring, star
c) star, ring
d) ring, bus

3) Which of the following are true about Token Ring networks?
a) Collisions occur as a normal part of their operation.
b) Only a machine with a free token can transmit a new data packet.
c) In the event of a break in the cable connecting a machine to the MAU, the entire network shuts down.
d) Token Ring can use either UTP or STP cabling.

4) Assuming that every node can send and receive data with every other node, what type of network is shown in Figure 3.15?
a) Ethernet
b) Token Ring
c) ARCnet
d) Sneakernet

FIGURE 3.15
Diagram for Review Question 4

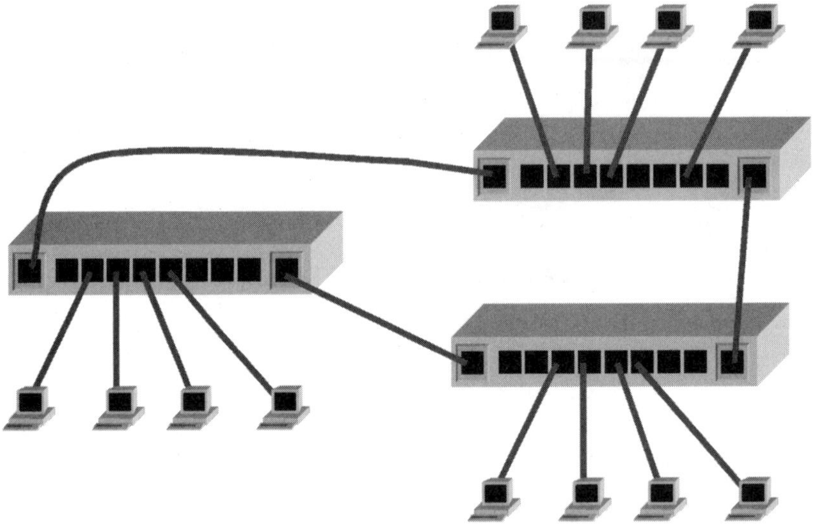

5) Assuming that every node can send and receive data with every other node, what type of network is shown in Figure 3.16
- a) Ethernet
- b) Token Ring
- c) ARCNET
- d) Sneakernet

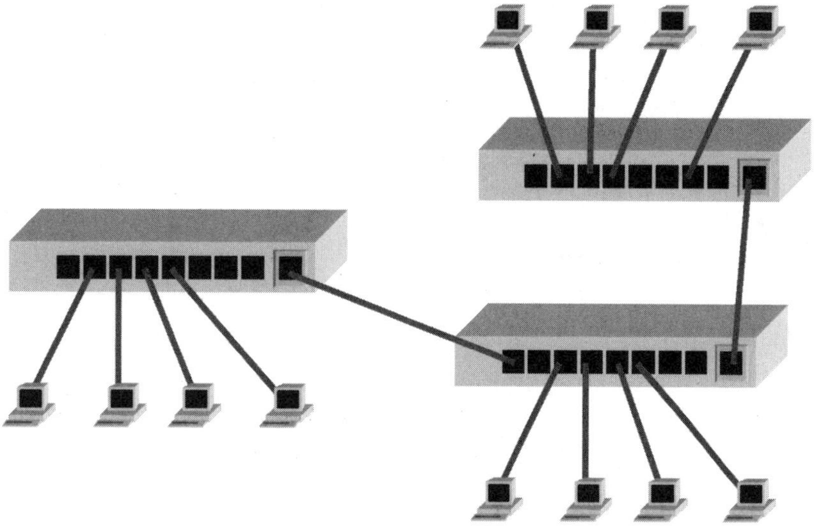

FIGURE 3.16
Diagram for Review Question 5

6) Philip calls Bob, a tech support technician, for help with a networking problem. Bob asks Philip to tell him what kind of network he uses. Philip responds that he uses UTP. This tells Bob that Philip:
- a) uses a Token Ring network.
- b) uses a 10BaseT network.
- c) uses a 10Base5 network.
- d) has not provided enough information for Bob to know what kind of network Philip uses.

7) Token Ring MAUs using STP can support up to _______ nodes.
- a) 1024
- b) 260
- c) 100
- d) 72

8) Token Ring MAUs using UTP can support up to __________ nodes.

a) 1024
b) 260
c) 100
d) 72

9) Token Ring MAUs use special ports called ________________ to connect to other MAUs.

a) Crossovers
b) Uplinks
c) Ring In and Ring Out
d) Repeaters

10) A node connected to its MAU using UTP can be ____________ from the MAU.

a) 100 meters
b) 100 feet
c) 45 meters
d) 45 feet

Review Answers

1) **B.** IEEE 802.5 is the IEEE standard for Token Ring. IEEE 802.3 is the standard for Ethernet. EIA/TIA 568A is a cabling standard for UTP cabling that is used in both Token Ring and Ethernet networks. IEEE 1284 is the IEEE standard for parallel communication.

2) **C.** Token Ring networks use a *star* physical topology and a *ring* logical topology.

3) **B** and **D.** Token Ring nodes only transmit new data packets if they have a free token. Token Ring can use either UPT or STP cabling. While collisions are a normal part of the operation of an Ethernet network, Token Ring's token-passing system prevents collisions from occurring. Because Token Ring uses a physical star topology, a break in the cable between the MAU and a device affects only that device, not the rest of the network.

4) **B.** The pictured network uses two cables to connect each hub to two other hubs. In order for this network to function properly, the hubs must be Token Ring MAUs connecting to each other via their Ring In and Ring Out ports. Ethernet networks use crossover cables to connect hubs and will not function properly (without bridges or routers) if there are multiple routers between nodes. ARCnet is an old, out-of-date networking technology not covered on the Network+ exams. Sneakernet is a slang term for carrying floppy disks around a building to transfer data.

5) **A.** The diagram shows a number of hubs daisy chained together. This would be a typical configuration for a 10BaseT Ethernet network with hubs connected by crossover cables. This diagram cannot show a functioning Token Ring network because there is no way for the connections shown to form a ring.

6) **D.** Because RJ-45 connectors can be used for either Token Ring or Ethernet, Philip has not provided enough information for Bob to know what kind of network Philip uses.

7) **B.** Token Ring MAUs using STP can support up to 260 nodes.

8) **D.** Token Ring MAUs using UTP can support up to 72 nodes.

9) **C.** Token Ring MAUs use special ports called Ring In and Ring Out to connect to other MAUs.

10) **C.** A Token Ring node using UTP can be up to 45 meters from the MAU.

CHAPTER 4

The OSI Model

The Open Systems Interconnect (OSI) model provides a precise terminology for discussing networks. Chapters 1–3 discussed two important networking technologies, Ethernet and Token Ring, and included a discussion of the jargon used with each technology. Unfortunately, the designers of Ethernet and Token Ring did not talk with one another when deciding what terms to use. An Ethernet hub and a Token Ring MAU, for example, perform roughly the same function, but the terms have no obvious similarity. As you delve deeper into networking, the jargon only gets worse. Terms such as protocol, gateway, and switch, for example, can have vastly different meanings depending on the context of the conversation. To prevent confusion, the International Organization for Standardization, known as the ISO, proposed the OSI 7-layer model.

NOTE

ISO is not an acronym. It derives from the Greek word "isos," which means "equal."

Protocols

The word protocol serves as a good example of this terminology confusion. In normal English, the term protocol usually refers to a formal procedure for doing something. A specific protocol, for example, exists for a meeting between two heads of state. If the President of Mexico comes to the United States to visit the US President, many issues have to be decided in advance. Does the US president meet the Mexican president at the airport or wait for him at the White House? Who walks into a joint press conference first? Who gets to make the announcement about a new agreement? Protocols supply the answers in advance. Networking protocols work the same way, setting the rules for communication in advance.

Even a simple exchange of data between two computers involves many distinct protocols. In computer networking, the term *protocol* describes any predetermined set of rules that define how two devices or pieces of software should communicate with each other. A single act on the part of a user actually involves multiple protocols. When Bobbie uploads a file from her computer to a server on the Internet, she thinks that she does a single thing. In reality, lots of things are happening behind the scenes. Assuming that she uses an FTP utility program like CuteFTP or WS_FTP32 to transfer the file, numerous protocols come into play. The File Transfer Protocol (FTP) describes how two programs running on different computers can exchange a file, while Transmission Control Protocol (TCP) describes how two computers can break that file up into smaller pieces on the sending machine and reassemble it on the receiving end. Internet Protocol (IP) determines the proper routing of the data across multiple routers, and Ethernet (or Token Ring) handles the actual delivery of the data packets (See Chapters 1-3 for more information about Ethernet and Token Ring). The OSI model provides a more precise terminology that clarifies the relationships between the various protocols used.

NOTE

For more detail about TCP/IP-specific protocols, such as FTP, TCP, and IP, see Chapter 6.

The Seven Layers

Most network documentation uses the OSI 7-layer model to define more precisely the role played by each protocol. OSI provides a common jargon that network techs can use to describe the function of any network protocol. The OSI model breaks up the task of networking computers into seven distinct layers, with each layer addressing some essential task:

- Layer 1: Physical
- Layer 2: Data Link
- Layer 3: Network
- Layer 4: Transport
- Layer 5: Session
- Layer 6: Presentation
- Layer 7: Application

Each layer defines a challenge in computer networking and the protocols that operate at that layer offer solutions to those challenges. The OSI model encourages a modular design to networking, meaning that each protocol should deal with a specific layer and have as little as possible to do with the operation of other layers. Each protocol should know the protocol handling the layer above it and the layer below it, but should be oblivious of the protocols handling the other layers. Keep in mind that these layers are not laws of physics—anybody who wants to design a network can do it in any way. While many protocols fit neatly into one of the seven layers, others do not.

NOTE

Be sure to memorize both the name and the number of each OSI layer. Network techs use terms such as "layer 4" and "transport layer" synonymously.

Layer 1: What do these electrical signals mean? The Physical Layer

Layer 1, the physical layer, defines the physical form taken by data that travel across a cable. While the other layers will deal with ones and zeros, the physical layer defines the rules for turning those ones and zeros into electrical signals going out over a copper cable (or light going out over a fiber optic cable, or radio waves generated by a wireless network, etc.). Figure 4.1 shows the process by which the sending NIC turns a string of ones and zeros into an electrical signal, and the receiving NIC turns it back into the same string of ones and zeros. Both ends of the transmission must agree in advance on the physical-layer rules or communication is not possible. The physical layer adds no additional information to the data packet—it simply transmits the data provided by the layers above it.

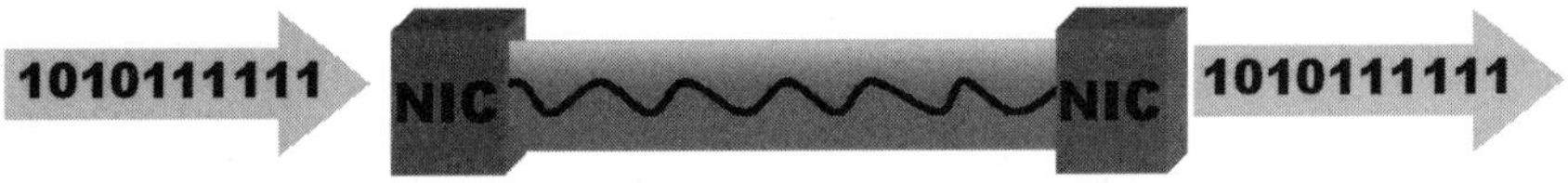

FIGURE 4.1 *The physical layer turns binary code into a physical signal and back again.*

Repeaters, discussed in Chapters 1 and 2, operate purely at layer 1 in the OSI model. The repeater takes the electrical signal received from one segment of cable, converts it into binary code, and then converts the binary code back into a physical signal on the other segment. Because a standard Ethernet hub is nothing more than a multi-port Ethernet repeater, it also functions as a layer-1 device.

KEY EXAM FACT

TIP

Repeaters operate at layer 1, the physical layer.

Layer 2: How do devices use the wire? The Data Link Layer

The data link layer, layer 2, defines the rules for accessing and using the physical layer. It provides a way to identify devices on the network, to determine which machine should use the network at a given moment, and to check for errors in the data received from the physical layer.

Ethernet and Token Ring protocols deal with issues at both the physical and data link layers. Ethernet, for example, uses MAC addresses to identify machines on the network, CSMA/CD to determine which machine should send its packet at a given time, and the CRC code to check for errors. Token Ring resolves the same issues using MAC addresses, token passing, and FCS code.

The separation between the physical and data link layers explains how Ethernet and Token Ring can run on so many different types of physical cabling. When devising a new cabling system, network engineers can make changes at the physical layer without altering the data link layer. In Token Ring, for example, the token-passing system remains the same whether the network uses UTP or STP cabling. In Ethernet, CSMA/CD controls access to the cable whether the network uses 10BaseT, 10Base5, or 10Base2. Provided some combination of hardware and software can be designed to take the binary data generated by the data link layer and transmit it using the physical layer, the use of any type of cabling imaginable becomes possible.

Protocols that operate at the physical and data link layers do not concern themselves with the meaning of the data they carry in the data field of their packets. Chapters 1-3 discussed the packets created by Ethernet and Token Ring networks, but left the field defined as "data" intentionally vague. Ethernet and Token Ring function like the truck drivers employed by UPS or the Post Office. As long as the box doesn't tick, the truck driver could not care less about the contents of the box. The driver simply moves the box from point A to point B. Similarly, an Ethernet or Token Ring device pays no attention to the contents of the data field, whether it contains a print job, a file being saved, or something really important like a game of hearts. The job of "filling the boxes" falls to the protocols operating at layers 3 through 7.

Layer 3: How do packets get from A to B? The Network Layer

The network layer adds information to the packet that determines how routers move a data packet from its source on one network to its destination on a different network. See Figure 4.2. The packet contains the data to be transferred, the network layer information, and the data link information. See Figure 4.3. The "data," however, contain information about additional layers as well.

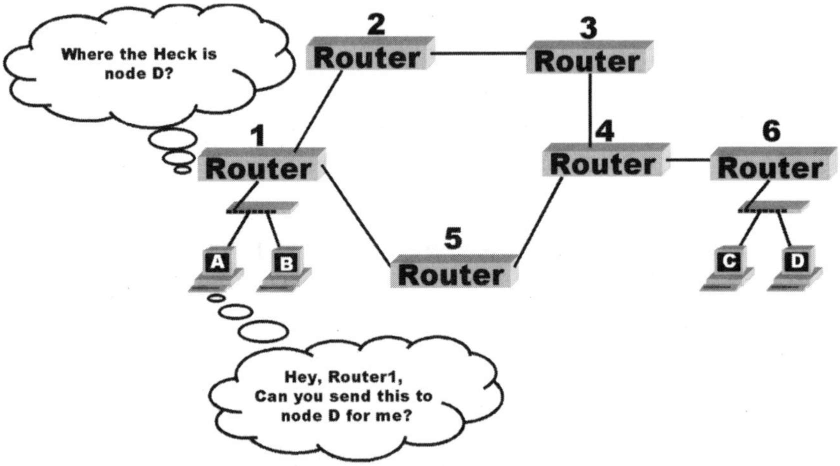

FIGURE 4.2
Routers need more information on how to move data from one network to the next.

FIGURE 4.3
The data surrounded by data link and network-layer information.

TIP

EXAM TIP

For the Network+ exam, be sure to know what type of device operates at each of the first three layers of the OSI model.

Layer 1– Physical–repeater
Layer 2–Data Link–bridge
Layer 3–Network–router

Layer 4: Breaking data up and putting it back together. The Transport Layer

The transport layer breaks data received from the upper layers into smaller pieces for "transport" within the data packets created at the lower levels. Ethernet, for example, limits the size of a packet to less than 1500 bytes, including the overhead of the various layers of the OSI model. To transfer a chunk of data larger than 1500 bytes, the data must be broken into smaller pieces on the sending node and reassembled at the receiving node. See Figure 4.4. The protocols that typically handle this job have names like NetBEUI, IPX, and TCP. These protocols also handle other functions, such as checking for errors.

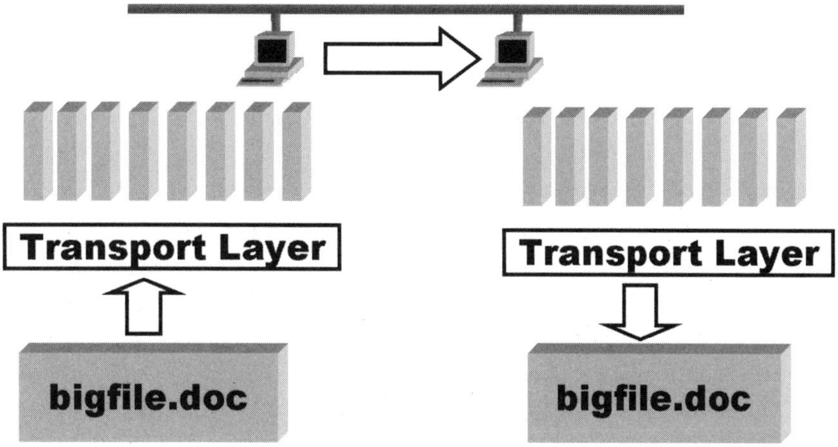

FIGURE 4.4
At the transport layer, large pieces of data must be broken up into smaller chunks on the sending machine and reassembled on the receiving machine.

The transport layer's function shares similarities with the process of shipping a large piece of machinery. See Figure 4.5. First, the shipper must break the machine down into components that will fit into shipping crates that can fit into the shipping company's trucks. Before the packages are sent, instructions should be included to tell the receiving party how to reassemble the machine. Once the boxes have been packed, they can be addressed and shipped using a variety of shipping companies: UPS, Federal Express, the US Postal Service. In the same way, transport-layer packets can be "shipped" by almost any combination of data link and physical protocols. The transport layer protocols (NetBEUI, IPX, TCP) do not care whether the network uses Ethernet, Token Ring, or some other technology.

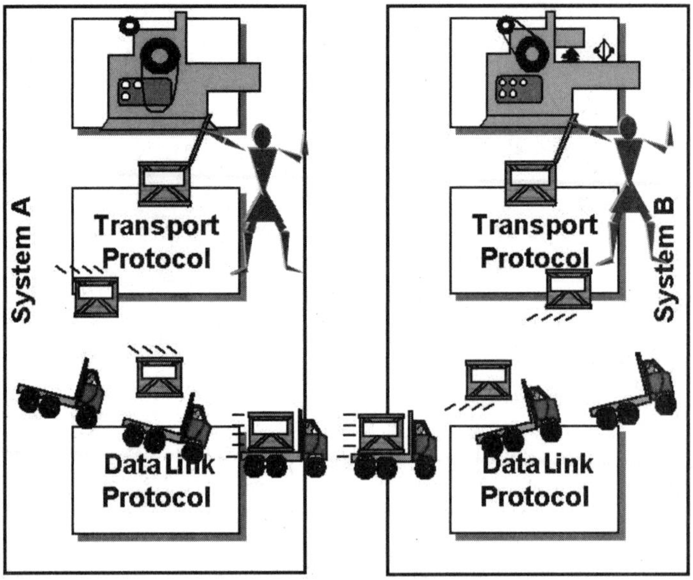

FIGURE 4.5
A file must be broken up into pieces small enough to fit inside the data packet, and must be reassembled on the receiving end.

The transport layer acts as a catchall layer that guarantees smooth communication between the lower layers (1–3) and the upper layers (5–7). The lower layers concern themselves with moving data from point A to point B on the network, without regard for the actual content of the data. The upper layers deal with specific types of requests from users and applications. This separation allows applications using the network to remain blissfully unaware of the underlying hardware.

Layer 5: How do machines keep track of who they are talking to? The Session Layer

The session layer manages the connections between machines on the network. In Figure 4.6, machine A receives one file from machine B, another from machine C, and sends a third file to machine D. Machine A needs some means to track its connections so that it sends the right response to the right computer. Protocols such as NetBIOS and Sockets give machines the means to track and manage connections. A computer managing connections is like a short order cook keeping track of orders. Just as a cook must track which meals go with which ticket, a computer on a network must track which data should be sent out to which machine. See Figure 4.7.

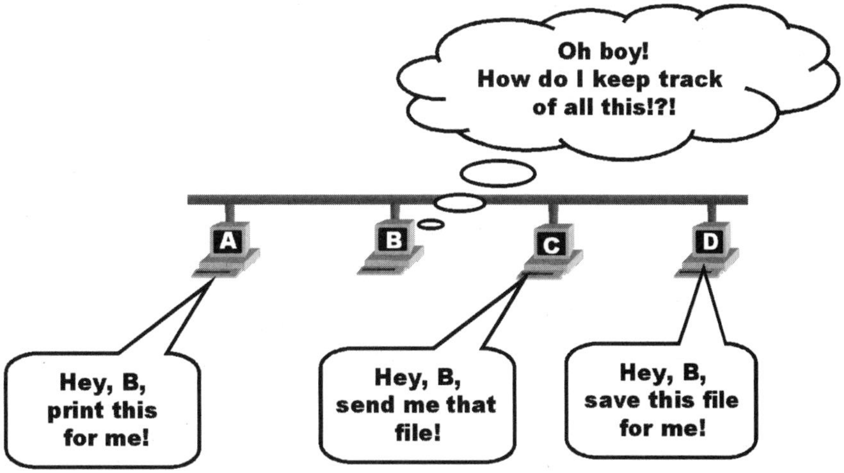

FIGURE 4.6
On a network, a machine must manage multiple connections.

NOTE
For a more detailed discussion of NetBIOS and Sockets, see Chapter 5.

FIGURE 4.7 *A machine on a network must keep track of the "orders" it must fill.*

Layer 6: What language is this? The Presentation Layer

The presentation layer allows different types of computers to communicate with each other despite the fact that they use different methods to store and express the same data.

Most computer systems, for example, store text. In a DOS or Windows 9x system, text is stored as a series of 8-bit codes known as ASCII (American Standard Code for Information Interchange), but a Windows NT system uses 16-bit Unicode to store text. The Windows 9x system would store the letter "A" as 01000001, while the Windows NT system would store the same letter "A" as 0000000001000001. The end-users, of course, do not care about the difference between ASCII and Unicode—they just want to see the letter "A." The presentation layer smoothes over these differences.

The presentation layer can also include data encryption. As discussed in Chapters 1-3, machines on Ethernet and Token Ring networks can be set to capture all data passing them on the network cable. To prevent sensitive data from being stolen off the wire, programs operating at the presentation layer can encrypt the data. Windows NT encrypts domain login passwords, for example, before sending them out over the network.

The OSI model treats the presentation layer as a distinct layer, but most real-world network operating systems (NOSs) fold presentation-layer functions into programs that handle either application or session layer functions as well. Because most network operating systems handle presentation layer issues at a very low level, usually only programmers need to be aware of the exact details.

NOTE

Although not purely network protocols, Adobe Systems' PostScript printer language and Acrobat file format handle a typical presentation-layer problem, enabling users to view or print the same file even if they use different operating systems or printers. PostScript is a device-independent printer language designed to ensure that any two PostScript-compatible printers will produce exactly the same output regardless of the manufacturer. A given document printed on an Apple LaserWriter or a Hewlett-Packard LaserJet will look identical despite the differences in the actual printer hardware and the device drivers running them. A user can create a word processing document on a Windows NT Workstation and e-mail that document to another user who uses a Macintosh computer. Provided they both use PostScript-compatible printers, their printouts of the file should be identical. Adobe's Acrobat file format takes device independence a step further, allowing any system running an Acrobat viewer to view and print an Acrobat file (*.pdf) precisely as the author intended, regardless of the operating system or printer used. PostScript and Acrobat are both presentation-layer tools that hide the differences between systems.

Layer 7: How do programmers write applications that use the network? The Application Layer

The application layer in the OSI model provides a set of tools that programs can use to access the network. Application-layer programs provide services to other programs—they are not the programs the users themselves see. Think about Web browsing. Bob launches his browser, either Netscape or Internet Explorer (or maybe even Opera), to access a Web site. These programs use the Hyper Text Transfer Protocol (HTTP) to request data (usually HTML documents) from a Web server. HTTP is not an executable program. It is a protocol, a set of rules, that allows two other programs—the Web browser and the Web server—to communicate with each other.

The APIs used by Microsoft networking also operate at the application layer. An *API* is an Application Program Interface, a special set of commands that allows applications, such as Microsoft Word, to request services from the operating system. When Microsoft Word displays the Network Neighborhood in the Close As dialog box shown in Figure 4.8, it does not access the network directly. Instead, it uses the networking APIs. By providing a standard set of APIs that operate at the OSI's application layer, Microsoft makes it easy for programmers writing applications like Microsoft Word or Lotus 1-2-3 to access the network without knowing any of the details of the network.

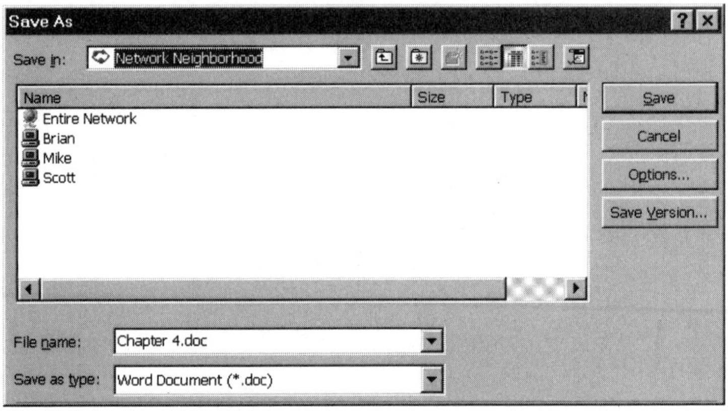

FIGURE 4.8
Microsoft Word's Save As dialogue box.

OSI and Going from A to B

Descriptions of the communication between two machines on a network become more precise when the OSI model is used as a frame of reference. Figure 4.9 shows two machines, WATSON and HOLMES, separated by a router. In this example, HOLMES is a *server*, a machine that shares its resources across the network. WATSON is a *client*, a machine that accesses shared resources stored on a server. Brent sits down at WATSON and uses Microsoft Word to save a file named BAKER.DOC in a shared directory on HOLMES. Let's take a simplified look at what happens next using the OSI model.

To handle application- and presentation-layer issues, Microsoft Word calls to an API that creates a Server Message Block, or SMB. The SMB contains the command telling HOLMES to save the file. *SMB* is a special message format used by Microsoft networks for handling file and print sharing messages between clients and servers. WATSON adds the SMB information to the data being sent, as shown in Figure 4.10.

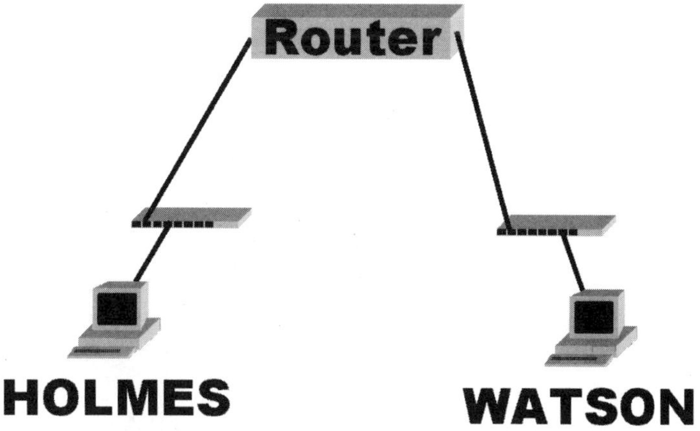

FIGURE 4.9
HOLMES and WATSON, separated by a router.

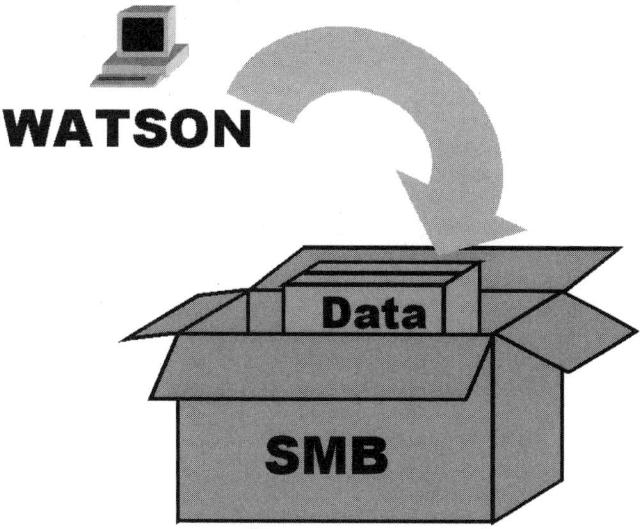

FIGURE 4.10
WATSON creates a Server Message Block.

At the session layer, the client WATSON must establish a connection with the server HOLMES (the SMB packet created above contains a request to save the file, but a connection must be established before that request can be sent). In Microsoft networking, the NetBIOS protocol establishes and manages connections (see Chapter 5 for more detail on NetBIOS). WATSON adds NetBIOS information to the packet, as shown in Figure 4.11, to request and manage a connection between WATSON as the client and HOLMES as the server.

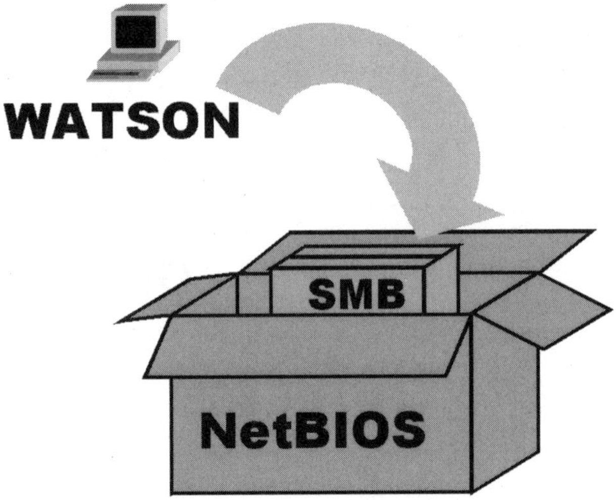

FIGURE 4.11 *WATSON adds NetBIOS information to the packet.*

At the transport layer, WATSON must then break the BAKER.DOC file into pieces small enough to fit into the packets used by whatever network-layer protocols will be used. In this example, WATSON uses the UDP (User Datagram Protocol) as its transport protocol (see Chapter 7 for more information about UDP). UDP adds additional information to the packet so that the pieces can be properly reassembled when they reach HOLMES. See Figure 4.12.

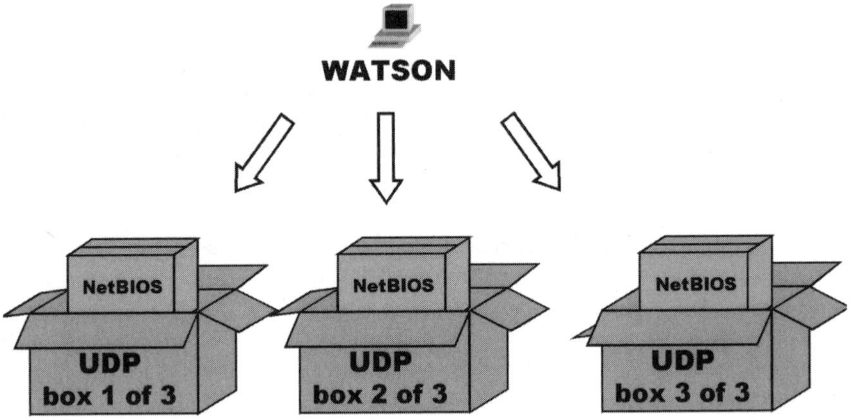

FIGURE 4.12 *WATSON breaks the NetBIOS package into smaller pieces.*

At the network Layer, WATSON must add information to the packet to tell any routers on the network how to direct the data packet to its destination. In this example, WATSON uses the IP protocol, discussed in more detail in Chapter 7, to add routing information to the packet. See Figure 4.13.

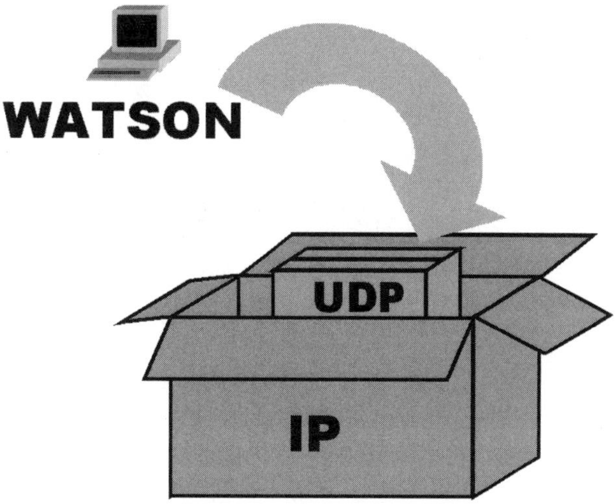

FIGURE 4.13
A data packet with application-, presentation-, session-, transport-, and network-layer information.

At the data link layer, WATSON hands the packet off to a network card driver. WATSON uses an Ethernet network card, so the NIC driver creates an Ethernet packet like the one described in Chapter 1. See Figure 4.14.

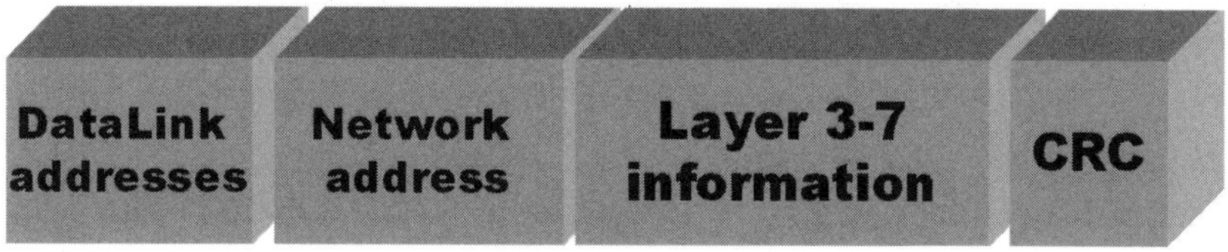

FIGURE 4.14
An Ethernet packet.

At the physical layer, the NIC driver then instructs the NIC itself to convert the ones and zeros of the data packet into electrical signals that it can transmit over the network cable. Notice that the physical layer is the only layer that adds no additional information to the data packet.

On the receiving end, HOLMES processes the data packet in reverse order, starting with the physical layer. After converting the physical signal into binary code, HOLMES examines the data link information, comparing the MAC address contained in the packet to its own MAC address. If the addresses do not match, HOLMES discards the packet.

In this case, the addresses do match, and HOLMES continues to read the packet. HOLMES decodes the information contained at each layer, finally passing the SMB originally created on WATSON to the program that controls HOLMES' file server functions. HOLMES then saves the file, completing the transaction.

The HOLMES-WATSON transaction described above, although simplified a great deal, demonstrates the complexity involved in every network transaction. By breaking the tasks involved into manageable pieces, network designers can make adjustments and improvements to protocols operating at one layer without forcing themselves to rewrite the entire system every time they make a change.

The average tech, of course, does not design networks from scratch. Drivers written by companies like Novell, Microsoft, and 3Com handle most of the details alluded to in the WATSON-HOLMES example, and the tech can get away with ignoring the more intricate details of each layer. For the average network tech the OSI model has more to do with describing the tools provided by others than with describing everyday duties. Terms flung about with imprecise abandon, such as "switch" and "gateway," suddenly gain precision when discussed in terms of the OSI model.

NOTE Don't expect every piece of network software and hardware to fit neatly into the OSI model. The OSI model is a theoretical construct, not a law of nature.

Switches and Gateways

Marketing people have abused the terms "switch" and "gateway" to the point that the terms have no precise meaning out of context. A *switch* is any device that filters and forwards traffic based on some criteria. A *gateway* is any device that enables two dissimilar systems to communicate. Unfortunately, these terms by themselves lack precision. Specifying the level in the OSI model at which switches and gateways function provides the necessary context for understanding their proper role in a network.

Switches

Marketing people use the term "switch" to refer to both bridges and routers (see Chapter 2 for a discussion of bridges and routers). Routers and bridges both filter and forward traffic between network segments, but make their decisions based on different information. The OSI model provides network techs the precise terminology needed to clarify the distinction between the different kinds of switches.

Layer 2 Switches/Bridges

Layer 2 switches, a.k.a. bridges, forward and filter data packets between segments based on the MAC addresses contained in each packet. Although technical manuals and certification exams predominately use the term "bridge," those who market networking hardware have decided that "layer 2 switching" sounds sexier and more high tech than "bridging." Just remember that a layer 2 switch and bridge are the same thing and you will do fine.

Bridges can process packets faster than other types of switches can because they have less information to process. When a packet hits a bridge, the bridge runs the packet through the first physical and data link layers of the OSI model and never even looks at the rest of the information in the data packet. Because bridges process less of the data packet than switches operating at layer 3 and above, they require less-powerful processors and tend to be less expensive. Unfortunately, the simplicity of bridges has its downside: the simple set of rules they employ cause them to forward all broadcast traffic to all segments.

Layer 3 Switches/Routers

Layer 3 switches, a.k.a. routers, filter and forward traffic based on the network addresses added to the data packet by network-layer protocols such as IP and IPX (see Chapter 5 for a discussion of IP and IPX). Because the architect who designs the network assigns the network-layer addresses, layer 3 switching gives network architects more control over the flow of traffic. Specifically, layer 3 switches filter broadcast traffic, confining it to the network on which it originates. Routers must process data all the way up to the network layer. Because they process more of the data packet, routers typically require faster processors than bridges in order to achieve acceptable performance.

NOTE

If you read the trade journals, you will see lots of hype about a new technology: layer 4 switching. Using the information added at the transport layer to determine which packets belong with each other, a layer 4 switch can assign a higher priority to data transmissions between specific machines, guaranteeing those machines a faster, more reliable connection. Layer 4 switches require more processing power than switches operating at the lower layers because the layer 4 switch must examine more layers of data. Layer 4 switching is a relatively new technology, and is not covered on the Network+ exam.

Gateways

A *gateway* is any device that allows two systems to communicate even though they use different protocols at some layer in the OSI model. A gateway can theoretically operate at any of the OSI model layers, but usually operates at either the network or the application layer.

Routers (layer 3 switches) can act as gateways between networks using different physical and data link layers. Figure 4.15 shows a router connecting an Ethernet and a Token Ring network. When forwarding a data packet from the Ethernet to the Token Ring network, the router takes the layer 3 through 7 data from the incoming Ethernet data packets and places them into new Token Ring data packets.

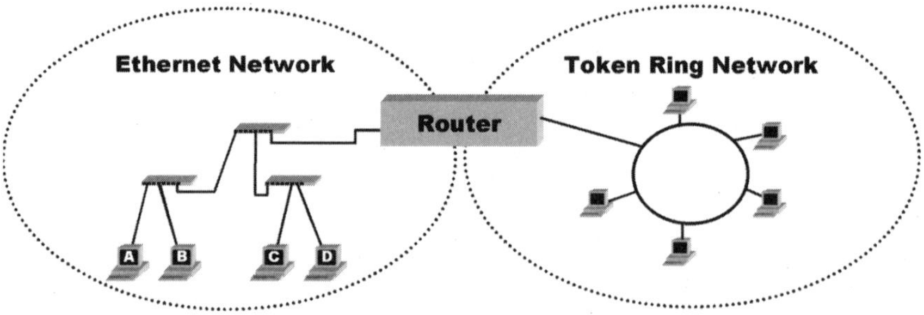

FIGURE 4.15
A router can act as a gateway between different types of networks.

NOTE

Routers in TCP/IP-based networks are frequently referred to as gateways. In other types of networks, the term router is preferred.

Gateways operating at the application layer allow client systems designed to communicate with one type of server to communicate with a different type of server. Microsoft's Gateway Services for NetWare, for example, enables machines configured to access NT servers to access NetWare servers without installing any additional software. The clients send a request to an NT server running Gateway Services for NetWare. The NT server translates the client's request into its NetWare equivalent. When the NetWare server responds, the NT server translates the NetWare response into its Microsoft equivalent.

TIP

EXAM TIP

While you need to know the names and basic functions of all seven layers of the OSI model, the Network+ exam focuses most of its attention to the first five layers where the boundaries between layers are more distinct.

It would be difficult for CompTIA to ask detailed questions about which protocols function at the presentation and application layers, because reputable sources disagree on how some protocols, such as SMB, fit into the OSI model. While SMB is described here as spanning the application and presentation layers, other documentation will place it entirely in one or the other. Remember that the OSI model is a theoretical description of how things should work. Many of the protocols in common use today predate the widespread adoption of the OSI model.

OSI Summary

CompTIA demands that Network+ certification candidates familiarize themselves with the OSI model because the OSI model acts as the *lingua franca*, the common language, of the networking industry. Without the OSI model as a common point of reference, network techs would wander aimlessly through a wilderness of vague terminology. The remaining chapters of this book discuss a wide variety of networking protocols and use the OSI model to clarify the role played by each. Chapter 5 will discuss the three dominant network protocol suites used today: NetBEUI, IPX/SPX, and TCP/IP.

NOTE

A *protocol suite* is a set of protocols, commonly used together, that operate at various levels of the OSI model.

Review Questions

1) A router operates at the ______________ layer of the OSI model.
   a) Application
   b) Network
   c) Data Link
   d) Transport

2) A bridge operates at the ______________ layer of the OSI model.
   a) Application
   b) Network
   c) Data Link
   d) Transport

3) A repeater operates at the ________________ layer of the OSI model.
   a) Presentation
   b) Network
   c) Data Link
   d) Physical

4) A ________________ allows clients and servers that use different protocols to communicate with each other without installing additional software.
   a) Repeater
   b) Bridge
   c) Gateway
   d) Router

5) Layer 4 is the ___________ layer.
a) Application
b) Data Link
c) Physical
d) Transport

6) The data link layer is layer _____ in the OSI model.
a) 3
b) 2
c) 5
d) 6

7) A layer 2 switch is also called a ______________.
a) Repeater
b) Router
c) Bridge
d) Gateway

8) A layer 3 switch is also called a _____________.
a) Repeater
b) Router
c) Bridge
d) Server

9) Ethernet operates at which of the following levels? (Choose 2)
a) Application
b) Data Link
c) Transport
d) Physical

10) The presentation layer is layer _______ in the OSI model.
a) 3
b) 2
c) 5
d) 6

Review Answers

1) **B.** Routers operate at the network layer.

2) **C.** Bridges operate at the data link layer.

3) **D.** Repeaters operate at the physical layer.

4) **C.** Gateways allow dissimilar systems to communicate with each other.

5) **D.** Layer 4 is the transport layer.

6) **B.** The data link layer is layer 2.

7) **C.** A bridge is a layer 2 switch.

8) **B.** A router is a layer 3 switch.

9) **B** and **D.** Ethernet operates at the physical and data link layers.

10) **D.** The presentation layer is layer 6.

CHAPTER 5

Protocol Suites

Applying the OSI model to real world networking strikes fear into the hearts of many novice network techs. Visions of individually selecting protocols for each layer reduce them to tears. The existence of protocol suites makes all of this pain, suffering, and gnashing of teeth unnecessary. A *protocol suite* is a set of protocols designed to work together. While Chapter 4 discussed individual protocols operating at specific layers in the OSI model, network techs deal most directly with the protocol suites.

The three major protocol suites—NetBEUI, IPX/SPX, and TCP/IP—offer varying degrees of ease of use, efficiency, and flexibility. Programmers delve into the nitty-gritty of the individual protocols to create protocol suites—techs install and troubleshoot the protocol suites given them by the programmers. The name of each protocol suite refers to one or more of the major protocols used in that suite. The TCP/IP suite, for example, includes Transmission Control Protocol (TCP) and Internet Protocol (IP) as well as dozens of others, including File Transfer Protocol (FTP), and Internet Control Message Protocol (ICMP). Each of the major protocol suites provides a different mix of efficiency, flexibility, and *scalability*, the ability to support network growth. NetBEUI works best for small networks without routers, IPX/SPX provides support for integrating with Novell NetWare, and TCP/IP provides a complex, robust, and open solution for larger networks.

NetBEUI

NetBEUI provides a fast, simple set of network protocols appropriate for use in smaller LANs. Although OS/2, LANtastic, and certain other Network Operating Systems (NOSs) support NetBEUI, NetBEUI primarily exists to support Microsoft networking using Windows NT or Windows 9x. (See Chapter 7 for more details about Windows 9x, Windows NT, and other NOSs). NetBEUI's speed and ease of use make it a good choice for small networks that do not require advanced features such as routing. The NetBEUI protocol suite consists of two main protocols: NetBIOS and NetBEUI, which operate at the session layer and the transport layer, respectively. See Figure 5.1.

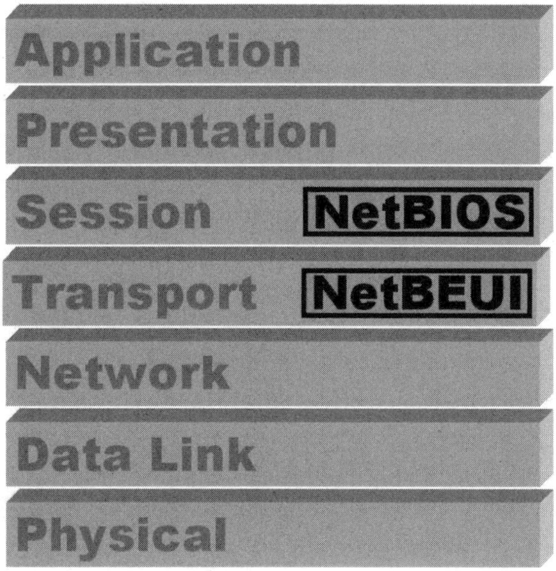

FIGURE 5.1
NetBIOS operates at the session layer, NetBEUI operates at the transport layer.

NOTE The term NetBEUI can refer either to the NetBEUI protocol suite, or specifically to the NetBEUI transport-layer protocol.

NetBIOS

NetBIOS handles the session-layer functions for NetBEUI networks. As discussed in Chapter 4, the session layer manages connections between machines. A server often communicates with several machines simultaneously, and must employ some system to track each of the "conversations" in which it participates. Because of its role in Microsoft networking, NetBIOS often handles the session layer in other protocol suites as well. (See the discussions of IPX/SPX and TCP/IP below.) NetBIOS manages connections based on the names of the computers involved.

Machines using NetBIOS take on a name for every function they perform. In a Windows 98 system, for example, the Network Control Panel applet lists the network name of the system. See Figure 5.2. Although this looks like a single name, a machine running the NetBIOS session-layer protocol takes this name and uses it as the basis for its NetBIOS names. A *NetBIOS name* is a special name that identifies both a specific machine and a particular function that it performs.

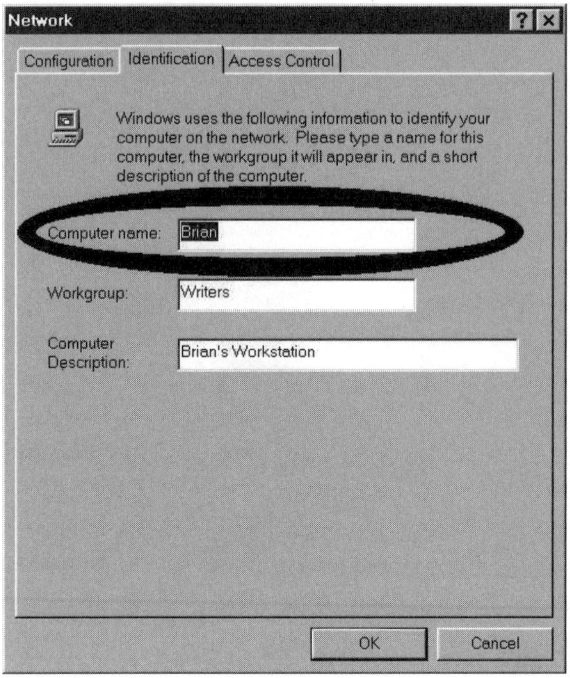

FIGURE 5.2
The Network Control Panel applet in Windows 98 displays the computer's name.

A NetBIOS name consists of the name entered in the Control Panel Network applet, with a special suffix added to the end. The name entered in the Control Panel can contain up to 15 characters. Each character represents a single 8-bit ASCII code. The 8-bit ASCII code 01100101 (often represented in hexadecimal format as 65h), for example, represents the capital letter A. NetBIOS limits the name to 15 bytes, or characters, because it reserves the 16th byte for a special code that defines the role the machine will play on the network.

The two most common roles played by computers on a network are client and server. A *client* is a machine that can access resources being shared by other computers on a network. A *server* is a machine that can share its resources with other machines on a network. Table 5.1 lists the common 16th-byte codes used to define the server and client functions of a machine. Do not worry about memorizing all the functions and 16th-byte codes listed in the table—they will not appear on the Network+ exam. Instead, let's look at the three most commonly used extensions to understand how NetBIOS manages connections between machines.

TABLE 5.1

NetBIOS names and functions

Unique Names	
16th Byte	Function
<00>	Workstation Service name; the name registered by clients on the network
<03>	Messenger Service Name; used by applications such as WINPOPUP and NET SEND to deliver messages
<1B>	Domain Master Browser
<06>	RAS server
<1F>	NetDDE Service
<20>	File and Print Server
<21>	RAS client
<BE>	Network Monitor agent
<BF>	Network Monitor utility

Hannah, a friendly neighborhood network tech, installs three machines on her network: a single Windows NT Server named FRED and two Windows 98 systems named BARNEY and DINO. Hannah configures FRED and BARNEY to act as both clients and servers, and configures DINO only as a client. FRED has at least two names:

FRED<00>, identifying FRED as a client.
FRED<20>, identifying FRED as a file and print server.

Barney also has two names:

BARNEY<00>, identifying BARNEY as a client.
BARNEY<20>, identifying BARNEY as a file and print server.

DINO, in contrast, simply registers as a client, DINO<00>.

NOTE

Any real machine using NetBIOS on a Microsoft Network will actually register several more names that support additional, less-obvious functions. Those additional names have been left out of this discussion for the sake of simplicity.

Hannah does not specifically set the machines to use these names—she simply installs the server or client software and a NetBIOS program operating in the background determines the names automatically based on the name Hannah enters in the identification tab of the Network Control Panel applet. On FRED, the Windows NT system, Hannah specifies the NetBEUI protocol on the Protocols tab of the Network Control Panel applet (see Figure 5.3) and specifies the computer name FRED on the Identification tab (see Figure 5.4). Notice that she does not install the NetBIOS session-layer and NetBEUI transport-layer functions separately—she simply installs "NetBEUI." On this screen, Microsoft has made the unfortunate decision to title the tab "Protocol" instead of "Protocol Suite" and refers to the "NetBEUI protocol suite" as simply "NetBEUI." Don't be fooled—when Hannah adds "NetBEUI," she actually installs two protocols: NetBIOS at the session layer and NetBEUI at the transport layer. By default, Windows NT installs both a server and workstation (i.e. client) component, displayed on the Services tab in Figure 5.5, and FRED is ready to roll.

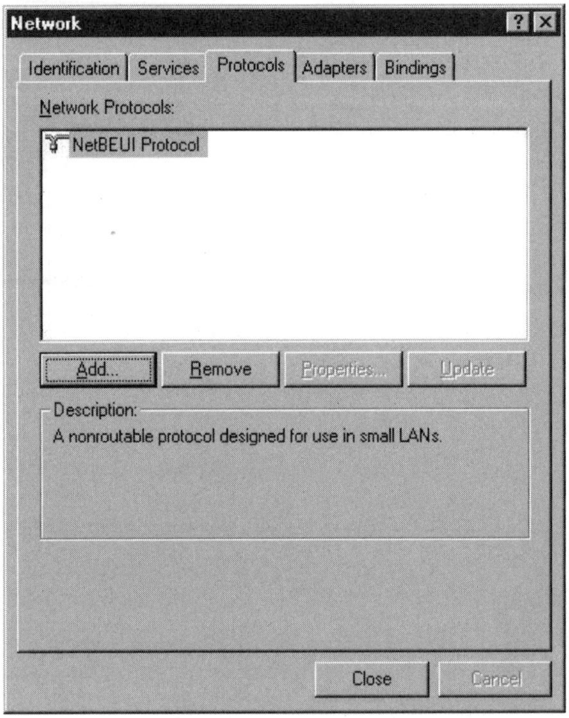

FIGURE 5.3

The Protocol tab of Windows NT's Network Control Panel applet.

FIGURE 5.4

The Identification tab of Windows NT's Network Control Panel applet

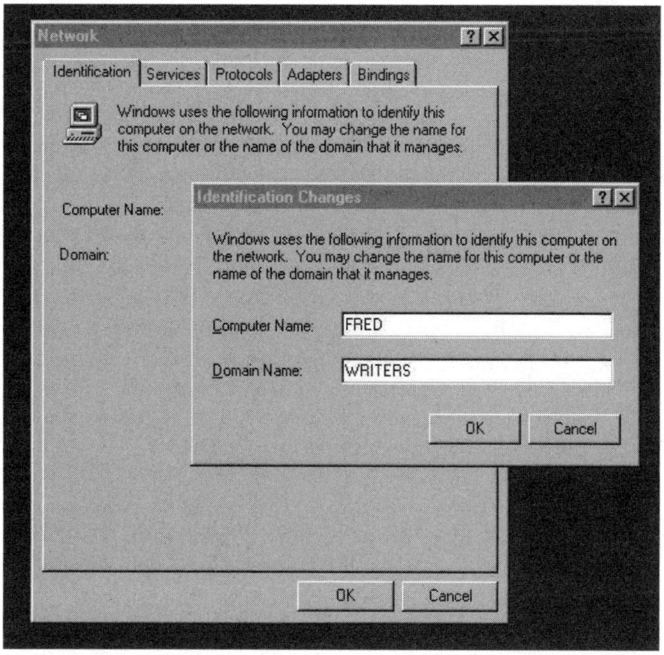

FIGURE 5.5

The Services tab of Windows NT's Network Control Panel applet.

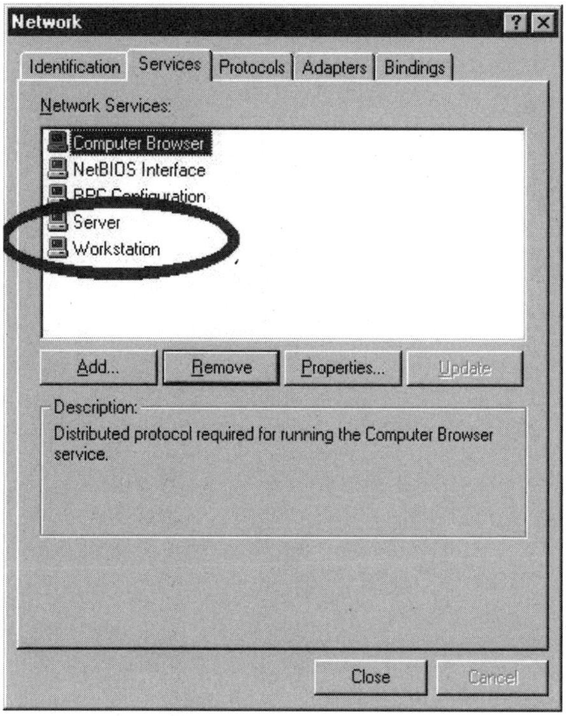

NOTE

The tradition in the industry of referring to entire protocol suites by the name of one or two of its constituent protocols has caused much unnecessary confusion. Unfortunately, it is too late to go back to the early 1980s and force the networking industry to adopt clearer terminology. Read carefully whenever the word protocol comes up–sometimes this means protocol, sometimes it means protocol suite.

The process of setting up BARNEY as both a client and a server involves roughly the same steps, with the addition of specifically adding the server function. While Microsoft assumes that all installations of Windows NT Server should be servers and installs the Server component by default, it also assumes that network techs will often install Windows 9x systems as clients only. On BARNEY, Hannah installs Client for Microsoft Networks, File and Print Sharing for Microsoft Networks, and NetBEUI (Figure 5.6). Notice that NT calls its server component "Server," while Windows 98 calls its server component "File and Print Sharing for Microsoft Networks." While the names and the layout of the control panel change between operating systems, the essential functions do not—FRED and BARNEY function as both clients and servers. After configuring DINO as just a client by installing NetBIOS and the Client for Microsoft Networks, Hannah has a three-node network and she and her coworkers sit down to do some work.

NOTE

Some techs make a distinction between the term *protocol suite*, a set of protocols used together, and *protocol stack*, the actual software that implements the suite on a particular operating system. For example: Windows NT and Windows 98 can both use the NetBEUI suite, but they use different NetBEUI stacks. In many contexts, however, writers ignore the distinction and use the terms interchangeably.

When Hannah sits at BARNEY and accesses a file on FRED, the NT server, both BARNEY and FRED must keep track and manage the connection. To open the connection, BARNEY the client, a.k.a. BARNEY<00>, opens up a connection with FRED the server, also known as FRED<20>. See Figure 5.7. As FRED begins to send the requested file to BARNEY, another user, Barbara, sits down at DINO and opens another file on FRED, as shown in Figure 5.8. Each of the computers keeps track of the "conversations" taking place using the NetBIOS names, as shown in Figure 5.9.

FIGURE 5.6

Install File and Print Sharing, Client for Microsoft Networks, and the NetBEUI protocol suite on the same screen in Windows 9x.

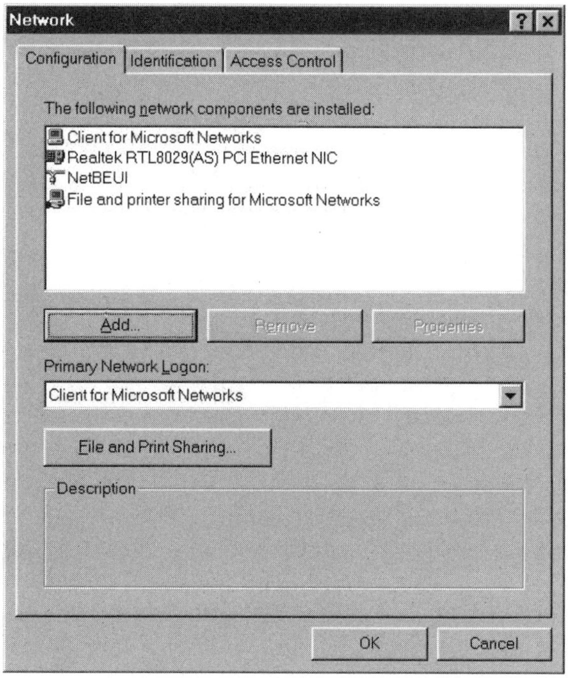

FIGURE 5.7

BARNEY opens a connection with FRED.

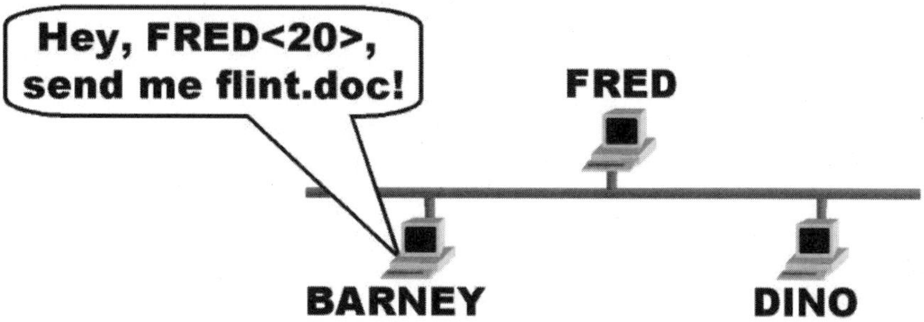

By using a different NetBIOS name for each function, machines can better track multiple connections between the same two machines. When Barbara sits at FRED and opens a file on BARNEY, FRED<00> establishes a connection with BARNEY<20>. (Note that even though FRED runs the Windows NT server operating system, it still can function as a client computer.) At the same time, Hannah sits at BARNEY and opens a file on FRED, causing BARNEY<00> to establish a connection with FRED<20>. The use of NetBIOS names that correspond to the server and client functions enables FRED and BARNEY to hold two (or more) simultaneous conversations. See Figure 5.10.

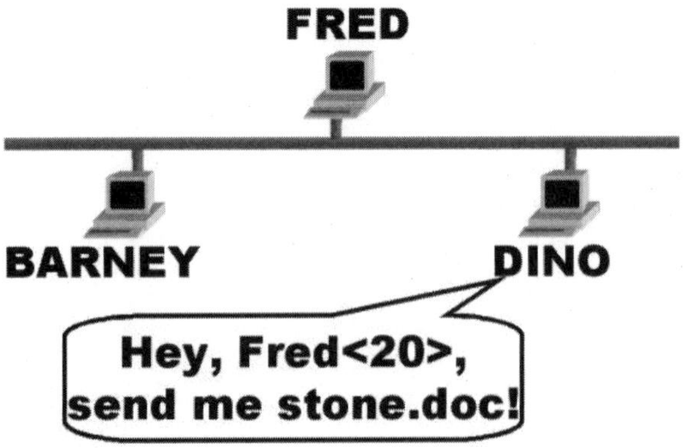

FIGURE 5.8
DINO opens a connection with FRED.

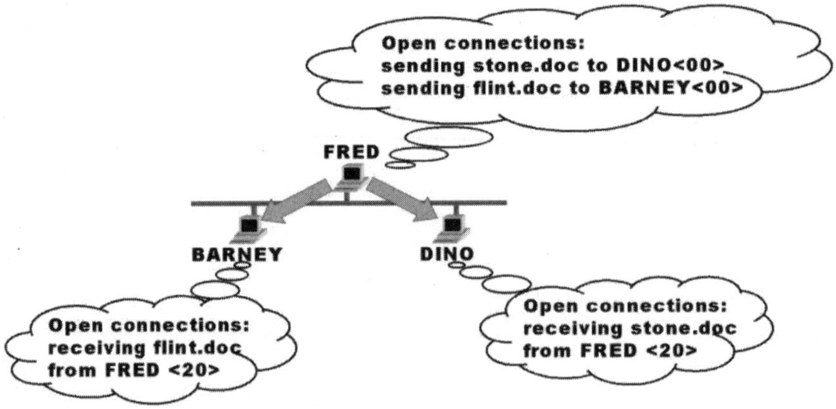

FIGURE 5.9
FRED, BARNEY, and DINO use NetBIOS names to track their connections.

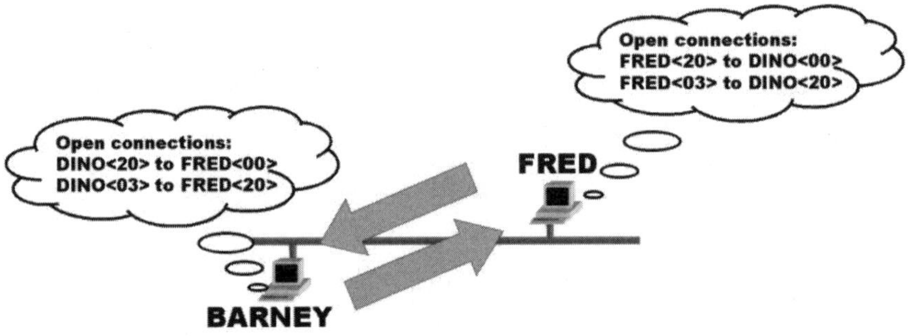

FIGURE 5.10
A single machine can function in more than one capacity at a time.

A machine requires a NetBIOS name for each function it performs—without the name, the other nodes cannot establish a connection. When Hannah sits at BARNEY and attempts to open a file on DINO,

BARNEY cannot establish the connection. DINO has no server function—it acts only as a client. When DINO receives a request for a connection with DINO<20>, DINO does not even bother to send a refusal message back to BARNEY. DINO<20> does not exist—DINO responds to DINO<00> or nothing at all. See Figure 5.11.

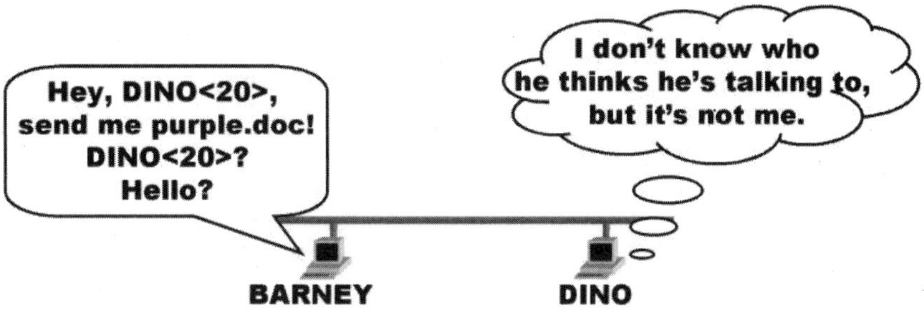

FIGURE 5.11 *DINO ignores BARNEY because DINO<20> is not one of its NetBIOS names.*

While NetBIOS provides an adequate means for managing connections on a small network, it does not scale well for larger networks. The base NetBIOS name for each computer must be unique—there cannot be two machines named DINO. NetBIOS uses a *flat name space*, meaning that every machine has a single name drawn from a single pool. Imagine a world without last names. No two people could have the name Mike, or Bob, or Johnny. Instead, people would have to come up with unique names like Johnny5, Fonzie, and Bluto. Given a dozen people, finding unique names presents no problem. Placing a few thousand people in the same flat name space creates a big problem. In real life, most people have as a many as three or four names, preventing this from becoming a problem. In the world of NetBIOS, unfortunately, its designers made no provision for "last names."

The flat name space frequently requires administrators to use bizarre, nondescriptive names and creates administrative headaches. NetBIOS names cannot be terribly descriptive. Bob's network has a single server, so calling that machine SERVER makes sense. But Wally's network has 20 servers, including 10 accounting servers, 5 Web servers, 4 file servers, and an e-mail server. Wally usually refers to one of his servers as "Accounting Server 7" in conversation, but he cannot use that as the NetBIOS name for the machine. Remember, NetBIOS names must contain 15 or fewer characters (not counting the special 16th character that designates the machine's function). Instead of "Accounting Server 7," Wally ends up naming the server ACCOUNTSERV7. The problem of coming up with unique names becomes more extreme in large WAN environments run by multiple administrators. While Wally could easily keep track of his 20 servers and guarantee that he never assigned two machines the same name, ensuring name uniqueness in a large WAN becomes an administrative nightmare. In a WAN run by 40 different administrators, guaranteeing that no two administrators ever assign the same name to any two of their 5000+ machines requires extensive planning and ongoing communication. Once a network becomes large enough, network architects prefer a more scalable naming scheme, such as the TCP/IP protocol suite's Domain Name Service (DNS). (See Chapter 6.)

Within the NetBEUI protocol suite, NetBIOS handles the session-layer function of managing connections. Its reliance on a flat name space makes it difficult to use in large WAN environments, but its simplicity makes it an ideal choice for smaller LANs. As long as the network tech assigns every computer a unique name, NetBIOS does a fine job. Once NetBIOS establishes a connection, it passes the packet down to the NetBEUI protocol, operating at the transport layer.

NetBEUI

NetBEUI functions at the transport layer within the NetBEUI protocol suite, breaking larger chunks of data into smaller pieces on the sending machine and reassembling them on the receiving end. See Figure 5.12. NetBEUI requires no setup by the network tech other than installation of the protocol. While this simplicity makes NetBEUI attractive for smaller networks, it deprives NetBEUI of an ability vital to larger networks: routing.

NetBEUI skips the network layer and communicates directly with the data-link layer, depriving itself of routing capability. As discussed in Chapter 4, routing occurs at the network layer. Network-layer protocols add additional addressing information to each data packet. This extra network-layer address tells a router how to find the destination network. When a router receives a NetBEUI packet, it cannot find the information it requires and discards the packet. See Figure 5.13. NetBEUI can work with bridges, however, which operate at the data-link layer. See Figure 5.14. In the early 1980s, network architects frequently used NetBEUI because of its simplicity. As the typical network grew and came to include routers, NetBEUI (both the individual transport-layer protocol and the protocol suite) became an increasingly less common choice, supplanted by more scalable protocol suites such as IPX/SPX and TCP/IP.

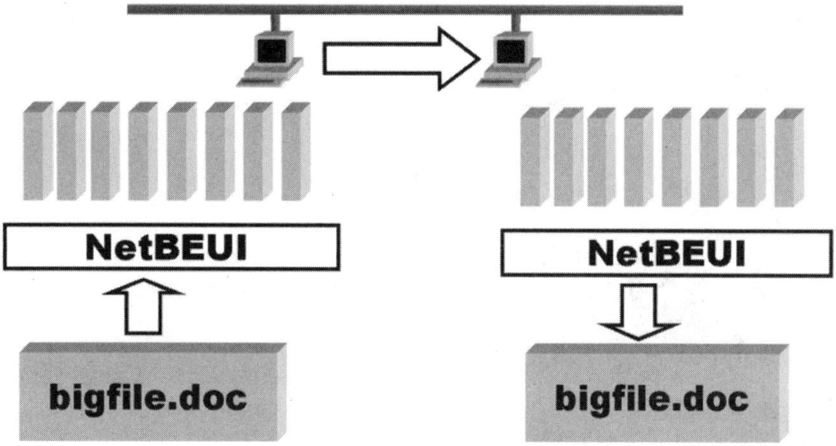

FIGURE 5.12 *NetBEUI breaks the file into smaller pieces for transmission and reassembles the pieces on the receiving end.*

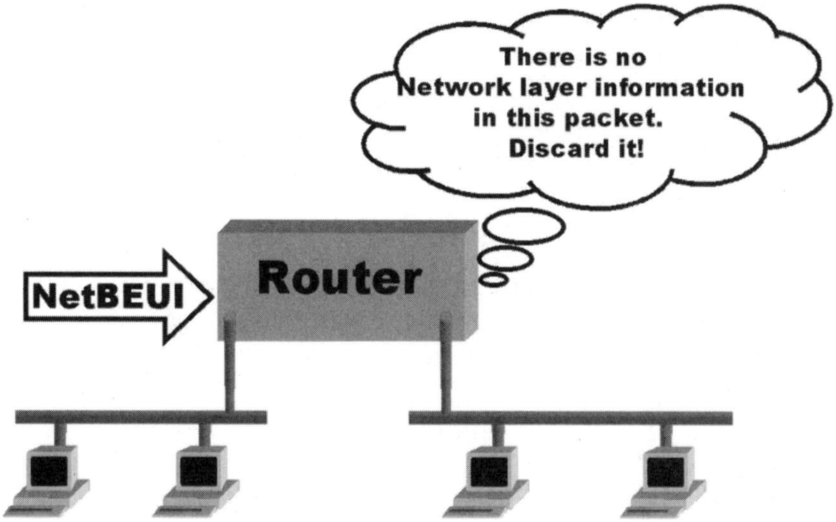

FIGURE 5.13 *Routers discard NetBEUI packets.*

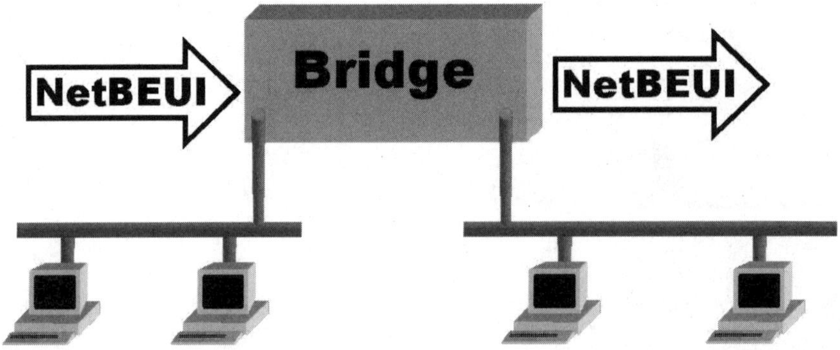

FIGURE 5.14
Bridges operate at Layer 2, the data-link layer, and can filter and forward NetBEUI packets using the MAC addresses contained in the data packet.

NOTE

The NetBEUI protocol suite's lack of any network-layer protocol illustrates the key weakness of the OSI model: not everyone follows it.

IPX/SPX

Novell's IPX/SPX protocol suite, used primarily by Novell NetWare-based networks, provides a more scalable solution for networks than NetBEUI. (See Chapter 7 for an overview of Novell NetWare.) While the NetBEUI protocol suite provides services at the transport and session layers, IPX/SPX includes a wide variety of protocols operating at layers three (the network layer) through seven (the application layer). Although the protocol is strongly associated with Novell, Microsoft supports IPX/SPX through its own version of the protocol, NWLink. Microsoft-based clients and servers can use IPX/SPX for communicating with both Microsoft and Novell NetWare servers. Although more scalable than NetBEUI, in very large networks IPX/SPX bogs down due to excessive traffic.

In a Novell NetWare network, IPX/SPX operates at layers 3-7 of the OSI model. Figure 5.15 shows some of these protocols in relation to the OSI model. At the network layers, the Internetwork Packet eXchange (IPX) protocol handles routing data packets between networks. At the transport layer, Sequenced Packet eXchange (SPX) handles the process of breaking data into smaller chunks on the sending machine and reassembling data on receiving machine. Server Advertising Protocol (SAP) handles the session layer, and the NetWare Core Protocol (NCP) handles a variety of presentation- and application-layer issues.

NOTE

The Network+ exam does not require knowledge of the individual protocols that make up the IPX/SPX suite.

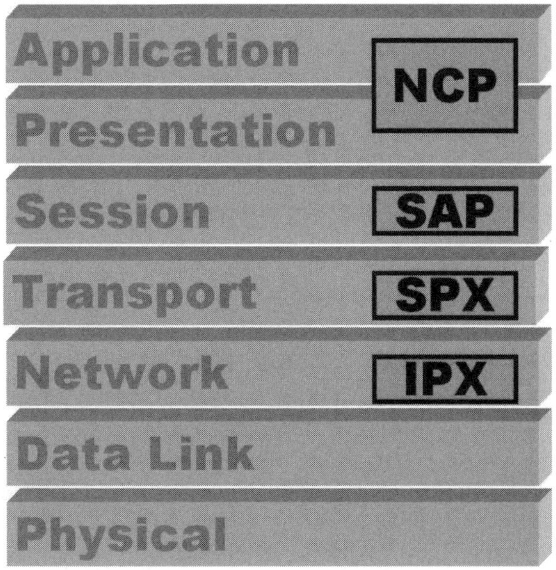

FIGURE 5.15
IPX/SPX includes protocols operating at OSI layers 3–7.

Microsoft takes advantage of the widespread industry support of IPX/SPX with its own version of the protocol suite, referred to as either "IPX/SPX-compatible protocol" or NWLink. See Figure 5.16. Rather than add routing support to NetBEUI, Microsoft simply adopted a proven routable protocol that already existed. Microsoft NOSs, including Windows 95, Windows 98, and Windows NT, use IPX/SPX for two purposes: to connect to NetWare servers and to provide transport- and network-layer functions for Microsoft networking. In communication between two Microsoft-based systems, Microsoft does not use the IPX/SPX protocol suite's application-, presentation-, or session-layer protocols, relying instead on traditional Microsoft networking protocols such as NetBIOS. See Figure 5.17.

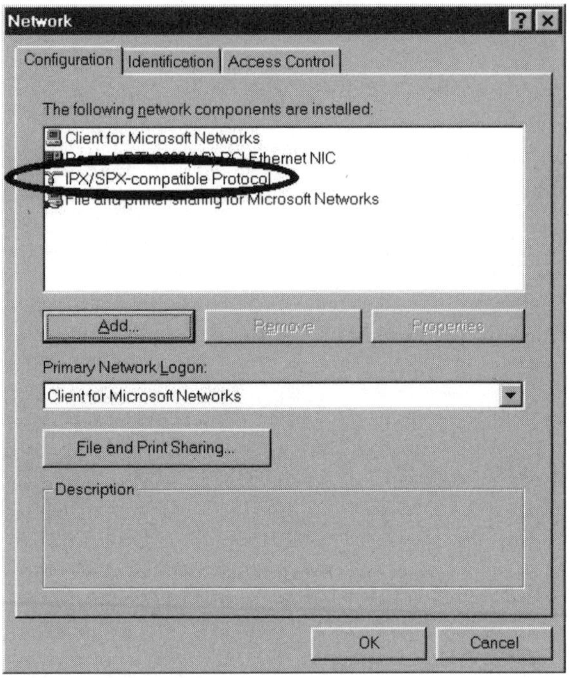

FIGURE 5.16
Microsoft calls its version of the IPX/SPX protocol suite either "IPX/SPX-compatible transport" or NWLink.

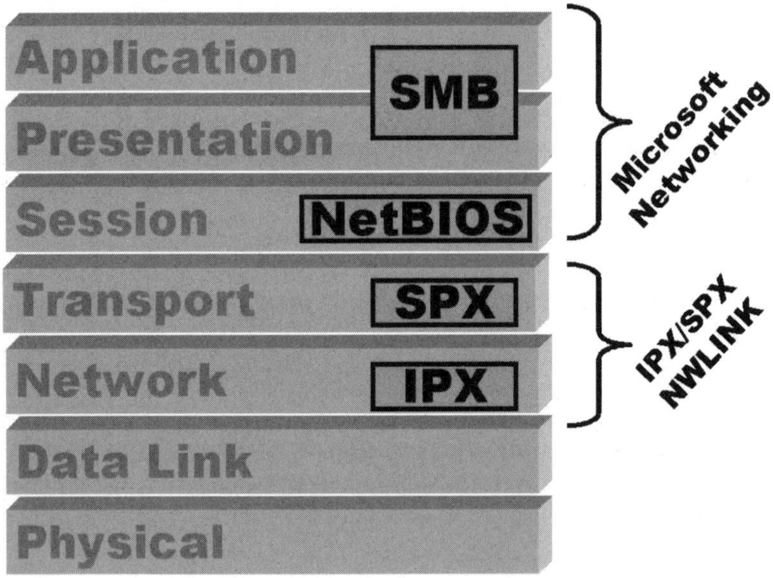

FIGURE 5.17
Microsoft clients and servers use only a subset of the IPX/SPX protocol suite.

Unlike NetBEUI, which requires no configuration beyond assigning each computer a name, IPX/SPX requires the network tech to configure IPX properly. IPX packets, created at the network layer, can use several formats that vary depending on the data-link layer protocol used. IPX running on top of Ethernet, for example, can use one of four data structures, called *frame types*: Ethernet 802.3, Ethernet II, Ethernet 802.2, or Ethernet SNAP. If two nodes use different frame types, they cannot communicate. See Figure 5.18. In the days of DOS-based network clients, network techs set the frame type manually for each system on the network. Windows 9x or Windows NT systems simplify the process by automatically detecting IPX traffics by default, configuring each machine to use whichever frame type is first detected on the network. See Figure 5.19. Problems arise, however, when a network uses more than one frame type. Each Windows 9x or NT system automatically configures itself to use the first frame type that it detects, resulting in mismatched frame types. See Figure 5.20. To ensure that every system uses the same frame type, use the network control panel applet, shown in Figure 5.21. The structural details of the different frame types do not affect the network tech—simply configure all systems to use the same frame type.

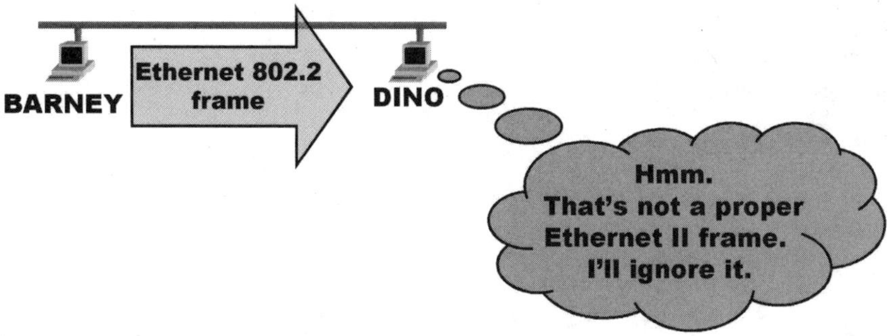

FIGURE 5.18
Two nodes using IPX ignore each other's packets if configured to use different frame types.

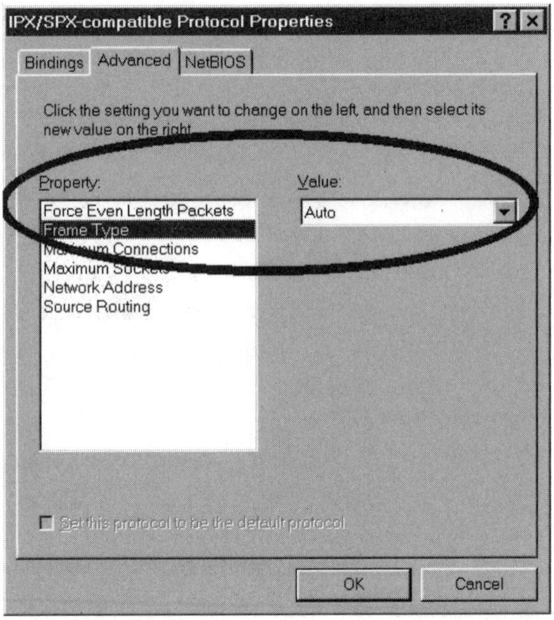

FIGURE 5.19 *Windows 9x and NT systems automatically detect the frame type in use on the network.*

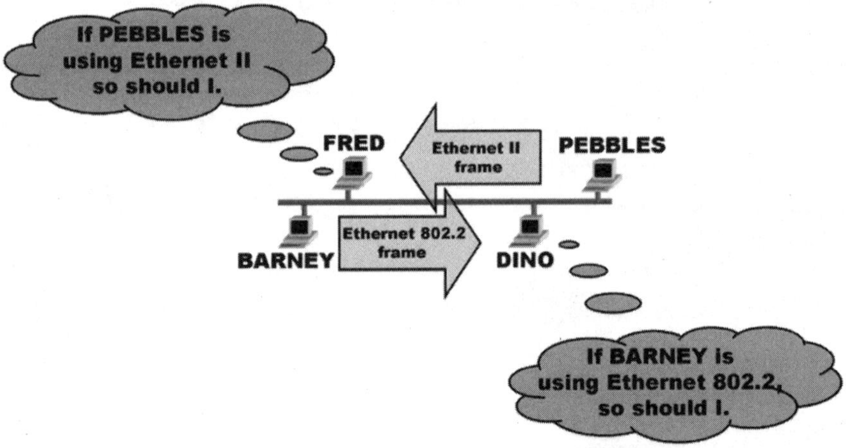

FIGURE 5.20 *Windows 9x and NT systems sometimes detect different frame types.*

IPX/SPX, although routable, does not scale well for large WANs. Novell designed IPX/SPX to support the NetWare operating system, which treats NetWare servers as the ultimate focus of the network. In a NetWare environment, servers are servers, clients are clients, and the twain never meet. Unlike NetBEUI, which assumes that a machine can function as both client and server, IPX/SPX assumes that a proper network consists of a few servers and a large number of clients. The servers use the Server Announcement Protocol (SAP) to create and maintain connections. While this configuration works well on small and medium-sized networks, as a network grows to include hundreds of servers and thousands of clients, SAP traffic increases, slowing down the network. Until recently, the danger of excessive SAP broadcasts had no impact on the typical network tech—most networks did not have enough servers for SAP broadcasts to cause congestion. As large networks become common, however, IPX/SPX's reliance on SAP broadcasts becomes more of a problem, leading most WAN designers to adopt a more scalable alternative: TCP/IP.

FIGURE 5.21
Setting the frame type manually.

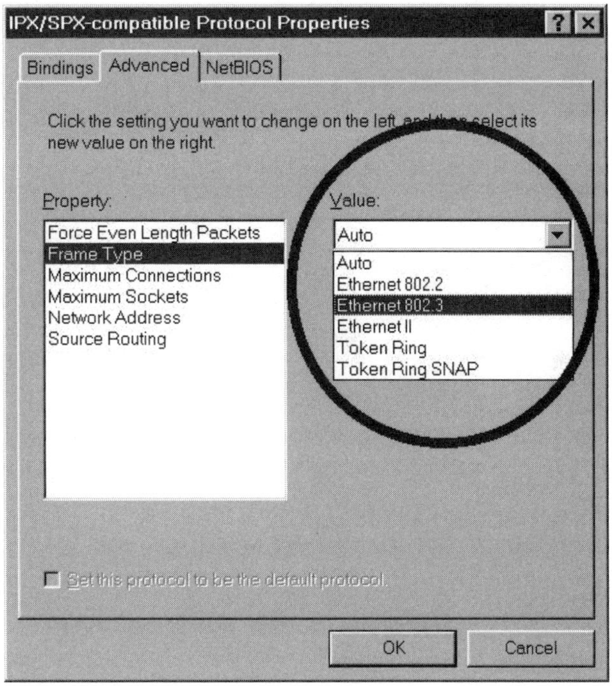

TCP/IP

The TCP/IP protocol suite offers a more scalable solution, but requires significantly more configuration on the part of the network tech. While it was originally a UNIX networking protocol suite, its use as the protocol suite of the Internet has prompted both Microsoft and Novell to embrace TCP/IP. Unlike NetBEUI and IPX/SPX, TCP/IP is an open standard, not controlled by any one company.

A series of documents called Requests for Comment, or RFCs, defines each protocol within the TCP/IP suite. These documents, freely available on the Internet, provide all the information needed to write programs that conform to the TCP/IP standard. The open nature of these protocols makes TCP/IP an attractive environment for developing new protocols. If TCP/IP has no protocol that provides a desired function, any skilled programmer can write a new protocol, publish an RFC, and add it to the TCP/IP suite. This flexibility fostered the evolution of the Internet from a simple, geographically dispersed network for transferring e-mail and data files into the Internet of today, with its World Wide Web pages, real-time audio broadcasts, instant messaging, secure credit card transactions, and more wonders to come. The ability to add new protocols to meet new needs gives TCP/IP a flexibility that the other protocols cannot match.

NOTE

Chapter 6 will cover TCP/IP configuration in detail.

Review Questions

1) When using NetBIOS, how long can the computer name be?

a) 8 characters
b) 12 characters
c) 15 characters
d) 256 characters

2) NWLink is Microsoft's version of ___________.

a) NetBEUI
b) NetBIOS
c) IPX/SPX
d) TCP/IP

3) The____________________ are documents that define the various protocols of the TCP/IP protocol suite.

a) Knowledge Base
b) TLAs
c) RFCs
d) TCPs

4) NetBIOS operates at the ________________ layer.

a) Data Link
b) Network
c) Transport
d) Session

5) NetBEUI operates at the ________________ layer.

a) Data Link
b) Network
c) Transport
d) Session

6) Travis, using a Windows 95 computer named TRACK3, complains that he cannot connect with another Windows 95 computer named SALES3. Jim, the friendly neighborhood network tech, determines that TRACK3 can connect successfully with other machines that reside on the same side of the router, but not with any machines on the far side of the router. Which of the following is the most likely cause of Travis's problem?

a) TRACK3 is connected to the network with a bad cable.
b) TRACK3's network card has failed and needs to be replaced.
c) TRACK3 is running NetBEUI.
d) TRACK3 is running NetBIOS.

7) Which of the following protocols are routable? (choose all that apply)

a) NetBEUI
b) IPX/SPX
c) TCP/IP

Review Answers

1) **A.** 15 characters, NetBIOS reserves the 16th byte for special codes that define the function of the machine on the network.

2) **C.** IPX/SPX

3) **C.** RFCs, RFC stands for Request for Comment.

4) **D.** Session

5) **C.** Transport

6) **C.** TRACK3 is running NetBEUI. NetBEUI is a non-routable protocol. Because TRACK3 can communicate with some other machines on the network, a bad cable or NIC is unlikely to cause the symptom described.

7) **B** and **C.** IPX/SPX and TCP/IP.

Chapter 6

TCP/IP

In the movie *The Graduate*, a friend of the family pulls Ben, Dustin Hoffman's character, aside and tells him one word the friend believes will guarantee a successful career for young Ben: "plastics." If that same conversation took place today, the word would be "TCP/IP." All major operating systems, including UNIX, Windows 95/98, Windows NT, and Novell NetWare, support TCP/IP. UNIX has relied on TCP/IP as its primary networking protocol suite since its earliest versions. Microsoft and Novell, on the other hand, began to shift their focus from their traditional protocol suites, NetBEUI and IPX/SPX, to TCP/IP because of the ever-increasing importance of the Internet, the "big daddy" of TCP/IP networks. A network tech must understand TCP/IP to work with any current NOS, and the Network+ exam justifiably stresses TCP/IP concepts and skills, including basic addressing and routing, managing connections, name resolution, and proper use of TCP/IP troubleshooting utilities.

Addressing

Internet Protocol (IP) handles network-layer issues for all TCP/IP traffic, defining the rules for moving data between hosts across a routed network. A *host* is any machine that can be the source or recipient of data. Not only is IP part of the name of the TCP/IP protocol suite, it is the suite's foundation. Not all TCP/IP traffic uses the Transmission Control Protocol (TCP), but all TCP/IP traffic uses IP. For this reason, network techs sometimes refer to TCP/IP-based networks as simply "IP networks."

NOTE

A *host* is any device that can be either the source or destination of a data packet.

Every host on a TCP/IP based network has a logical address known as its *IP address*. A *logical address* describes both a specific network and a specific machine on that network, in contrast to a *physical address*—like a MAC address—that merely identifies the machine without reference to its location. IP addresses function like mailing addresses. Just as a mailing address helps the post office to deliver mail to its intended recipient,

IP addresses provide the information routers and other devices need to deliver IP packets. A mailing address, such as 3130 Rockabilly Way, provides two pieces of information: a street (Rockabilly Way) and a specific house on that street (3130). A mail carrier examines the address and extracts those two crucial pieces of information—the street and specific house—and delivers the mail. A router on an IP network extracts similar information from an IP address—the network and the specific host on the network—and delivers the packet accurately.

NOTE

Network techs use the term *logical address* when referring to IP addresses to distinguish them from MAC addresses, which they refer to as *physical addresses.*

In an IP-based network, the network architect assigns each network a *network ID* number. This takes the place of the name that people would use to define each network. Cliff has an intranet in his building, consisting of two networks. The east wing of the building has, appropriately, the east wing network, and the west wing has the west wing network. See Figure 6.1.

FIGURE 6.1
Two networks separated by a router.

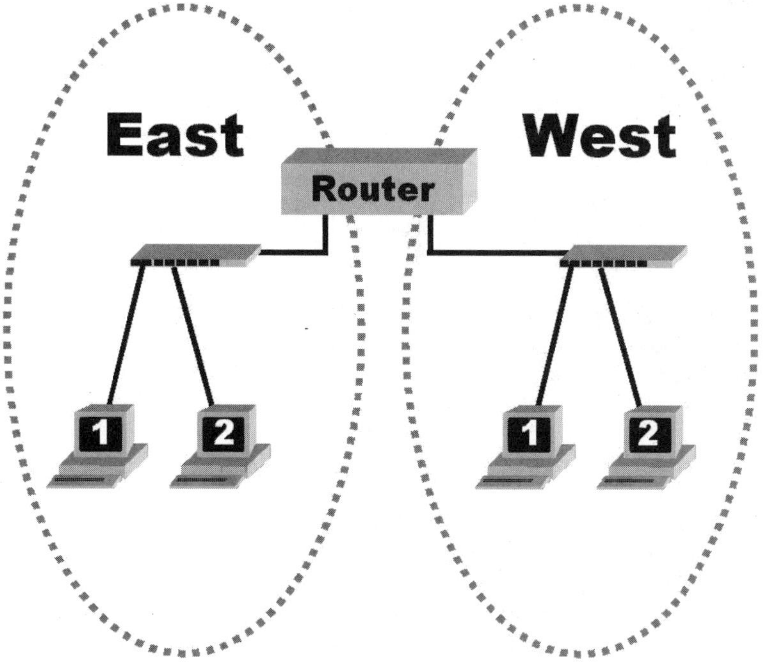

Because devices such as routers cannot handle destinations like "east wing," Cliff assigns ID numbers to each network—the east wing network gets the network ID of 192.168.49.0; the west wing network gets the network ID of 192.168.50.0, as shown in Figure 6.2. Now Cliff can refer to the first computer in the east wing as "host 1 on network 192.168.49.0." and the second computer in the west wing as "host 2 on network 192.168.50.0."

NOTE

The trailing zero in the network ID numbers is not part of the network address—it serves as a placeholder. The network ID numbers could just as easily be expressed as 192.168.49.*x* and 192.168.50.*x*. Why use zero instead of x to represent the placeholder? Because those who designed IP said so.

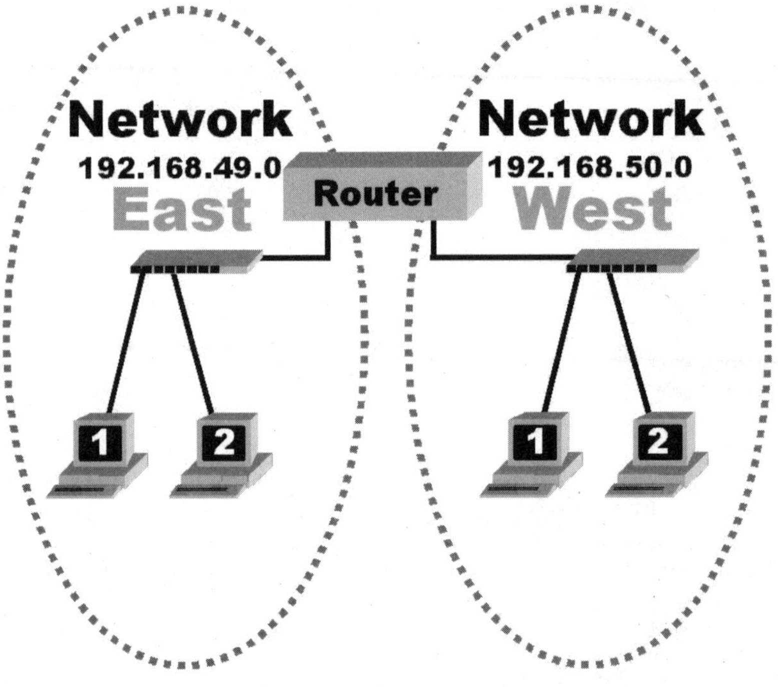

FIGURE 6.2

Cliff assigns each network its own identifying number.

The computers themselves, however, need these designations reduced to pure numbers. Cliff generates the IP address of each machine by taking the network ID of the network on which it lies and replacing the place-holding zero with the host ID of the specific machine. Instead of "host 2 on network 192.168.50.0," the computers refer to that machine simply by its numerical IP address: 192.168.50.2. The *host ID* is the part of the IP address that specifies the individual machine, not the network in general. Using this system, each device has a logical address, its IP address, that both identifies it as an individual and specifies the network on which it resides, as shown in Figure 6.3.

FIGURE 6.3

Each machine has an IP address that describes it as a specific host on a specific network.

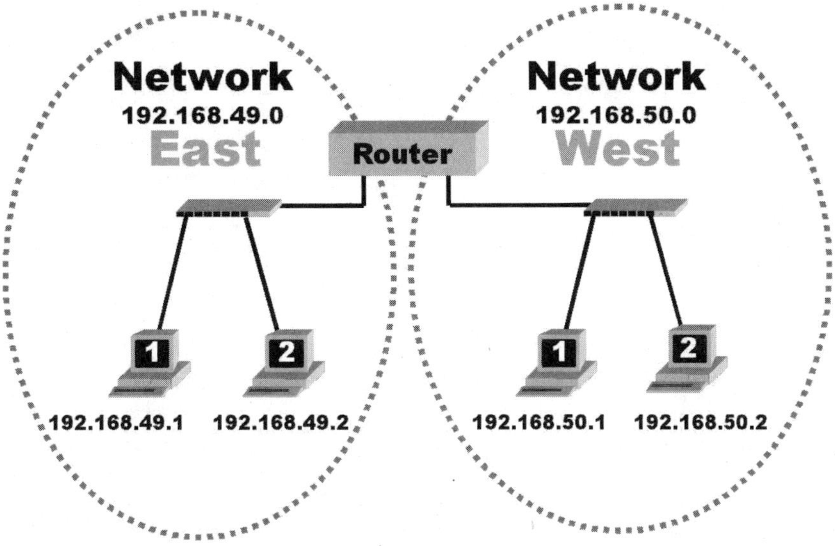

Cliff's two networks can have no more than 254 hosts. Each decimal digit in an IP address must fall between 0 and 255, and the numbers 0 and 255 are reserved for special purposes. As seen in the example above, the address 192.168.50.0 refers to the east wing network as a whole, and does not refer to any specific host on the network. The address 192.168.50.255 has another meaning—it designates a packet as broadcast. All hosts on network 192.168.50.0 respond to packets sent to 192.168.50.255, as shown in Figure 6.4. If Cliff's network stands alone and does not connect to the Internet, Cliff can add additional networks of 254 devices or fewer as needed, as long as he ensures that no two networks share the same network ID and no two devices share the same IP address.

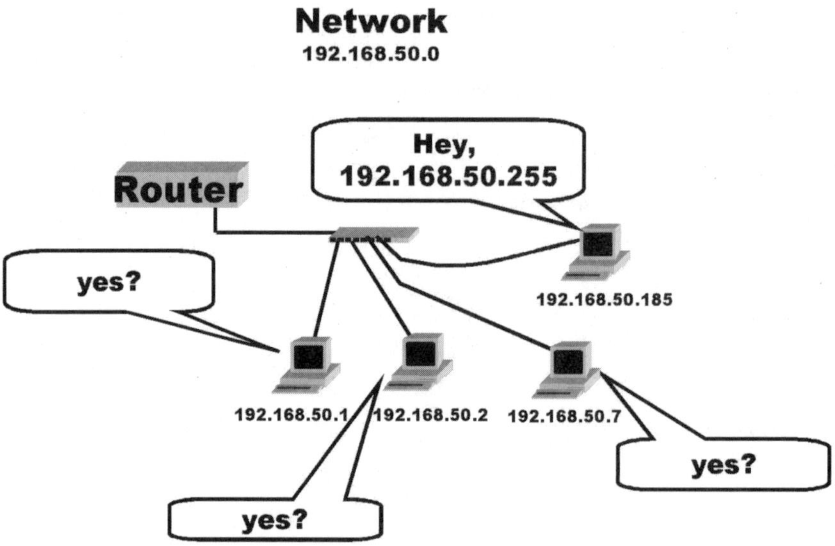

FIGURE 6.4
Every host on a network receives a broadcast packet.

NOTE

Each digit in an IP address must fall in the range 0-254 because each digit actually represents an 8-bit binary number, and there are 256 possible 8-bit numbers. For example, the decimal number "50" in the address 192.168.50.2 is shorthand for the binary value 00110010. The entire IP address 192.168.50.2 represents a 32-bit value, 11000000 10101000 00110010 00000010.

The binary values for IP addresses have important implications for more advanced TCP/IP topics not covered on the Network+ exam. For a more detailed discussion of IP addressing, consult 3Com's "Understanding IP Addressing: Everything You Ever Wanted To Know" at **http://www.3com.com/nsc/501302.html** or "Connected: an Internet Encyclopedia" at **http://www.freesoft.org/CIE/Course/index.htm**. (Note that both addresses are case-sensitive.)

If Cliff's network connects to the Internet, however, he must ensure that none of his networks share the same address as any other network connected to the Internet. (Imagine the confusion that would happen if two houses had the same street and same number for their address.) To avoid duplicate addresses, any network architect who wishes to connect his network to the Internet must obtain an unused block of addresses from a central authority known as the Internet Network Information Center, or InterNIC. InterNIC keeps track of all of the addresses currently in use and assigns blocks of previously unassigned addresses to organizations based on their size. Small organizations, like the one run by Cliff in the preceding example, get small blocks while larger organizations like Microsoft and Coca-Cola receive larger blocks. InterNIC calls these blocks of addresses *licenses*.

InterNIC assigns blocks of addresses in one of three sizes. A Class A network has 16.7 million possible addresses, a Class B network has 65,534 possible addresses, and a Class C license (like the ones used by Cliff in the example above) has 254 possible addresses. The first decimal value of an address determines its class. All addresses between 1.x.x.x and 127.x.x.x. are Class A addresses; all addresses between 128.x.x.x and 191.x.x.x. are Class B addresses; and all addresses between 192.x.x.x and 223.x.x.x are Class C addresses. Table 6.1 shows the addresses that correspond to each class. As Table 6.1 shows, all addresses above 224.x.x.x. belong to two special classes that are never used for individual machines. (The Network+ exam does not cover the uses of multicast and experimental IP addresses.) Virtually all the Class A and B licenses have already been assigned, leaving new networks that wish to connect to the Internet fighting over the remaining Class C licenses. Organizations that cannot acquire enough valid addresses must employ devices such as proxy servers (discussed later in this chapter) to connect to the Internet.

TABLE 6.1
IP address classes.

	First Decimal Value	Addresses	Hosts per Network
Class A	1–127	1.0.0.0–127.0.0.0	16.7 Million
Class B	128–191	128.0.0.0–191.255.0.0	65,546
Class C	192–223	192.0.0.0–223.255.255.0	254
Class D	224–239	224.0.0.0–239.255.255.255	Multicast Addresses
Class E	239–255	240.0.0.0–255.255.255.254	Experimental Addresses

The class of an address determines another important variable: its *subnet mask*. The subnet mask determines which part of an IP address refers to the network ID and which part refers to the host ID. Table 6.2 shows the class licenses and their corresponding default subnet masks.

An IP address has four values, called *octets* (because each represents an 8-bit value), separated by periods. For each octet, if the corresponding value in the subnet mask equals 255, that octet refers to the network ID. If the corresponding value equals zero, then the octet refers to the host ID. The default subnet mask for the address 192.168.50.2, a Class C address, is 255.255.255.0. The address 192.168.50.2 translates to mean "host 2 on network 192.168.50.0." For the Class B address 187.12.54.123, the default subnet mask is 255.255.255.0. Address 187.12.54.123 translates to "host 54.123 on network 187.12.0.0." Table 6.3 shows other examples of translating IP addresses into their equivalent network and host IDs.

TABLE 6.2
Class licenses and their corresponding default subnet masks.

Class	Default Subnet Mask
Class A	255.0.0.0
Class B	255.255.0.0.
Class C	255.255.255.0
Class D	Multicast Addresses
Class E	Experimental Addresses

TABLE 6.3
Translating IP addresses and subnet masks into network and host IDs.

IP Address	Subnet Mask	Default Network ID	Host ID
210.35.156.198	255.255.255.0	210.35.156.0	198
195.25.210.12	255.255.255.0	195.25.210.0	12
180.220.215.19	255.255.0.0	180.220.0.0	215.19
155.35.123.99	255.255.0.0.	155.35.0.0	123.99
142.98.189.222	255.255.0.0	142.98.0.0	189.122.
85.123.225.19	255.0.0.0	85.0.0.0	123.225.19

TIP

EXAM TIP:

The Network+ exam does not require candidates to break down addresses into their network ID and host ID components, but it does require candidates to know the addresses included in each class , the default subnet masks, and the approximate number of hosts allowed by each class. Before taking the exam, be able to recreate Tables 6.1 and 6.2 on a blank sheet of paper.

The Loopback: A Special Address

TCP/IP sets aside a special address, 127.0.0.1, for internal testing. This is the *loopback address*; messages sent to 127.0.0.1 never leave the sending machine. Instead, they are redirected back to the sending machine. The command "PING 127.0.0.1" is often used to confirm that a tech has properly installed TCP/IP on a system. (See below for more on the PING command.)

Routing

IP addresses exist to provide routers the information they require to deliver each data packet to its intended recipient. A router examines each data packet, determines its destination network, and forwards it on to that network. For routers to do their job, hosts on the network must send them the packets that need to be forwarded to other networks, and the router must know how to find every other network within the *internetwork*, the larger "network of networks" within which it operates.

Routers do not grab traffic off the network and forward it automatically—the hosts on the network must ask the router to forward the traffic for them. When sending data across a router to other networks, a host explicitly sends IP packets to its nearest router, which then forwards the packet to its final destination. In a TCP/IP network, a host's nearest router is called its *default gateway*.

The IP address for a host's default gateway must lie on the same network as the host. In the network that Cliff built, there is only a single router, but that router has two IP addresses (192.168.49.50 and 192.168.50.50) and the hosts on the network treat each IP address as a separate logical device. See Figure 6.5. Devices on the 192.168.49.0 (east) network must use 192.168.49.50 as their default gateway, while devices on the 192.168.50.0 network must use 192.168.50.50 as their default gateway. In other words, a host will always use the "near side" address of the router as its default gateway setting.

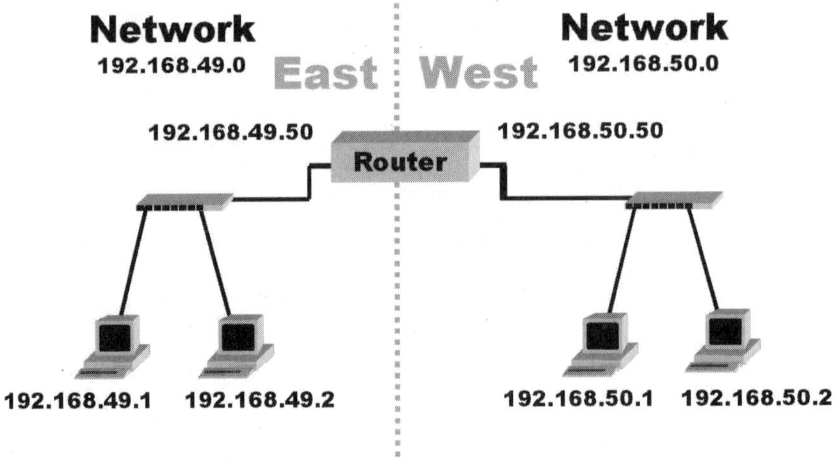

FIGURE 6.5
A router will have two or more IP addresses.

To communicate using TCP/IP across a routed network, a network tech must configure three settings on every host: the IP address, the subnet mask, and the default gateway. Figure 6.6 shows the IP address tab from the Windows NT Network Control Panel applet. If the network tech enters a correct IP address and subnet mask but leaves the default gateway setting blank (or enters the wrong default gateway address), then the system can only communicate with other hosts on the same network. When communicating with hosts on other networks, a host must send data bound for other networks to its default gateway and trust that the default gateway, a router, knows how to find the packet's destination.

Routers must learn the location of the other networks within their internetwork. The router in Figure 6.5 above, has no trouble finding both the 192.168.49.0 (east) and the 192.168.50.0 (west) networks because it attaches directly to both of them. The routers shown in Figure 6.7, however, have a more difficult job because they must forward traffic to a number of networks to which they have no direct attachment. Sergio, the network tech in charge of the routers, can use two basic methods to teach each router about the location of the other networks: static and dynamic routing.

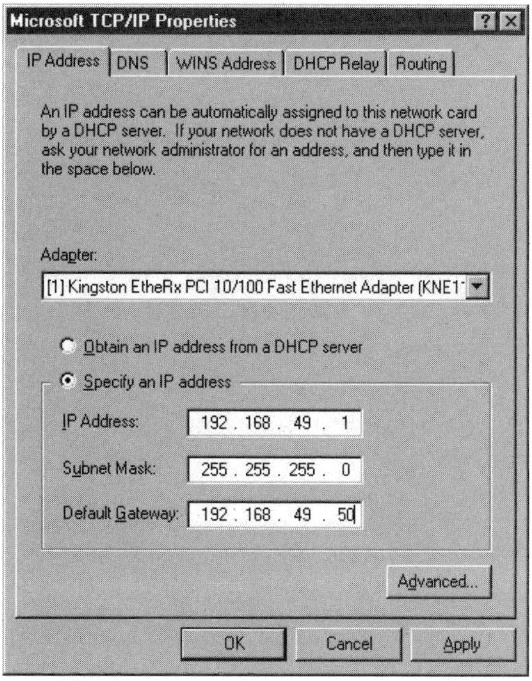

FIGURE 6.6

The IP Address tab from the Network Control Panel applet in Windows NT.

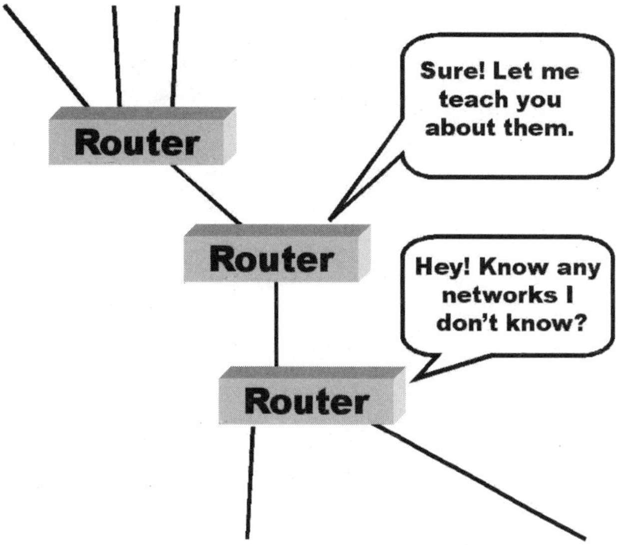

FIGURE 6.7

Routers must learn about networks to which they are not directly attached.

Static routing requires a network tech to sit at each router and manually enter a route to each network within the internetwork. The commands used vary from router to router depending on the brand, but all supply the same essential information. To configure Router 1 in Figure 6.7, above, so that it can route traffic to the network 203.250.2.0, Sergio must enter in a command telling Router 1 something like this: "All traffic bound for network 203.250.2.0 should be forwarded to Router 3." Notice that Router 1 does not need to know exactly which router the packets follow after reaching Router 3. Router 1 simply needs to know how to find the next router in the chain between itself and network 203.250.2.0. Using static routing, Sergio must configure each router manually, entering in at least one command defining a route for each network within the internetwork. Sergio, being lazy like most of the rest of us, would prefer to automate this process using dynamic routing.

With *dynamic routing*, each router in an internetwork automatically exchanges information with every other router, building a list of routes to the various networks. The routers build this list, called a *routing table*, by sending out messages to other routers on the network informing them of the networks that they can reach. For example, Router 1 sends a message to Router 2 and Router 3 that says "I know how to get to network 195.123.11.0!" Router 2 and Router 3 then add an entry to their routing tables that says: "To reach network 195.123.11.0, forward packets to Router 1." Although dynamic routing increases traffic between the routers, it relieves network administrators of the task of manually configuring the routers.

Static routing works best for small internetworks that rarely change, while dynamic routing works best in larger internetworks that change frequently. In a small internetwork with relatively few routers to configure, the network tech should take the time to set any necessary routes manually. In addition to eliminating dynamic routing traffic between the routers, static routing gives the network tech control over the routes used. In a larger internetwork with dozens or hundreds of routers, updating manual configurations becomes so time consuming that some type of dynamic routing becomes essential. Network architects can choose from a variety of dynamic routing protocols, with names like Router Information Protocol (RIP), Open Shortest Path First (OSPF), Exterior Gateway Protocol (EGP) and Border Gateway Protocol (BGP). Each dynamic routing protocol has advantages and disadvantages in terms of ease of use and efficiency. As a general rule, the larger the network managed by a routing protocol, the more complex its configuration becomes.

TIP

EXAM TIP:

Routers configured with *static routing* require manual configuration of routes; routers configured with *dynamic routing* protocols communicate with each other and automatically calculate routes on their own.

The Transport Layer: TCP and UDP

With IP handling the job of routing packets between hosts, the job of handling the transport layer issues falls to two main protocols: Transmission Control Protocol (TCP) and User Datagram Protocol (UDP). End-users sitting at their desks do not concern themselves with choosing a transport-layer protocol for a particular application—the programmers who designed the applications choose the appropriate protocol. TCP is a connection-oriented protocol, whereas UDP is a connectionless protocol.

TCP functions as a *connection-oriented* protocol, establishing a connection between two hosts before transmitting data, and verifying the receipt of the data before closing the connection. Think of TCP and other connection-oriented protocols as analogous to phone calls. When Carl calls American Express on the phone to complain about his bill, he waits until they answer before he begins discussing his complaint. Only after ensuring that they understand his complaint does Carl hang up. TCP connections work the same way. The sending host establishes a connection, sends the data, confirms the reception of the data, and then closes the connection. See Figure 6.8. Connection-oriented protocols such as TCP work best for situations where data must be delivered accurately and within a specific period of time, but generate additional traffic while establishing the connection. When sending less-critical data, or data that can be resent later without causing problems, most networks use a connectionless protocol like UDP.

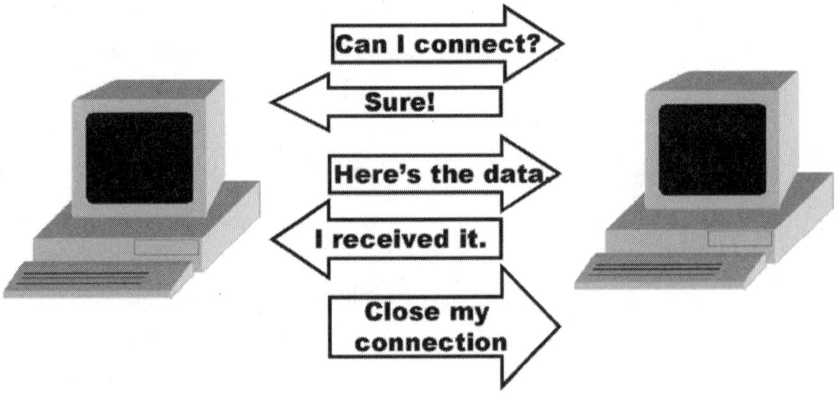

FIGURE 6.8 *Connection-oriented protocols like TCP must establish connections before sending data.*

UDP does not create connections—it just sends the data and they arrive. See Figure 6.9. While TCP functions like making a phone call, UDP functions like mailing a letter. When Carl mails his check to American Express to pay his bill, he does not know for certain that American Express receives the check. Carl trusts that the U.S. Postal Service reliably delivers the mail. Carl accepts the small chance that the letter will be lost, and waits until somebody like American Express complains before he considers the possibility that his envelope has not arrived. Just as Carl relies on the U.S. Postal Service, network architects (usually) trust the reliability of the networks they build. Because applications can resend most data in the event that it does not arrive in good shape (just as Carl can resend his check), network programmers prefer connectionless protocols like UDP for most data transmissions. Given the same amount of time, UDP can transmit more data than TCP because it dispenses with the time-consuming process of establishing and managing a connection.

TIP

EXAM TIP:

TCP is connection-oriented; UDP is connectionless.

Network programmers choose UDP or TCP for their application based on the way the application uses the network. Applications that send short bursts of data typically use UDP because of its low overhead. Applications that send larger pieces of data typically use TCP because the cost of establishing the connection becomes less significant as the amount of data sent over that connection grows. Regardless of which transport-layer protocol the programmer chooses, the devices at either end of the transmission need a session-layer protocol to keep track of the incoming and outgoing data packets.

FIGURE 6.9
Connectionless protocols like UDP just send the data and hope it gets there.

Managing Connections at the Session Layer

TCP/IP networks currently support two distinct session-layer protocols: NetBIOS and Sockets. Microsoft operating systems using TCP/IP employ NetBIOS names to track connections, while traditional Internet functions such as Web browsing use Sockets, the traditional TCP/IP session-layer protocol. Network techs and architects must understand the distinction between NetBIOS and Sockets applications to secure their networks properly and to configure correctly the two name-resolution services that operate in TCP/IP networks: WINS and DNS.

TIP

EXAM TIP:

Although CompTIA claims to be "vendor-neutral," TCP/IP questions on the Network+ exam generally assume that the client system uses a Microsoft operating system such as Windows 9x or Windows NT.

NetBIOS

NetBIOS, discussed in more detail in Chapter 5, manages connections between machines using *NetBIOS names*. NetBIOS names combine the computer's "simple name" with a series of special codes defining the roles that the machine can perform on a network: server, client, etc. A machine named SCOTTJ, for example, that functions as both a client and a server, would have at least two names: SCOTTJ<20> as the server and SCOTTJ<00> as the client.

Microsoft operating systems use NetBIOS for file- and print-sharing functions regardless of the protocol suite used. By maintaining NetBIOS as the session-layer protocol, Microsoft avoids rewriting programs operating at higher layers that rely on NetBIOS. Programs like Windows Explorer function identically whether the network uses TCP/IP, IPX/SPX, or NetBEUI.

Sockets

The Sockets standard manages connections based on an IP address and a port number. The IP address identifies the machine at the other end of the connection, and the *port number* identifies the function being performed. Each function has its own application-layer protocol (discussed individually below). Table 6.4 lists the most common application-layer protocols in the TCP/IP suite and their corresponding port numbers. A *socket*, a combination of a port number and an IP address, uniquely identifies a connection.

Sockets function much like NetBIOS names, defining both the host on the other end of the connection and its role in the connection. Where NetBIOS would define a connection with a NetBIOS name and an extension designating a function, a Sockets application defines a connection in terms of a socket, made up of an IP address and a port number. When Clara uses her Web browser to connect to **www.microsoft.com**, her computer sends a request to Microsoft's web server requesting a connection at port 80, the default port number for HyperText Transfer Protocol (HTTP). Web browsers use HTTP to transfer web pages between a web server and a browser. The server sends the requested page, using the socket to keep track of the connection. See Figure 6.10.

TABLE 6.4

The most common application-layer protocols.

Port Number	Service	Description
20	FTP DATA	File Transfer Protocol and Data. Used for transferring files
21	FTP	File Transfer Protocol and Control. Used for transferring files
23	TELNET	Telnet, used to gain "remote control" over another machine on the network
25	SMTP	Simple Mail Transfer Protocol, used for transferring e-mail between e-mail servers
69	TFTP	Trivial File Transfer Protocol, used for transferring files without a secure login
80	HTTP	HyperText Transfer Protocol, used for transferring HTML (HyperText Markup Language) files (i.e. Web Pages)
110	POP3	Post Office Protocol, version 3, used for transferring e-mail from an e-mail server to an e-mail client
119	NNTP	Network News Transfer Protocol, used to transfer Usenet news group messages from a news server to a news reader program
137	NETBIOS-NS	NetBIOS Name Service, used by Microsoft Networking
138	NETBIOS-DG	NetBIOS Datagram Service, used for transporting data by Microsoft Networking
139	NETBIOS-SS	NetBIOS Session Service, used by Microsoft Networking
161	SNMP	Simple Network Management Protocol, used to monitor network devices remotely
443	HTTPS	HyperText Transfer Protocol, Secure

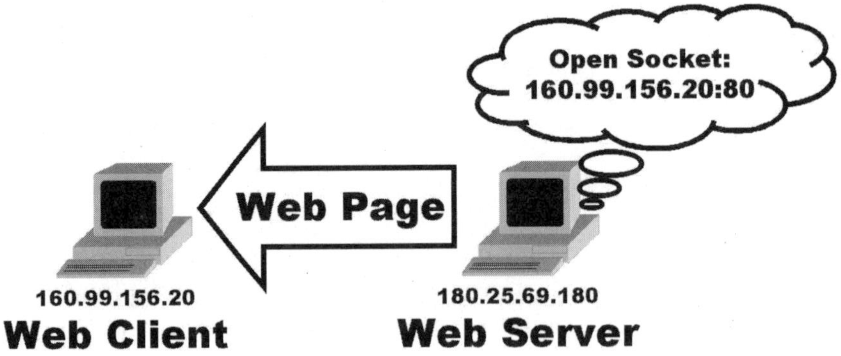

FIGURE 6.10
Sockets track connections by IP address and port number.

A good network tech knows the function and port numbers of the most common Internet qpplication-layer protocols, including:

- **HTTP (port 80)**
  Web servers use HyperText Transfer Protocol to send Web pages to clients running Web browsers such as Internet Explorer or Netscape Navigator.
- **FTP (ports 20 and 21)**
  File Transfer Protocol (FTP) transfers data files between servers and clients. All implementations of TCP/IP support FTP file transfers, making FTP an excellent choice for transferring files between machines running different operating systems (Windows to UNIX, UNIX to Macintosh, etc.). FTP uses port 21 for control messages and sends the data using port 20. FTP servers can require users to log in before downloading or uploading files. Most operating systems include a command line: FTP Utility.
- **TFTP (port 69)**
  Trivial File Transfer Protocol (TFTP) transfers files between servers and clients. Unlike FTP, TFTP requires no user login. Devices that need an operating system but have no local hard disk (e.g. diskless workstations and routers) often use TFTP to download their operating systems.
- **SMTP (port 25)**
  Simple Mail Transfer Protocol (SMTP) sends e-mail messages between clients and servers or between servers. From the end-user's perspective, SMTP handles outgoing mail only.
- **POP3 (Port 110)**
  Post Office Protocol version 3 (POP3) enables e-mail client software (e.g. Outlook Express, Eudora, Netscape Mail) to retrieve e-mail

from a mail server. POP3 does not send e-mail—SMTP handles that function.

- **SNMP (Port 161)**
  Simple Network Management Protocol enables network management applications to monitor devices remotely.
- **Telnet (Port 23)**
  Telnet allows a user to log in remotely and execute text-based commands on a remote host. Although any operating system can run a Telnet server, techs typically use Telnet to log into UNIX-based systems.
- **NetBIOS (Ports 137, 138, 139)**
  Although NetBIOS handles the session-layer issues, for compatibility with the TCP/IP suite its functions are rerouted to ports 137, 138, and 139.

Network techs must know the default port numbers in order to work in a modern TCP/IP environment. Memorizing Table 6.4 before taking the Network+ exam will not just help you pass the exam. Having those port numbers at your fingertips also enables you to configure client software, proxy servers, routers, and firewalls properly.

Proxy Servers

Most programs that rely on application-layer protocols within the TCP/IP suite come preconfigured to use the default port numbers for those applications. Figure 6.11, for example, shows Microsoft's Outlook Express and its POP3 and SMTP settings. In some cases, a server will use non-standard port numbers for these protocols and a network tech must modify the client's configuration to match before the client can communicate with that server. Web browsers, as shown in Figure 6.12, also require a port setting when connecting to the Internet through a proxy server.

A *proxy server* acts as a go-between, fetching data from servers on the Internet on behalf of clients on the local network. When using a proxy server, the client application does not try to connect directly to the server. Instead, it sends a request to the proxy server, asking it to fetch the requested data from the server. See Figure 6.13. Proxy servers typically accept requests for Web (HTTP), FTP, and e-mail (POP3 and SMTP) resources, but do not support requests for other TCP/IP application protocols unless the proxy server vendor specifically adds support. Proxy servers can enhance both the performance and security of a network.

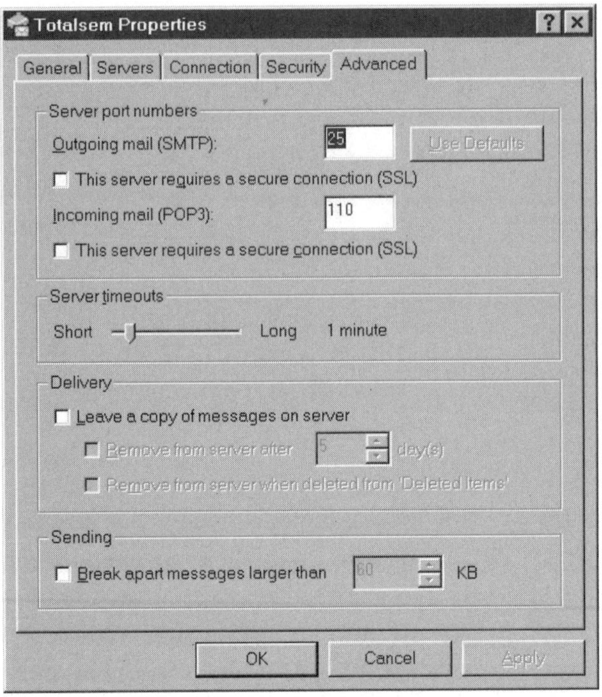

FIGURE 6.11
Microsoft Outlook Express Advanced Properties tab.

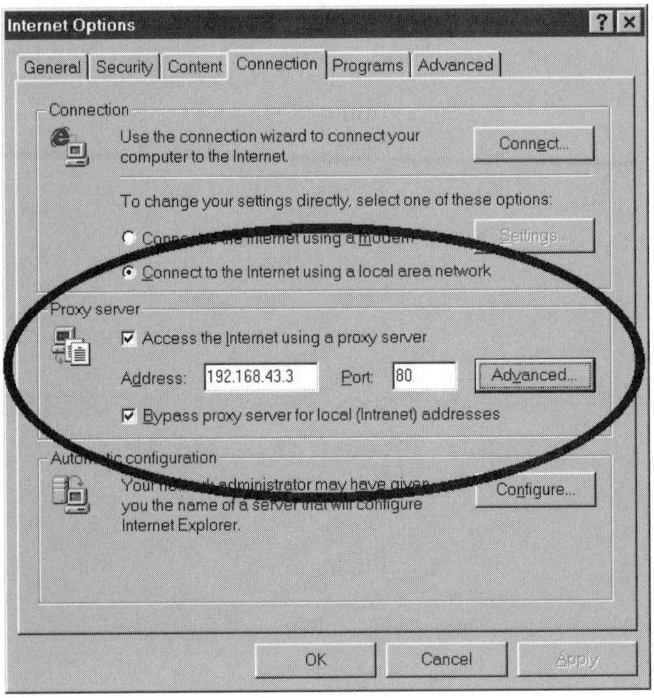

FIGURE 6.12
Microsoft Internet Explorer Connection Properties tab.

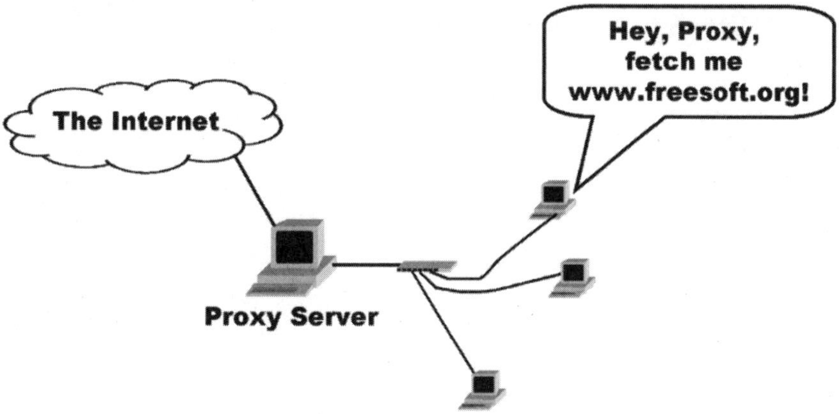

FIGURE 6.13
A client using a proxy server never accesses the Internet directly.

Proxy servers improve the performance of a network by cutting down on the traffic caused by multiple users requesting the same data. If three users on Sherman's network all go to **www.cnnsi.com** to check the latest baseball scores, Sherman's network downloads the same information from the Internet three times, as shown in Figure 6.14.

When a proxy server is used, however, the proxy server keeps a copy of the page the first time a user requests it. See Figure 6.15. When another host requests the same page, the proxy server gives the client that *cached* copy instead of contacting the Web server again, cutting down on the amount of traffic going across the Internet and providing a faster response to the client. See Figure 6.16.

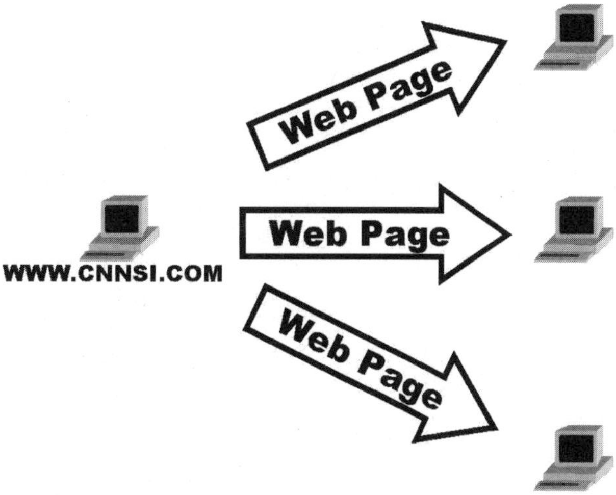

FIGURE 6.14
If three users request the same Web page, it travels across the Internet three times.

FIGURE 6.15
A proxy server keeps a copy of a requested file just in case another host asks for the same data.

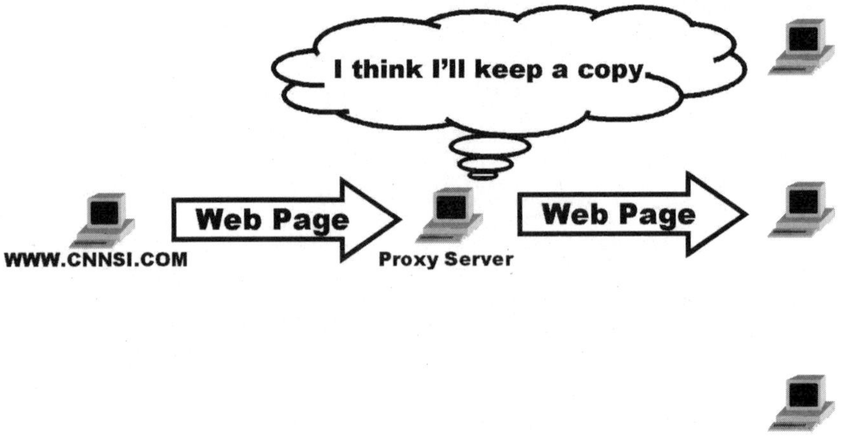

FIGURE 6.16
A proxy server delivers its cached copy.

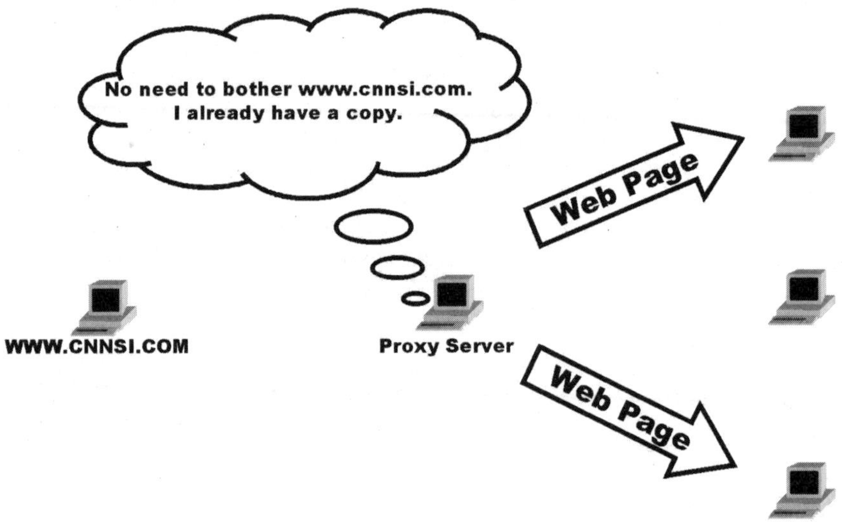

Proxy servers enhance the security of a network by hiding individual hosts on the local network from hosts on the Internet at large. Figure 6.17 shows three computers, MO, LARRY, and CURLEY, protected behind a proxy server. As far as the hacker lurking somewhere in the dark recesses of the Internet with his computer NEO can tell, MO, LARRY, and CURLEY do not exist. The hacker can only see the proxy server. By limiting the number of machines that directly connect to the Internet, wise network techs ease their own workloads. Properly securing a single machine, the proxy server, consumes much less time and effort than properly securing hundreds of individual machines on a network. A proxy functions therefore, as a type of *firewall*.

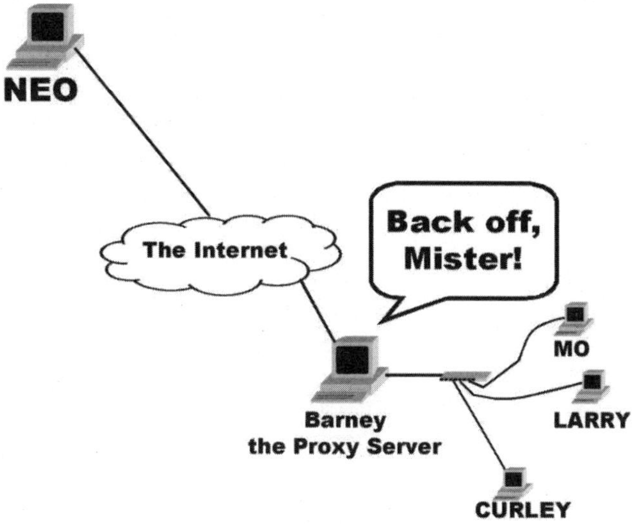

FIGURE 6.17 *The proxy server acts as a firewall, protecting MO, LARRY, and CURLEY from the hacker sitting at NEO.*

Firewalls

Firewalls restrict traffic between the local network and the Internet (or other external network) while still allowing some level of access to the Internet. Firewalls can restrict in either direction, in or out. Some firewalls, such as proxy servers, keep unwanted and potentially dangerous traffic out while still allowing users on the network the benefits of Internet access. Other devices, such as routers, can cut off access to certain portions of the Internet, thus placing limits on what users can do from the inside.

Routers as Firewalls

Routers can function as firewalls for networks by restricting traffic based on port numbers. Rufus, the network manager for the Bayland Widget Corporation, connects his company's LAN to the Internet so that customers can visit the Bayland Widget Corporation's Web site and so that the tech support and accounting departments can communicate with customers via e-mail. See Figure 6.18. Rufus immediately receives complaints from his customers that the Web server responds slowly or not at all, and that their requests for help via e-mail take too long as well. A quick stroll through the accounting and tech support departments leads Rufus to the conclusion that both customer complaints share the same root cause: the accountants and support technicians spend too much time surfing the Web and not enough time working. Web browsing keeps the router so busy fetching the latest sports scores and stock quotes from the Internet that the router cannot handle its business-related functions. Rufus decides to configure his router to stop these shenanigans.

A router can be configured to block packets bound for certain ports. Rufus configures his router to block all outgoing traffic bound for port 80 (HTTP), the port used for Web browsing. The router still allows incoming connections on port 80 (HTTP), enabling users from outside the network to access the company Web server. E-mail traffic, using port 25 (SMTP) and port 110 (POP3) can still pass through the router unimpeded, allowing the accountants and support technicians to use e-mail normally. Configuring the router to filter traffic based on port numbers enables Rufus to control how employees of the Bayland Widget Corporation use the Internet.

FIGURE 6.18 *The Bayland Widget Corporation's network, connected to the Internet.*

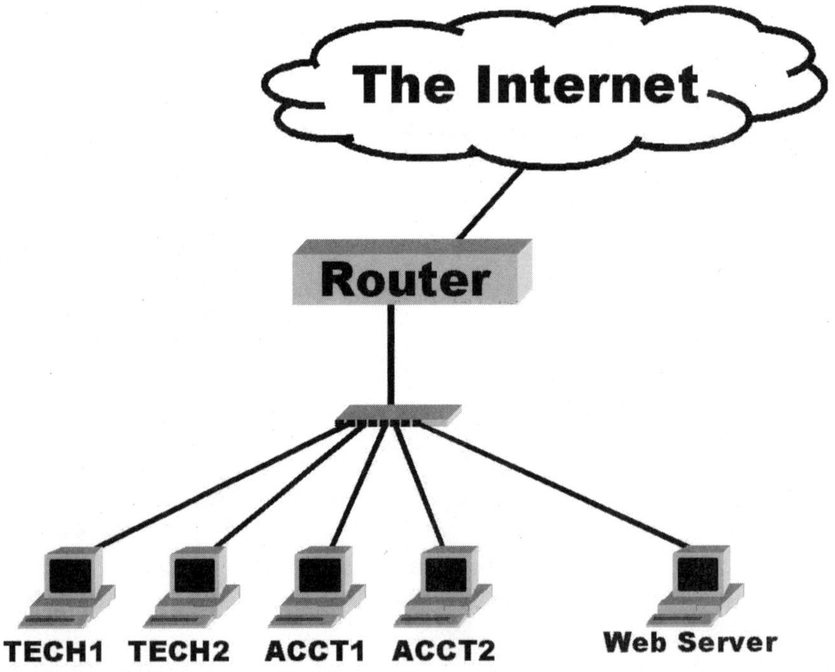

NOTE

The Network+ exam covers the basic concept of a firewall but does not delve into advanced firewall configuration. Firewalls in the "real world" go far beyond proxies and port filtering.

Name Resolution

The discussion of IP addresses and sockets above assumed that the IP address of the destination host was known. The human beings and software applications that actually use the computers, however, rarely think of computers by their addresses. They do not want to use numbers like 129.168.43.3 to refer to their servers; they prefer to use a name like CASSIUS. They don't want to access the Total Seminars Web site at 207.222.216.40; they want to type "http://www.totalsem.com" into their Web browsers. TCP/IP networks require some means of "name resolution" so that people can use names instead of numbers, but the computers can still determine the addresses they need. In a simple network, name resolution is trivial—a system can simply broadcast on the network to get the name of a particular system. When routing becomes involved, however, broadcasting is no longer a viable option—routers do not forward broadcasts. TCP/IP networks can use two separate name resolution method tools, DNS (Domain Name System) and WINS (Windows Internet Name Service), depending on the types of applications supported on the network.

DNS and WINS essentially provide directory assistance for TCP/IP networks. Just as Bob might call directory assistance to find out Mike Meyers' phone number, a host on a TCP/IP network contacts a DNS or WINS server to find out the IP address of another host on the network. DNS and WINS servers store a list of names and their corresponding IP addresses. The two different name services exist because Sockets and NetBIOS applications use names and addresses in different ways.

Sockets Applications and DNS

TCP/IP Sockets-based applications, such as Web browsers and e-mail client programs, do not require that computers have names in order to function. Because these applications manage connections based on a socket, composed of an IP address and a port number, an IP address serves as all the identification the program requires. People, however, prefer names.

TCP/IP networks employ names like **www.totalsem.com** or **ftp.usgs.gov** to specify computers. These user-friendly names, better known as "host names," provide a method of accessing other hosts far easier than using difficult to remember IP addresses. In a vast IP-based network such as the Internet, using names presents two challenges. First, names must be unique to avoid confusion. Second, every host on the network (or Internet) must have the ability to translate any name quickly into its corresponding IP address. The Domain Name Service (DNS) standard addresses these challenges by providing a hierarchical name space and a distributed database of names and addresses.

DNS uses a *hierarchical name space*, an imaginary structure of all possible names that could be used within a single system. In a *flat name space*, such as the NetBIOS name space, all names have to be absolutely unique. No two machines can ever share the same name under any condition. A flat name space can be extremely confining. A large organization with computers and networks spread among several cities, for example, would have to make sure that all its administrators know all the names used in the entire corporate network in order to ensure that no two machines have the same name.

A hierarchical name space offers a better solution and a great deal more flexibility by giving machines a longer, more fully descriptive name. The personal names people use every day are examples of hierarchical name spaces. Most people address the town postman, Ron Samuels, as simply "Ron." When his name comes up in conversation, people usually refer to him as Ron. The town troublemaker, Ron Falwell, and Jim's son Ron who went off to New York, obviously share first names with the postman. In some conversations, people need to distinguish between the good Ron, the bad Ron, and the Ron in New York City (who may or may not be "the ugly"). They could at that point use the more "Middle Ages" style of address, and refer to the Rons as Ron the Postman, Ron the Blackguard, or Ron the Lost; or, they could use a more typical address and include the Rons' surnames in their discussion. "That Ron Samuels; he is such a card!" "But that Ron Falwell; he is one bad apple." You might visualize this as the "people name space," illustrated in Figure 6.19. There is no confusion between the many people named Ron as long as their full names (or *fully qualified* names) differ.

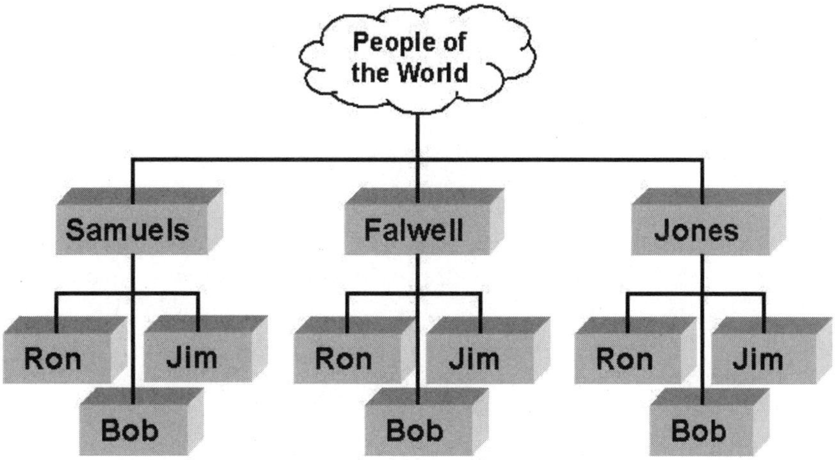

FIGURE 6.19
The "people of the world" name space.

Another name space most people already know is the hierarchical file name space used by DOS and Windows File Allocation Table (FAT) volumes. Hard drives formatted with FAT use a hierarchical name space, enabling creation of as many files named DATA.TXT as required, as long as they exist in different paths. In the example shown in Figure 6.20, C:\DATA\CURRENT\DATA.TXT and C:\DATA\BACKUP\DATA.TXT can both exist on the same system, but only because they have been placed in different directories. While the files might both be called DATA.TXT, their fully qualified names are C:\DATA\CURRENT\DATA.TXT and C:\DATA\BACKUP\DATA.TXT.

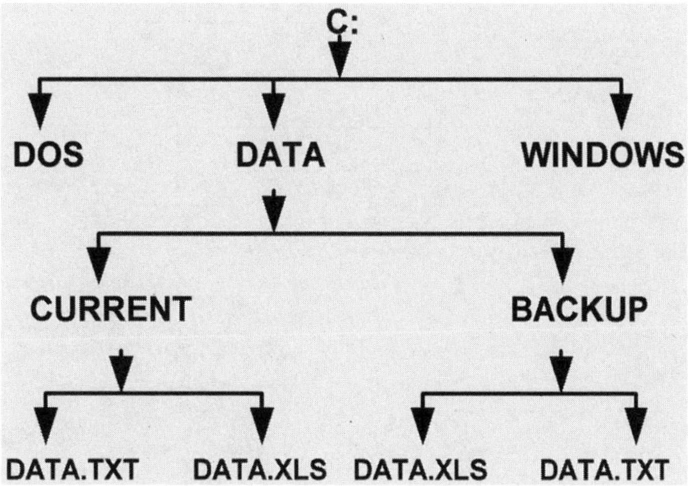

FIGURE 6.20
The "file system name space" used by FAT and NTFS.

If files were stored in a flat name space, where each file required a single unique name, naming files would quickly become a nightmare. Software vendors would have to avoid sensible descriptive names such as README.TXT, because they would almost certainly have been used already. In fact, an organization of some sort would probably have to assign names out of the limited pool of possible file names. With a hierarchical name space, such as that used by FAT, naming is much simpler. The DNS name space works in the same fashion. The server name "www" exists in most organizations. If DNS used a flat name space, however, only the first organization with the name could have used it. Because DNS naming appends *domain names* to the server names, however, the servers **www.totalsem.com** and **www.microsoft.com** can both exist.

DNS names such as **www.microsoft.com** must fit within a worldwide hierarchical name space, meaning that no two machines should ever have the same fully qualified name. The DNS name space must be managed manually by network administrators. In order to allow decentralized administration, the DNS name space is broken up into domains.

A *DNS domain* is a specific branch of the DNS name space, as shown in Figure 6.21. The DNS name space starts at the root, shown here as—" "—a set of blank quotation marks. The machine named ACCOUNTING has a fully qualified domain name of **accounting.texas.microsoft.com**.

FIGURE 6.21
The DNS name space.

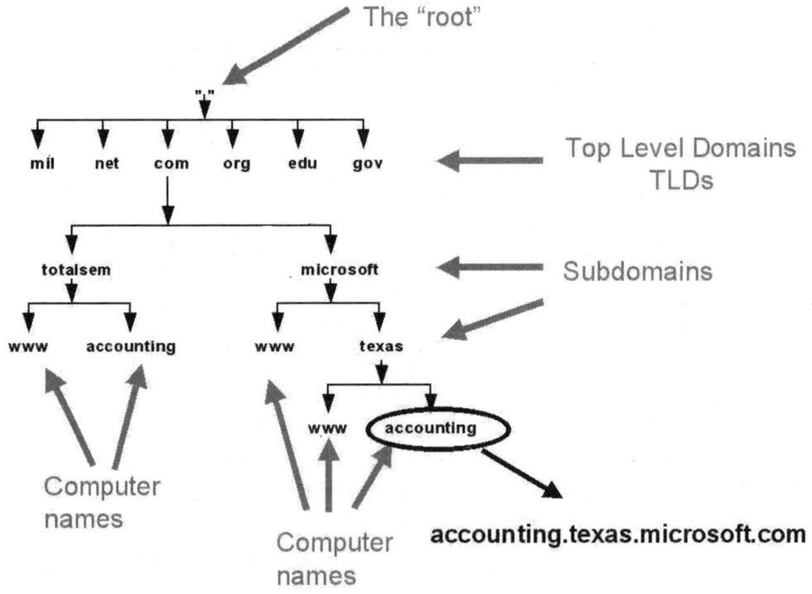

The DNS name space is a hierarchical tree, similar in many respects to the file name space used by FAT volumes. FAT volumes can have several "trees," the roots of which have names such as "C:" or "D." The DNS naming tree has a single root, usually left unnamed. The InterNIC (Internet Network Information Center) controls the root domain, sometimes referred to with a pair of empty quotation marks. The InterNIC does not have to know the name of every computer in the world. Instead, it delegates authority for particular subdomains to other organizations. InterNIC contracts with Network Solutions (**www.networksolutions.com**), for example, to maintain the .com subdomain.

There are a variety of subdomains similar to .com in the Internet world. Table 6.5 shows the common top-level subdomains used in the United States. This first level of subdomains, including the .com, .org, and .net domains, are often referred to as TLDs (top-level domains).

TABLE 6.5 *Common top-level subdomains.*

Top level domain	Refers to:
.com	Originally intended for companies involved in commercial activities, but anyone can register a .com address.
.net	Companies involved in providing network access, such as Internet service providers (ISPs), but anyone can register a .net address.
.org	Organization not involved in commerce, especially non-profit organizations, but anyone can register a .org address.
.mil	United States military organizations.
.edu	United States educational institutions, especially higher education.
.gov	United States Federal government organizations.

NOTE

In Figure 6.21, above, **accounting.texas.microsoft.com** specifies a particular host named "accounting" in the **texas.microsoft.com** domain. Although **texas.microsoft.com** in this example is technically a subdomain, the term domain and subdomain are commonly used interchangeably.

Name Resolution

Programs like Internet Explorer accept names such as **www.microsoft.com** as a convenience to the end-user, but utilize the IP address that corresponds to the name to create a connection. In Figure 6.22, IE displays the same Web page whether the IP address or the DNS name **www.microsoft.com** is used. In fact, even when you type in **www.microsoft.com**, Internet Explorer must resolve that name to the IP address 207.46.131.137 to make a connection to Microsoft's Web server. It can resolve the name in three ways: by broadcasting, by consulting a locally stored text file named HOSTS, or by contacting a DNS server.

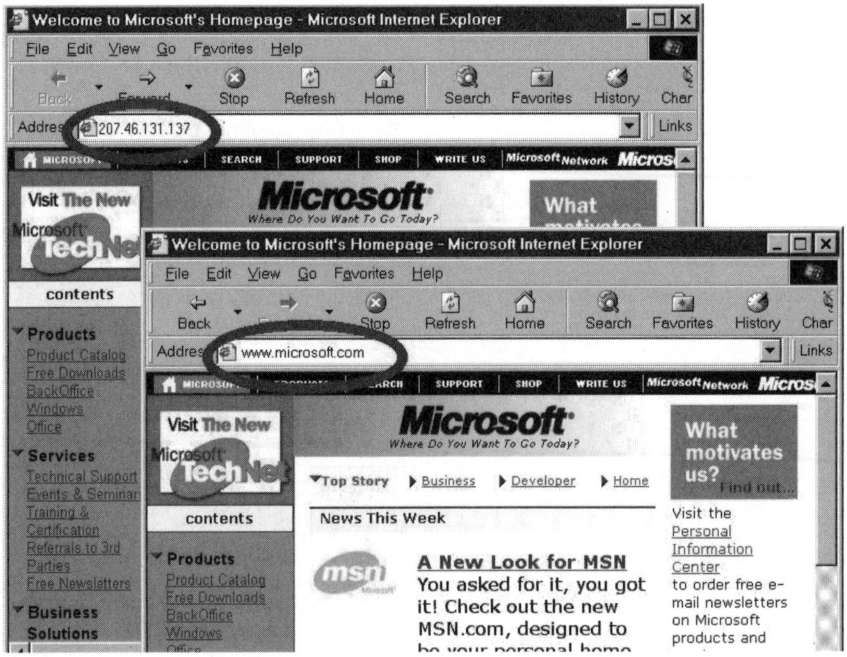

FIGURE 6.22
Internet Explorer (and other sockets-based applications) can use either names or addresses.

With a *broadcast*, a host sends a message to all the machines on the network, saying something like "If your name is JOESCOMPUTER, please respond with your IP address." All the networked hosts receive that packet, and JOESCOMPUTER should respond. Broadcasting works fine for small networks that contain no routers, but cannot provide name resolution across routers. Routers do not forward broadcast messages to other networks, as illustrated in Figure 6.23.

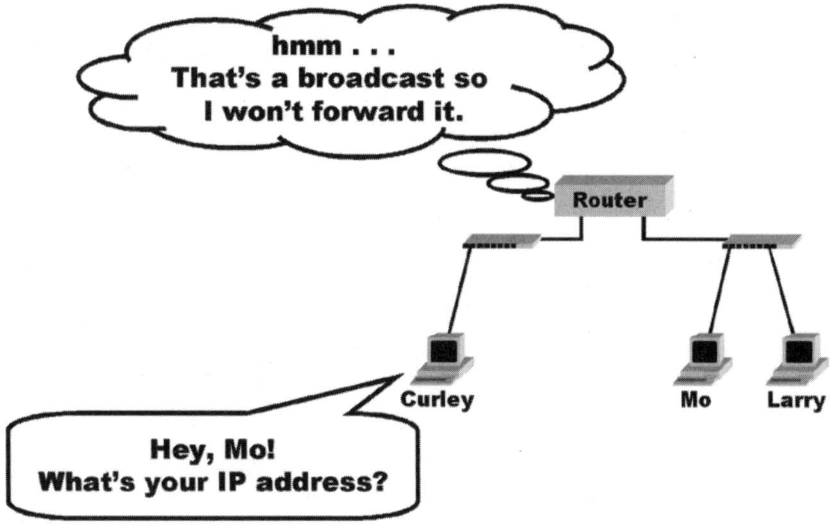

FIGURE 6.23
Name resolution by broadcast does not work across routers because routers do not forward broadcasts.

A HOSTS file functions like a little black book, listing the names and addresses of machines on a network just as a little black book would list the names and phone numbers of people. A typical HOSTS file looks like this:

```
109.54.94.197     stephen.totalsem.com
138.125.163.17    roger.totalsem.com
127.0.0.1         localhost
```

When a program tries to resolve a name, it consults the local machine's HOSTS file to see if it contains an entry for the name specified. HOSTS files represent a throwback to the early days of the Internet, when very few machines connected to the Internet and changes were rare. As new hosts connected to the Internet (or any other TCP/IP network), administrators manually updated the HOSTS file on each machine. Today, the Internet changes too rapidly for manually maintained HOSTS files to keep up. While HOSTS files are still supported, network administrators rarely use them except as stopgap measures when DNS is unavailable.

NOTE

Notice that the name "localhost" appears in the HOSTS file as an alias for the loopback address, 127.0.0.1.

In most cases, hosts resolve domain names using DNS. To resolve the name **www.microsoft.com**, the host contacts its DNS server and requests the IP address, as shown in Figure 6.24. The local DNS server may not know the address for **www.microsoft.com**, but it does know the address of a DNS root server. The root servers, maintained by the InterNIC, know all of the addresses of the top-level domain DNS servers. The root servers would not know the address of **www.microsoft.com**, but they would know the address of the DNS server in charge of all .com addresses. The ".com DNS server" would also not know the address of **www.microsoft.com**, but it would know the IP address of the microsoft.com DNS server. The microsoft.com server would know the IP address of **www.microsoft.com**, and would send that information back to the local DNS server. Figure 6.25 shows the process of resolving a fully qualified domain name into an IP address.

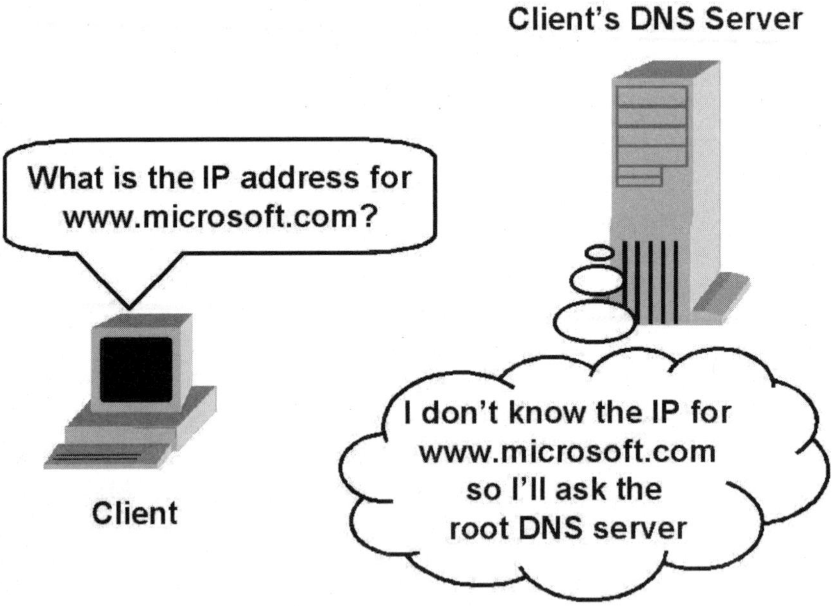

Client's DNS Server
What is the IP address for www.microsoft.com?
Client
I don't know the IP for www.microsoft.com so I'll ask the root DNS server

FIGURE 6.24
A host contacts its DNS server.

No single machine needs to know every DNS name, as long as every machine knows whom to ask for more information. The distributed, decentralized nature of the DNS database provides a great deal of flexibility and freedom to network administrators using DNS. DNS still requires an administrator to type in each name and address, just as with a HOSTS file. Maintaining a DNS database, however, has two key advantages over maintaining the same information in the form of HOSTS files. First, the database is centralized: an administrator adds new entries once on the DNS server rather than walking around the network to add new entries to each machine. Second, the database is distributed, meaning that no single administrator must maintain a database that knows about every other machine in the world. A DNS server simply has to know where to go for more information. Unfortunately, NetBIOS-based applications cannot take advantage of DNS.

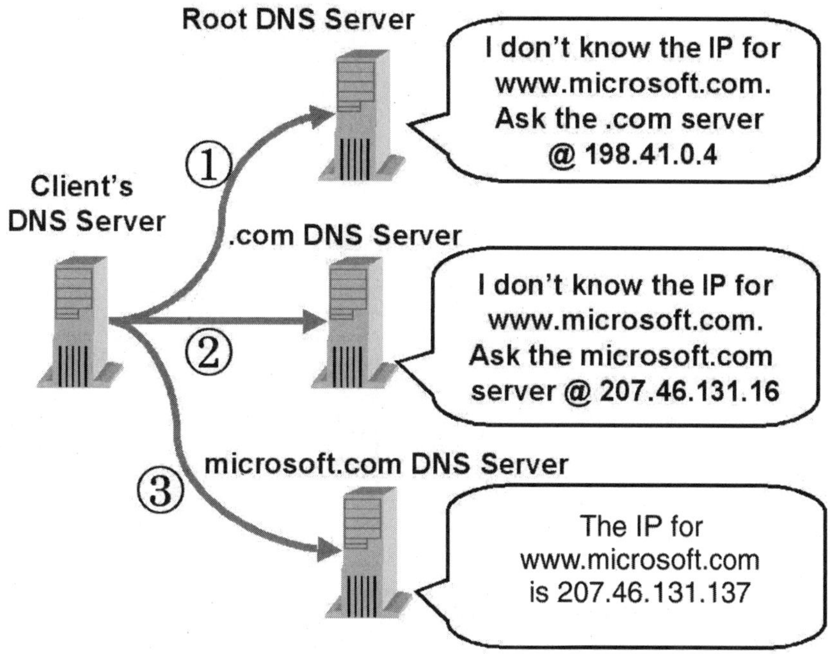

FIGURE 6.25
A DNS server resolves the name by contacting other DNS servers.

NetBIOS Applications and WINS

NetBIOS applications include basically every program that has the word Microsoft in front of its name except Microsoft Internet Explorer. Because NetBIOS-based applications can run over protocol suites other than TCP/IP, NetBIOS applications themselves must remain aloof from details like IP addresses that only exist in a single protocol suite. These programs use NetBIOS names instead of sockets when connecting to talk to other computers. The need for compatibility with non-TCP/IP networks prevents NetBIOS-based applications from taking advantage of DNS. NetBIOS applications must find their own way: Windows Internet Naming Service (WINS).

NOTE

WINS servers only exist in Microsoft-based TCP/IP networks.

When a WINS client (i.e., any machine using WINS) boots up, it sends a message to its specific WINS server (usually specified in the control panel) registering its name and IP address. In Figure 6.26, SALES1 and ACCOUNT2 register their addresses with their WINS server (SALES3). The WINS clients do not broadcast their registrations, but send them directly to the IP address of their WINS server: 200.72.20.15. The WINS client does not care about the NetBIOS or host name of the WINS server. It just needs to know where to send the registration data.

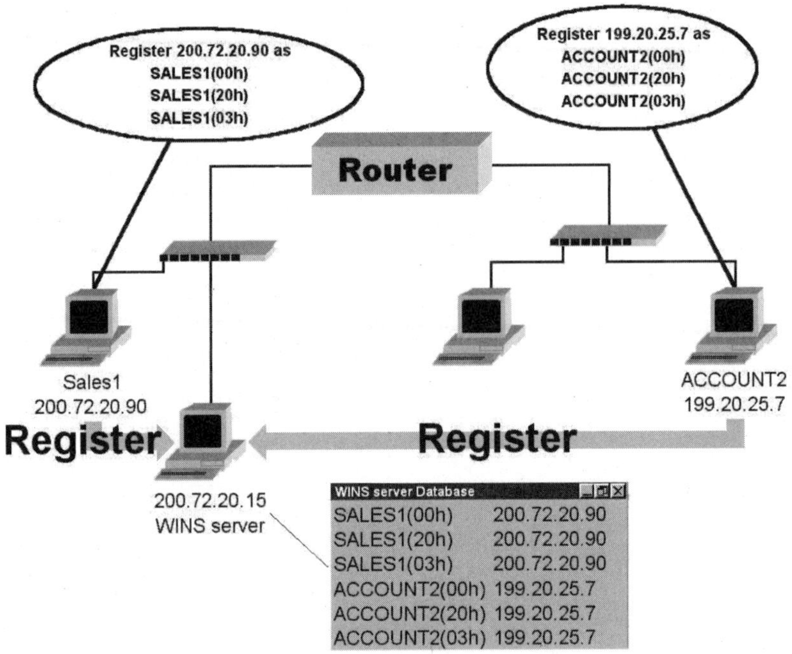

FIGURE 6.26
WINS clients register with a WINS server.

After registering with the WINS server, the WINS clients have a means of determining the IP address that corresponds to a particular NetBIOS name. They contact the WINS server. In Figure 6.27, SALES1, a WINS client, contacts the WINS server to determine the IP address that corresponds to the NetBIOS name ACCOUNT2.

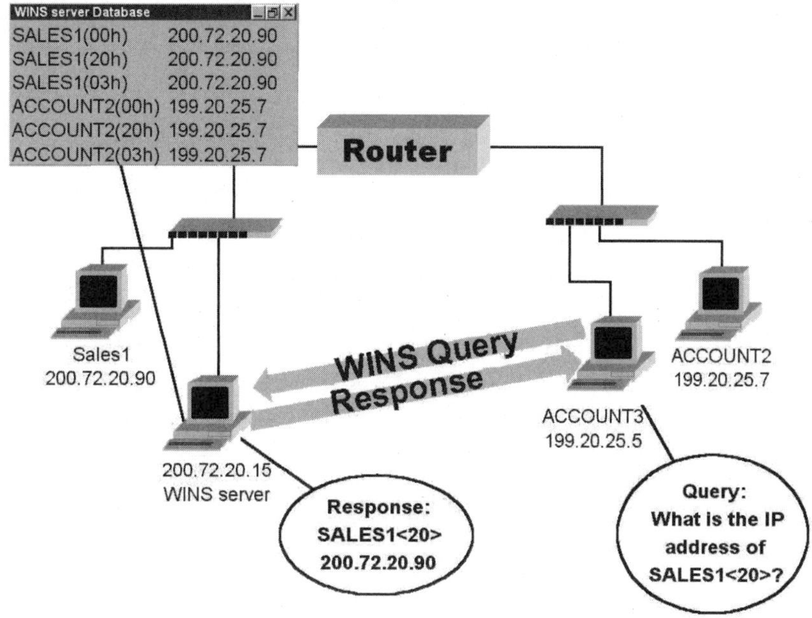

FIGURE 6.27
A WINS client requests IP address information from a WINS server.

Once SALES1 has the address, it no longer has to rely on a broadcast to reach ACCOUNT2. Because ACCOUNT2 lies on the far side of the router, a broadcast would not work anyway. WINS allows NetBIOS-based applications to direct their packets to specific IP addresses instead of depending on broadcasts, as shown in Figure 6.28.

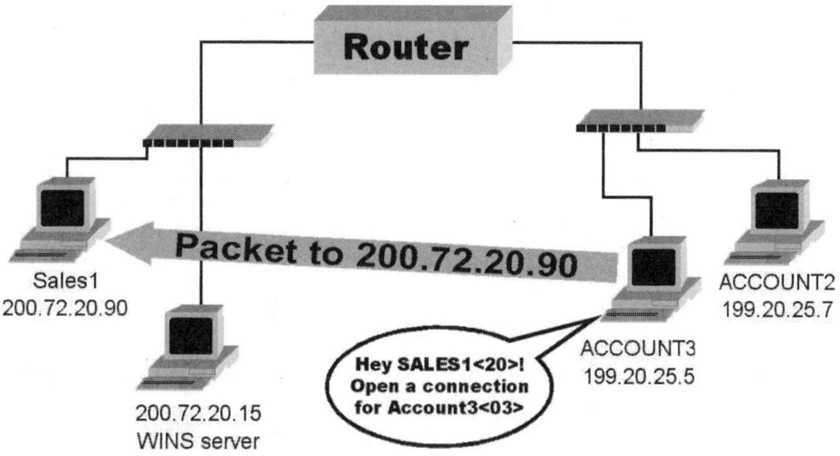

FIGURE 6.28
ACCOUNT3 can contact SALES1 directly using its IP address.

WINS has another vital task on a NetBIOS-based network—ensuring name uniqueness. In a DNS-based network, applications manage connections using sockets, a combination of an IP address and a port number. The name of a computer has nothing to do with how the computer communicates, but is merely a convenience to the user. While duplicate computer names might confuse the human beings using the network, they do not affect the computers because the computers do not identify other computers by name, only by IP address and port, or socket.

NetBIOS networks, however, rely on the NetBIOS names (and their 16th Byte/extensions) to manage connections. If two computers share the same NetBIOS name, the computers themselves can become confused. To avoid this confusion, NetBIOS networks demand that all computers have unique names.

In a small, non-routed network, keeping names unique presents no real challenge. Upon booting up, every machine running NetBIOS broadcasts its name to the network. If another computer already uses that name, that computer will send a message to the new computer on the network, telling the new computer to get off the network, as shown in Figure 6.29. The user of the machine that has its name refused sees the error message shown in Figure 6.30.

FIGURE 6.29

If another machine with the same NetBIOS name hears the broadcast, it kicks the newcomer of the network.

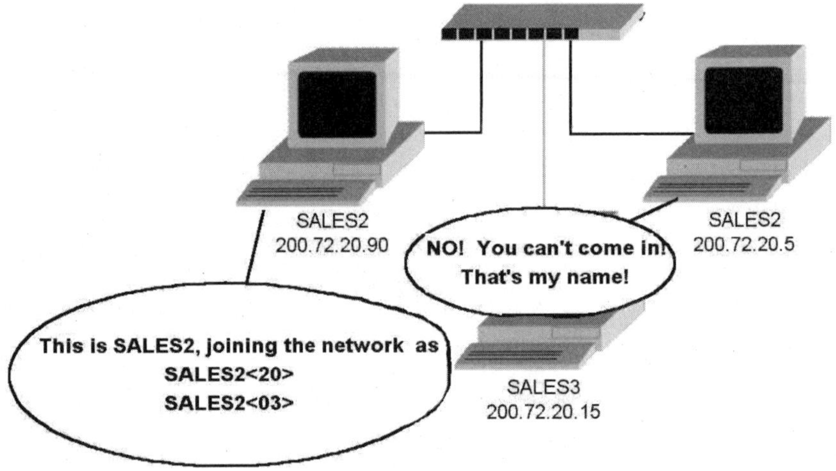

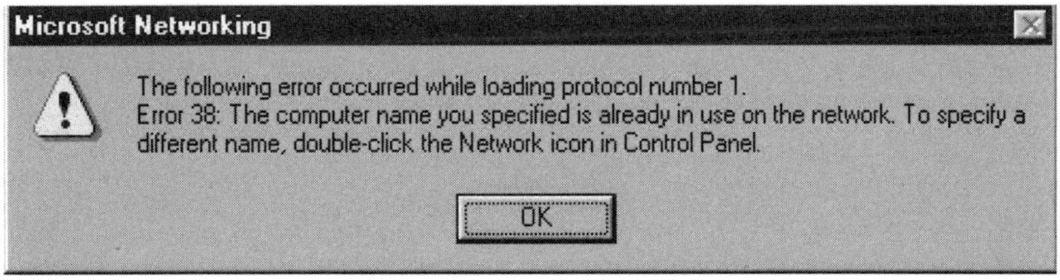

FIGURE 6.30
When a new machine tries to use a duplicate name, an error message pops up.

In a routed network, NetBIOS can create interesting problems. A computer's bootup broadcast—"This is my name"—will not reach machines on the far side of a router, leaving open the possibility of duplicate names on the network. Figure 6.31 shows two machines announcing themselves as SALES2. Because they sit on opposite sides of the router, they do not hear each other's announcements. Other machines on the network have no way to distinguish between the two machines named SALES2, even though they have different IP addresses—NetBIOS does not use IP addresses to manage connections.

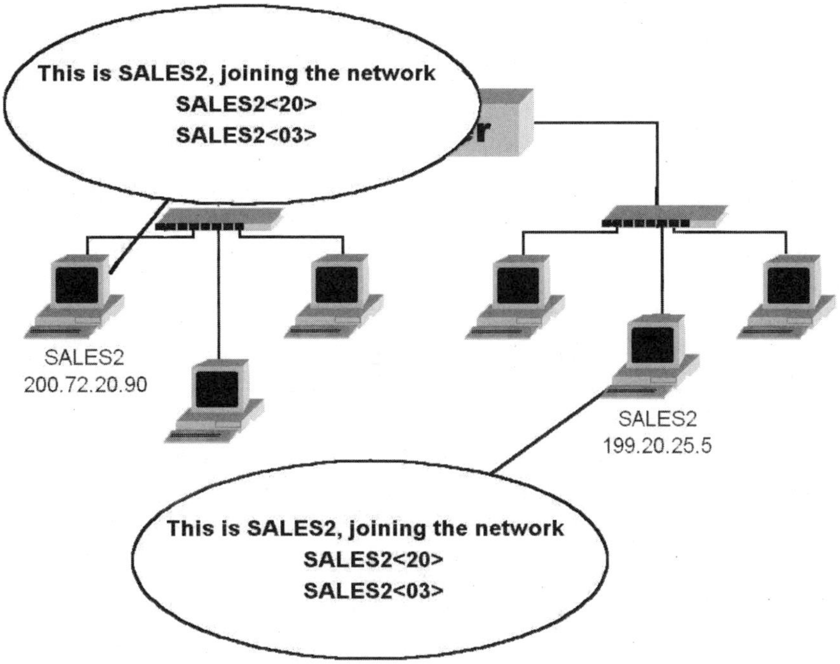

FIGURE 6.31
Machines separated by a router cannot detect that they are using the same NetBIOS name by broadcasting.

A WINS server solves the problem of duplicate NetBIOS names on a routed network, because it does not allow a machine to register a NetBIOS name already in use anywhere on the network, as shown in Figure 6.32. The machine attempting to register a NetBIOS name that is already being used receives the same error message shown in Figure 6.30 above.

FIGURE 6.32 *WINS prevents duplicate NetBIOS names, even when machines lie on opposite sides of a router.*

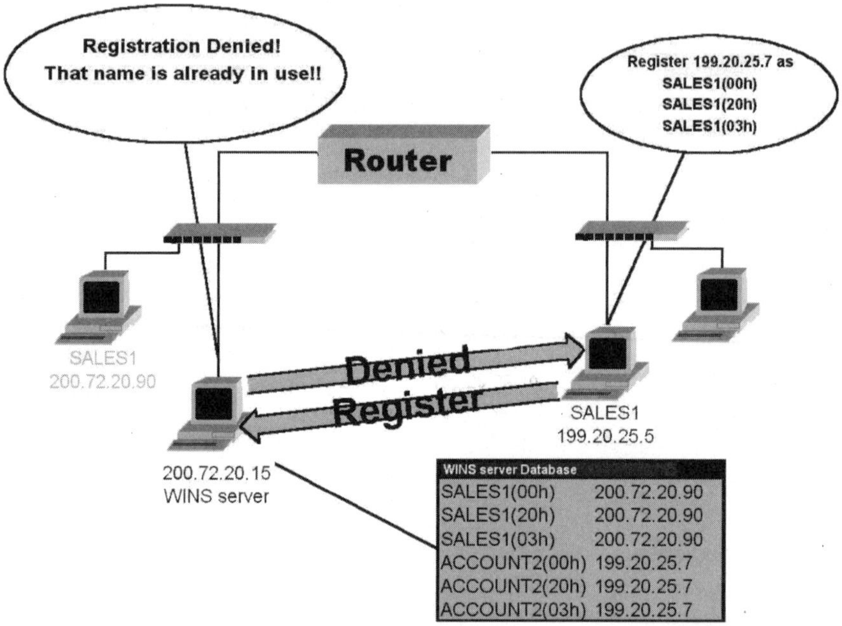

In the absence of a WINS server, a file called LMHOSTS offers another means of resolving names to IP addresses. This is very similar to the way that a HOSTS file functions for DNS host names. Where a WINS server acts much like directory assistance, the LMHOSTS file acts like a little black book of phone numbers. The WINS server provides a centralized database to which every machine can refer, while the LMHOSTS file exists on each machine's individual hard drive and exists for that machine's exclusive use.

NOTE

The LMHOSTS file can resolve NetBIOS names to IP addresses, but cannot guarantee unique NetBIOS names across a routed network.

WINS servers are the preferred and recommended method for handling NetBIOS name resolution. While LMHOSTS files can be used, they cannot guarantee unique names. In addition, administrators must manually edit the LMHOSTS files of each machine should the network change. Typically, LMHOSTS files are used when a WINS server cannot easily be added to the network because of cost or other factors.

DNS versus WINS

DNS and WINS serve a similar function on a TCP/IP based network, providing centralized databases of names and addresses for hosts on the network to consult. Although they are similar, several key differences exist. The DNS name space is hierarchical, whereas the NetBIOS namespace used by WINS is flat. Administrators must maintain DNS databases manually, whereas WINS builds its databases as clients register. The key difference, however, lies in the types of applications that use each service. TCP/IP sockets-based applications (Web browsers, e-mail clients, etc.) use DNS, while Microsoft-based NetBIOS applications (Network Neighborhood, the Save As dialog box in Microsoft Word) use WINS. Table 6.6 summarizes the distinctions between DNS and WINS.

TABLE 6.6
DNS vs. WINS.

	DNS	**WINS**
Used by:	Sockets Applications	NetBIOS Applications
Database built:	Manually	Dynamically
Text file alternative:	HOSTS	LMHOSTS

DHCP

With so many settings (IP address, subnet mask, default gateway, DNS servers, WINS servers) to specify, the typical TCP/IP network administrator can spend days properly configuring each host manually. Fortunately, TCP/IP provides a protocol that takes much of the drudgery out of TCP/IP configuration: Dynamic Host Configuration Protocol (DHCP). DHCP servers distribute settings to other machines on the network, freeing the network tech from the wear and tear inflicted by manual configuration. Machines that can handle this automatic configuration are called, appropriately, DHCP clients; most network client software can be set up to accept DHCP.

When a DHCP client boots up, it sends out a broadcast message requesting its configuration. If a DHCP server receives that message, it returns the appropriate values to the DHCP client, as shown in Figure 6.33. The DHCP server keeps track of the addresses it assigns to ensure that it does not assign the same address to two machines.

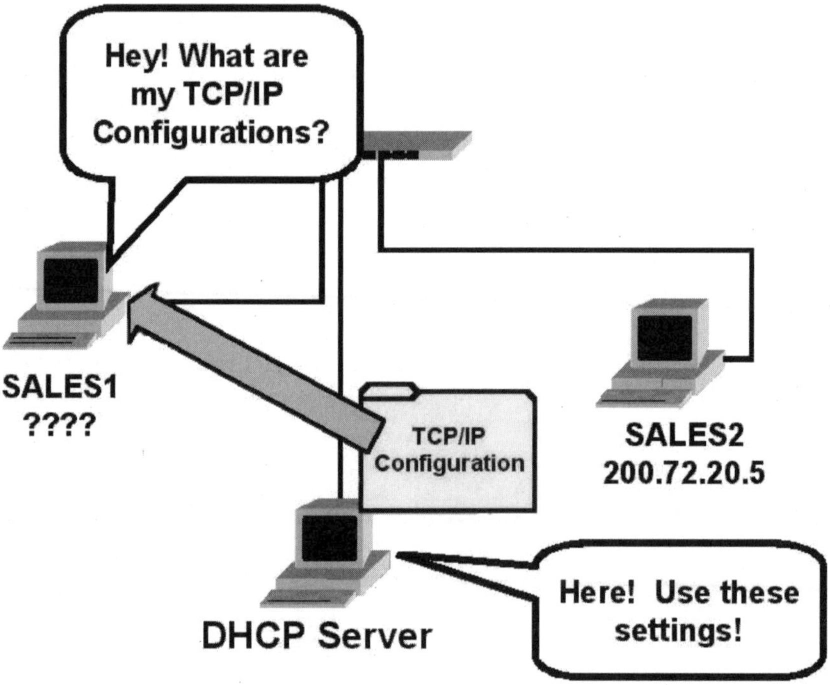

FIGURE 6.33 *A DHCP server can supply the appropriate configuration upon request.*

When using DHCP, network techs may need to check the configuration of specific machines to ensure that the DHCP server has assigned the appropriate configuration. Every operating system that supports TCP/IP will include a utility that displays the current TCP/IP configuration. In Windows 95 or 98, for example, run the WINIPCFG program from a command line to display the screen shown in Figure 6.34. On a Windows NT system, the command IPCONFIG /ALL displays similar information:

```
C:\>ipconfig /all
Windows NT IP Configuration
```

```
    Host Name . . . . . . . . . . : sales2
    DNS Servers . . . . . . . . . : 192.168.42.254
    Node Type . . . . . . . . . . : Hybrid
    NetBIOS Scope ID. . . . . . . :
    IP Routing Enabled. . . . . . : No
    WINS Proxy Enabled. . . . . . : No
    NetBIOS Resolution Uses DNS : Yes
Ethernet adapter EC2T1:
    Description . . . . . . . . . : PCMCIA Ethernet Card
    Physical Address. . . . . . . : 00-E0-98-01-4A-19
    DHCP Enabled. . . . . . . . . : Yes
    IP Address. . . . . . . . . . : 192.168.42.10
    Subnet Mask . . . . . . . . . : 255.255.255.0
    Default Gateway . . . . . . . : 192.168.42.254
    DHCP Server . . . . . . . . . : 192.168.42.254
    Lease Obtained. . . . . . . . : Thursday, October 15,
1998 10:16:02 AM
    Lease Expires . . . . . . . . : Friday, October 16,
1998 10:16:02 AM
C:\>
```

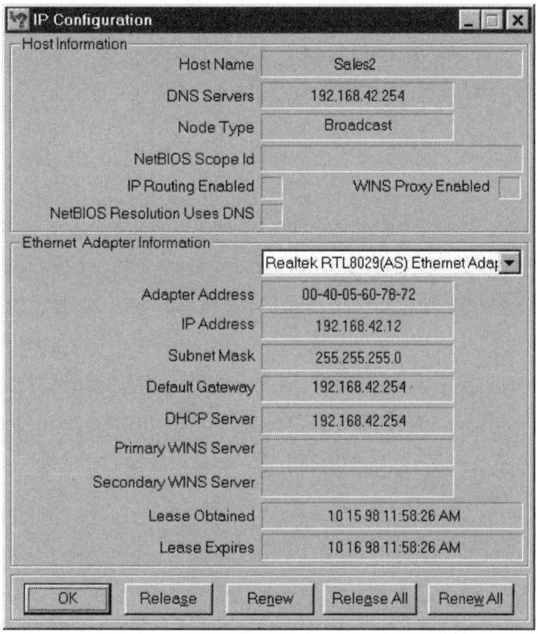

FIGURE 6.34

The Windows 9x WINIPCFG utility.

In UNIX, the command used to display this information can vary, but is usually IFCONFIG. Regardless of the operating system, a utility exists that can display the current configuration.

Utilities

TCP/IP—in all OS flavors—comes with a powerful set of troubleshooting utilities with which all network techs should familiarize themselves. Before sitting down to take the Network+ exam, make friends with these utilities: PING, TRACERT (TRACEROUTE), ARP, NETSTAT, and NBTSTAT.

PING

The PING utility tests connections between two hosts. To test the connection between two hosts, sit at one of them and type in "PING" followed by the name or IP address of the other host. PING uses Internet Control Message Protocol (ICMP) to determine if the other machine can receive the test packet and reply. A host that can be reached will respond back, and the PING command will report success:

```
C:\>ping notes01.totalsem.com

Pinging notes01 [192.168.43.4] with 32 bytes of data:

Reply from 192.168.43.4: bytes=32 time=1ms TTL=128
Reply from 192.168.43.4: bytes=32 time<10ms TTL=128
Reply from 192.168.43.4: bytes=32 time<10ms TTL=128
Reply from 192.168.43.4: bytes=32 time=1ms TTL=128
Ping statistics for 192.168.43.4:
    Packets: Sent = 4, Received = 4, Lost = 0 (0% loss),
Approximate round trip times in milli-seconds:
    Minimum = 0ms, Maximum =  1ms, Average =  0ms
```

or:

```
C:\>ping 192.168.43.4

Pinging 192.168.43.4 with 32 bytes of data:
```

```
Reply from 192.168.43.4: bytes=32 time<10ms TTL=128
Reply from 192.168.43.4: bytes=32 time<10ms TTL=128
Reply from 192.168.43.4: bytes=32 time<10ms TTL=128
Reply from 192.168.43.4: bytes=32 time<10ms TTL=128
Ping statistics for 192.168.43.4:
    Packets: Sent = 4, Received = 4, Lost = 0 (0% loss),
Approximate round trip times in milli-seconds:
    Minimum = 0ms, Maximum =  0ms, Average =  0ms

C:\>
```

Read the messages PING reports back when it cannot reach another machine—they can contain important clues about the source of the problem. If PING cannot turn a name into an IP address, for example, it will report back "Unknown host" or some similar message, indicating that PING was unable to determine the proper IP address for the name used. (The exact message returned by the PING command varies depending on the operating system.) If PING determines an IP address (either because the tech specified one or because PING resolved it using DNS) but cannot reach the specified address, PING will display a different message, such as "Destination host unreachable." "Unknown host" means "I don't know the IP address!" "Destination host unreachable" means "I can't get to that IP address."

NOTE Some people claim that PING stands for Packet InterNet Groper, but most people think it refers to the sound from those old Hollywood submarine movies. Know what PING does; do not worry about what it stands for. For a discussion of the origins of the PING program, see **http://ftp.arl.mil/~mike/ping.html.**

TRACERT

TRACERT (or TRACEROUTE on some operating systems) traces the route between two hosts. When PING fails, TRACERT can track the problem down to a specific router. TRACERT lists each router between the host and the destination:

```
C:\>tracert www.totalsem.com
```

```
Tracing route to totalsem.com [207.222.216.40]
over a maximum of 30 hops:

1   138 ms   140 ms 123 ms  houtx-pm83.netcom.net
[163.179.40.126]
2   139 ms   121 ms 130 ms  hougw1.netcom.net
[163.179.40.33]
3   141 ms   117 ms 119 ms  h5-0-2.dfw.netcom.net
[163.179.233.69]
4   149 ms   137 ms 135 ms  f3-0.dal-tx-gw1.netcom.net
[163.179.1.129]
5   124 ms   121 ms   141 ms  totalsem.com
[207.222.216.40]

Trace complete.
```

ARP

The ARP utility helps diagnose problems associated with the Address Resolution Protocol (ARP). TCP/IP hosts use the ARP protocol to determine the physical (MAC) address that corresponds with a specific logical (IP) address. The ARP utility, when used with the –a option, displays the IP and MAC addresses currently known by the host:

```
C:\>arp -a

Interface: 192.168.43.5 on Interface 0x1000002
  Internet Address      Physical Address      Type
  192.168.43.2          00-40-05-60-7f-64     dynamic
  192.168.43.3          00-40-05-5b-71-51     dynamic
  192.168.43.4          00-a0-c9-98-97-7f     dynamic
```

NETSTAT

NETSTAT enables the network tech to examine the current sockets-based connections on a specific host:

```
C:\>netstat
```

```
Active Connections
  Proto  Local Address   Foreign Address       State
  TCP    brian:1030      BRIAN:1274            ESTABLISHED
  TCP    brian:2666      totalsem.com:pop3     TIME_WAIT
  TCP    brian:2670      totalsem.com:pop3     TIME_WAIT
  TCP    brian:2672      www.cnn.com:80        TIME_WAIT
  TCP    brian:2674      www.nytimes.com:80    ESTABLISHED
  TCP    brian:2460      MARSPDC:nbsession     ESTABLISHED
  TCP    brian:1273      NOTES01:2986          TIME_WAIT
  TCP    brian:1274      RIAN:1030             ESTABLISHED
```

NBTSTAT

NBTSTAT enables a network tech to check the current NetBIOS name cache, which shows the NetBIOS names and corresponding IP addresses that have been resolved by a particular host:

```
C:\ >NBTSTAT -c

Node IpAddress: [192.168.43.5] Scope Id: []
              NetBIOS Remote Cache Name Table

    Name            Type       Host Address    Life [sec]
---------------------------------------------------------

WRITERS     <1B>  UNIQUE     192.168.43.13      420
SCOTT       <20>  UNIQUE     192.168.43.3       420
VENUSPDC    <00>  UNIQUE     192.168.43.13      120
MIKE        <20>  UNIQUE     192.168.43.2       420
NOTES01     <20>  UNIQUE     192.168.43.4       420
```

When properly used, NBTSTAT helps network techs diagnose and troubleshoot NetBIOS problems, especially those related to NetBIOS name resolution. NBTSTAT enables the network tech to determine if the WINS server has supplied inaccurate addresses to the WINS client.

Using command line utilities such as PING, TRACERT, ARP, NETSTAT, and NBTSTAT, an experienced network tech can diagnose most TCP/IP problems quickly and begin working on solutions. If two hosts can PING each other by address but not by name, for example, the wise network tech know to leave the routers alone and concentrate on name resolution (DNS, WINS) issues instead.

Conclusion

To function effectively as a network tech, learn TCP/IP. Supported by most operating systems, the TCP/IP suite provides excellent tools for integrating multiple operating systems within the same network. Its importance will continue to grow as the Internet continues to increase its importance in both business and everyday life.

Review Questions

1) A host is:

a) Any server on a TCP/IP network.

b) Any device on a TCP/IP network that can send or receive data packets.

c) A device on a TCP/IP network that forwards data packets to other networks.

d) A device on a TCP/IP network that resolves names to IP addresses.

2) Before it can communicate with another host on a different network, a TCP/IP host must have which of the following settings configured correctly?

a) IP address

b) Subnet mask

c) DNS server

d) Default gateway

3) Which of the following commands would produce the following output?

```
Active Connections

 Proto   Local Address     Foreign Address       State
 TCP     brian:1030        BRIAN:1274            ESTABLISHED
 TCP     brian:2666        totalsem.com:pop3     TIME_WAIT
 TCP     brian:2670        totalsem.com:pop3     TIME_WAIT
 TCP     brian:2672        www.cnn.com:80        TIME_WAIT
 TCP     brian:2674        www.nytimes.com:80    ESTABLISHED
 TCP     brian:2460        MARSPDC:nbsession     ESTABLISHED
 TCP     brian:1273        NOTES01:2986          TIME_WAIT
 TCP     brian:1274        BRIAN:1030            ESTABLISHED
```

a) NBTSTAT
b) ARP
c) NETSTAT
d) TRACERT

4) Which of the following commands will display a list of machines and their corresponding IP and MAC addresses?
a) NETSTAT
b) NBTSTAT
c) ARP
d) PING

5) Donnie complains that he cannot connect to **www.cnnsi.com**. Marie, the network administrator, suspects the network's DNS server could be causing the problem. Which of the following steps could help her determine if the DNS server is to blame for Donnie's problem?
a) Run DNSDIAG from Donnie's computer.
b) Run NBTSTAT from Donnie's computer.
c) PING **www.cnnsi.com** by both its name and IP address from Donnie's computer.
d) Run NETSTAT from Donnie's computer.

6) What port number does HTTP use?

a) 443
b) 110
c) 80
d) 43

7) What port number does SNMP use?

a) 80
b) 110
c) 119
d) 161

8) What port number does NNTP use?

a) 80
b) 110
c) 119
d) 161

9) Fred worries that hackers may be trying to break into his network. To prevent these break-ins, Fred should install:

a) A DNS server.
b) A WINS server.
c) A firewall.
d) A router.

10) The address 127.0.0.1 refers to:

a) The default gateway.
b) The default DNS server.
c) The local machine.
d) The default WINS server.

Review Answers

1) **B.** Any device on a TCP/IP network that can send or receive data packets is called a host.

2) **A, B, and D.** A host on a TCP/IP network must have its IP address, subnet mask, and default gateway correctly configured before it can communicate with hosts on other networks.

3) **C.** NETSTAT displays the current TCP/IP connections for a host.

4) **C.** The ARP command can display the MAC and IP addresses known by a TCP/IP host.

5) **C.** If Marie can PING **www.cnnsi.com** by its IP address but not by its name, then the problem is that Donnie's machine cannot properly resolve the name **www.cnnsi.com** into its corresponding IP address. Marie could also look for clues in the failure messages that the PING utility generates when it fails to reach an address.

6) **C.** HTTP (HyperText Transfer Protocol) uses port 80.

7) **D.** SNMP (Simple Network Management Protocol) uses port 161.

8) **C.** NNTP (Network News Transport Protocol) uses port 119.

9) **C.** Fred should install a firewall, a device that keeps unwanted and potentially dangerous traffic out while still allowing users on the network the benefits of Internet access.

10) **C.** The address 127.0.0.1, known as the loopback or localhost address, refers to the local machine.

CHAPTER 7

Network Operating Systems

Once upon a time, building a network was a simple task. The intrepid network tech went to a single large company like IBM and said, "Give me a network." The vendor then provided everything needed: servers, clients, NICS, hubs, etc. Everything worked together, at least in theory, because everything came from a single company that controlled the design of all the components. Today, network techs cannot live in that fairy tale world.

A typical large-scale network includes products from many vendors. On the hardware level, a network designer can select Ethernet or Token Ring hardware from a wide variety of vendors, trusting that the products comply with standards such as IEEE 802.3 and IEEE 802.5 (see Chapters 1-3). A computer with an Ethernet NIC from 3Com needs no alteration to communicate with a computer using an Ethernet NIC from SMC. At the operating-system level, the choices become more complex, with each of the major operating-system choices offering its own approaches to the common tasks performed by all networks. While each of the major network operating systems (NOSs) offers similar features, details of implementation vary greatly.

Network Operating System Features

All NOSs share the same fundamental goal: to enable *users*, the human beings who sit at the computers, to get work done. The routes to that goal vary, depending on the nature of the work. Some networks enable users to share files and printers, while others supply users with access to sophisticated applications that execute on a server. Before choosing the right network operating system or systems for a network, evaluate the roles that need filling (clients, file and print servers, and application servers) and the level of security desired. (Figure 7.1)

Roles

The majority of networks consist of *clients*, the machines at which users sit and do work. Client systems run applications such as word processors, spreadsheets, and web browsers while providing access to resources on the network. Most networks today use a Microsoft operating system such as Windows 95 or Windows NT Workstation as their client operating system, although UNIX workstations dominate in some settings.

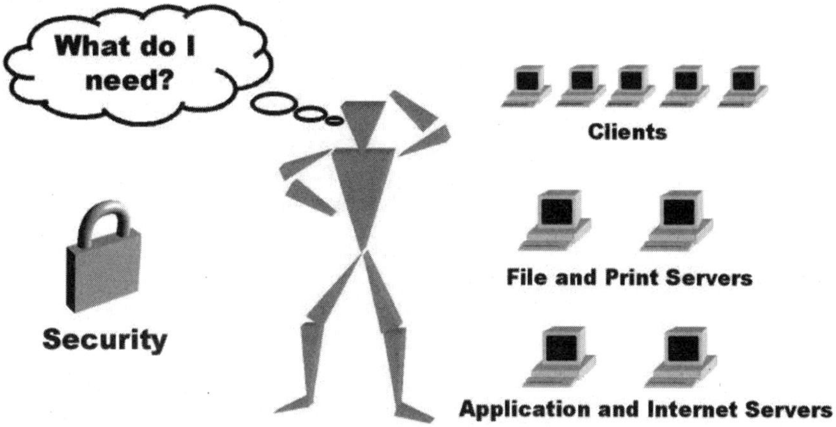

FIGURE 7.1 *Assessing network needs.*

File and print servers, as the name implies, provide clients access to data files and printers stored on the server. In small environments that require little or no security, such as a home network, a single system frequently acts as both client and server. In these networks, called *peer-to-peer* networks, every system can act as both client and server. Because end users have physical access to the servers, peer-to-peer networks typically provide little or no security and work best in very trusting environments. In *server-based* networks, one or more systems act as dedicated file or print servers. A *dedicated server* does not function as a client—it exists to serve the needs of other systems. Because they can be physically isolated from the end users, dedicated servers can offer far greater security (see the Security section below).

Application servers provide clients with access to the results generated by applications run on the server itself. Examples of application servers include Web servers, e-mail servers, and database servers. Think about how a Web site like **www.webopaedia.com** works. Webopædia maintains an encyclopedia of computer technology terms. When a user, sitting at a client system, types in a search term and clicks on "GO," as seen in Figure 7.2, the server searches its database and sends the client the search results. All the searching takes place on the server. The client system only receives the answer.

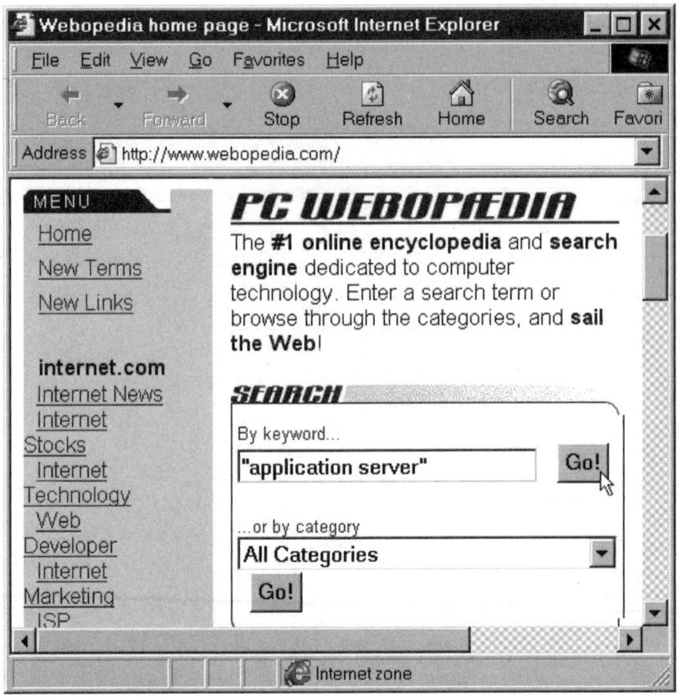

FIGURE 7.2
A Web browser accessing a database.

Running an application on an application server rather than on each client system offers three key advantages. First, application servers make efficient use of network traffic. Rather than having each client download the entire database and perform its own search, the database stays on the server. Client to application server communication (and vice versa) uses only a minimal amount of network bandwidth. Second, only a single copy of the database exists, which makes it easy to maintain and back up the database. When Bill makes a change to a database stored on the server, Roger can immediately access that data because only one copy of the database actually exists. Third, a single, very powerful server can provide access to a large database for much less expensive, less powerful systems, thus reducing costs. Cheap, out-of-date 386 and 486 computers running a client application such as a Web browser can access the database and achieve acceptable levels of performance because the heavy lifting of searching and sorting the database occurs on the server—the client merely displays the results.

ABCD TERMINOLOGY

Terminology Alert!

"Client-server" can have at least two distinct meanings. A *client-server network* has dedicated server machines and dedicated client machines. A *client-server application* performs some part of its processing on an application server rather than on the client systems.

Security

Network security involves protecting a network's users from their two greatest enemies: the "bad guys" and themselves. When most people think about security issues, they immediately have images of some hacker attempting to break into the network and steal company secrets. For many organizations, especially those connected to the Internet, such threats exist. Network security, however, includes the issue of "user-proofing" the network—preventing users from accidentally destroying data or granting access to unauthorized individuals. Basic security issues common to all networks include the level of security, the proper use of passwords, and the centralization of control.

Share-Level Security

A network designer can choose from two levels of security: share level and user level. With *share-level control*, a network administrator assigns each shared resource a password. Each user attempting to access the resource must supply the password. Network administrators usually consider share-level control to be weak and difficult to manage. If Carey, an intrepid network administrator, assigns the password "FICUS" to the payroll database stored on one of his servers, he must give that password to every user who must use that database. Unfortunately, if the accountants Greg, Bobby, and Peter all know the password, it is usually not too long before Mike the salesman learns it as well. After all, you know how bad Bobby is about putting his passwords on those little yellow sticky notes. If Carey learns about this breach of security, he must not only change the password—he must also tell it to Greg, Bobby, and Peter. Worse yet, the poor users may need to remember hundreds of different passwords. While share-level control can provide some benefit for small, trusting companies with few computers and few users, large networks require a more sophisticated scheme: *user-level security*.

User-Level Security

Under user-level security, a network administrator creates an account for each user. A *user account* defines the rights and privileges of a specific person's access to a computer system or network. A user who sits down at the computer, supplies an account name and password, and the computer checks that account name and password against its security database. If the password used matches the password listed for that user account in the database, the computer assumes from that point forward that the user is who she says she is and grants all the rights and privileges assigned to that user account. If Carey the intrepid network administrator employs user-level security instead of share-level security, he assigns Greg, Bobby, Peter, and Mike individual user account names and passwords. Since Bobby needs to remember only a single password to access all his resources, he probably will not need to use those treacherous sticky notes and will be less likely accidentally to inform others of his password.

To avoid the excessive workload of assigning specific rights to each user individually, network administrators organize users with similar needs into *groups*. Carey assigns Greg, Bobby, and Peter to the ACCOUNTS group and Mike to the SALES group. Carey can then assign the ACCOUNTS group permission to access the accounting database and any other appropriate databases. By virtue of their membership in ACCOUNTS, Greg, Bobby, and Peter can all access the accounting database. If the company hires more accountants, Carey simply creates new user accounts and adds them to the ACCOUNTS group. By virtue of their membership in that group, they can access all the resources that accountants should be able to access. The use of groups greatly eases the burden on the network administrator. Carey creates a group for every job description and then simply places users into the appropriate groups (Figure 7.3). In large organizations with hundreds of employees with similar needs, the time and effort saved quickly becomes significant.

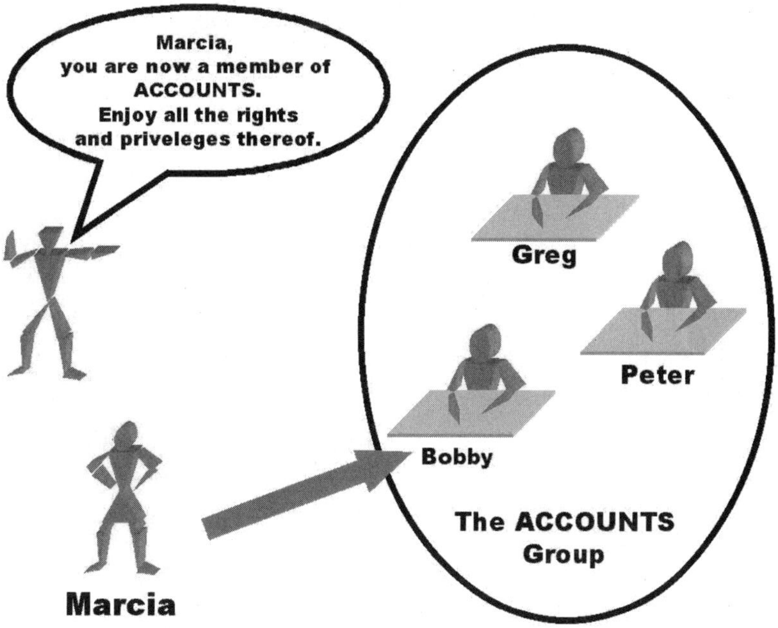

FIGURE 7.3
Groups enhance efficiency.

In most instances, a user's rights are cumulative, meaning that a user receives the sum of the rights granted to his user account and the rights granted to any of the groups to which he belongs. Greg, for example, belongs to both the MANAGERS and ACCOUNTANTS groups. Carey sets up a shared folder on a server and assigns the MANAGERS group the right to add files to the folder, the ACCOUNTANTS group the right to read (but not alter or delete) files in that folder, and Greg as an individual the right to modify files that already exist in that folder. As a result, Greg can add files, read files, and modify files in that directory because of his individual and group rights (Figure 7.4).

Passwords

Of course, user-level security works well only when users keep their passwords secure. Passwords should never be written down where another user might find them and users should never reveal their passwords to anyone, even the administrator of the network. In most cases, the administrator can reset a user's password without knowing the old password. Many end-users, however, remain unaware of this and fall prey to one of the oldest hacker tricks in the book: the fake tech support phone call. In a large organization, most users will not know every network support technician. A hacker simply calls up one of these hapless users and says, "This is Bob from tech support. We're upgrading the forward deflector grid and we need your password so we can reset it when we're done." A shocking number of users will simply give out their password when asked over the phone. A large part of password security lies in educating network users about the proper care and feeding of their passwords.

FIGURE 7.4
Rights are cumulative.

First, teach users to pick good passwords. A good password cannot be guessed easily. Passwords should never be based on any information about the user that can be easily obtained. If Herman lives at 1313 Mockingbird Lane, is married to Lilly, and has a pet named Spot, for example, he should never use these passwords:

mockingbird
dribgnikcom (mockingbird spelled backwards)
lilly
yllil (Lilly spelled backwards)
spot
tops (Spot spelled backwards)

Ideally, a password should not be a real word at all. Hackers probing a network often run password-guessing utilities that simply try common dictionary words at random. Network administrators can reduce the effectiveness of such password-guessing programs by requiring all passwords to be longer than 6-8 characters. Hackers have a more difficult task when guessing longer passwords because there are many more possible combinations.

The most secure passwords contain a combination of letters and numbers. The following list contains "strong" passwords:

gr78brk
tnk23wqk
100bobotw

A good network administrator should assume that, given enough time, some users' passwords will become public knowledge. To limit the impact of these exposed passwords, a careful network administrator sets passwords to expire periodically, usually once every 30 days or so. Should a password become public knowledge, the gap in network security will automatically close when the user changes his password.

TIP

EXAM TIP:

A strong password should:

- be longer than 6–8 characters.
- contain both letters and numbers.
- not be based on easily guessed information.
- change on a regular schedule.

Choosing the Right Operating System

Microsoft, Novell, and UNIX all provide strong NOS solutions that address the goals of networking, including access to shared resources and security. While Microsoft clients dominate the role of desktop clients, Microsoft, Novell and UNIX compete for the server NOS market.

Microsoft Windows 9x and NT

Microsoft competes for NOS market share with two distinct product lines: Windows 9x and Windows NT. Windows 9x functions as a flexible desktop NOS, capable of connecting to virtually any type of server.

Windows NT, in contrast, can function as both a powerful client and a full-featured server NOS.

Window 95 and 98

Microsoft Windows 95 and 98, collectively known as Windows 9x, provide basic file- and print-sharing functions, but little security by themselves. A network tech can configure a Windows 9x as simply a client, or as both a client and a server. As a server, however, Windows 9x uses share-level control, making it significantly less secure than more sophisticated server operating systems such as Windows NT, Novell NetWare, or UNIX. Windows 9x's key appeal lies in its ability to connect to virtually any other kind of server, including Windows 9x, Windows NT, Novell NetWare, and UNIX.

To connect to a server running any Microsoft NOS, a Windows 9x client must have the Client for Microsoft Networks installed, shown in Figure 7.5. Because Microsoft maintains a high degree of compatibility with its older network operating systems, Client for Microsoft Networks enables a Windows 9x system to communicate with any of the following types of servers:

- Microsoft LAN Manager
- Windows for Workgroups
- Windows 95
- Windows 98
- Windows NT 3.x
- Windows NT 4.x
- Windows 2000.

Windows 9x also ships with the Microsoft Client for NetWare Networks, which enables connectivity with Novell NetWare servers. The Microsoft Client for NetWare Networks requires IPX/SPX-compatible transport and enables a Windows 9x client to connect to resources on the server. The Microsoft Client for NetWare Networks that comes with Windows 9x has two key weaknesses. First, it cannot connect to NetWare servers via TCP/IP. As Novell joins the rest of the networking industry in its headlong stampede into the world of TCP/IP, Windows 9x clients running the Microsoft Client for NetWare Networks get left behind. Second, the Microsoft Client for NetWare Networks does not understand Novell Directory Services (NDS), NetWare's default security and directory system for NetWare 4 and 5. (See below for a discussion of NDS.)

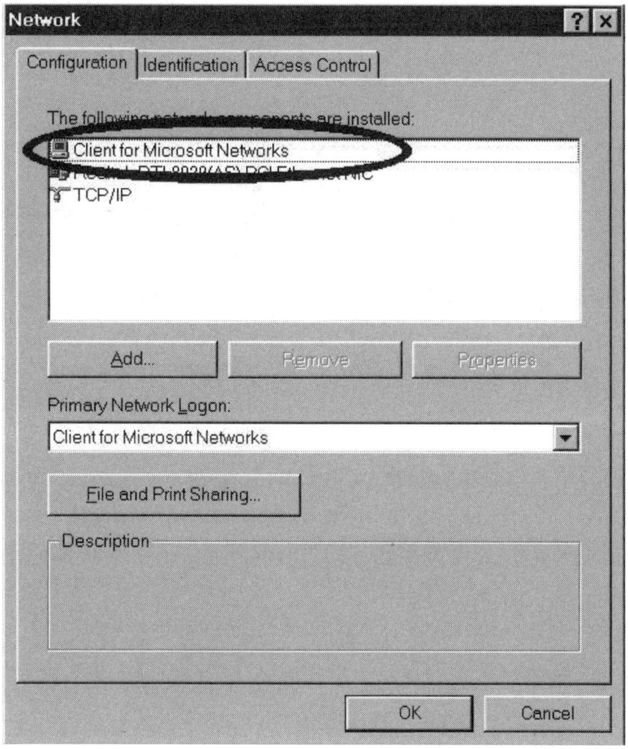

FIGURE 7.5
The client for Microsoft Networks.

Novell, however, provides an alternative to Microsoft's Client for NetWare Networks. Novell's Client32 enables Windows 9x clients to connect to a NetWare server using either IPX/SPX or TCP/IP and provides full support for NDS. Novell calls the current version, which replaces the original Client 32, "Client v3.1 for Windows 95/98." Techs, as a general rule, prefer shorter names, and simply refer to whatever client software Novell provides for Windows 9x clients as "Client32."

NOTE

To download Novell client software, go to **http://www.novell.com/download/**.

Windows NT Workstation

Windows NT Workstation offers the same user interface as Windows 95 but with greatly enhanced security and stability. A knowledgeable "power user" can often defeat most security measures on a Windows 9x machine by directly accessing the *registry*, the database that defines all settings, including security settings, on a Windows 9x system. Windows NT Workstation, in contrast, follows a more robust security model and an able network administrator can prevent even power users from digging into the internals of the system. Windows NT Workstation also provides a more stable platform for running applications. While applications can still lock up, Windows NT Workstation does a better job of protecting programs from each other—rarely will the failure of one program on an NT Workstation crash other programs.

Windows NT Workstation can also function effectively as a NetWare client. Microsoft provides its own NetWare client software, Client Services for NetWare (CSNW). As with Windows 9x's Client for NetWare Networks, CSNW cannot connect to NetWare servers via TCP/IP and does not fully support NDS. Novell provides its own client software for NT, Client 4.11b for Windows NT Networks, usually referred to simply as Client32. The Novell Client32 can connect to a NetWare server using TCP/IP and fully supports NDS.

User Profiles

Windows 9x and Windows NT support the use of user profiles, which enhance both the usability and security of a network. *User profiles* are a collection of settings that correspond to a specific user account and follow the user regardless of the computer at which he sits. User profiles allow each user to customize the working environment. Each user's preferences for wallpaper, desktop layout, etc., remain consistent from session to session. The ACME Rocket Corporation runs three shifts. Elmer, Marvin, and Wiley work different shifts and share the same computer. When each of them logs in to the Windows 9x computer at the beginning of his respective shift, Windows 9x loads the appropriate configuration from the user's profile. If the profiles exist on the local hard drive, they affect only that computer. A savvy network administrator will store the profiles on a network server (NT, NetWare, or other

NOS), enabling the profiles to follow the user regardless of where they sit. When Wiley transfers to the day shift, he can use a different computer and still enjoy all his customized settings. As much as Elmer, Marvin, and Wiley enjoy the benefits of user profiles, Sylvester the network admin likes them even more. Sylvester can use profiles to place restrictions on how Elmer, Marvin, and Wiley use their computers. When the boss, Sam, complains that employees spend too much time playing solitaire, Sylvester edits their profiles so that they cannot run the solitaire program anymore. Sylvester can also restrict use in other ways, preventing them from:

- running other programs
- changing their desktop icons and wallpaper
- loading new programs.

User profiles offer a consistent look and feel to the end user and control to the network administrator.

TIP

EXAM TIP:

A *profile* is a set of configuration settings specific to an individual user. Profiles can be stored locally or on a server. Administrators can use profiles to place restrictions on what users can do with their computers.

Windows NT Server and Domain-Based Networking

Windows NT Server, Microsoft's server product, offers all the features of Windows NT Workstation plus enhancements that strengthen it as a server. Microsoft optimized Windows NT Server to put a higher priority on serving requests over the network than on serving the requests of a user sitting at his own keyboard. Windows NT Server possesses the ability to join a common security environment called a domain and can fill a variety of needs on the network in addition to its file- and print-sharing functions.

Windows NT enables multiple servers to join a group of servers, called a *domain*, that share a common security database. In the bad old days of computer networking, a user needing to access more than one server would need a separate user account on each server. Maintaining multiple user accounts for each user created a huge burden on administrators (who had to create and maintain all those accounts) and on end-users (who had to remember multiple user account names and passwords). Fortunately, someone came up with the idea of a *single login*, which enables a user to log in once and access all their resources, regardless of the server on which the resource resides. Microsoft implements the single login through domains.

In an NT domain, special servers known as *domain controllers* store a common security database called the *Security Access Manager (SAM)* database. When a user logs in to the domain, a domain controller checks the user name and password. When Penelope logs in successfully to the domain, the domain controller issues her an *access token*, the electronic equivalent of an ID badge. Whenever she attempts to access a resource on any server on the domain, her computer automatically shows the server her access token. Based on the access token, the server then decides whether or not to grant her access (Figure 7.6).

FIGURE 7.6
Access token at work.

NOTE

In Windows NT, all computers within a domain share a common security database. Each user logs in once to access all of their resources within the domain.

Novell NetWare

The continued use of older versions testifies to the power and stability of Novell NetWare. Many organizations upgrade their client software, but continue to use their existing NetWare 3.x and 4.x servers, following those ancient words of wisdom: "If it ain't broke, don't fix it." Network techs should familiarize themselves with three significant versions of NetWare: NetWare 3.x, NetWare 4.x, and NetWare 5.x.

NetWare 3.x and the Bindery

NetWare 3.x offers solid file- and print-sharing capabilities using the IPX/SPX protocol suite, but lacks a centralized security database. Each NetWare 3.x server maintains its own security database, called the *Bindery*. When a user logs in, the NetWare server compares the user name and password to its Bindery database and then determines which resources it will share with the user. NetWare 3.x works best in networks that require only a single server, because each server maintains its own Bindery database independently. A user accessing resources on three different servers requires three separate user accounts and passwords (Figure 7.7). NetWare 3.x's reliance on IPX/SPX also limits its use as more and more networks adopt TCP/IP as the protocol of choice.

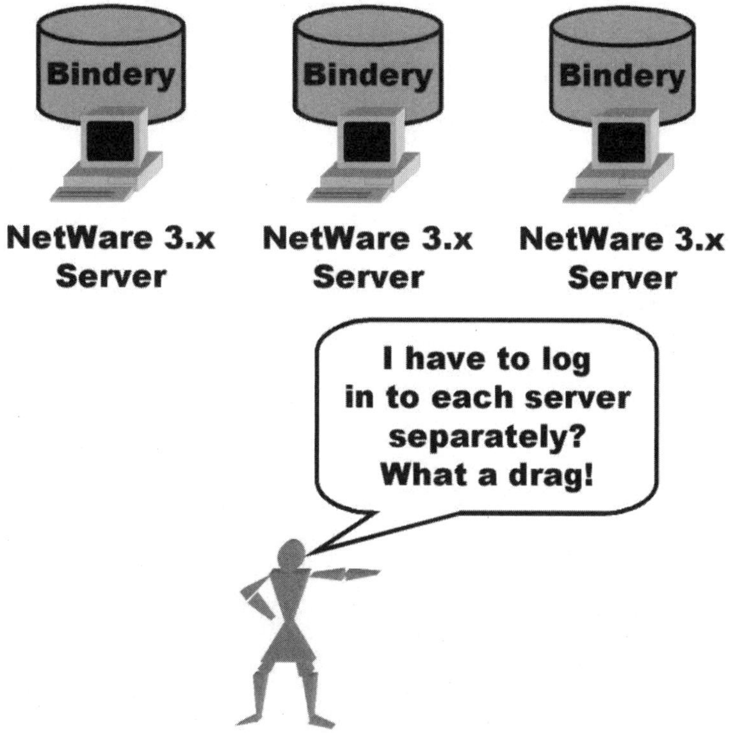

FIGURE 7.7 *NetWare 3.x Servers maintain separate Bindery databases.*

TIP

EXAM TIP:

While it is possible to add TCP/IP support to a NetWare 3.x server, NetWare 3.x servers running TCP/IP rarely occur "in the wild." For the purposes of the Network+ exam, assume that all NetWare 3.x servers use IPX/SPX as their sole networking protocol.

NetWare 4.x and NDS

NetWare 4.x built on the success of NetWare 3.x by adding two key features: Novell Directory Services (NDS) and TCP/IP encapsulation. *Novell Directory Services (NDS)* organizes all user and resource information in a database referred to as the *NDS tree*. This acts as a centralized security database, enabling users who "log in to the directory" to access all their resources anywhere on the network. NetWare 4.x also supports TCP/IP, allowing NetWare servers and clients to place IPX packets inside TCP/IP packets, a process known as *encapsulation* (Figure 7.8). NetWare's basic design assumes the use of IPX/SPX, and encapsulation enables Novell to use TCP/IP without massively redesigning the NOS. Encapsulation, however, hurts performance by adding an additional layer of protocol information to each packet.

I can encapsulate an IPX/SPX packet!
TCP/IP Packet
IPX/SPX Packet

FIGURE 7.8
NetWare 4.x and TCP/IP encasulation.

TIP

Exam Tip:

Windows NT enables users to log in once and access all their resources by logging in to the NT *domain*.

NetWare 4.x (and 5.x) enable users to log in once and access all their resources by logging in to the *NDS tree*.

NetWare 5.x

NetWare 5.x removes the need for TCP/IP encapsulation, enabling NetWare to run TCP/IP natively. *Native TCP/IP* means that NetWare 5 no longer needs to use IPX/SPX at all (although it can for backward compatibility). Because NetWare 5 can "speak" TCP/IP natively, it performs far more efficiently when using TCP/IP than NetWare 4 did.

NOTE

NETWARE SUMMARY:

For the Network+ exam, familiarize yourself with the protocols and security databases used by each version of NetWare, as shown in Table 7.1.

TABLE 7.1

NetWare security database and protocol.

NetWare version	Security Database	Protocol(s)
NetWare 3.x	Bindery	IPX/SPX
NetWare 4.x	NDS	IPX/SPX or TCP/IP
NetWare 5.x	NDS	IPX/SPX or TCP/IP

UNIX and Linux

UNIX, the mainstay of universities and scientific computing, becomes more important for the average network tech in the trenches as the importance of the Internet continues to grow. Originally, the Internet consisted of a few UNIX-based systems at a few universities spread around the world. The basic Internet protocols (FTP, HTTP, DNS, ARP, etc.) originated in the world of UNIX and were only later ported to other operating systems. UNIX comes in many flavors, but they generally share certain features. The flexibility of UNIX and the rise of open-source variants such as Linux and Free BSD, makes UNIX an NOS that network techs ignore at their peril.

Many Flavors

The wide variety of UNIX versions, known as *flavors*, arose because Bell Labs made UNIX available to universities and allowed the universities to modify the operating system to meet their own needs. The freedom the universities enjoyed encouraged rapid development, leading to such critical technologies as TCP/IP-based networking; but it also created significant distinctions between versions. Today, major variations include Sun's Solaris, IBM's AIX UNIX, Hewlett-Packard's HP UNIX, and BSD. While all versions of UNIX have a similar look and feel, a program written for one flavor often requires significant revision before it can run on another. Fortunately, the typical network tech can safely leave the distinctions between UNIX flavors to the programmers. From the network tech's point of view, all versions of UNIX look more alike than different.

TIP

EXAM TIP:

The Network+ exam does not cover the differences between versions of UNIX.

Sharing Files

UNIX systems can share files across a network in a variety of ways, including File Transfer Protocol (FTP), Network File System (NFS), and SAMBA. FTP, as discussed in Chapter 6, enables two TCP/IP hosts to transfer files across the network. All implementations of TCP/IP support FTP, making it an excellent choice for moving files from a UNIX host to a machine running another operating system such as Windows 9x, Windows NT, a different flavor of UNIX, or even Macintosh.

Network File System (NFS) enables two UNIX systems to treat files and directories on another UNIX host as though they were local files. Fred needs to access the /mark/projects/current directory on Mark's UNIX system, MARK1. Fred *mounts* the /mark/projects/current/ directory to his own file systems as /markstuff/, adding it to the local directory structure. As far as any program on Fred's UNIX machine can tell, the files in the /markstuff/ directory are local files. NFS enables his UNIX machine to share files transparently, adding network directories to the local directory structure. Unfortunately, Windows-based machines don't get to play—they don't come with an NFS client.

UNIX systems, however, can pretend to be Microsoft clients and servers using SAMBA, which enables UNIX systems to communicate using Server Message Blocks (SMBs). (See Chapter 5 for more information about the SMB protocol.) To a Windows-based system running a client for Microsoft Networks, a UNIX system running SAMBA looks just like any Microsoft server. (See Figure 7.9)

FIGURE 7.9
That's some disguise!

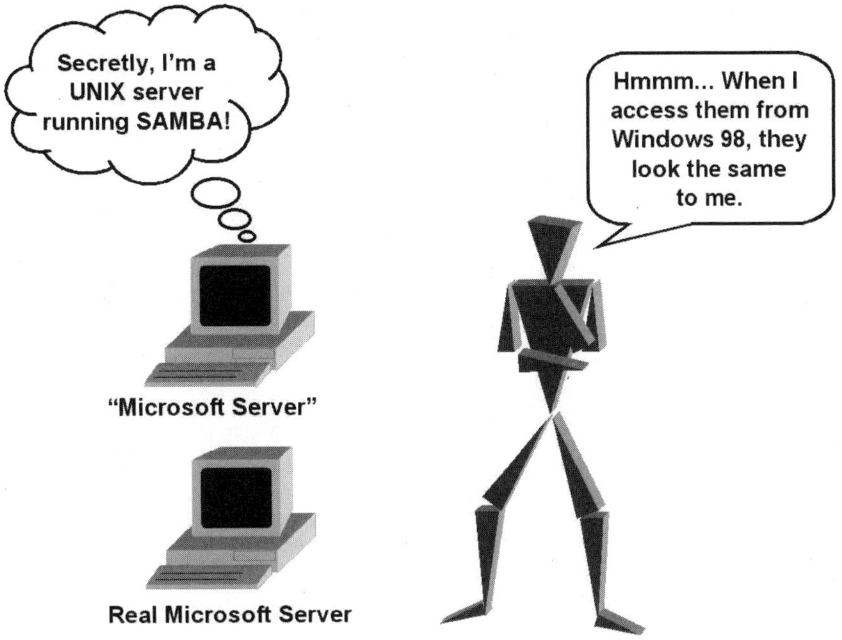

Web Applications

Although facing increasing competition from Windows NT and NetWare, UNIX remains the server of choice for providing Internet-based services such as Web browsing and e-mail. The protocols used originated in UNIX versions and many organizations that use NetWare or Windows NT for their file- and print-sharing needs rely on UNIX for their Internet services.

Open Source UNIX

If you have not heard of Linux yet, you need to read the newspaper a little more often. Linus Torvalds, while a student, expressed his frustration with the high cost of most versions of UNIX by building his own. Torvalds licensed his UNIX clone, dubbed *Linux*, in a unique way. Linux is an *open source* operating system, meaning that anyone who purchases a copy receives full access to its *source code*, the building blocks of the operating system. Free access to the source code gives software developers tremendous power to modify the operating system to meet their needs, and has led to the rapid development of a wide variety of applications, including some of the most commonly used Web and e-mail servers on the Internet. In most cases, both the Linux operating system and Linux applications are available for free download from the Internet, although vendors such as Red Hat and Caldera charge for support services. For all intents and purposes, Linux is a full-featured clone of UNIX.

Conclusion

As a network tech, prepare yourself to support and maintain multiple operating systems. Always remember, however, that the goal of all network operating systems remains the same: help the human beings who use computers get their work done.

Review Questions

1) May wants to allow Mary Jane and Peter to view and modify a database stored on her server. She wants Betty to be able to view the database but not modify it, and Jonah should not have any access to the database whatsoever. Each user should have his or her own password. What kind of security should May implement?

a) High level
b) Share level
c) User level
d) SMTP level

2) Which of the following would be the most secure password for a user named Walter Schwarz?

a) walter
b) wschwarz
c) wishbone
d) tail51hctc

3) When using a common security database, Microsoft Windows NT machines must be organized into:

a) An NDS tree.
b) A domain.
c) A ring.
d) A web.

4) When using a common security database, Novell NetWare servers must be organized into:

a) An NDS tree.
b) A domain.
c) A ring.
d) A web.

5) On a Windows 95 system, which of the following combinations can enable the Windows 95 system to connect to a NetWare 4.x server?
(Choose all that apply.)

a) Microsoft Client for NetWare Networks and IPX/SPX
b) Microsoft Client for NetWare Networks and TCP/IP
c) NetWare Client 32 and IPX/SPX
d) NetWare Client 32 and TCP/IP

6) On a Windows 95 system, which of the following combinations can enable the Windows 95 system to take full advantage of NDS? (Choose all that apply.)

a) Microsoft Client for NetWare Networks and IPX/SPX
b) Microsoft Client for NetWare Networks and TCP/IP
c) NetWare Client 32 and IPX/SPX
d) NetWare Client 32 and TCP/IP

7) Bernie needs to download a word processing file from a UNIX server on his network to his Windows 9x machine. To transfer the file, he should use:
a) POP3.
b) FTP.
c) NFS.
d) SMTP.

8) NetWare 3.x servers store user account and password information in a database called the:
a) Domain.
b) NDS tree.
c) Bindery.
d) National Register of Historic Places.

9) Which of the following NOSs support TCP/IP?
a) Windows 9x
b) Windows NT
c) Novell NetWare 4.x
d) UNIX

10) A user profile:
a) Stores a photo of the user on the network for identification purposes.
b) Stores the user's passwords.
c) Contains customized settings and restrictions that apply for a specific user regardless of the machine at which they sit.
d) Tracks the activities of a user for later analysis by network administrators.

Review Answers

1) **C.** User-level security allows administrators to assign different rights and permissions to each user, with each user using his or her own unique password. Share-level security assigns a password to each resource, but would not fulfill May's needs because share-level security would require Mary Jane and Peter to use the same password to access the database. SMTP refers to Simple Mail Transfer Protocol, an e-mail protocol that has nothing to do with securing files on a server. "High-level" security is a bogus term that has no specific meaning.

2) **D.** The best passwords avoid using easily guessed personal information like names (walter, wschwarz) or words that appear in the dictionary (wishbone), and combine numbers and letters.

3) **B.** Windows NT systems that belong to the same domain share a common security database.

4) **A.** Novell NetWare servers use Novell Directory Services when sharing a common security database. Servers sharing that database exist within an NDS tree.

5) **A, C,** and **D.** The Microsoft Client for NetWare Networks can only connect to NetWare servers running IPX/SPX, not TCP/IP. (This question assumes that the NetWare 4.x server can run either TCP/IP or IPX/SPX.)

6) **C** and **D.** The Microsoft Client for NetWare Networks cannot take full advantage of the features of NDS.

7) **B.** All TCP/IP hosts can transfer files using FTP. Post Office Protocol version 3 (POP3) and Simple Mail Transfer Protocol (SMTP) move e-mail, not word processing documents, around the network. Network File System (NFS) is a file-sharing protocol used between UNIX hosts, and is not supported natively by Windows 9x. SAMBA, although it would work, is not listed as a choice.

8) **C.** Each NetWare 3.x server has its own security database called the Bindery. NetWare 4.x and 5.x servers share a common NDS database, and Windows NT servers share a domain database. If you choose answer D, seek professional help immediately.

9) **A, B, C,** and **D.** All these operating systems support TCP/IP as a protocol suite.

10) **C.** A user profile contains customized settings and restrictions that apply for a specified user regardless of the machine at which the user sits. A user's password is not part of their profile—the user must log in using a valid user account name and password before the user profile can be applied.

CHAPTER 8

The Complete Network PC

The job of networking demands fundamental hardware differences between a PC that connects to a network and a PC that does not. The designers of the personal computer probably never considered the PC as a device to participate in a network but cannot be blamed for such thinking. The original PC simply did not pack the necessary firepower to function in any but the most primitive of networks. The first PCs used tiny (less than 10 megabyte) hard drives—or only floppy drives—and the 4.77 MHz Intel 8088 could not handle the many calculations demanded by even the most basic network operating systems. The mainframe-centric world of IBM created the PC to work primarily as an individual computer, a "standalone" system, or to perform as a "dumb terminal" for mainframe access. While networks were not part of the original PC concept, ongoing improvements in the power and the phenomenal flexibility of PCs enabled them to move easily from a world of individual, standalone systems, into the interactive world of connected, networked machines. Even though any standalone PC transforms nicely into a networked machine, the different jobs of a standalone versus a networked machine require significantly different hardware in each. What are these requirements? What hardware does a networked PC need that a standalone PC can live without? The network functions themselves supply the answers (Figure 8.1).

FIGURE 8.1

Networked PCs need more hardware.

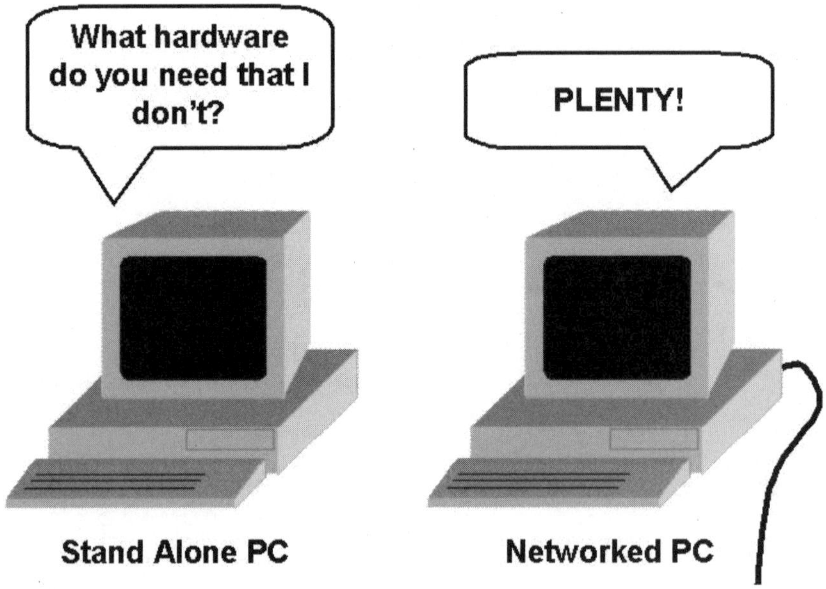

A network PC has four significant functions. First, it must connect to the network. This connection usually runs through a cable of some type, but wireless networks are becoming more common. Second, if the PC shares data, the PC needs to protect that shared data by creating more than one copy of the data. The copies are most often created using multiple storage devices working together. Third, and again only if the PC shares data, it needs specialized hardware that enables it to share the data as quickly as possible. A sharing PC often uses a number of different hardware technologies to increase the speed at which it shares its resources. A good example of a speed technology is a specialized network card that enables faster data access. The fourth and last function unique to a network PC is reliability. The shared resources of the network must be available whenever another system accesses them. The network PC must use special hardware to prevent a sharing system from failing to provide shared resources. Reliability means methods to make sure the PC does not stop working due to a failed component. These hardware devices manifest themselves in items such as redundant power supplies or air conditioning units. Together or separately, every network PC has at least one of these four functions (Figure 8.2).

FIGURE 8.2

The four network functions.

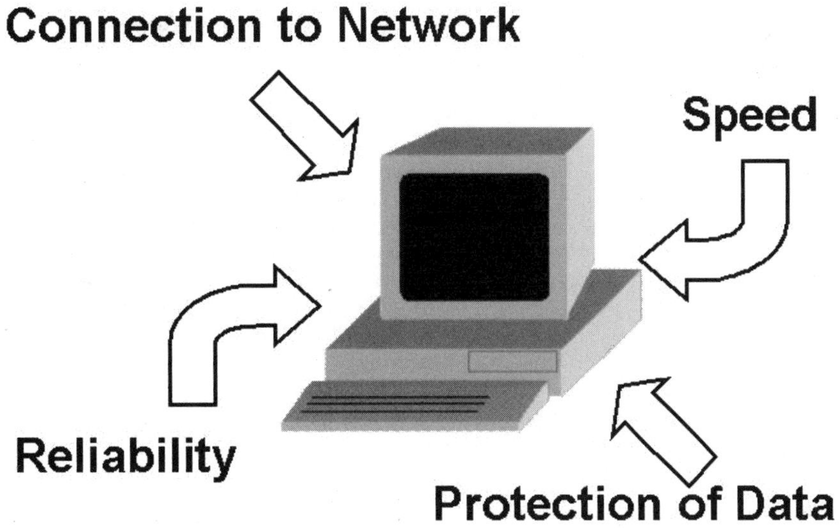

The process of deciding which functions appear in a network PC is determined by the job of that particular system. The biggest line of demarcation is between systems that share resources (servers) and systems that only access the server's shared resources (workstations). The hardware requirements for a workstation and a server differ fundamentally. The only specialized function of a workstation is connecting to the network via a NIC. Workstations do not share resources, so they have little need for reliability, speed, and data protection beyond that already built into any standalone PC. Servers, on the other hand, use all the functions, creating the need for highly specialized systems full of specialized hardware to provide most, if not all, of these four network functions. The incorporation of the specialized hardware usually makes a server system stand out compared to a workstation, especially if you purchase a premade server system (Figure 8.3).

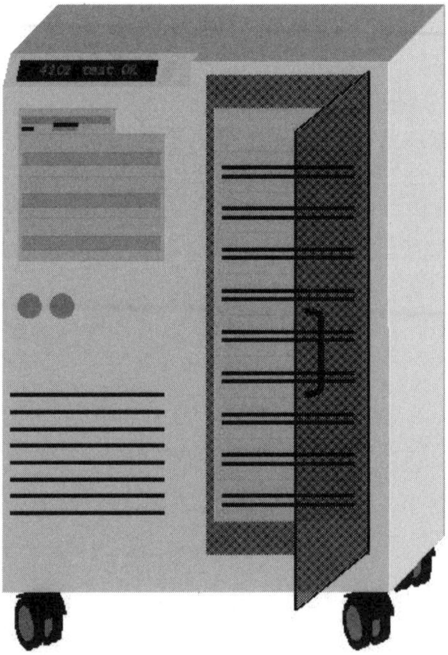

FIGURE 8.3 *Typical network server.*

Keep in mind that there is no requirement for a serving system to have the extra hardware. Virtually any PC can act as a serving system—as long as you are willing to put up with lack of reliability, slower response times, and the higher potential for data loss. Equally, in peer-to-peer networks, some, most, or all of the systems act as servers. It is usually logistically impractical and financially imprudent to give every user in a peer-to-peer network a powerful server system (although if you did, you'd be extremely popular!). A good network person considers the network functions of a particular system to determine which ones the system actually needs and then balances the needed network functions against cost, time, and support needs to determine what hardware a particular system needs (Figure 8.4).

FIGURE 8.4
Do I really need this for a workgroup printer?

All networked PCs need at least one of these four network functions: connections, reliability, speed, and data safety. In this chapter, we explore these four network functions in detail and tour the wide variety of hardware, software, and organization solutions used in today's networks to fulfill the needs of these four functions.

Connecting to a Network

A network PC must communicate with other networked PCs. There can be little argument that the connecting to the network function is the first and certainly the most obvious function of a networked PC. Network cards or Network Interface Cards (NICs) (Figure 8.5) are the most common way to connect a PC to a network.

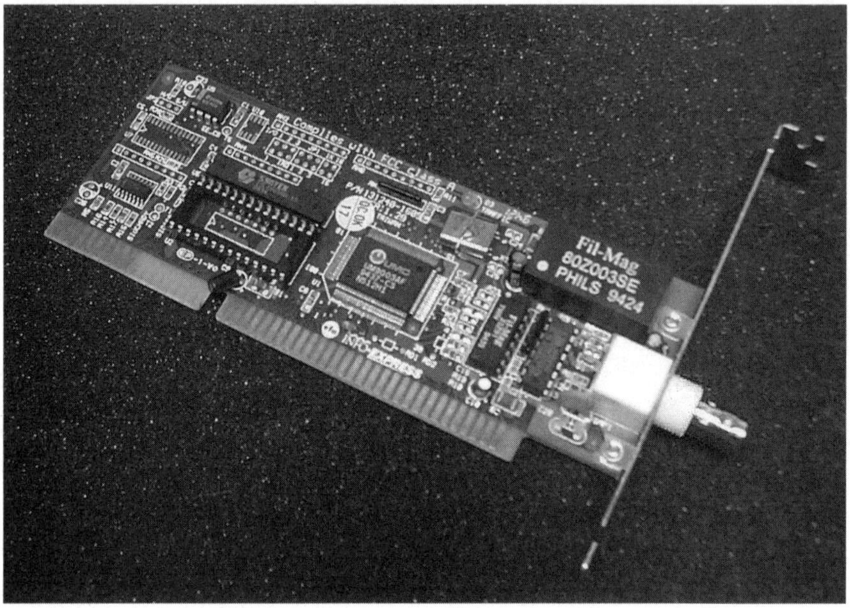

FIGURE 8.5
A typical NIC.

Using NICs is the most common, but not the only method for connecting PCs to networks. Other methods include using wireless networks (in reality, wireless networks are simply special NICs connected to a radio or infrared transmitter/receiver), modems, and serial-to-serial ports (Windows calls this a "Direct Cable Connection"). We will look at all these connections and learn that they share many issues. We can then look at how to use (or not use) these connections in a network, so that when it comes time to plug something in, we do it correctly.

The Connectors

Have you ever heard the phrase "Don't reinvent the wheel?" The creators of network cards must have this cliché printed on their ceilings! There are very few NIC connections designed from scratch just for PC networks. In fact, the specially designed connections are so rare that the Network+ exam does not cover them and you almost certainly will never see one in your career. With that in mind, we will just say that no NIC connector is designed from scratch. If all NIC connections take the form of previous connector designs, what are the chances that there might be two or three identical connectors on the back of a PC? The probability is very high. Techs must therefore know ALL of the connectors that might connect PCs to networks, regardless of whether or not they are currently used in network connections. Later, we can look at the individual network connections to appreciate which types of connections are commonly used to enable one PC to network to another.

All network connectors fit into one of four different families: BNC, RJ, DB, and fiber. Before we start memorizing which connector goes with what NIC, we should understand these connectors; this will make the memorization process trivial.

BNC Connectors

BNC stands for either *British Naval Connection* or *Bayonet Neil-Concelman*, depending on whom you ask. Which ever is correct, BNC connectors are among the oldest connectors used on NICs. BNC connectors are used with coaxial cable (See Chapter 1). The tubular look of a BNC connector makes it very distinct (Figure 8.6).

FIGURE 8.6

BNC connector.

If you see a BNC connector on a NIC, you can almost always assume a 10Base2 (thin Ethernet) card. Two other types of cards also used (use) the BNC connector. The first was a type of network technology called

ARCnet. ARCnet is an old, rarely used network technology and is not covered on the Network+ exams, although you may see it on the exam as a wrong answer. Another use of BNCs is in an old IBM terminal emulation adapter known as a 3270. A 3270 terminal emulation card would enable a PC to switch between being a PC and a dumb terminal. 3270 emulation is even older than ARCnet and has been rendered completely obsolete in the PC world by network cards. Make your life easy—if you see a BNC connector sticking out of the back of a card, assume that it is 10Base2 and you will be right 98% of the time—and 100% right on any Network+ questions.

RJ Connectors

RJ (*Registered Jack*) connectors are the most common connectors on NICs. They are also the most common connector used in telephones. RJ connectors use Unshielded Twisted Pair (UTP—see Chapter 2) wiring. While there are many different sizes of RJ connectors, only two ever appear on the back of a PC. The first is the RJ-11 (Figure 8.7).

FIGURE 8.7
RJ-11.

RJ-11 is the exclusive domain of modems. Many years ago, RJ-11s appeared on a few proprietary network technologies, but they have all since disappeared. RJ-11 connectors use four-wire cables, the two inner connectors for one phone line and the outer ones for a second line. Most home phone systems only have one line per jack, so the outer lines do nothing. The six-wire version is known as the RJ-12. RJ-12s certainly do exist, usually for more complex telephone systems, but are virtually nonexistent in the PC world.

Far more common is the RJ-45, the standard network connection for many different types of networks. Ethernet, Token Ring, and even the old ARCnet networks all have at least one version that uses RJ-45 connectors (Figure 8.8).

FIGURE 8.8
RJ-45.

RJ-45 connectors have eight wires. Many types of network technologies only use four wires, so it is not at all uncommon to see an RJ-45 with only four wires used.

DB Connectors

DB connectors are the "D"-shaped connectors used for hundreds of different connections in the PC and network world and come in a number of different forms. They can be "male" (pins) or "female" (sockets); they can have different numbers of pins or sockets (9-, 15-, and 25-pin are most common); and they usually have two rows of pins, although there are a few exceptions. Figure 8.9 shows a 25-pin, female DB connector. We call this, appropriately, a "female DB-25."

FIGURE 8.9
Female DB-25.

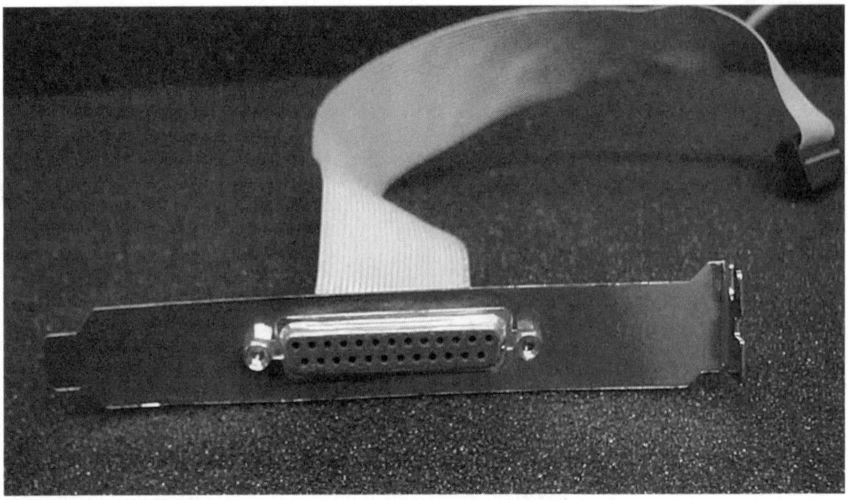

Figure 8.10 shows a male DB-25.

FIGURE 8.10
Male DB-25.

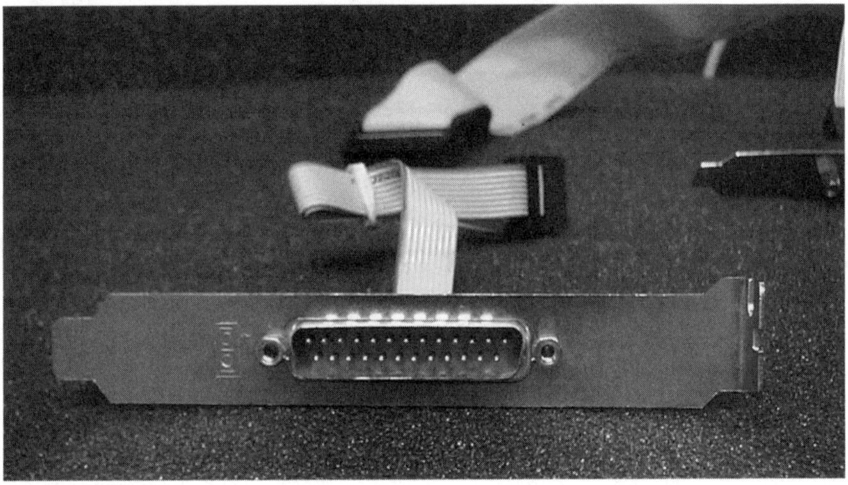

The most common DB connectors in the networking world are the female DB-15 connectors used on 10Base5 Ethernet networks and the female DB-9s used on older Token Ring cards. The Network+ exam assumes that you know these connectors as well as the standard connectors used in the back of PCs, such as the female DB-25 (parallel ports) and the male DB-9 or DB-25 (serial ports). See Figure 8.11.

FIGURE 8.11
Serial and parallel ports on the back of a PC.

Be aware that the multi-function aspect of DB connectors can lead to confusion because totally different devices could use the exact same DB connector. 10Base2 NICs, joysticks, and MIDI (Musical Industry Digital Interface) cards, for example, all use the female DB-15 connector. If you see a female DB-25, it might be a parallel port or a SCSI connector (see SCSI later in this chapter).

How is it possible to determine the function of one of these connectors? The trick is first, to know that female DB-25 and DB-15 connectors are notorious for multiple uses. Second, know the functions of these connectors. Almost every PC has a soundcard which will have a female DB-15. It will also have microphone and speaker connections. Figure 8.12 shows a typical soundcard. Note the microphone and speaker connections.

Figure 8.13 shows a 10Base5 card. Will a 10Base2 have speaker connections? Of course not! Familiarity with the functions of these connections means it takes little more than common sense to know "which connector is which!"

FIGURE 8.12
Soundcard connections.

FIGURE 8.13
10Base5 card.

Another connector to watch for is the "Centronics" connector. These are not DB connectors, but tend to get dumped in with DB when techs discuss connectors. Centronics connectors are the D-shaped connectors on the back of printers. They do not have true pins. Instead, they utilize a single "blade" that contains some number of flat tabs that make the connection. Though these connectors do not truly have pins, the term "pins" is still used with Centronics to reflect the number of tabs. Centronic connectors have both female and male versions but only come in two common sizes: 36-pin ones on the back of printers and the increasingly rare 50-pin connectors used with SCSI devices. Figure 8.14 shows the female 36-pin Centronics printer connector.

FIGURE 8.14

36-pin Centronics.

Make sure to know all the DB connectors—even if they are not used for network connections. Network+ loves to make questions that include bizarre combinations such as "male DB-35" in an effort to catch those who don't know their connectors. DB (and Centronics) connectors are common on every PC and can have multi-function aspects that make for some absolutely excellent (or tricky, depending how you look at it) questions that are easy to miss unless one is familiar with the connector uses.

Fiber Optic

Fiber optic cabling has its own unique connectors. Didn't this whole "connectors" section start with the premise that no network connections are unique and that the same connectors used for NICs can be found in other devices? Didn't we just show some examples of this multiple use idea with BNC, RJ, and DB connectors?

Yes we did. But what would the computer business be without the obligatory exception! Combining fiber optics and PC networks is a recent phenomenon. The PC industry had a large part in the process of figuring out how fiber would be used to connect PCs. Fiber optics existed before PC networks, but the existing connectors were somewhat strange and hard to use. To jumpstart fiber on PCs, the industry created special connectors that are tough, easy to stick on to the end of a piece of fiber optic cable, and easy to insert and remove. This makes the exception to the rule a good one. Let's look the fiber optic connectors.

The fact that the PC industry participated in the development of fiber optic cabling kept fiber optics connectors from suffering the "too many different connectors" headache we have seen with earlier network connections. There are only two common types of fiber optic connections, the "SC" and the "ST" connectors (Figure 8.15).

FIGURE 8.15
SC and ST connectors.

Both are common and interchangeable. No networking technology is locked into one or the other. 100BaseTX and 100BaseT4 networks, for example, use either or both types of connectors.

In networks, fiber optics mostly connect hubs, switches, and routers, rather than going directly to PCs. Although rare, "fiber to the desktop" is utilized in situations where speed and security become more important than cost. Fiber optic NICs are very expensive (Figure 8.16).

The ST and SC connectors control the overwhelming majority of fiber installations within the world of PC networking, but are certainly not the only connectors. Some fiber networks use a special networking topology called Fiber Distributed Data Interface (FDDI). FDDI networks use a unique connector (Figure 8.17).

FIGURE 8.16

A fiber optic NIC with SC connectors.

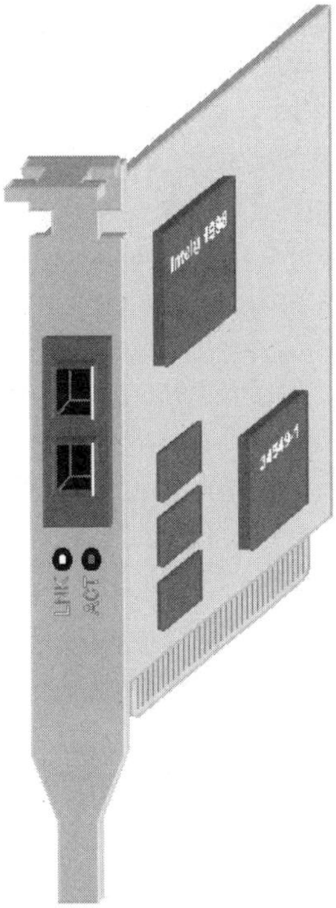

FIGURE 8.17

FDDI connectors.

FDDI connectors are rare, but you may see them on the exam as a possible type of fiber optic connection.

Adding network connections to a standalone PC requires you to "know your connections!" Many connections on a standalone PC are unique. The one-of-a-kind female, three-row DB-15 video connector cannot be confused with any other connector. The classic "AT"-style keyboard connector has no other type of connector anything like it on a PC. When network functions are added to the PC, the variety of connectors can sometimes get confusing. Mentally separate all these connectors into four groups: BNC, DB, RJ, and fiber. This will facilitate the process of memorizing these different connectors for the exam, and for your work. Armed with the understanding of these many connectors—or at least being able to tell one from the other—we can now look at the ways PCs connect to networks and match up the networking technology to the connector.

It is easy, and incorrect, to assume that "connecting to the network" instantly means using a NIC. The NIC is certainly the most common method for taking a standalone PC and hooking it to a network cable, but many other methods to connect to a network exist. Modems run a not-too-distant second to NICs for network connections. Literally millions of PCs connect to the Internet daily via dialup modems. Modems and NICs perform nearly all of the network connections in PC networks. There is one more, rarely used but of interest to Network+: serial port-to-serial port connections. Let's look at all three, starting with NICs.

The NICs

The NIC provides the PC with a method of sending and receiving data from other systems by connecting the PC to the network's cabling structure. Every combination of networking technology and cabling will have its own type of NIC. For the most part, these cards cannot be interchanged. Every PC in a 10BaseT network, for example, uses a 10BaseT card. Every PC in a 100BaseTX network uses a 100BaseTX card. A 4-megabit Token Ring network uses nothing but 4-megabit Token Ring NICs. Each combination of topology, cable, and connections for a particular network technology requires a different NIC, and they are in no way compatible.

But what would a rule be in the PC world without the inevitable exceptions? Some NICs work with more than one network technology/cable/connection. Figure 8.18 shows a common example. Note the BNC and the RJ-45 connector. This card works with either a 10BaseT or a 10Base2 Ethernet network. These multiple-connector cards are generically known as "combo cards."

FIGURE 8.18
Typical Ethernet combo card.

There are a number of different types of combo cards. Figure 8.19 shows a card that can run 10BaseT, 10Base2, and 10Base5.

Combo cards are for the most part limited to Ethernet. Other network technologies either use one type of connector exclusively or, as in the case of Token Ring, often use media filters at the MSAU or NIC to enable differently connected cards to work together (Figure 8.20).

Many NICs operate at more than one speed using the same network technology. Any NIC that can run at more than one speed is called a "multi-speed" NIC. These cards are very popular today, especially NICs that run in 10BaseT and 100BaseT networks. Some multi-speed NICs will automatically detect and adjust themselves to the speed of the network without any configuration. These multi-speed cards are often referred to as "Auto-sensing" NICs. Many network administrators prefer to use these cards in 10BaseT networks as a hedge against the chance that they might one day upgrade their networks to 100BaseT. A network of PCs using auto-sensing 10/100BaseT NICs can change from a 10BaseT to a 100BaseT simply by changing out the hubs (assuming the cabling is correct). The card shown in Figure 8.21 is a multi-speed, auto-sensing NIC. It works on either a 10BaseT or a 100BaseTX network.

FIGURE 8.19
Ethernet three-way combo card.

FIGURE 8.20
Token Ring media filter.

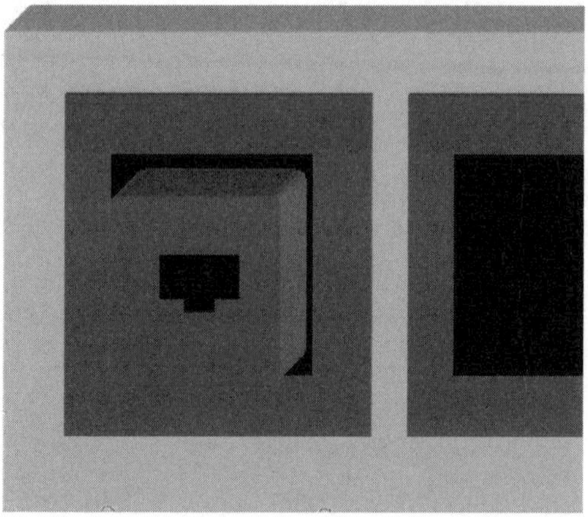

Multi-speed is in no way limited to Ethernet networks. Many Token Ring NICs can switch between 4 megabits and 16 megabits. They can also be auto-sensing.

FIGURE 8.21
Multi-speed NIC.

NICs that run in different cabling or speeds of the same networking technology are very popular and quite common. No NIC yet invented, however, can operate with more than one network technology. For example, no one has yet made a NIC that can handle both Ethernet and Token Ring. If you have a Token Ring network, you will buy Token Ring NICs. If you have an Ethernet network, you will purchase Ethernet NICs.

As you might imagine, there are hundreds of different types of NICs. While most NICs are unique to a particular network technology, cabling type, or speed, some NICs can handle more than one type of cable, more than one speed, or both. As a person who wants to pass the Network+ exam and also work on networks, you must be able to identify these different network cards quickly. In some cases, different network cards look absolutely identical at first glance and you must inspect them closely for proper identification. These next few sections will match up the types of NICs to the different network technologies, cables, and speed, and give you some rules and tricks of identification so that you don't make silly mistakes like buying 2200 100BaseT4 cards when you should have purchased 2200 100BaseTX cards. (Not that *anyone* has actually *done this*!)

Ethernet NICs

Ethernet NICs are by far the most common NICs today. It is difficult to get an absolutely dependable statistic, but probably safe to say that 95% of all new installations use Ethernet in one way or another. Ethernet is also the most complicated topology by virtue of the vast number of cable types and speeds. While this has been covered in Chapters 1 and 2, here we will consolidate all the different connectors and inspect their separate nuances. We will also throw in a few types of Ethernet not yet covered—you need not know these for the test, but you may see the terms. A rundown of the different types of Ethernet and their connections follows.

10Base5 (ThickNet)

10Base5 NICs use a female, 15-pin DB connector, as shown in Figure 8.22. Officially, this connector is called a "DIX" (Digital-Intel-Xerox) connector. The DIX connector goes to the AUI (Attachment Unit Interface). The AUI is the cable and a device called the "transceiver." As a result, many people call the DIX connector the AUI.

FIGURE 8.22
DIX connector.

10Base2 (ThinNet)

10Base2 NICs have a BNC connector, as shown in Figure 8.23. The BNC connector attaches to the network cable via a "T" connector.

FIGURE 8.23

BNC connector.

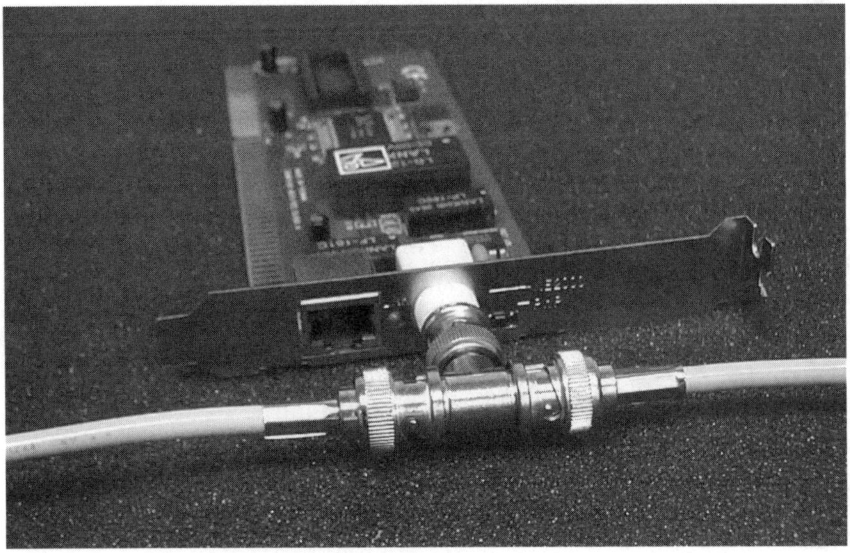

10BaseT

10BaseT NICs all use the RJ-45 connector. The cable runs from the NIC to a hub or a switch (Figure 8.24).

FIGURE 8.24

RJ-45 connector.

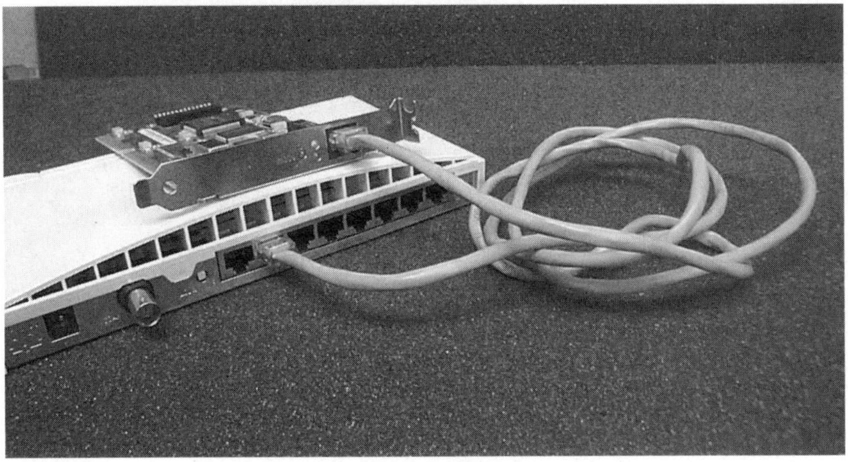

100BaseTX, 100BaseT4, 100BaseVGAnyLAN

100BaseTX, 100BaseT4, and 100BaseVGAnyLAN are three competing networking technologies for running Ethernet at 100 megabits per second. All of them use RJ-45 connectors. The difference between these technologies is in the quality and the number of wires used in the network cabling (see Chapter 2).

10BaseFL, 100BaseFX

The 10BaseFL and 100BaseFX standards are the most common (>99%) of the implementations for running Ethernet over fiber optic cable. As their names suggest, 10BaseFL runs at 10 megabits per second while 100BaseFX clips along at 100 megabits per second. Either SC or ST connections are used on their NICs, even by cards from the same manufacturer (Figure 8.25).

FIGURE 8.25
100BaseFX card.

Gigabit Ethernet

Gigabit Ethernet defines a number of network technologies, all under the Ethernet banner, that have data transfer rates of 1000 megabits per second. These very fast new standards are rapidly becoming popular where speed is important. All require very powerful and very expensive switches and live in the world of network backbones. There are very few Gigabit Ethernet NICs. While Gigabit Ethernet is fantastically fast, from a connection standpoint, it uses the standard RJ-45 (copper-based 1000BaseT) or an ST/SC connector (fiber optic-based 1000BaseSX or 1000BaseLX).

Token Ring NICs

In this Ethernet-centric world, many network users tend to look at IBM's Token Ring as yesterday's papers. This is wrong. Granted, finding a new Token Ring installation is about as easy as 50-yard-line tickets to a Packers/Dallas football game, but Token Ring continues to enjoy a huge installed base. If you need proof that Token Ring is alive and well, simply browse any of the leading NIC manufacturers' Web sites. Notice that they all continue to sell Token Ring cards, because the demand still exists. Token Ring is most definitely doing fine.

Token Ring NIC connectors come in two types. The older and still quite common connector is a female DB-9. This cable runs from the back of the PC to an MSAU (Multi-Station Access Unit). Figure 8.26 shows a typical MSAU.

FIGURE 8.26
Token Ring DB-9.

The newer and increasingly more common connector is an RJ-45. The Token Ring powers-that-be realized that to keep market share, they needed to make Token Ring more compatible with the existing UTP cables in the walls of so many offices today. Thus Token Ring incorporated the RJ-45 (Figure 8.27).

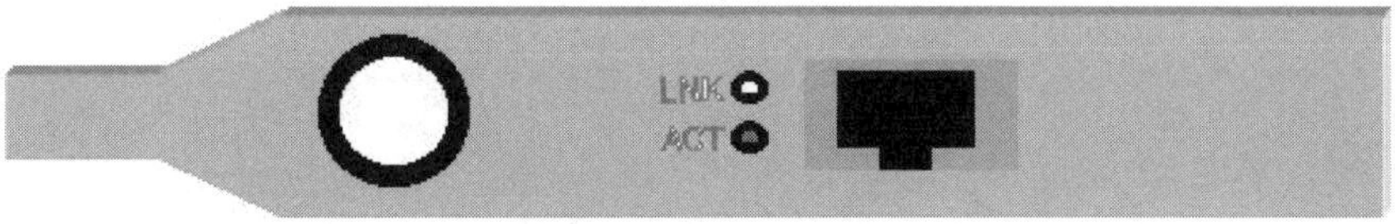

FIGURE 8.27
Token Ring RJ-45.

This Token Ring card suddenly looks a lot like a 10BaseT card, doesn't it?

The problem of trying to recognize what type of connector goes with what NIC is complicated by the realization that lots of networking technologies use the exact same connector—in particular the RJ-45. How is it possible to tell whether the NIC in your hand with an RJ-45 connection is for 10BaseT, 100BaseTX, or Token Ring? The answer is that you can't always tell, although there are some clues. An RJ-45/BNC combo card, for example, pretty well guarantees that the RJ-45 is for 10BaseT. In addition, most cards will have some information printed on the card itself. Everybody who makes Token Ring cards gives them a Token Ring sounding name. If you see a word like "TokenLink" printed on the card you have a reliable clue. Last, you should know if you have a Token Ring or an Ethernet network.

Separating between Token Ring and Ethernet is usually fairly easy. But now that you know you have an Ethernet RJ-45 NIC, how do you know if it is 10BaseT, 100BaseTX, etc? This is harder. First of all, know your network and the cards that you buy. If you don't buy 100BaseTX cards, then it's not going to be 100BaseTX. Then, know your model numbers. Every NIC has a manufacturer's model number that you can use to determine the exact capabilities of the card. The model number is always printed on the card. Last, pray that the NIC is plug-and-play (PnP) and stick it in a Windows 95/98 system. The PnP should recognize the card and give you some text clue about what type of card you have (Figure 8.28).

FIGURE 8.28 *Windows 98 plug-and-play.*

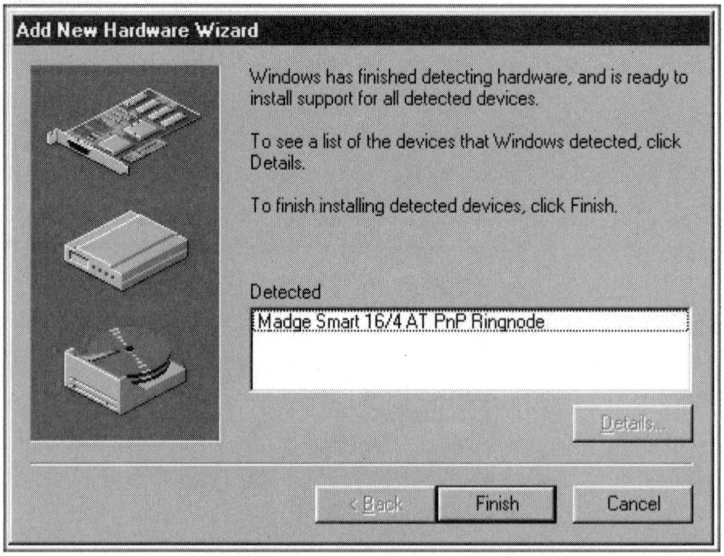

Do You See the Light?

Almost every NIC made today has some type of lights—really LEDs (Light Emitting Diodes)—shining on the back of the card (Figure 8.29). (Now that you know they are really LEDs, call them "lights" just like all the other network techs.) NICs with lights are usually limited to Ethernet network technologies that use RJ-45 (10BaseT, 100BaseT, etc.) and to Token Ring cards. Don't be surprised if an old 10Base2 card has no lights. In most cases, NICs with lights will have two of them. These lights make troubleshooting a NIC much easier, giving you clues about what's happening. One light is a connection light. It tells you that the NIC is connected to a hub (or MSAU in Token Ring). Hubs also have a connect light, enabling you to check the connectivity at both ends of the cable. If a PC cannot access a network, it is nice to look in the back and be sure that the cleaning person did not accidentally unplug the card during the night.

FIGURE 8.29
Typical lights on 10BaseT NIC.

Don't laugh! When a network problem arises, especially a problem with a networked PC that ran well previously, the first item to check (depending on the symptom) is whether it is plugged in or not. There have been too many situations where some overly certified network honcho did not have the common sense to check such basic things as whether or not the connect light is lit!

The second light is the activity light. It will flicker erratically when the card detects network traffic. The activity light is a lifesaver for detecting problems. The connection light will sometimes lie. If the connection light is good, the next step is to try to copy a file or something to create network traffic. If the activity light does not flicker, there is a problem.

There is no guarantee that a NIC will even have these lights. They can be any color and sometimes there might only be one light. Lights are extremely handy troubleshooting tools; refer to the troubleshooting chapter for more details on how to use the lights to detect network trouble.

The Modems

Modems (Modulator Demodulator) stand second only to NICs as the most common way to connect PCs to networks. For some reason, the idea of a modem as a network connection confuses those new to networking. They want to separate the idea of dialing up from using a NIC. This problem tends to show up more in techs who remember the days when a modem was used to dial up private bulletin boards, before the Internet became so common. All network operating systems look at a modem as nothing more than another type of NIC. Windows 95/98 even shows the modem as an adapter in the Network Properties window. Go to a networked Windows 95 or 98 system with a modem installed and right-click on Network Neighborhood; select Properties. This displays something like Figure 8.30.

Modems take analog serial data (the phone line) and turn it into digital serial data. There are two types of modems, internal and external. Internal modems go inside the PC and external modems are small boxes that connect to the PC via a serial port (Figure 8.31).

Once a modem has turned the analog phone signal into a digital signal, the data must then be changed to a digital format that the PC can understand. That's where the serial port comes in. The serial connector leads to a special chip called a UART (Universal Asynchronous Receiver/Transmitter) (see Figure 8.32).

The UART takes digital serial data from the modem and converts it into parallel data that makes sense to the PC. A serial port is really just a connection to a UART. External modems do not have UARTs and must connect to a serial port on the PC. Internal modems are really a UART and a modem on one card. An internal modem, therefore, brings its own UART to the PC. There are many types of UARTs, but the only one worth purchasing—and by now the only one you *can* buy—is called a 16550 UART. The 16550 can run serial ports at 115,600 bits per second—faster than the fastest modems.

FIGURE 8.30

Network properties in Windows 98.

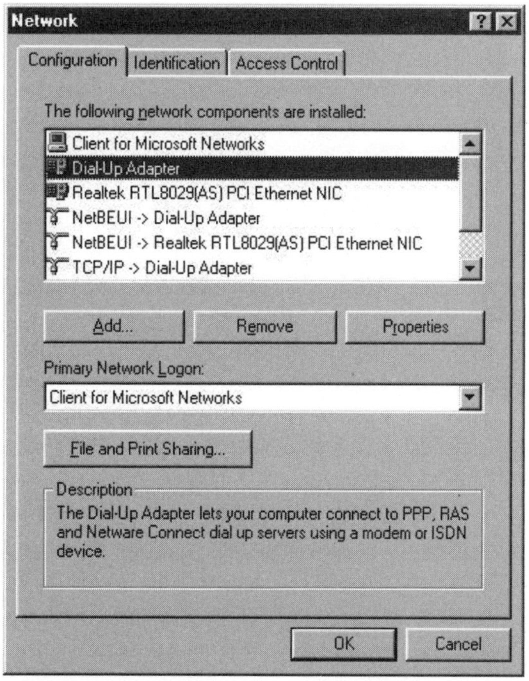

FIGURE 8.31

Internal and external modems.

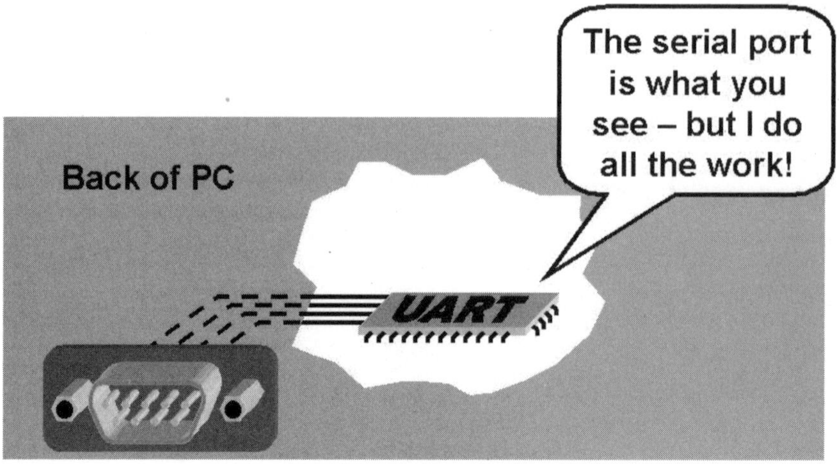

FIGURE 8.32
UART and serial port.

Phone lines have a speed based on a unit called a *baud*, a cycle per second. The fastest baud rate a phone line can achieve is 2400 baud. Modems can pack multiple bits of data into each baud. A 33.6K bps (bits per second) modem, for example, packs 14 bits into every baud. (2400 x 14 = 33.6K) It is technically incorrect to say, "I have a 56K baud modem." You should say, "I have a 56K bps modem." But people use the term baud instead of bps so often that the terms have become functionally synonymous.

Looking at a modem as nothing more than another NIC makes sense. Modems have a few extra requirements during installation, but generally they still need the same items a NIC does. The other nice thing about modems is that there is only one type of connection—good old RJ-11 (Figure 8.33).

One RJ-11 connector goes to the phone jack; the other makes it possible to install a telephone. Compared to NICs, modems are trivial to identify. Modems come in a number of speeds and other important controls. Refer to Chapter 9 for details on modems.

System Resources

This section assumes you know your system resources. If you are not aware of system resources, the short descriptions given here are sufficient to pass the Network+ exam. Any good tech, however, should know them in better detail. For those who do not, here is the condensed version. For a detailed study of system resources, get *A+ Certification Exam Guide* by Mike Meyers.

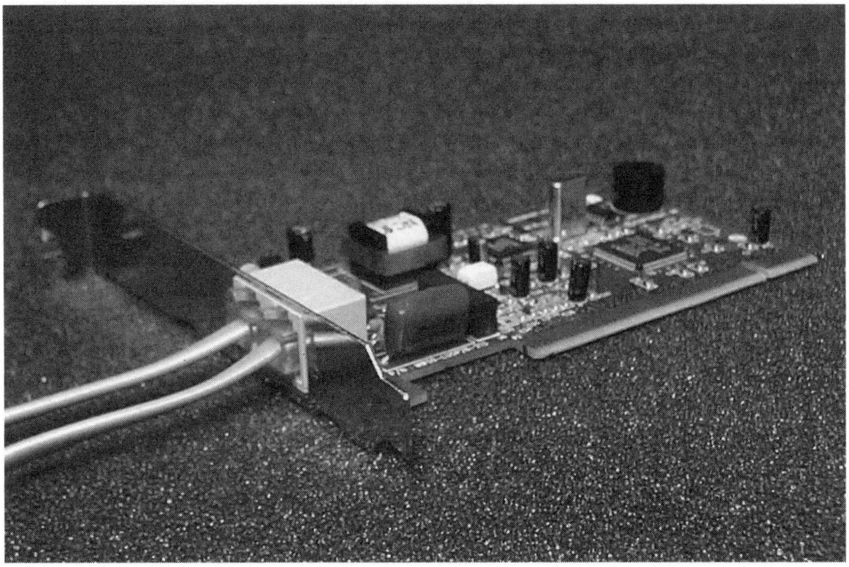

FIGURE 8.33
Internal modem, showing RJ-11.

Modems and NICs require system resources in order to function properly. Don't worry about *how* to set these resources at this point; just be aware that they exist. We will examine the process of setting system resources next.

"System resources" is a Microsoft term, now part of tech vernacular, that describes four totally different PC functions. The first of these functions is the *Interrupt Request (IRQ)*. Every device that wants to tell the CPU that it needs to talk to that particular device must have an assigned IRQ. Virtually every device in the PC uses an IRQ. Certainly, all NICs and modems must have an assigned IRQ. There are a number of IRQs on a PC, but required devices such as hard drives and floppy occupy many. Here is the complete IRQ list and the devices that use them:

IRQ	Default function	Available?
IRQ 0	System timer	No
IRQ 1	Keyboard	No
IRQ 2/9	Open for use	Yes
IRQ 3	Serial ports	Yes
IRQ 4	Serial ports	Yes
IRQ 5	Second parallel port	Yes
IRQ 6	Floppy drive	No
IRQ 7	Primary parallel port	No
IRQ 8	Real-time clock	No
IRQ 10	Open for use	Yes
IRQ 11	Open for use	Yes
IRQ 12	Open for use	Yes
IRQ 13	Math-coprocessor	No
IRQ 14	Primary hard drive controller	No
IRQ 15	Secondary hard drive controller	No

Don't let this table deceive you. Only one device can use a particular IRQ. If you have installed a sound card using IRQ 10, for example, you cannot use IRQ 10 for your NIC. Be aware of the fact that if the default device is not using an IRQ, the IRQ is open for use. Looking again at the table, note that IRQ 5 is for a second parallel port. Most PCs do not have a second parallel port. IRQ 5, therefore, is pretty much always available on a PC.

The second, and also required, system resource is called the *I/O Address*. *Every* device in the PC has an I/O address. Think of the I/O address as the "phone number" for a particular device. A four-digit hexadecimal number designates I/O addresses. Here are a few examples of common I/O addresses on a PC:

0060	Keyboard
01F0	Primary hard drive controller
03F0	Floppy-drive controller
0300	NIC

Both NICs and modems absolutely require I/O addresses and IRQs. If you install either of these, you must give the NIC or modem an unused I/O address and IRQ. There are two other system resources that NICs *might* need: a *DMA channel* and a *memory address*. Modems need only an I/O address and an IRQ; they never need these other two system resources.

DMA stands for "Direct Memory Access" and is used by a few devices, notably sound cards and the floppy drive, to talk directly to RAM without any intervention by the CPU. Many years ago, DMA was a popular method of speeding up a device, but with today's very fast computers, it is rarely used (aside from the two exceptions already noted). A DMA channel is a wire used by the device to perform a DMA. There are seven DMA channels on the PC:

DMA Channel	Default Function	Available?
DMA 0/4	System	No
DMA 1	Open for Use	Yes
DMA 2	Floppy Drive	No
DMA 3	Open for Use	Yes
DMA 5	Open for Use	Yes
DMA 6	Open for Use	Yes
DMA 7	Open for Use	Yes

Modern NICs rarely require DMA, but be aware that DMA is a system resource and that a NIC might need to have a DMA assigned when it is installed. DMA channels should be treated exactly like IRQs: no two devices should ever share a DMA channel.

The fourth and last system resource is the *memory address*. Some NICs must have a tiny amount of RAM set aside for their own use. The memory address is the location of this "set aside" RAM. Memory addresses are defined by two eight-digit memory addresses. Very few devices except video cards still use memory addresses in modern PCs. Here is an example of a memory location used by the video card:

000A0000-000AFFFF Video Graphics

Most NICs today do not require memory addresses, but a number still do.

It is not critical to understand exactly *what* a system resource is. Just remember that there are four of them: IRQ, I/O address, DMA, and memory address, and that all NICs and modems will need an I/O address and an IRQ. Only NICs might need a DMA channel or a memory address.

When the people at IBM first invented the PC, they realized that some users might have trouble setting IRQs and I/O addresses. To make device configuration easier, IBM defined preset combinations of I/O addresses and IRQs for the serial and parallel connectors. IBM called these preset combinations *ports* to reflect that the serial and parallel ports would function as *data portals*. They called serial ports *COM ports* and the parallel ports *LPT ports*. These ports are still used today. Here's the list of ports as defined by IBM:

Port Name	I/O address	IRQ
COM1	03F8	4
COM2	02F8	3
COM3	03E8	4
COM4	02E8	3
LPT1	0378	7
LPT2	0278	5

Ports enable people to install serial and parallel devices without having to worry too much about resources. If you want to install an external modem, for example, you simply plug it into one of the two built-in serial ports. In the original IBM PC, the first serial port was preset as I/O address 03F8 and IRQ4 (COM1). The other serial port was preset as I/O address 02F8 and IRQ3 (COM2). This configuration is common today. Plug the modem into one serial port or the other and then configure the modem software to look on the correct port simply by selecting the appropriate COM port number from a list. Internal modems came (and still do) with their own built-in serial port. Instead of setting an I/O address and an IRQ on an internal modem, you set a COM port on the modem. You do not have to know that selecting a COM port actually sets the I/O address and IRQ, you just set the COM port and it works. COM and LPT ports were a handy item years ago, and remain useful today.

Ports can also cause confusion. Philip's system has a serial mouse installed on COM1. That means that IRQ 4 is used. No other device can use IRQ 4. If you accidentally installed, say, a modem and used IRQ 4, his computer would lock up the moment he tried to use either the mouse or the modem. That is, as we say in the business, a "bad" thing. But it was easy to do since nobody knew that COM1 was, by definition, I/O address 03F8 and IRQ4. The few techs who understood this back in the "bad old days" made a mint.

To make matters worse, notice that COM1 and COM3 share IRQ4 while COM2 and COM4 shared IRQ3. That means that you cannot have a device using COM1 and COM3 (or COM2 and COM4) at the same time. If you try, they will lock up.

Fortunately, most internal modems can use non-standard IRQs for their COM ports. Mabel's PC, for example, has devices installed on COM1 and COM2. You need to install an internal modem in her system. The modem must have a COM port. You set it to COM3 (and create a potential IRQ conflict), but then set the IRQ to something like IRQ 10. Assuming that no device uses IRQ 10, everything works perfectly.

Before Windows 95, the process of installing devices, including NICs and modems, was only performed by techs with an intimate knowledge of system resources and ports. The introduction of Windows 95 brought a powerful new standard called *plug-and-play (PnP)*. PnP is a combination of smart PCs, smart devices, and smart operating systems that automatically configures all the necessary system resources. With plug-and-play operating properly, there is no need to know anything about system resources or ports. The computer handles all of these details automatically. All new—and not so new—NICs and modems are PnP.

If PnP is so great, why even discuss system resources? Three issues require network technicians to have a thorough understanding of resources. First and perhaps most shocking, PnP does not always work perfectly and occasionally requires a little manual configuration. Second, millions of older devices came out before PnP. These "legacy" devices require you to understand system resources in detail. Third, and possibly the most important, Network+ tests you on system resources. Know your resources!

Installing Modems and NICs

Now that we have a basic understanding of system resources, we can march through the process of installing NICs and modems. Any device installed in a PC must have three things. First, it must be physically installed. Second, it must be assigned unused system resources—either by plug-and-play or manually. Third, you (or PnP) must install the proper drivers for the card.

Physical Connections

First, plug the card in. One thing is sure, if you do not plug the NIC or modem into the computer, it is not going to work! Fortunately, physically inserting the modem or NIC into the PC is the easiest part of the job. If the card is not PnP, however, you must determine the available system resources and then find out how to set resources before installing the card. The best way to determine available unused resources is a third-party utility such as Touchstone's CheckIt. If you install on Windows 95/98, use the Device Manager to determine open resources by clicking on the Computer icon, as shown in Figure 8.34.

FIGURE 8.34

Device manager.

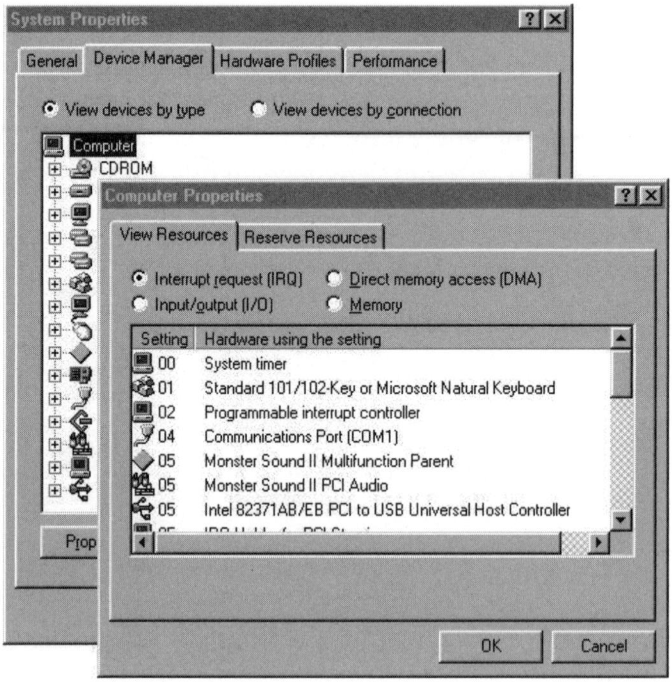

After settling on the open resources you want to use, determine how to set those resources for your non-PnP card. This is normally done with a special software utility on the driver disk or through tiny jumpers on the card (see Figure 8.35).

FIGURE 8.35
Typical jumpers.

If the card is PnP, you may still need to deal with jumpers. Many PnP cards can have the PnP turned on or off on the card by a jumper. Read the documentation to be sure about jumpers before you install the card.

Most PCs today have two types of expansion slots in the PC. The first, and most common, are the *PCI (Peripheral Component Interconnect)* type. These are 32-bit, fast, self-configuring expansion slots and virtually all new NICs sold today are of the PCI type—and with good reason. PCI's speed enables the system to take full advantage of the NIC (Figure 8.36).

Still present are the old *ISA (Industry Standard Architecture)* slots. These slots date back to the old, 80286 powered IBM "AT" computer and have not changed since then. They are 16-bit and very slow. Most modern PCs still have a few of these old expansion slots, because lots of devices still do not need the speed of PCI and a few slots ensures compatibility. Most modems continue to be ISA—although every modem manufacturer now has PCI modems. There are also still a number of ISA NICs manufactured. ISA is definitely going, but not yet gone (Figure 8.37).

FIGURE 8.36
PCI slots.

FIGURE 8.37
ISA slots.

Techs disagree about whether to buy PCI or ISA. The general consensus is always try to buy PCI NICs. Modems' relatively slow speeds make them good candidates for ISA, although many people worry that ISA will fade away soon. If they buy a PCI modem, they will not be stuck with outdated technology if their next PC doesn't come with ISA slots.

External modems connect to the PC through an available serial port. Almost all PCs come with two serial ports, which are often the male 9-pin type. Most external modems come with a 25-pin connector. That means you will probably need a 9-to-25-pin converter, available at any computer store. Do yourself a favor when you buy an external modem. Before you head for the store or phone, check the serial connectors on the back of the PC. When you get ready to purchase the new external modem, look at the modem's serial connector and the cable that comes with the modem to be sure you can connect. If you're ordering by phone, ask the salesperson. Buy what you need to make the connection. It sure beats getting the new modem home and then realizing the modem won't plug into one of your serial ports!

Watch out for electrostatic discharge—a.k.a. static electricity. Always use proper grounding techniques when working inside the PC. Try to use a grounding strap. If that is not available, touch the power supply before working on the PC to discharge yourself (Figure 8.38).

FIGURE 8.38

Touching the power supply.

At this point, do not bother trying to connect the NIC to the network or the modem to the phone line. We need to test the device first to make sure it is in good shape before trying to contact another system.

Drivers

Every NIC and modem comes with a set of drivers on a floppy disk or CD-ROM. You must install the proper driver. Without the correct driver, the device is not going to work. A popular trick is to copy the drivers onto the PC's hard drive and install from there. That way, if you ever need the drivers again, you will not need to rummage around for the driver disk.

Watch for updated drivers. Try to avoid using any drivers that come with Windows; they tend to be out of date. Drivers are constantly being updated. Check the manufacturer's Web site or at least always use the driver disk.

Assigning Resources

Once you have installed the NIC or modem, start the PC and assign resources. If the system, card, and operating system are all PnP, this is simple. The system will boot, recognize the PnP device, and prompt for the driver disk (Figure 8.39). The rest is automatic, although you will probably need to reboot.

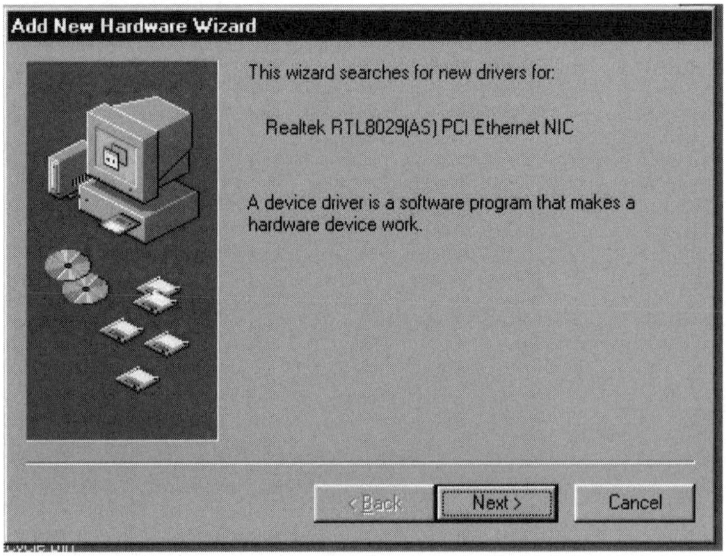

FIGURE 8.39
PnP in action.

If the card is non-PnP, then you have still more work to do. You need to set the resources on the utility that came with the disk. These utilities are almost always DOS programs. Figure 8.40 shows a typical utility.

FIGURE 8.40

NIC configuration utility.

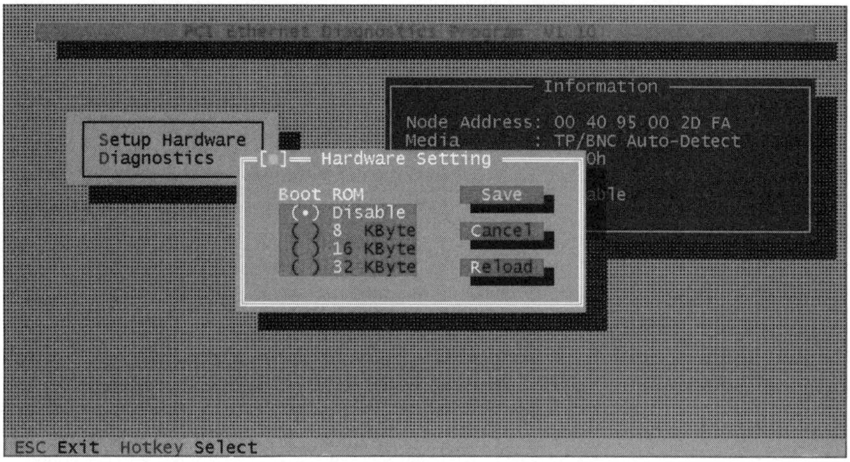

Setting resources for a non-PnP NIC requires a two-step process. First, install the DOS driver and configure the card resources with the setup utility. Second, boot to Windows, go to Device Manager, and set the system resources. The setup utility configures the card; you also need to tell Windows what resources that card requires.

Card Diagnostics

The driver disk provides the most powerful tool to check a NIC. Every NIC's driver disk has a handy utility to test the card. This may be the same utility used to set system resources. Look on the driver disk for it. Like the configuration utility, the testing utilities are usually DOS programs. Here is an example of a diagnostic program in action (Figure 8.41).

Modems rarely have a diagnostic disk. To test a modem, use the popular shareware application Modem Doctor, written by Hank Volpe. It comes in DOS and Windows versions and is the best modem tester available (Figure 8.42).

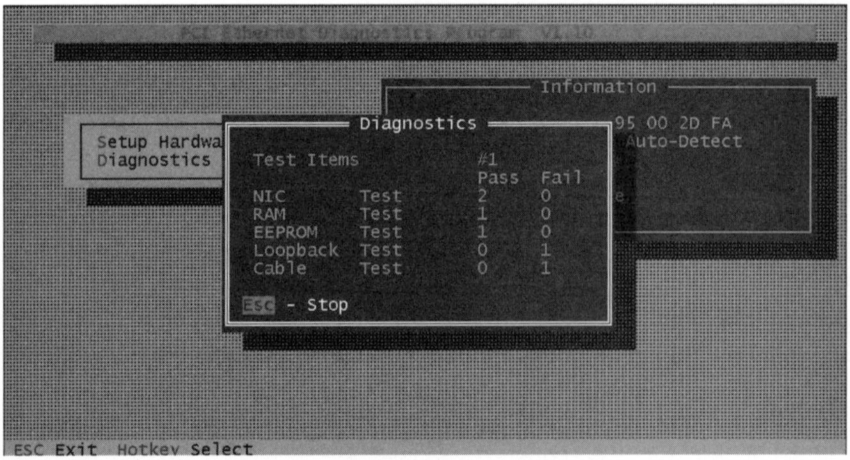

FIGURE 8.41

Diagnostic program.

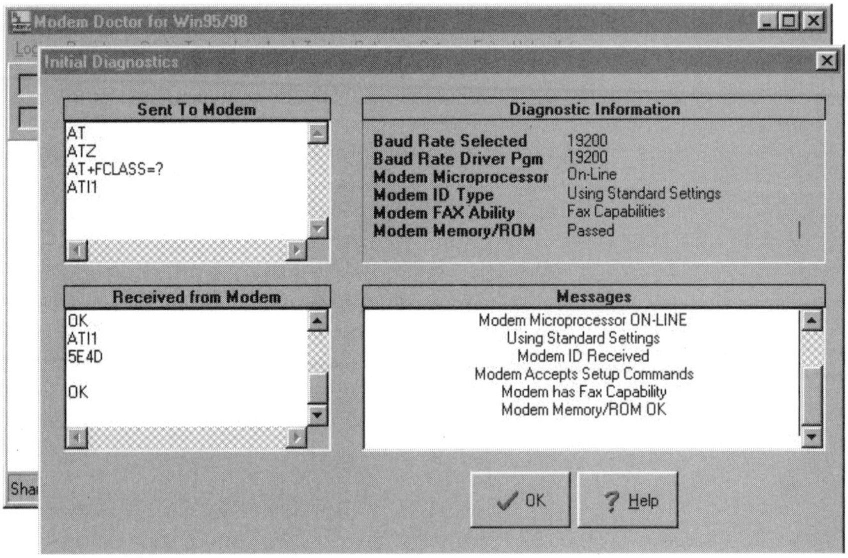

FIGURE 8.42

Modem Doctor.

Once the NIC or modem has tested out properly, you are ready to plug in the network cable or phone line. This will be covered in the next chapter.

Buying NICs and Modems

Be sure always to purchase name-brand modems and NICs. For NICs, stick with big names such as 3Com or Intel. The NICs are better made, have extra features, and are easy to return if defective. It is also easy to replace a missing driver and to be sure that the drivers work well. For modems, try the 3Com (U.S. Robotics) brand.

The type of NIC you purchase really depends on the network. Try to think about the future and go for multi-speed cards if the wallet will accept the extra cost. Always try to stick with the same model of NIC. Every different NIC means another set of driver disks you need to haul around. Keeping the same model of NIC makes driver updates easier.

Buying the right modem is fairly easy. Be sure to get the fastest modem possible. Currently, the fastest modems run at 56Kbps under the V.90 standard. (See the next chapter for details on modem standards.)

Direct Cable Connections

No doubt, NICs and modems are the most common method to connect PCs together. There is one other method—called direct cable connection—that should be addressed for completeness.

All versions of Windows come with the software to enable the direct serial port-to-serial port, parallel-to-parallel, or infrared-to-infrared connection between two PCs called a *direct cable connection*. To connect via serial ports, you need to string a special cable called a *null modem* cable between two PCs. The PCs can then share hard drives, but nothing else. Direct cable connections with serial are very slow at a maximum of 115,600bps, but are a quick, cheap alternative to buying two NICs. Parallel connections require a special *bidirectional* parallel cable.

Protection of Data

The single most important part of most networks is the shared data. The main motivation for networks is the ability for many users to access shared data, which might be as trivial as pre-made forms or as critical as accounts receivable. The sudden loss of data in their networks would cripple most organizations. Computers can be replaced and new employees hired, but it is data that makes most organizations function. Certainly, any good network must include a solid backup plan, but restoring backups takes time and effort. Unless the data are continually backed up, the backups will always be a little dated. Backups are a "last-resort" option. Businesses have failed after the loss of data—even with relatively good backups. The shared data of a network, therefore, should have better protection than the fallback of laboriously having to restore potentially dated backups. A good network must have a method of protecting data so that if a hard drive fails, a network technician can bring the data instantly, or at least very quickly, back online. This requires some sort of "instant backup" or automatic copy of the data stored on a second drive.

Now you need to come up with a way to make data redundant on the serving system. How do you do this? First, you could install a fancy hard drive controller that reads and writes data to two hard drives simultaneously (Figure 8.43). The data on each drive would always be identical. One drive would be the primary drive and the other drive, called the "mirror" drive, would not be used unless the primary drive failed. This process of reading and writing data at the same time to two drives is called *drive mirroring*.

FIGURE 8.43
Mirrored drives.

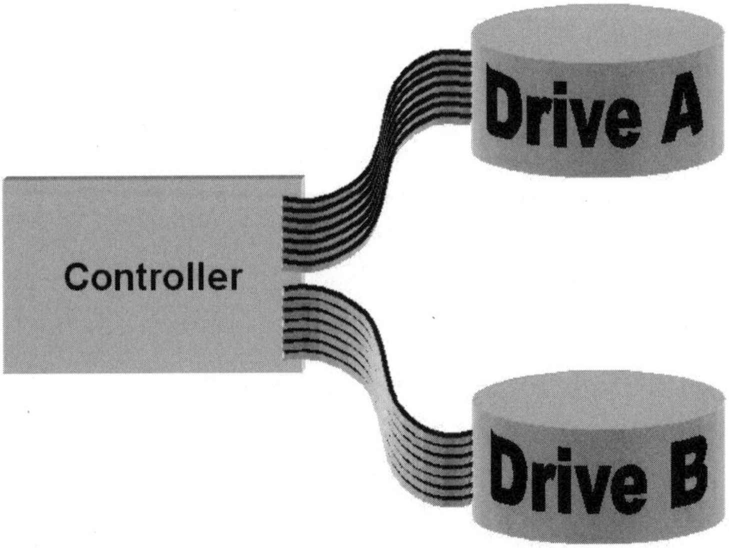

If you really want to make data safe, you can use two separate controllers for each drive. With two drives, each on a separate controller, the system will continue to operate even if the primary drive's controller stops working. This super-drive mirroring technique is called *drive duplexing* (Figure 8.44). Drive duplexing is also much faster than drive mirroring since one controller does not write each piece of data twice.

FIGURE 8.44
Duplexing drives.

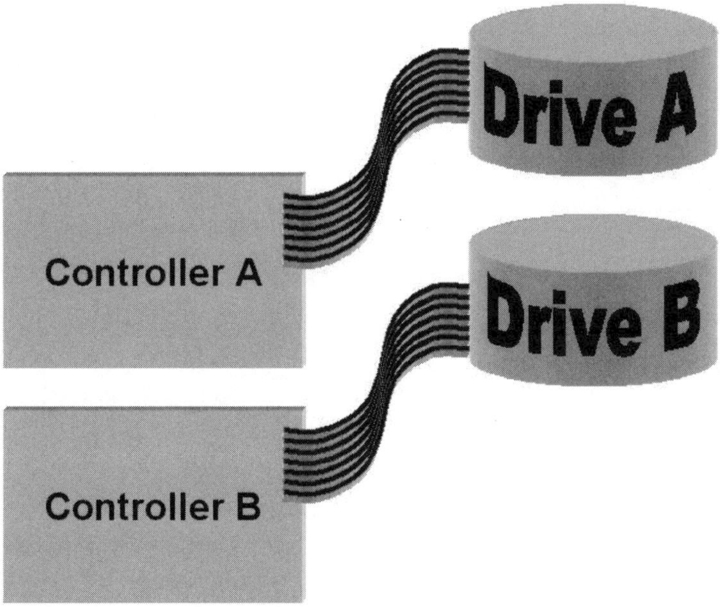

Even though drive duplexing is faster than drive mirroring, they are both slower than the classic one-drive, one-controller setup. The third and most common way to create redundant data is by a method called *disk striping with parity*. *Disk striping* (without parity) means to spread the data among multiple (at least two) drives. Disk striping by itself provides no redundancy. If you save a small Microsoft Word file, for example, the file is split into multiple pieces; half the pieces go on one drive and half on the other (Figure 8.45).

The only advantage of disk striping is speed—it is a very fast way to read from and write to hard drives. If either drive fails all data are lost. Disk striping is not something we ever want to do—unless we don't care about data. Nobody does disk striping.

Disk striping *with parity*, in contrast, protects data. It adds an extra drive, called a parity drive, that stores information that can be used to rebuild data should one of the data drives fail. Let's look at that same Microsoft Word document used earlier. The data are still stored on the two data drives, but this time a calculation is done on the data from each equivalent location on the data drives to create parity information on the parity drive. Parity data are created by a simple, but very accurate calculation. It is similar to dividing two numbers and storing the result of the division. The calculation is not important. The fact that the parity data can be used to rebuild either drive is *very* important.

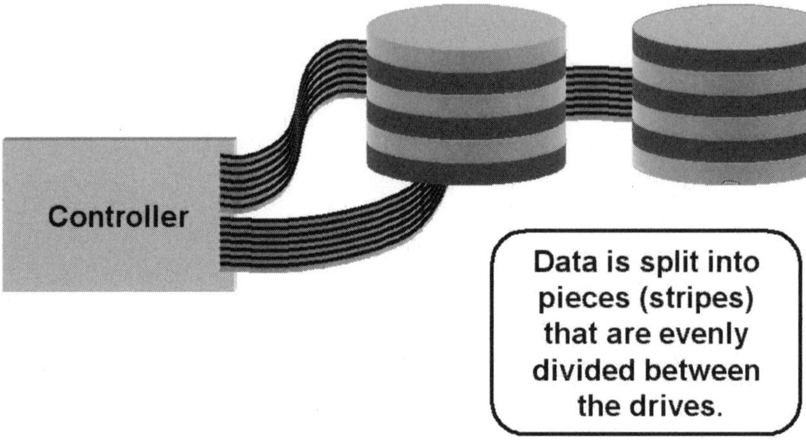
Controller
Data is split into pieces (stripes) that are evenly divided between the drives.

FIGURE 8.45
Disk striping.

Disk striping with parity must have at least three drives, but it is very common to use more than three. Unfortunately, the more drives used, the higher the chance one might fail. Drive striping with parity can only recover data if one drive fails. If two drives fail, you are heading for the backup tapes!

Disk striping with parity combines the best of disk mirroring and plain disk striping. It protects data and is quite fast. The majority of network servers use a type of disk striping with parity.

RAID

The many different techniques of using multiple drives for data protection and increasing speeds were organized by a couple of men at Berkeley back in the '80s. This organization was presented under the name RAID (Random Array of Inexpensive Devices or Random Array of Independent Devices). There are seven official levels of RAID, numbered 0 through 6. They are:

RAID 0	Disk striping.
RAID 1	Disk mirroring and disk duplexing.
RAID 2	Disk striping with multiple parity drives. Unused, ignore it.
RAID 3 and 4	Disk Striping with parity. The differences between the two are trivial.
RAID 5	Disk Striping with parity, but parity information is placed on all drives. This is the fastest way to provide data redundancy. RAID 5 is the most common RAID implementation.
RAID 6	RAID 5 with the added capability of asynchronous and cached data transmission. Think of it as a Super RAID 5.

No network tech says things like "We're implementing disk striping with parity." Use the RAID level. Say, "We're implementing RAID 5." It is more accurate and very impressive to the people in the Accounting Department!

Drive Technologies

Talking about RAID levels is like singing about football. You may sound good, but that does not mean you know what you are talking about. Remember that RAID levels are a general framework; they describe methods to provide data redundancy and enhance the speed of data throughput to and from groups of hard drives. They do not say *how* to implement these methods. There are literally thousands of different methods to set up RAID. The method used depends largely on the desired level of RAID, the operating system used, and the thickness of your wallet. Before we delve into these solutions, we should do a quick run-through of hard drive technologies to clarify a few terms.

EIDE

If you peek into most desktop PCs, you will find hard drives based on the ultra-popular EIDE (Enhanced Intelligent Device Electronics) standard. EIDE drives are always internal—inside the PC. PCs are designed to use up to four EIDE drives. EIDE drives can be identified by their unique 40-pin ribbon cable connection (Figure 8.46).

FIGURE 8.46
EIDE connections.

The price, performance, and ease of installation explain the tremendous popularity of EIDE drives. IDE, the predecessor to EIDE, was exclusively a hard-drive technology. EIDE can accept any type of storage device, including CD-ROMs, tape backups, and removable drives. Even with the ability to handle diverse devices, the PC cannot handle more than the maximum of four EIDE devices.

SCSI

SCSI (Small Computer System Interface) accomplishes much the same goals as EIDE—making hard drives and other devices available to the PC. However, it is not a hard-drive technology. Think instead of SCSI as a mini network that connects many different types of devices. Any type of storage device you can imagine comes in an SCSI version. SCSI manifests itself in PCs via a card called a *host adapter*. The host adapter then connects to SCSI devices in a daisy-chain (see Figure 8.47). An installed set of SCSI devices is called a *SCSI chain*.

Each SCSI device on the SCSI chain must have a unique SCSI ID. SCSI devices are numbered 0 through 7, with 7 usually reserved for the host adapter itself. More advanced versions of SCSI can support up to 16 devices (including the host adapter).

FIGURE 8.47

SCSI chain.

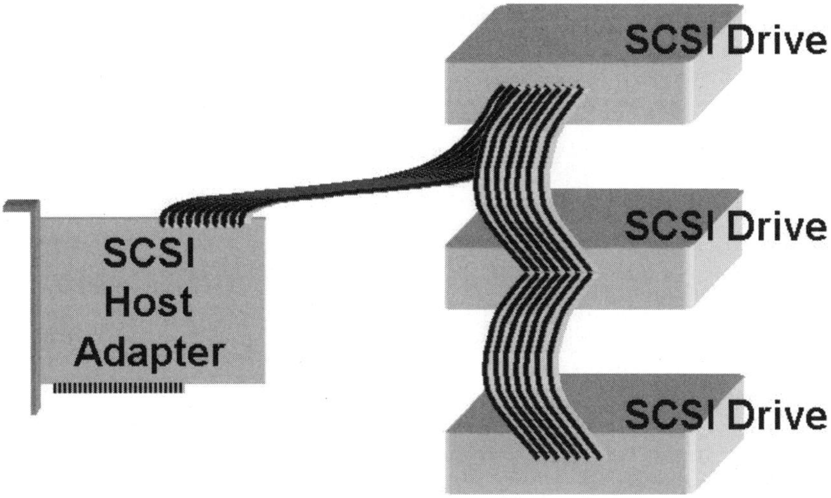

SCSI devices can be internal or external. Better host adapters come with an internal and an external connector, enabling both types of devices to exist on the same SCSI chain. Figure 8.48 shows a SCSI chain with both internal and external devices. Note that each device gets a unique SCSI ID.

FIGURE 8.48

Typical SCSI chain with internal and external devices.

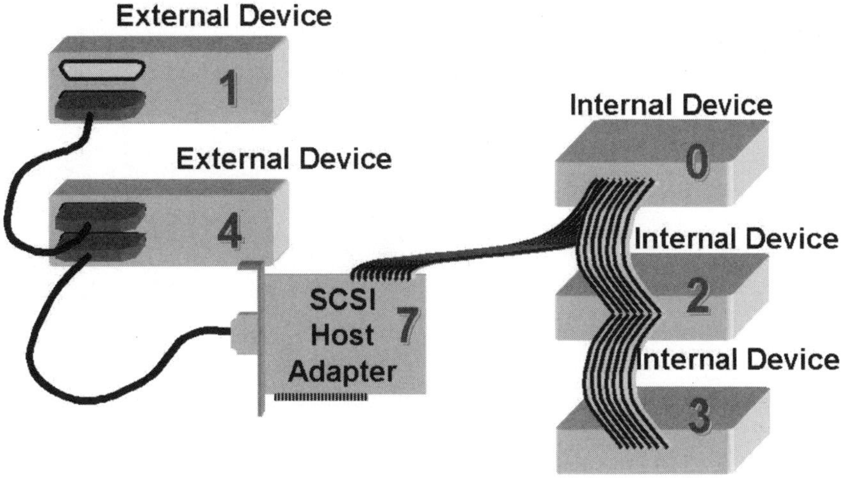

SCSI Connections

Fortunately, the Network+ exam is not interested in your ability to configure SCSI. The exam does demand that you know the many connections unique to SCSI devices. No other class of device has as many connections as SCSI. SCSI has been in existence for a long time and has gone through four distinct standard upgrades, and many variations within each standard, over the years.

SCSI devices can be both external (outside the PC) or internal (inside the PC). This gives SCSI drives an advantage over EIDE. There are two types of internal SCSI connections. Both of these are inserted into a ribbon cable, just like EIDE: the 50-pin "narrow" connection and the 68-pin "wide" SCSI. Figure 8.49 shows a typical 50-pin narrow connection with a ribbon cable attached.

FIGURE 8.49
50-pin "narrow" SCSI connection.

The oldest external SCSI connection is a 50-pin Centronics. Although it is dated, a large number of SCSI devices still use this connector. It looks like a slightly longer version of the printer Centronics (Figure 8.50).

Many host adapters use a female DB-25 connector. The DB-25 has been on Apple computers for many years, but is fairly new to PCs. This SCSI connector is identical to a PC parallel port. See Figure 8.51. If you plug your printer into the SCSI port, or a SCSI device into the printer, it definitely will not work—and in some cases may damage devices.

FIGURE 8.50 *50-pin SCSI Centronics connection.*

We may look the same, but we are totally different!
SCSI Port
Parallel Port

FIGURE 8.51 *Parallel and SCSI connections–both DB-25.*

Most modern SCSI devices now come with the special, SCSI only, "high density" DB connectors. High-density DB connectors look like regular DBs at first, but have much thinner and more densely packed pins. High density DB connectors come in 50-pin and 68-pin versions. The 50-pin version is much more common (Figure 8.52).

They Both Work!

Both EIDE and SCSI drives work beautifully for RAID implementations. People who are new to RAID immediately assume wrongly that RAID requires some special, expensive "stack of SCSI drives." It is certainly possible to spend money on fancy RAID boxes, but it is not necessary. RAID can easily be implemented using nothing but cheap EIDE drives and cheap, sometimes free, software. Further, RAID can use combinations of EIDE and SCSI, although trying to keep track of combinations of SCSI and EIDE drives is not recommended!

FIGURE 8.52
High-density DB-50.

Most people prefer SCSI drives for RAID. They tend to be faster than EIDE drives and more drives can be put into a system (7–15, rather than the 4 of EIDE). The only drawback with SCSI is cost—hard drives are more expensive and you often must purchase a host adapter as well. When speed outweighs cost as a factor—and it usually does for servers—SCSI implementations win. Finally, if serious speed and extra bells and whistles are required, you can install any number of expensive "stack of SCSI drives" solutions.

RAID Implementations

All RAID implementations are either hardware or software methods. Software is often used when price takes priority over performance. Hardware is used when speed and data redundancy are required. The most famous software implementation of RAID is the built-in RAID software that comes with Windows NT/Windows 2000. The NT Disk Administrator can configure drives for RAID 0, 1, or 5, and it works with EIDE and or SCSI (Figure 8.53).

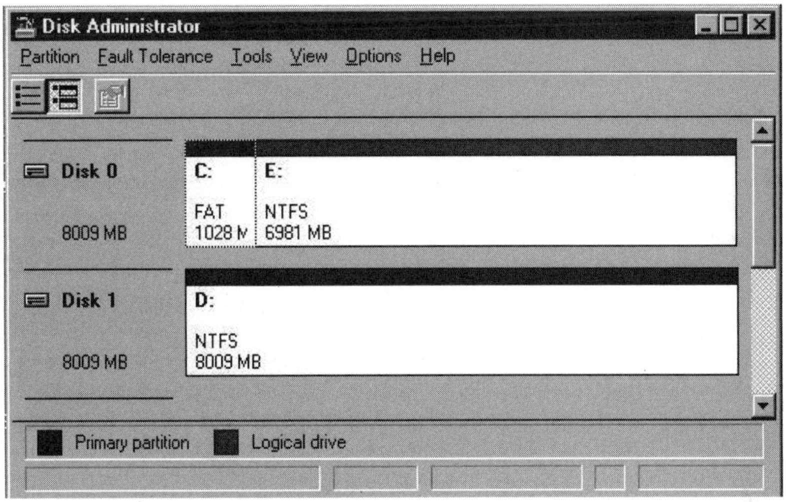

FIGURE 8.53

NT disk administrator.

NT is not the only software RAID game in town. There are a number of third-party software programs available that can be used with other operating systems. There are even third-party software RAID solutions for NT that add a number of extra features beyond what Disk Administrator provides.

Most techs and administrators prefer hardware RAID. Software RAID works for very small RAID solutions, but tends to run quite slowly and usually requires shutting down the PC to reconfigure and replace drives. When you *really* need to keep going, when you need RAID that does not even let the users know there was ever a problem, hardware RAID is the only answer. Since most organizations fit into this latter category, most RAID in the "real world" is hardware based. There are a large number of hardware RAID solutions, and almost all of them rely on SCSI. SCSI can do one thing that EIDE still cannot do—assuming that you have the right type of host adapter, you can yank a bad SCSI drive off an SCSI chain and replace it with another one without even rebooting the server. This "hot-swapping" process is very common in hardware RAID (Figure 8.54).

RAID provides data redundancy. To implement RAID requires deciding the level of RAID to use and whether to go the hardware or software route. For the exam, make sure you can quote the different levels of RAID and know your SCSI connections.

FIGURE 8.54

Hot-swapping a drive.

Tape Backup

Various RAID solutions provide data redundancy to a certain degree, but to secure server data fully, nothing beats a tape backup. If the RAID solution works properly, that tape backup can happily collect dust on an offsite shelf somewhere. In the event of a catastrophic hardware crash, however, such as when two drives in your disk stripe with parity suddenly go to the hardware heaven in the sky, only that tape can save the day.

Magnetic tape is the oldest of all methods for storing data with computers. Who hasn't seen an episode of the old TV shows like "Time Tunnel" or "Voyage to the Bottom of the Sea" and watched the old reel-to-reel tapes spinning merrily in the background? The reel-to-reels are gone, replaced by hard drives, and tapes are now relegated to the world of backup. Nothing can beat magnetic tape's ability to store phenomenal amounts of data cheaply and safely.

Every properly designed network uses a tape backup, so every network tech must learn to use them. The type of tape backup implemented varies from network to network, as do the methods for backing up data. This section covers the types of tape backup; refer to the Troubleshooting chapter for the methods.

There are a dizzying number of tape backup options, each with different advantages and disadvantages. They basically break down into three major groups: QIC, DAT, and DLT. All the groups similarly use cartridge tapes—"square" tapes like fat audio cassettes—but the physical cartridge size, capacity, recording method, tape length, and speed vary enormously.

QIC

QIC (*Quarter Inch Tape*) is an old standard and rarely used in any but the smallest of networks. QIC was one of the first standards used for PC backups, but has gone through many evolutions in an attempt to keep up with the demand for increased capacities over the years. The earliest versions of QIC could store about 40 megabytes—fine for the days when tiny hard drives were the rule, but unacceptable today. There have been a number of increases in QIC capacities, as high as 2 gigabytes, but QIC has fallen out of favor as a desired tape standard. Imation Corporation created an improved QIC format called Travan that is quite popular, again on smaller networks, with capacities up to 8 gigabytes. Under the Travan banner, QIC lives on as a tape backup option. Older QIC/Travan drives used a floppy connection, but EIDE or SCSI connections are more common today.

DAT

DAT (*Digital Audio Tape*) was the first tape system to use a totally digital recording method. DAT was originally designed to record digital audio and video, but has easily moved into the tape backup world. DAT tapes have much higher storage capacities than QIC/Travan tapes—up to 24 gigabytes—and are popular for medium-sized networks. DAT drives use an SCSI connection.

DLT

DLT (*Digital Linear Tapes*) are quickly becoming the tape backup standard of choice. DLT is a relatively new standard that has massive data capacity (up to 70 gigabytes). DLT is very fast, incredibly reliable, and quite expensive compared to earlier technologies. When the data are critical, however, the price of the tape backup is considered insignificant. DLT drives use an SCSI connection.

Data Redundancy Is the Key

Data redundancy provides networks with one of the most important things they need—security. Improper preparation for the day a server hard drive dies leads to many quickly prepared résumés for the suddenly out-of-work network technician. When the data are important enough (and when aren't they), providing data redundancy via RAID solutions is required for the properly designed network.

Speed

A system providing a resource to a network has a tough job. It needs to be able to handle thousands, millions, even billions of transactions over the network to provide that shared resource to other systems. All this work can bring a standard desktop PC to its knees. Anyone who has taken a regular desktop PC and shared a folder or a printer and watched the PC act as though it just shifted into first gear can attest to the fact that sharing resources is a drain on a PC. Systems that share resources, and especially dedicated servers, require more powerful, faster hardware to be able to respond to the needs of the network.

There are a number of methods for making a serving system faster. Making a good server is not just a matter of buying faster or multiple CPUs. You cannot just dump in tons of the fastest RAM. Fast CPUs and RAM are very important, but there are two other critical areas that tend to be ignored—a good server needs fast drives and fast NICs.

Fast NICs

The first place to look for making a server faster is the NIC. Placing the same NIC in your server that you place in your workstations is like putting a garden hose on a fire hydrant—it just is not designed to handle the job. There are a number of methods for making the NIC better suited to the task. You can increase the megabits (the data throughput), make the NIC smarter, make the NIC pickier, and make the NIC do more than one thing at a time.

Increase the Megabits

Mixing 10-megabit and 100-megabit Ethernet on your network can optimize network performance. The trick is to have the server part of the network run at a faster speed than the rest of the network. If you have a 10BaseT network, you can purchase a switch that has a couple of 100 megabit ports. Put a 100BaseT NIC in the server and connect it to one of the 100BaseT connectors on the switch. The server runs at 100 megabits while the workstations run at 10 megabits (Figure 8.55). This optimizes the server speed and, since the server does most of the work in the network, optimizes your network as well.

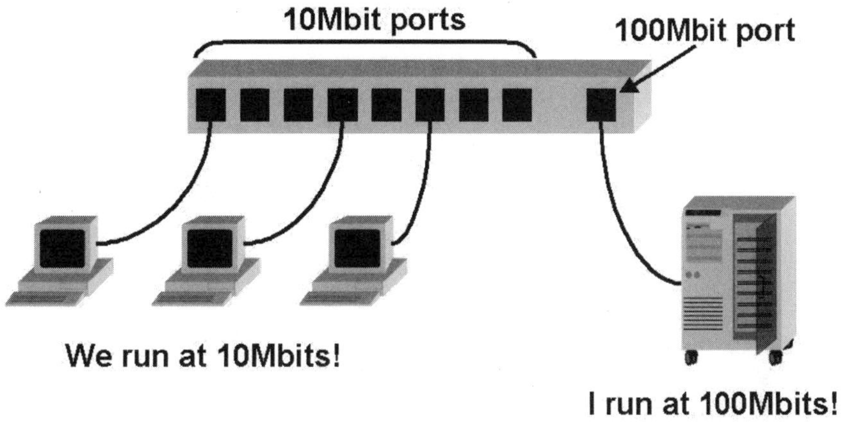

FIGURE 8.55
Server at 100 megabits per second; workstations at 10 megabits per second.

Smarter NICs

Most NICs still need the CPU to handle most of the network job, but several companies make powerful NICs with onboard processors that take most of the work away from the CPU. Every NIC manufacturer has a different method to provide this support and those methods are outside the scope of this book. From a network person's standpoint, just buy a special "server NIC," plug it in, and enjoy the benefits of faster response times.

Full-Duplex NICs

Most network technologies consist of send and receive wires, and most NICs can handle only sending or receiving at a given moment. Full-duplex NICs can send and receive data at the same time, which practically doubles the speed of the network card. Make sure that your server NICs are full duplex, but be warned that you may need to upgrade the server's hub to take advantage of full duplex!

Making the NIC better is one of the easiest upgrades to a server as it usually means only yanking out an inferior NIC and replacing it with something better. At worst, you may even replace a hub or switch. Make your NIC better and you will see the results.

Make the Drives Faster

The other way to make a server faster is to make the process of getting the data to and from the shared drives faster. There are two options here. The first is to get fast drives. Using run-of-the-mill EIDE drives in a busy serving system is not smart. Try using high-performance SCSI drives on a fast controller. It makes a big difference. Second, use RAID 5. Since you probably need it for data protection anyway, you will also enjoy the speed.

It's Not Just Hardware

The demands of networking require servers to have better hardware than a run-of-the-mill standalone PC. Improving CPUs, adding RAM, using powerful NICs, and running fast hard drives all work together to make the serving PC more powerful. But hardware is not the only answer. Good maintenance such as defragging and setting up good disk caches also plays an important role. Many times slow resource access is due to poor network design and is not the fault of the serving system. Be careful about throwing hardware at the slow access issues; it can often be money *not* well spent!

Reliability

The last network function, primarily for serving systems, is reliability. The shared resource must be there when the user needs it. Reliability is achieved by providing a secure environment for the server and by adding redundant hardware to compensate for failed components. There is a nasty tendency to confuse reliability with data protection. All the pretty RAID systems will not do any good if somebody steals the server. Tape backups are useless if the power supply dies. Clearly, other technologies are needed to keep the serving system reliable. There is no logical order to explaining these technologies and safeguards, so we will cover them in no particular order.

Good Power

All the components in the PC run on DC current electrical power. Without clean, steady, DC power, the components stop working. There are a number of steps that electrical power must take between the power company and those components. At any given moment, if one of those steps fails to do its part, the PC no longer works. You can take several actions to safeguard your hardware to make sure this does not happen, starting with the power company.

Electrical power in the U.S. is a wonderful commodity. Electrical service is fairly reliable, and the electricity is generally of high quality. Most people in the U.S. can count on good electrical service 98% of the time. It's that 2% that will get you! Electrical power sometimes stops (power outages) and sometimes goes bad (electrical "spikes" and "sags"). Additionally, techs (and non-techs alike) can ruin perfectly good electricity on their own by overloading circuits with too much equipment. You can protect the servers from problems of power outages, electrical spikes, and overloaded circuits with several important technologies—dedicated circuits, surge suppressors, UPSs, and backup power.

Dedicated Circuits

A *dedicated circuit* is a circuit that runs from the breaker box to only certain outlets. In most homes and offices, a circuit might have many jobs. The circuit that runs your PC might also run the office water cooler and the big laser printer. Using too many devices on one circuit causes the power to sag. A sag can cause your computer to do nothing, lock up, or spontaneously reboot. It all depends on how lucky you are at that moment. Dedicated circuits keep this from happening. In most cases, dedicated circuits have outlets with bright orange faceplates to let you know that they are dedicated. This will (theoretically) prevent some uninformed person from plugging a photocopier into the circuit.

Surge Suppressors

It almost sounds silly to talk about suppressors these days, doesn't it? Does anyone really need to be convinced that all PCs, network and standalone, need surge suppressors? An electrical surge—a sudden increase in the voltage on a circuit—can (and will) destroy an unprotected computer. Every computer should plug into a surge suppressor!

UPS

A UPS (*Uninterruptible Power Supply*) is standard equipment for servers. Many UPSs also provide protection from spikes and sags. Most UPSs provide only a few minutes of power, enough to enable the server to shut down cleanly. All servers will have a UPS.

Backup Power

For real reliability, get a backup power supply. There are a number of small battery-based backup systems that will provide a few hours of protection. If you want something that will last for a few days, however, you will need a gasoline/diesel generator backup system.

Environment

Keep the server room locked at all times. Get a card lock or combination lock doorknob and make sure that only the right people have access. Keep the humidity low, but not too low—around 40% is about right for most electronics. Keep the room a little on the cool side—right around 68 degrees is just about perfect, although most PCs can handle up to 80–85 degrees before overheating becomes a problem. Check with the system's manufacturer for recommendations.

Redundant Components

Many components inside the system can be made redundant. It is common to find servers with redundant power supplies, so that a power supply can be removed without even shutting down the PC. You can buy NICs that work together in the same PC, covering for one or the other if one dies—there are even NICs that can be replaced without rebooting the PC. Placing hard drives on separate controllers—like the drive duplexing discussed earlier in this chapter—provides excellent redundancy.

Last, there are methods for making the entire server redundant. There are a number of methods where two or more servers can be mirrored, providing the ultimate in reliability, assuming the cost is bearable.

How Much Reliability Do You Need?

Reliability is like any security system—expensive, boring, a pain to administer; and you never have enough when you need it. Measure the cost of being down vs. the cost of reliability to make your decision. You might be surprised to find that it is a lot cheaper to be safe than sorry.

Putting Them All Together

There is no such thing as the perfect, complete network PC. Certainly every network PC needs to connect to the network; but data protection, speed, and reliability are functions that vary tremendously depending on network size, types of data and applications, the existing network cabling system, demands of growth, and of course, available funds. The Network+ exam does not assume that you can build the perfect network PC, but it does expect you to have a feel for the available options. When it comes time to build or buy that system, you can act as an advocate for your network, to ensure that you get as close to that perfect network PC as possible.

Review Questions

1) A NIC with both an RJ-45 and a BNC connector is probably a(n) ________ NIC.

a) Ethernet
b) Token Ring
c) ARCnet
d) Modem

2) Which of the following network technologies does NOT utilize RJ-45 connectors?

a) 10BaseT
b) 10Base2
c) Token Ring
d) 100BaseT4

3) A card with two RJ-11 jacks is most probably a ________.

a) 3270 emulator card
b) Modem
c) 100BaseT4 NIC
d) Token Ring NIC

4) Which of the following is not a fiber optic connector?

a) ST
b) SF
c) SC
d) FDDI

5) John's PC, networked with a 10BaseT NIC, ran perfectly yesterday. Today he can't access the network. Everyone else on the network can see each other, but not John. You look at the NIC and notice both lights are off. You should first:

a) Try copying a file from another machine over the network.
b) Verify the hub is turned on.
c) Replace the card.
d) Make sure the NIC is connected to the hub.

6) The part of the serial port that converts digital serial data to a format the PC can understand is called the ________.

a) COM port
b) Chipset
c) UART
d) Modem

7) Which of the following IRQs would most probably be available for a NIC?

a) IRQ 4
b) IRQ 5
c) IRQ 6
d) IRQ 7

8) You have a floppy disk that came with your new NIC. The floppy probably contains all of the following EXCEPT:

a) Drivers
b) Configuration utility
c) Diagnostic utility
d) Driver update utility

9) Disk mirroring is under which level of RAID?

a) RAID 0
b) RAID 1
c) RAID 2
d) RAID 3

10) Which of the following connectors are used with SCSI? (Choose all that apply.)

a) 50-pin Centronics
b) 36-pin Centronics
c) Female DB-15
d) Female DB-25

Review Answers

1) **A.** The BNC gave it away. Only an Ethernet combo card would have an RJ-45 and BNC connector.

2) **B.** 10Base2 only uses a BNC connector.

3) **B.** Only a modem has two RJ-11 jacks.

4) **B.** There is no such thing as an "SF" fiber optic connector.

5) **D.** The connect light is off, so the NIC is not connected to a working hub. Everyone else is working, so the hub is fine.

6) **C.** The UART converts digital serial data to a format the PC can understand.

7) **B.** All of these IRQs have a predefined use, but IRQ 5 is for a second parallel port. As most PCs do not have a second parallel port, IRQ 5 is the most likely to be open for use.

8) **D.** There is no such thing as a driver update utility.

9) **B.** Disk mirroring is under RAID level 1.

10) **A** and **D.** Both 50-pin Centronics and female DB-25 connectors are used with SCSI.

Chapter 9

Connectivity Hardware

There is a huge difference between what we have learned about network hardware so far and how hardware is actually implemented in the real world. In Chapters 1, 2, and 3, we toured the most common network technologies used in today's (and yesterday's) networks. At this point you should be able to visualize basic network setup. For bus topologies like 10Base2, there is a cable, running in a ceiling or along the floor, with each PC connected somewhere along the bus. For star bus or star ring topologies like 10BaseT or Token Ring, in contrast, there is some type of box (e.g. hub, MSAU, switch) with a number of cables leading out spider-like to all the PCs on the network, as shown in Figure 9.1.

FIGURE 9.1 *What a lovely network!*

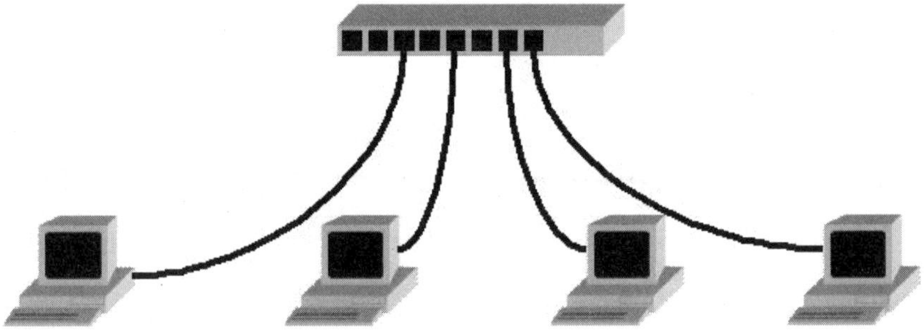

On the surface, such a network setup is absolutely correct, but does not have enough detail. Real-world networks do not look like that (Figure 9.2).

FIGURE 9.2 *Real world network mess.*

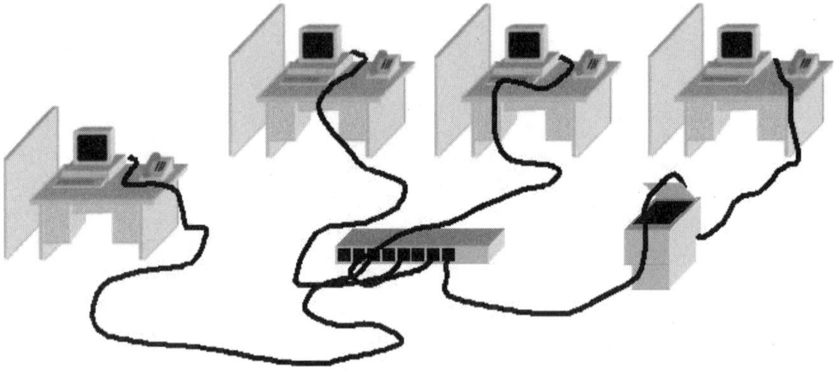

This chapter is designed to turn all the conceptual networks so far discussed in the book into real equipment. We will observe what real network hardware (hubs, switches, etc.) looks like and how it is implemented. We will turn the lines we've used to represent cables into functional wiring systems. Finally, this chapter provides how-to knowledge of cabling and networking devices.

The Network+ exam requires you to understand the basic concepts of designing a network and installing network cabling, and to recognize the components used in a real network. Network+ does not, however, expect you to be as knowledgeable as a professional network designer or cable installer. If you compare networks to automobiles, the goal of Network+ is not to test your abilities as an auto mechanic, but rather to test whether or not you have a solid understanding of how your automobile works and can talk intelligently to an auto mechanic.

Cable Basics—It All Starts with a Star

With that goal in mind, let's explore the world of connectivity hardware, starting with the most basic of all networks: a hub, some UTP cable, and a few PCs—a typical star network (Figure 9.3).

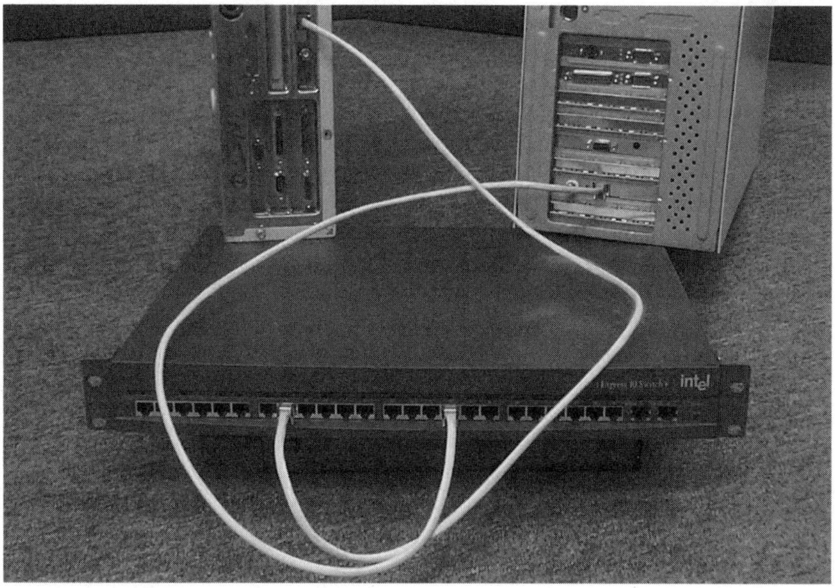

FIGURE 9.3
Photo of hubs and PCs.

Is the network in Figure 9.3 a star bus or a star ring? Is it Token Ring, 10BaseT or 100BaseTX? It doesn't matter. It could be any of these network technologies. If you have a 10BaseT network, what would you have to do to turn it into a Token Ring network? Replace the 10BaseT NICs in the PCs with Token Ring NICs and replace the 10BaseT hub with a Token Ring MSAU. The cable would stay the same, would it not? As far as the cabling is concerned, there is no difference between these topologies.

Many people find the idea that totally different network technologies like 10BaseT and Token Ring (assuming that it is using UTP) can use the same installed cables "just isn't right." For some reason, people want to think that because the network technology is different, the cabling must also be different. If you went back in time ten years, almost every networking technology had its own type of cabling. Over the years, UTP has edged out other cabling options. If an organization already has UTP cabling installed, it will not open to a network technology that does not use that UTP. If a network technology wants to exist, it must work with UTP. Token Ring originally used only STP cable, but changed to UTP to survive. All new network technologies use UTP—even the new Gigabit Ethernet standards. Virtually all of today's network technologies use UTP cabling in a star topology (Figure 9.4).

FIGURE 9.4

UTP–I'm the King!

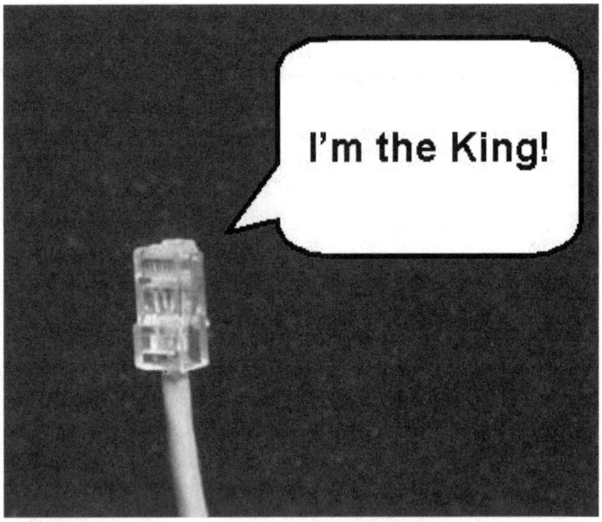

Only 10Base2 and 10Base5 networks break the pattern of UTP in a star, but they are both on the way out. The number of PCs using either of these technologies is a tiny minority compared to the UTP star technologies. 10Base5 is so rare now that it is probably safe to say that it is obsolete. 10Base2 still has a good following, but it will never be found in a true permanent installation—"in the walls" as network cabling people say. 10Base2 is still quite popular for temporary networks or for "quick and dirty" small networks, like a small two-PC office. Nevertheless, for the pretty network with the cable in the walls and the nice outlets, star topology UTP is the only way to go. The bus technologies do not exist in serious, permanent network installations (Figure 9.5).

FIGURE 9.5

The bus is dead.

Even though the bus is dead, that does not mean that older NICs are useless. Almost all older NICS can still connect to UTP. For 10Base5, add a transceiver to convert the 9-pin DIX (AUI) to RJ-45. 10Base2 does not have a transceiver but most hubs have an extra 10Base2 port, allowing an easy connection. Older STP Token Ring cards have converters that plug into the back of the Token Ring NIC, converting to RJ-45 (Figure 9.6).

Fiber optic cabling is a partial exception to the UTP/star dominance in network cabling. It uses a star topology, but does not use UTP cabling. Fiber optic cabling has properties that UTP just cannot match and is safe in its own special niche. We will see how fiber optics are used within the network later in this chapter.

The pure bus topology is dead, leaving us with only the star bus or star ring topologies using UTP. The most basic configuration for either of these topologies consists of a hub (or MSAU) with cables running out of it that connect directly to the PCs. We will call this the "basic star."

FIGURE 9.6
10Base 2 connection on hub.

NOTE

The rest of the chapter uses the term "hub" generically to mean either an Ethernet hub or a Token Ring MSAU. Note also that network techs often use MAU in place of MSAU.

The Basic Star

The basic star topology works well for a diagram, but falls apart spectacularly—as in Figure 9.2 above—when applied to a real world environment. Four basic problems are at work. First, the exposed cables running along the floor are just waiting for someone to trip over them, causing damage to the network and giving that person a wonderful lawsuit opportunity. Even if no accident ever takes place, just the acts of moving and stepping on the cable over time will cause failure. Second, the thousands of other electrical devices, if allowed to get too close to the cable, create interference that confuses the signals going through the wire. Third, such a setup limits the ability to make changes to the network. It is difficult to find out where one cable stops or starts. No one knows which individual cables in the huge pile of cables connected to the hub goes to his or her respective machine. Imagine the nightmare trying to troubleshoot the cables. Fourth, the only way to upgrade this network is to yank out all of the cables and replace them. Don't forget that while separate network technologies use UTP, there are subtle variances; if these are not addressed through some type of standardized cabling, upgrading the network will be impossible. The easiest example is the number of wires used. Assume you strung a 10BaseT network. 10BaseT only uses two pairs of wires so you bought UTP cable with two pairs and installed the network. Now you want to upgrade to 100BaseT4. Forget it; 100BaseT4 needs four pairs of wires, not two. Throw the cable out and buy some new cable!

There must be a better way to install a physical basic star network. A new installation method must provide safety: protecting the star from vacuum cleaners, clumsy coworkers, and electrical interference. The basic star needs extra hardware to allow for tight organization, so that making changes to the network becomes trivial. Last, the successful star network must have a cabling standard that provides both growing room for the network and the flexibility to upgrade to the next great network technology—whatever that may be.

The people who most wanted these standards were those who installed cable for a living. The first network cabling installers were all telephone people. Some very smart telephone installer who was forced into installing network UTP had a phenomenal idea. Telephone systems have outlets at each place where you want a telephone. All the phone cables are run in the walls to a central location. Phone systems also use a basic star (Figure 9.7).

FIGURE 9.7 *Installing telephone and network cabling is basically the same thing.*

If telephone systems use UTP in a basic star and network cabling use UTP in a basic star, why doesn't someone come up with some standard for UTP that would allow the same cabling to be used for either telephones or networks? That way you could install only one set of cables, significantly reducing the cost of adding cabling to a building. Of course, this standard would have to address the limitations for both network and telephone cable quality, distances, and distribution. Why do the same thing twice?

Structured Cabling to the Rescue!

The demand for a safe, dependable, and organized network motivated the Electronics Industry Association and the Telephone Industry Association (EIA/TIA) to develop a series of standards that have become the de facto standards used by everyone in the network installation business. EIA/TIA has developed many standards, but EIA/TIA 568 is considered the centerpiece of all the EIA/TIA cabling standards. This defines every aspect of putting cables into buildings. It standardizes acceptable cable types, the organization of the cabling system, guidelines for installation of the cable, and proper testing methods. The implementation of these standards is called *structured cabling*.

EIA/TIA 568 defines a series of terms that enable designers of structured cabling systems to talk in a standardized language that is not specific to telephones or networks. For example, network designers won't say "the network cable that runs to the PC" very often. They have no interest what you choose to do with the cable. They say things like "horizontal cabling" instead to imply that it is a cable running from a closet somewhere to an outlet in an office. These terms are extremely helpful to the cabling people, but can sometimes confuse a pure network person.

You don't have to learn these standards to pass the Network+ exam, but you do need a passing understanding of structured cabling to answer some questions. This chapter will make an abbreviated tour of network cabling from the structured cable viewpoint—just enough for you to get the idea of network cabling and certainly *not* enough for you to go out and install your own network cables. This abbreviated tour of structured cabling happily ignores critical aspects of EIA/TIA, as well as NEC, standards that are important to a real structured cabling system but are of no interest to the Network+ exams. If you want to become a structured cable designer, there are a series of certifications provided by an organization called BICSI (**www.bicsi.org**) that are the recognized certifications for that industry.

While we are talking about pulling cable, here is a bit of advice—DON'T! Installing proper structured cabling takes a startlingly high degree of skill. Thousands of pitfalls await the inexperienced network people who think they can install their own network. Pulling cable requires expensive equipment, a lot of hands, and the ability to react to problems quickly. Network people lose millions of dollars, and often their good jobs, by thinking they can do it themselves. Unless the network is tiny and the downside is low, let the pros install a solid structured cabling system for you. You set up the PCs and establish the network. Your organization will save money and you will save your job.

Structured Cable Network Components

The hardest part about understanding structured cabling takes place right at the beginning. Structured cabling works for telephones as well as networks, so you need to stop being a "network snob" for a moment and instead think about getting two cables from every place where a phone or networked PC resides to a central point. (See Figure 9.8.) Once you begin to think in these terms, structured cabling starts to make more sense.

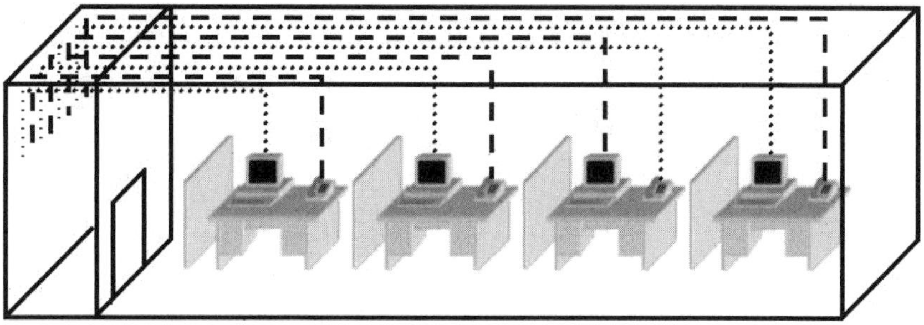

FIGURE 9.8
Structured cabling.

A successfully implemented basic star network has three essential ingredients—the equipment room, horizontal cabling, and the work area. All the cabling must run to a central location, the "equipment room." Structured cabling is not too interested in what equipment goes in there. You can put in a hub, MSAU, or a telephone system. The only important thing is that all the cables concentrate in this one area (Figure 9.9).

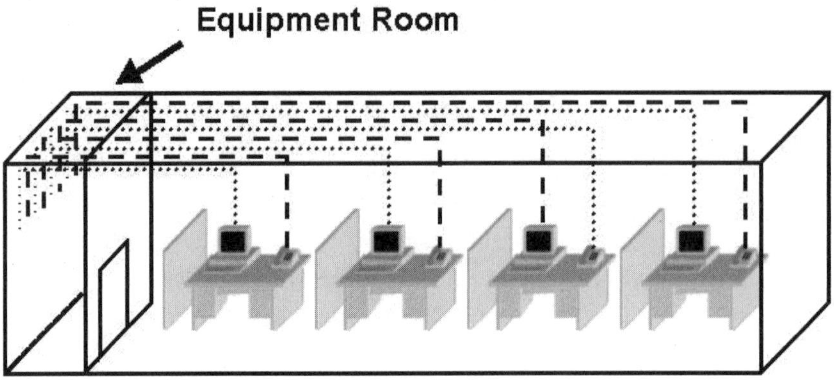

FIGURE 9.9
Equipment room.

From the equipment room, all cables run horizontally (for the most part) to the telephones or PCs. This cabling is appropriately called "horizontal cabling" (Figure 9.10). The other end of the horizontal cabling is the "work area" and is often simply an office that contains the telephones and PCs (Figure 9.11).

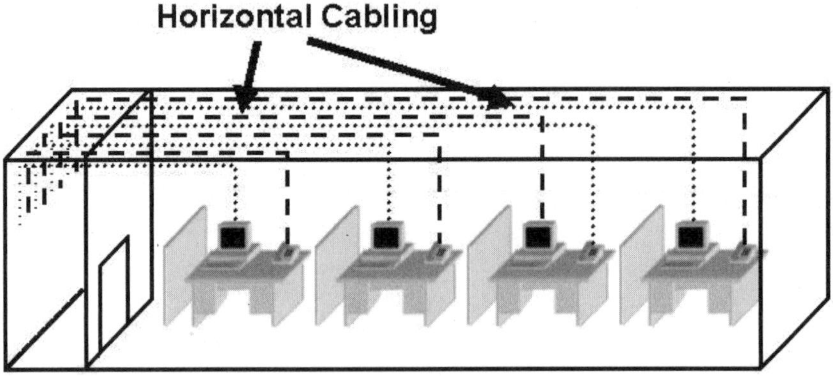

FIGURE 9.10
Horizontal cabling.

The basic star network functions with all three parts: the horizontal cabling, the equipment room, and the work areas. Each of these parts has a series of strict standards to use in order to assure that the cabling system is reliable and easy to manage. Let's look at each of the parts individually, starting with the horizontal cabling.

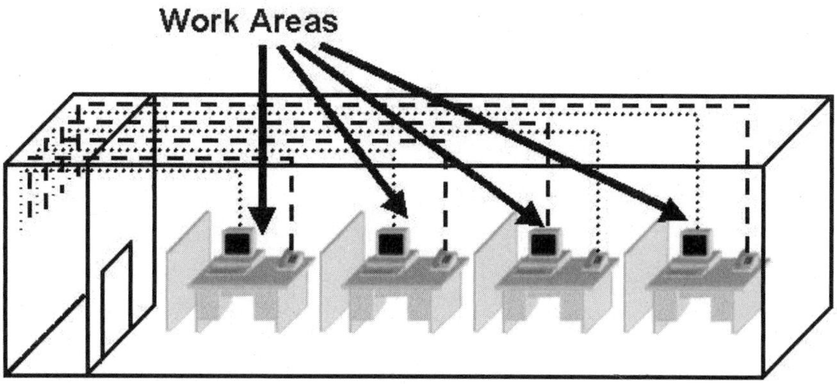

FIGURE 9.11
Work area.

Horizontal Cabling

EIA/TIA 568 recognizes three different types of cable used for horizontal cabling:

- Four-pair, 100 Ohm, 24 AWG, solid-core UTP
- 2-pair, 150 Ohm, 22 AWG, solid-core STP
- 2-fiber, 62.5/125 μm fiber optic

UTP

UTP comprises over 95% of all the new horizontal cabling installed today and that makes it very interesting to the Network+ people. Don't bother memorizing all the numbers and unknown acronyms. Here are a few of the more useful terms. "Ohms" is an electronic measurement of the cable's *impedance*. Impedance is (roughly) the amount of resistance to an electrical signal on a wire, and is used as a relative measure of the amount of data a cable can handle. The 24 AWG is the gauge, or thickness of the cable. Don't worry about those details. Do you remember the UTP CAT levels we discussed earlier in the book? Well, when you specify a CAT level of UTP, in reality you are also specifying the ohms and gauge, as well as a number of other critical criteria. You need to know the CAT levels, not details like impedance or wire gauge.

The CAT level alone does not completely describe UTP. CAT level ignores critical issues like the number of pairs or whether the individual wires are stranded (made from lots of tiny wires) or solid (made from one solid piece of copper). EIA/TIA has added these points to the specification. When specifying the cable to use, a network technician should care about the CAT level, the number of pairs, whether stranded or solid core is required, and one other critical component not covered by EIA/TIA 568 directly—the fire rating of the cable.

Fire Ratings

Did you ever see the movie *Towering Inferno*? A skyscraper goes up in flames due to evil engineers who use poor-quality electrical cabling. The fire reaches every part of the building due to burning insulation on the wires. Nobody wants a real towering inferno. Although no cables made today contain truly flammable insulation, insulation is made from plastic; if you get any plastic hot enough, it will make smoke and noxious fumes.

To reduce the fire risk, all cables—UTP, STP, and fiber—have fire ratings. The two most common fire ratings are "PVC" and "plenum." PVC (Polyvinyl Chloride) has no significant fire protection. If you burn a PVC cable, it makes lots of smoke and noxious gases. Plenum cable makes much less smoke and gas—and also costs about three to five times as much as PVC. Most city ordinances require the use of plenum-rated cable for network installations.

Back to UTP

There are five different CAT levels for UTP, as discussed extensively in Chapter 2. Here is the chart for review:

Category 1	Regular analog phone lines–not used for data communications
Category 2	Supports speeds up to 4 megabits per second
Category 3	Supports speeds up to 16 megabits per second
Category 4	Supports speeds up to 20 megabits per second
Category 5	Supports speeds up to 100 megabits per second

In the real world, network people only install CAT5 UTP, even if they can get away with a lower CAT level. Installing CAT5 is done primarily as a hedge against the day when the network upgrades to another type of networking technology that requires CAT5. Many network installers take advantage of the fact that a lower CAT level will work and bid a network installation using CAT3. Make sure you specify CAT5.

While CAT levels never seem to pose a problem for those just getting into network cabling, there always seems to be confusion about the number of pairs. Many people mistakenly assume that CAT5 means four pairs of cable. There is no correlation between CAT5 and the number of pairs. You can purchase CAT5 in many different pair combinations, so don't confuse them. The EIA/TIA 568 standard demands four pairs for two reasons. First, most of the up-and-coming network technologies, particularly the very high-speed ones, require four pairs of wires. Second, many advanced telephone systems require four wires. You should always get four-wire UTP.

The EIA/TIA standard defines the type of UTP to be used so precisely that the demand for anything but four-pair, CAT5 UTP has essentially collapsed. Almost every place UTP is pulled, you will find four-pair CAT5. The only choice left for horizontal UTP cabling is whether to use plenum or PVC. Next time you add a phone line to your house, check the cable—and don't be surprised if what you see is CAT5.

Installing UTP takes fairly serious work, but the cabling industry provides thousands of products that make the job fairly easy—for the professional. The most serious consideration for UTP is electronic and radio interference. Cable installers go to great lengths to make sure that UTP stays away from electric motors, fluorescent lights, power cables, etc. Most UTP installations take advantage of cabling trays or hooks suspended above drop ceilings to keep them away from potential interference sources.

The EIA/TIA standard sets the maximum distance from the equipment room to any one work area at 90 meters. For those of you who remember your cable distances from earlier chapters, almost all UTP based networking technologies allow 100 meters. Read on to find out where the other 10 meters went.

STP and Fiber

The Network+ exam barely touches STP or fiber cabling, but we will consider them for completeness. STP cabling does not blend well with the telephone side of structured cabling and is pretty much reduced to Token Ring and a few very high-speed networking technologies. There is nothing wrong with STP; in fact STP prices have dropped so much that if you look, you can find STP prices fairly close to UTP. But the UTP bandwagon is so full today that STP continues to disappear, with the few exceptions noted. It is extremely rare to see STP being used as horizontal cabling today.

Installing STP cable makes even the most experienced network tech shudder. Like UTP, STP is usually installed above drop ceilings on racks or hooks. It is less susceptible to electronic interference so the need to avoid potential sources diminishes. STP cable must have its shielding grounded or the shielding turns into a 90-meter antenna and usually causes significant problems for the network.

Fiber optic is rarely used as horizontal cabling due to its high price and the fact that UTP invariably is more than enough for most installations. A fiber optic cable has three components: the fiber itself, the *cladding*, which actually makes the light reflect down the fiber, and the insulating jacket. Fiber optic cabling comes in many different diameters of fiber and cladding, so cable manufacturers use a two-number designator to define fiber optic cable. The most common size of fiber optic cabling is 62.5/125m. Almost all network technologies that use fiber optic require two fibers. In response to the demand for two-pair cabling, two fibers are often connected together like a lamp cord—the popular "duplex" fiber optic cabling (Figure 9.12).

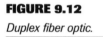

FIGURE 9.12
Duplex fiber optic.

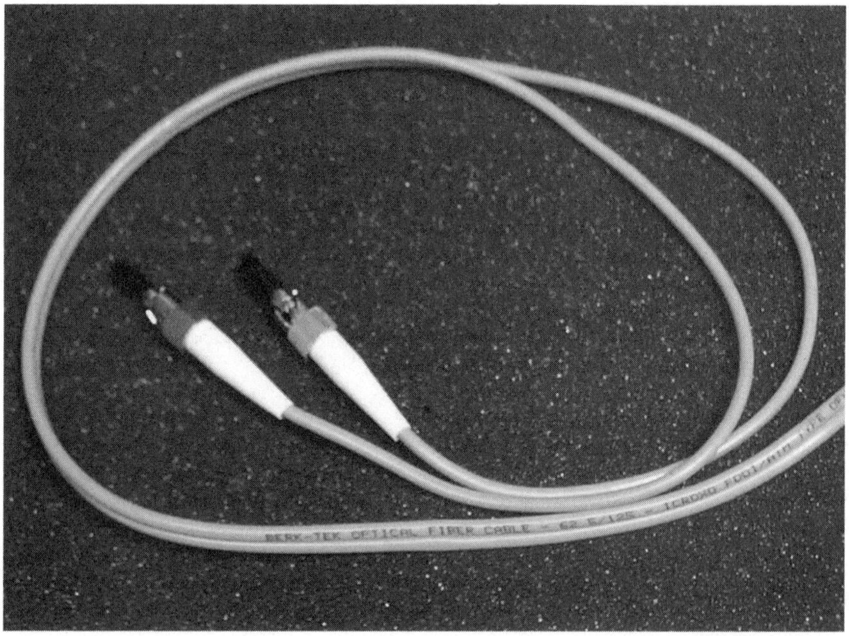

Light can be sent down a fiber optic cable as regular light or as laser light. Each type of light requires totally different fiber optic cables. Most network technologies that use fiber optics use LED (Light Emitting Diodes) to send light signals. These use *multimode* fiber optic cabling. Network technologies that use laser light use *single-mode* fiber optic cabling. Using laser light and single-mode fiber optic cables enable phenomenally high transfer rates and incredibly long distances. Single mode is currently quite rare. If you see fiber optic cabling, you can be relatively sure that it is multimode.

Installing fiber optic cabling is a love/hate scenario. On the plus side, since fiber optics do not use electricity, they can ignore the electrical interference issue. Also, fiber optic cabling can reach up to 2000 meters, depending on the networking technology used. The downside to fiber optic is actually getting it in the walls. Fiber optic cabling installations are tedious and difficult, although fiber optic manufacturers continually make new strides in easing the job. Fiber optic cabling is fragile and cannot be bent too much or the fiber optic will fail. Leave it to a professional cable installer.

Know Thy Cables

Concentrate on UTP—that is where Network+ will test you the hardest. Don't forget to give STP and fiber a quick pass over and know why you would pick one type of cabling over another. Even though Network+ doesn't test cabling knowledge too much, this is important information you will use in the real networking world.

Now that you are more comfortable with horizontal cabling and the types of cabling used, we will concentrate on the ends of the basic star, starting with the equipment room.

The Equipment Room

The equipment room is the heart of the basic star. All the cables from all of the PCs and telephones concentrate in this one area. It holds the hubs and the telephone equipment. All these together make the equipment room potentially one of the messiest parts of the basic star.

Even if you do a nice job of organizing the cables when they are first installed, networks change over time. People move computers, new work areas are added, network topologies are added or improved, etc. Without some type of organization, all the equipment and cables always decay into a nightmarish Gordian knot disaster, as shown in Figure 9.13.

FIGURE 9.13
Messy, messy!

Fortunately, the networking industry has developed a number of specialized components, under EIA/TIA guidelines, that make organizing the equipment room a snap. It might be fair to say that there are *too many* options. To keep it simple, we are going to stay with the most common equipment room setup and then take a short look at other fairly common options.

Every equipment room should store equipment in standard equipment racks. These provide a safe, stable platform for all the different components that reside inside the telecommunications closet. All equipment racks are 19" wide, but vary in height from 2–3-foot-high models that bolt onto a wall to the more popular floor-to-ceiling models (Figure 9.14).

FIGURE 9.14

Bare equipment rack.

Almost anything can be mounted into a rack. All hub manufacturers make rack-mounted hubs, switches, and routers that mount into the rack with a few screws. They come in a wide assortment of ports and capabilities. There are rack-mounted servers, complete with slide-out keyboards. Of course there are also rack-mounted UPSs to power the PCs and NICs (Figure 9.15).

NOTE

Be careful about the UPS. Most of the devices we call UPSs are not truly uninterruptible power supplies. They are Standby Power Supplies (SPSs). An SPS differs from a UPS because it does not provide continuous power. An SPS does nothing until it detects a power outage. If the power goes out for more than a few milliseconds, the SPS kicks in automatically. There is absolutely nothing wrong with SPSs—just make sure you know the difference and verify with the manufacturer that the SPS will work with your devices.

FIGURE 9.15
Rack mounted UPS.

The first item on the "proper equipment room" list is the *patch panel*. Horizontal cabling, once installed, should never be moved. Sure, cables can handle some rearranging, but taking a wad of cables and inserting them directly into the hubs means that every time a cable gets moved to a different port on the hub, or if the hub gets moved, the cable is going to be jostled. UTP horizontal cabling is solid core. It is pretty stiff. You will not have to move it too many times before some of those thin strands of solid copper start breaking and there goes the network. A patch panel consists of nothing more than a row of female connectors (ports). Every cable coming from the work areas connects directly to the back of a patch panel, as shown in Figure 9.16.

Not only do patch panels prevent the horizontal cabling from being moved, they are also the first line of defense for organizing the cables. All patch panels leave space in the front for labels and these are the network person's best friend. By placing a tiny label on the patch panel, the nightmare of "where does this cable go?" disappears. Purists can use the official, and rather confusing, labeling methodology; but most real-world networks simply use their own internal codes, as shown in Figure 9.17.

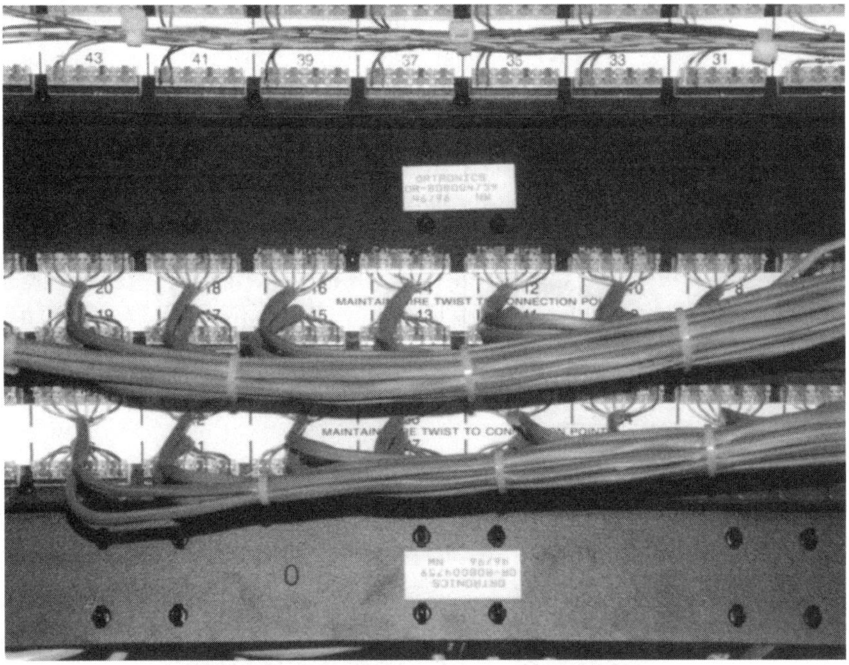

FIGURE 9.16

Back of patch panel.

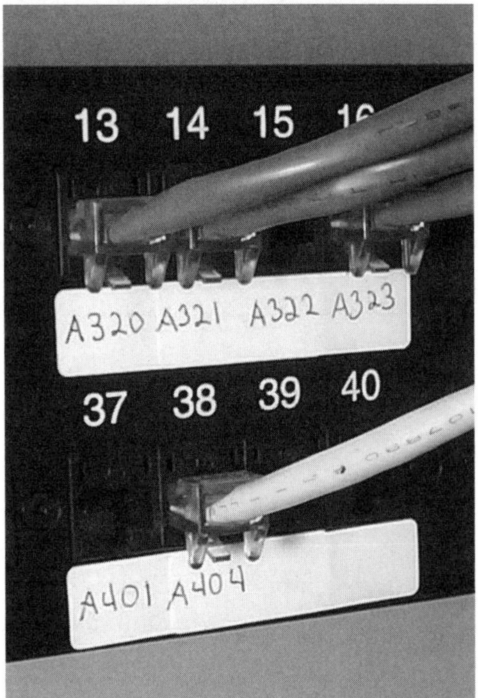

FIGURE 9.17

Labeled patch panel.

Patch panels come in a wide assortment of port types and numbers. There are UTP, STP, or fiber ports (some manufacturers combine different types on the same patch panel). You can get 8, 12, 24, 48, and higher ports. UTP patch cables also come with CAT ratings, so don't blow a good CAT5 cable installation by buying a cheap patch panel—get a CAT5 patch panel. Most manufacturers display the CAT level right on the patch panel.

Once the patch panel is installed, connect the ports to the hub through *patch cables*. These are short (2–5 ft) UTP cables, similar to horizontal cabling. Unlike horizontal cabling, they use stranded cable to enable them to accept much more handling. Patch cables also differ from horizontal cables because they ignore the EIA/TIA wiring schemes and instead wire straight through. Pin 1 on one connector goes to Pin 1 on the other, Pin 2 to Pin 2, etc. (Figure 9.18).

FIGURE 9.18
Typical patch cables.

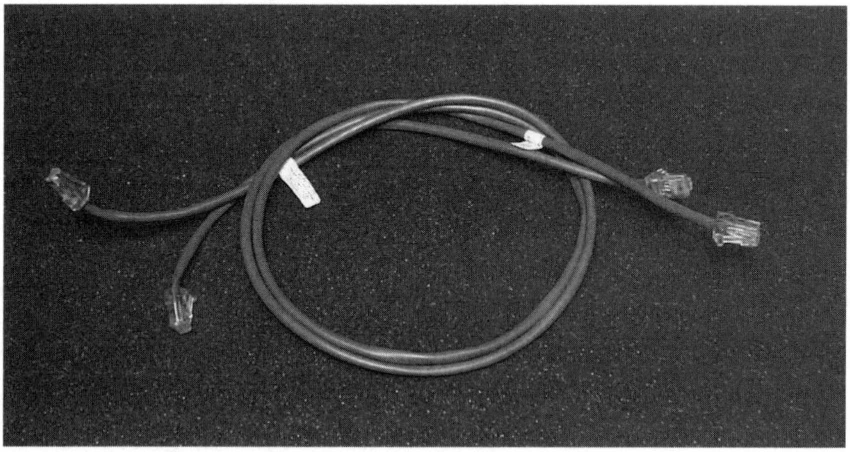

Even though you can make your own patch cables, most people buy premade cables. Making a good CAT5 connection with stranded cable is a little harder than with solid core, so buying CAT5 patch cables makes your life easier. Buying patch cables enables you to use different colored cables to facilitate organization (yellow is accounting, blue is sales, etc.).

An equipment room does not have to be a special room dedicated to computer equipment. You can use specially made cabinets with their own built-in equipment racks that sit on the floor or attach to a wall. You can use a storage room, as long as the equipment can be protected from the other items in the closet. Fortunately, the demand for equipment rooms has been around for so long that most offices have them ready to go.

Now, the basic star is certainly improving. The EIT/TIA horizontal cabling is installed and the equipment room configured. Now you need to address the last part of the structured cabling system, the work area.

The Work Area

From a cabling standpoint, the work area is nothing more than a wall outlet. It serves as the termination point for the network and telephone cables, providing a convenient insertion point for PCs and telephones. The wall outlet consists of nothing more than a female jack that connects to the cable, a mounting plate, and a faceplate. There are CAT5-rated jacks for wall outlets to go along with the CAT5 cabling in your network. Many network connector manufacturers use the same connectors in the wall jacks that they use on the patch panels. These modular jacks increase the ease of installation significantly.

Most work area outlets have two connectors, one for the network and one for the telephones. Many outlets use RJ-45 for both connections because RJ-11 jacks fit into RJ-45 and many phones use RJ-45 natively. Be sure to label the outlet to show the job of each connector (Figure 9.19).

FIGURE 9.19
Typical phone/data outlet.

A good outlet will also have some form of label that identifies its position on the patch panel. It sure saves a lot of work later to provide proper documentation.

The last step is connecting the PC to the outlet box. Here again most people use a patch cable. Its stranded cabling stands up to the abuses of moved PCs and the occasional kick (Figure 9.20).

FIGURE 9.20
Patch cord connecting PC to outlet.

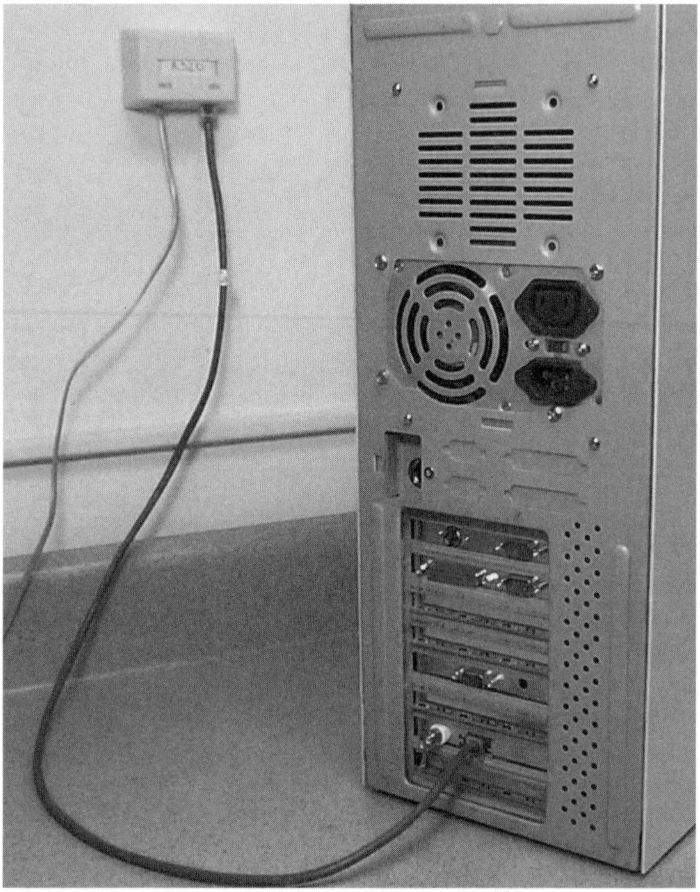

The work area may be the simplest part of the structured cable system, but is usually the source of most network failures. When a user cannot see the network and you suspect a broken cable, the first place to look is here.

Earlier we wondered why the EIA/TIA 568 specification only allowed UTP cable lengths of 90 meters instead of the 100 meters allowed by most networking technologies that use UTP. The answer is the patch cables. They add extra distance between the hub and the PC. That extra distance must be compensated for by reducing the horizontal cabling length.

The New Basic Star

EIA/TIA structured cabling methods transform the basic star into an ordered and robust network, rather than the cabling nightmare it was at the beginning of this discussion. None of this must be done to make a network function, though it should be done if the network is to run reliably and change easily with the demands of an organization. The extra cost and effort of installing a properly structured cabling system pays huge dividends by preventing the nightmare of trying to locate one bad cable and by protecting the network from accidental abuse by users.

Beyond the Basic Star

The basic hub with star is only acceptable in the simplest networks. In the real world, networks tend to have many hubs, and many networks span floors, buildings, states, and even countries. Let's take the basic star and, using structured cabling where applicable, go beyond it to see some of the equipment and strategies for more advanced, larger, and more efficient networks.

Be aware that this is only the lightest of touches on networking beyond the basic star. Network+ wants you to understand the concepts and does not intend for you to be the ultimate expert. Each of these more advanced network topics deserves its own chapter, if not its own book.

Getting a Little Switchy?

As PCs are added to the basic star running 10BaseT, the network traffic increases. As network traffic increases, users begin to notice a perceptible slowdown in network performance. One of the fastest and cheapest hardware solutions to too much traffic on a 10BaseT network is the addition of a switch. To change to a switched 10BaseT network, remove the hub and replace it with a switch. Nothing has to be done to the cards or the cabling. Certainly, switches are expensive compared to a hub, but the ease of installation and the instantaneous positive results make switches very popular today.

Switches, like hubs, come in a dizzying variety of shapes and sizes. From 20 feet away, a hub and a switch are identical. Most manufacturers use the same casing for equivalent hubs and switches. Figure 9.21 shows an Intel small-office hub next to a small-office switch; note that they are virtually identical.

FIGURE 9.21
Switches and hubs are similar.

The cost of switches motivates a good network technician to use switches as efficiently as possible. There are a number of strategies for implementing switches, each with different benefits. The three most common strategies are to switch *all* of the systems, switch the servers, or to use a switch as a bridge. Providing every PC a switched port gives the network incredible throughput, but it is expensive and overkill for all but the most heavily overworked networks.

To switch just the most accessed system(s) in any network—the servers—makes more sense for most networks. As described in Chapter 2, most networks that utilize switching go for a combined hub/switch with one or two switched ports for the server(s) and regular ports for the other PCs. Figure 9.22 shows the back of the hub displayed previously in Figure 9.21. Notice the two switched ports and the regular ports.

FIGURE 9.22

Back of switch showing ports.

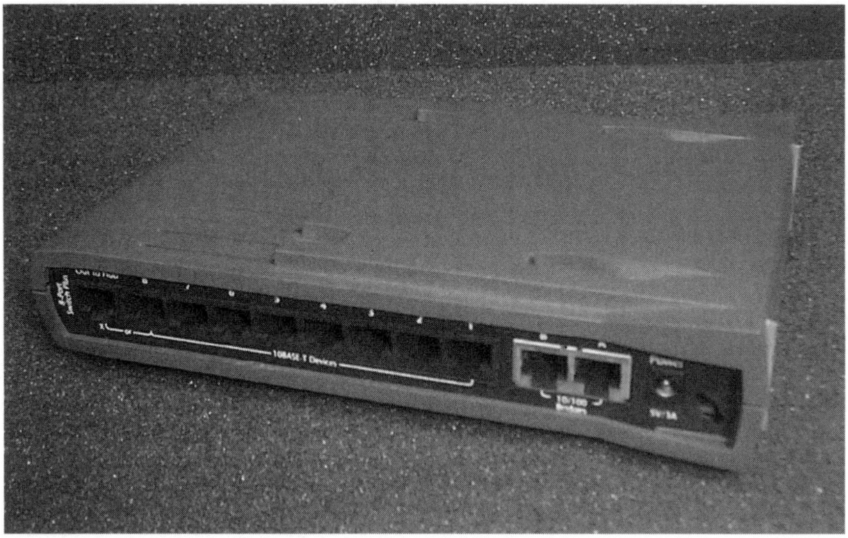

The third popular strategy is to use the switch as a bridge. This helps compartmentalize a fair-sized network and reduce internetwork traffic. The Bayland Widget Corporation's network, for example, has three hubs. Each hub serves a different department—Hub 1 is for Accounting, Hub 2 is for Sales, and Hub 3 is for Manufacturing. Each department has its own server and only rarely does someone from one department need to access another department's server. The hubs all cascade from a central, single hub (Figure 9.23).

FIGURE 9.23

Basic cascading hubs.

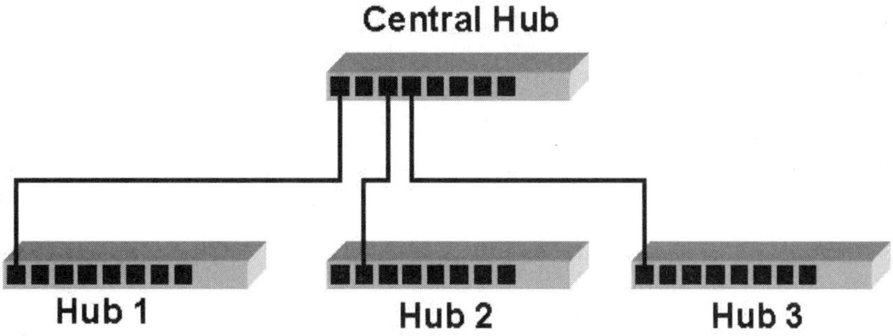

As the network currently stands, every other system on the network hears all traffic from all of the systems. Replacing the central hub with a switch keeps traffic between two systems in one department from spreading into the network in the other departments (Figure 9.24). Such a setup makes excellent sense for mid-sized to large networks.

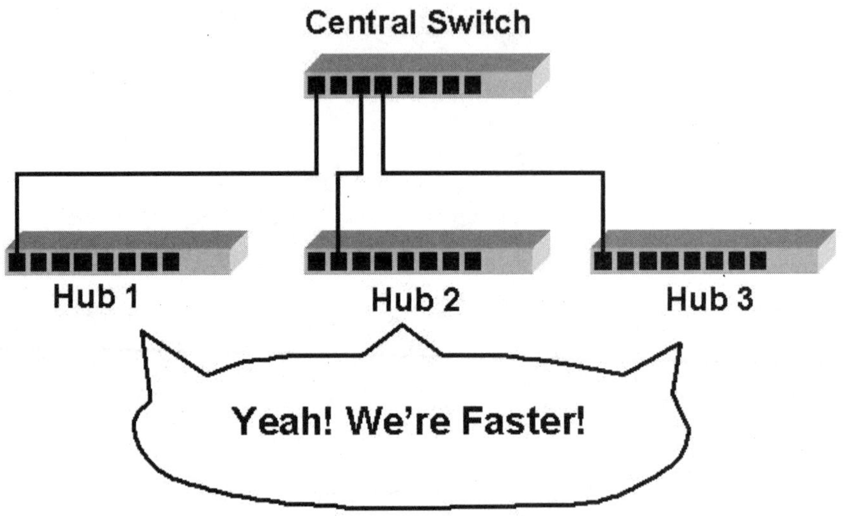

FIGURE 9.24
Adding a switch improves throughput.

Multispeed Networks

In Chapter 8, we touched on the concept of multispeed networks. Making a network faster with higher speed networking technologies is another good way to combat a slow network. Replacing a basic star's 10BaseT hub and 10BaseT NICs with 100BaseT, however, has no effect on the basic star. Making every PC in the network faster is usually overkill, the same as making every machine switched. The more common uses of combining high-speed with low-speed networks certainly will add new hardware to the basic star.

As mentioned in Chapter 8, you can purchase a multispeed hub, containing one or two 100BaseT hubs with 10BaseT hubs. Give the server a 100BaseT card and plug it into the 100BaseT port to improve performance (Figure 9.25).

FIGURE 9.25
Speeding up the server improves throughput.

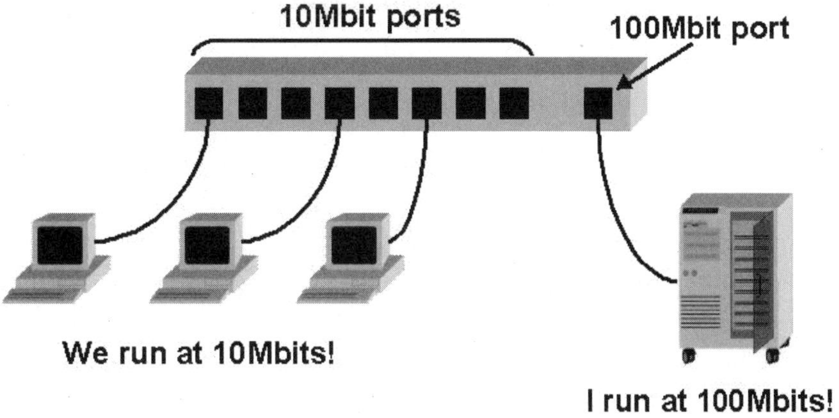

This is a fine strategy for smaller networks and it does not affect the basic star. Let's look again at the Bayland Widget Corp.'s three-department network and apply the concept of multispeed networks. Faster networks can be used in conjunction with slower networks to increase throughput. Again, replace the central hub, but this time with a 100BaseT hub. Add the servers to their individual 10/100 hubs or add them together to the 100BaseT hub. Each scenario provides roughly the same increase in throughput (Figure 9.26). The current popular strategy for improving network speed is to combine both high speed and switching into a scenario that looks something like the network in Figure 9.26.

FIGURE 9.26
Speeding up all the servers.

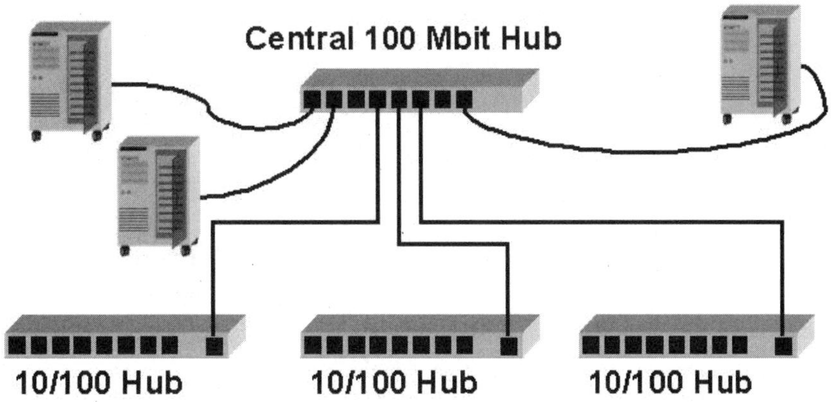

FIGURE 9.27
Combined switch and 100Mbit.

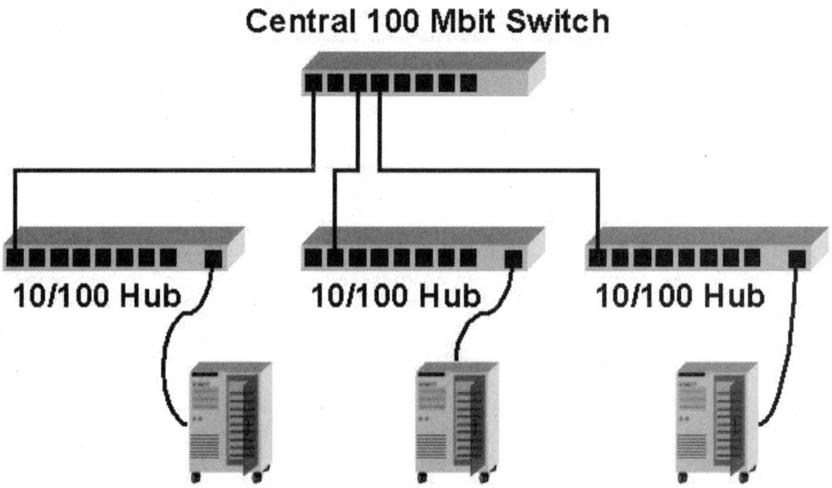

These advancements to the basic star have one item in common: a special set of cables designed to run better than the regular 10BaseT. These cables rarely go to a PC, unless it is a server. In a way, we have two separate types of networks: the individual networks connecting the PCs, and a single, high-speed network that ties together all the individual networks. This is the *backbone*, which is not one cable, but a group of cables running from a central point (usually a high-speed switch) to all the other switches or hubs. EIA/TIA does not care about hubs, switches, high speed or low speed, but does have a lot to say about backbones—in particular, how those backbones are cabled.

Multiple Floors, Multiple Buildings

Once a network breaks out of a basic star and begins adding more hubs/switches, certain demands start to surface:

1. The network will need multiple networks with multiple switches/hubs in multiple equipment rooms.
2. The multiple hubs/switches will need to be tied together with a "backbone cable."
3. The backbone must be able to support the demands of the combined networks.
4. Mission-critical servers will need to become centralized to simplify administration.

All these statements can combine into a single statement: "As networks grow, they take up more space." Adding significantly more PCs to a network usually implies adding work areas—more offices, cubicles, etc. More work areas means more equipment rooms, possibly on multiple floors. It means new buildings, requiring relatively long distances between any given server and the PCs that want to access it. It usually means more, and more powerful, servers to handle the increased demand. As more servers come into the network, the administrators of those servers want them placed together in a single room—a computer room—which enables the administrators to handle the mundane chores, such as backups, from one central location. The larger the network, the larger the space needed to support it.

The concept of structured cabling continues beyond the basic star. EIA/TIA provides a number of standards, centralized on EIA/TIA 568 and another important EIA/TIA standard, EIA/TIA 569, that address the issues of multiple equipment rooms, floors, and buildings.

Again, EIA/TIA does not think in terms of networks and has developed its own terminology for structured cabling beyond the basic star. With a little simplification, EIA/TIA's view of structured cabling breaks down into six main components: the equipment room, the horizontal cabling, the work areas, the backbone, the building entrance, and the telecommunication closets (Figure 9.28). The first three were discussed above in the basic star and occupy the same roles in a more complex network. Let's concentrate, therefore, on the last three.

NOTE

Don't bother memorizing these. Network+ is not going to quiz you on naming each of these parts of structured cabling. Do make a point to understand the equipment involved with each of these parts and how the parts interrelate. This is real-world knowledge required in the marketplace.

Telecommunications closets are really more for telephone systems than for networks, but are included here for completeness. This is where the individual phone cables running from the work areas are connected to the actual phone lines from the internal telephone system. Before the onset of more advanced telephone systems that handle this electronically, this was where lines were moved to change phone numbers in an office. Have you seen those little white connectors with all the phone lines punched into them? Those are called *punch-down blocks* and according to EIA/TIA should be located in a telecommunications closet for telephones (see Figure 9.29). Telecommunications closets are not supposed to have networking equipment in them so they are rarely seen for networks. Instead, larger networks will have a number of equipment rooms. From a networking standpoint, telecommunications closets do not strictly apply—especially for our very short dip into structured cabling.

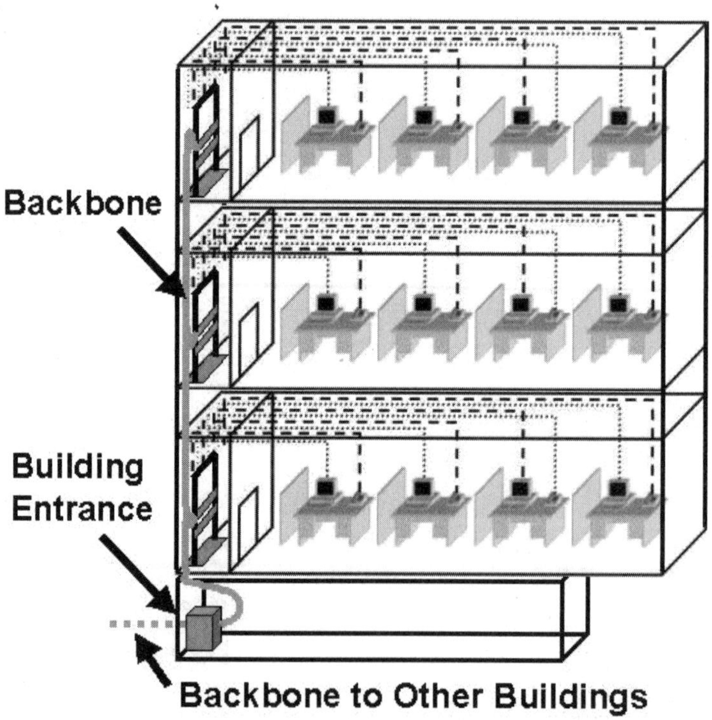

FIGURE 9.28
Backbone and building entrance.

Most networks use one equipment room per floor. If the room is centrally located in the building, the 90-meter distance will completely cover the floor space in most buildings. The "computer room" is nothing more than the main equipment room.

EIA/TIA specifies using UTP, STP, or fiber optics for backbones. UTP and fiber optics are very popular for backbones, whereas STP is rarely used. While any cable that meets the criteria for backbone (discussed above and in Chapter 2) is certainly a backbone cable, EIA/TIA thinks more of backbones as cables that vertically connect equipment rooms (often called risers) or horizontally connect buildings (interbuilding). EIA/TIA gives guidelines for backbone cable distances, but the ultimate criteria for the length of the cable depend on the networking technology used (Figure 9.30).

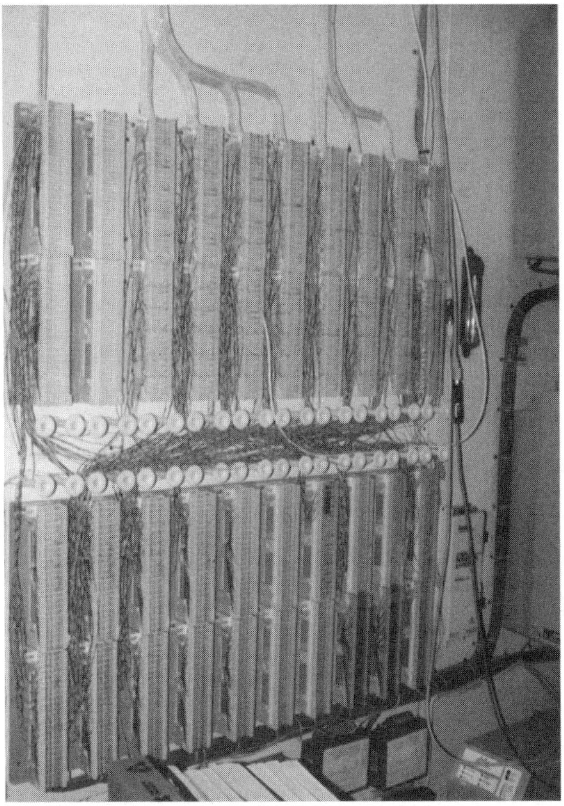

FIGURE 9.29
Punch down blocks.

Most riser backbones use either copper or fiber optic cables. The type of networking technology used determines which cabling type to use for the backbone. Only fiber optic should be used in interbuilding cables due to its imperviousness to electrical problems. Certainly, copper can be used between buildings, but it needs significant grounding to prevent the chance of damage from electricity.

The *building entrance* is where all the cables from the outside world (telephone lines, cables from other buildings, etc.) come into a building. EIA/TIA specifies exactly how the building entrance should be configured. We are not interested in any part of the building entrance other than the type of cable that should be used between buildings (fiber optic).

FIGURE 9.30 *Fiber optic backbone cables connecting into hubs.*

Network+ does not directly address structured cabling, but understanding structured cabling makes a lot of Network+ questions easier. For example, you will not be quizzed on the different types of fiber optic cable—but be ready to determine, as the Network+ objectives state: "when they are appropriate." Don't get hung up on how UTP horizontal cable is placed over drop ceilings, but do be aware of its susceptibilities to radio frequency and electronic interference. The goal here was not to turn you into a cable installer, but to give you a solid understanding of the concept of structured cabling—not only to pass the Network+, but also to be a good network support person.

The Tools of Cabling

If you like to play with fun tools, then get into the network cabling business. Most network cable installers carry an arsenal of tools to help in the installation and testing of new structured cabling systems. These tools range from inexpensive crimpers (the tools that put the connectors on the ends of the cables) to multi-thousand-dollar cabling testers that plug into two ends of a cable. The higher-end testers give acres of detailed information to ensure that the electrical properties of a cable pass a battery of EIA/TIA standards. These tools are indispensable to those who install cable and most of them require significant training to use and to understand.

Fortunately, Network+ does not expect you to know how to use most of these tools—especially the expensive ones. It does expect you to know how to use a few basic cable diagnostic tools so that you can answer the two biggest questions about cabling: "Is this cable good?" and "Is this the right cable?" You can determine if a cable is good with a cable tester. To locate a particular cable, you use a toner. Let's look at these two types of network tools.

Cable Testers

As the name implies, cable testers test cables. Before we can talk about cable testers, we must determine what makes a cable "bad." No doubt, if a hamster chews a piece of UTP in half, that cable should be considered bad. Any time a cable is cut through (any or all of the wires), there is a cable break. Other things also make a cable bad. How about if someone crimped one connector improperly, putting the individual colored wire pairs in an incorrect order? What if a perfectly good cable is run too close to an electric motor and is unable to properly move data? What if the distance between the hub and the PC is too long? These all can make a cable "bad."

Cable testers come with a wide variety of functions. Most network administrators staring at a potentially bad cable want to know the following:

- How long is this cable?
- Are any of the wires broken?
- If there is a break, where is it?
- Are any of the wires shorted together?
- Are any of the wires not in proper order (i.e., split or crossed pairs)?
- Is there too much electrical or radio interference?

Cable testers are designed to answer some or all of these questions, depending on the amount of money you are willing to pay. The low end of the cable tester market consists of devices that only test for broken wires. A wire that is not broken can conduct electricity—it has continuity. These cheap (less than $100) testers are often called "continuity testers." Some cheap testers will also test for split or crossed pairs and shorts (Figure 9.31).

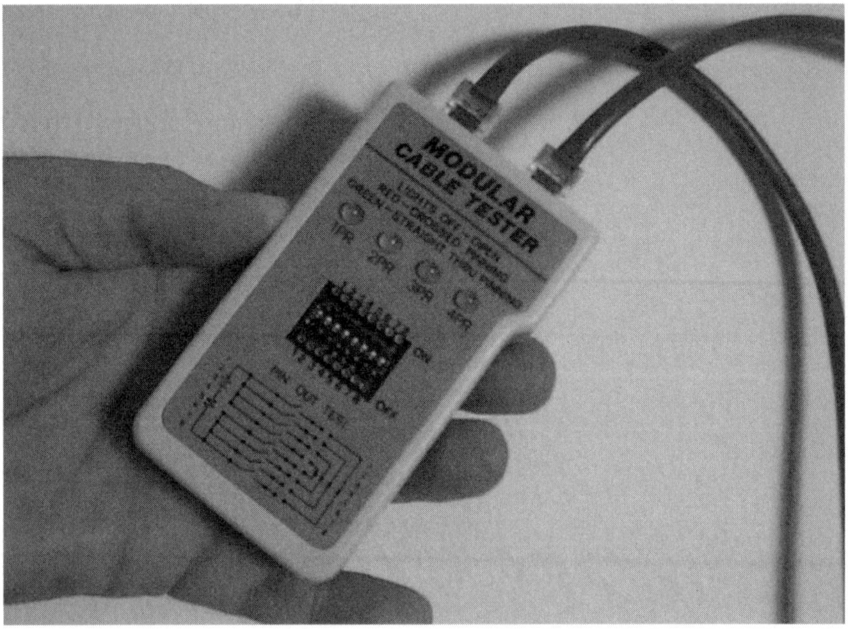

FIGURE 9.31
Simple cable tester.

These cheap testers usually require that both ends of the cable be inserted into the tester. That can be tough if the cable is already installed in the wall.

Medium-price (~$300) testers add the ability to tell the length of the cables. They also tell where a break is located. These are generically called *Time Domain Reflectometers* (TDRs) (Figure 9.32).

The medium-priced testers will have a small loopback device that gets inserted into the far end of the cable, enabling them to work with installed cables. These are the types of testers to have around.

Once you want to start testing the electrical characteristics of a cable, the price shoots up fast, into the $2000 and up range. These professional devices test the critical EIA/TIA electrical characteristics and are used by professional installers to verify installations. Some have powerful extras, such as the ability to plug into a network and literally draw a schematic of the entire network, including the MAC addresses of the systems, IP or IPX address, etc. These "super cable testers" might be better described as *protocol analyzers*. (Protocol analyzers are discussed in Chapter 11) (see Figure 9.33).

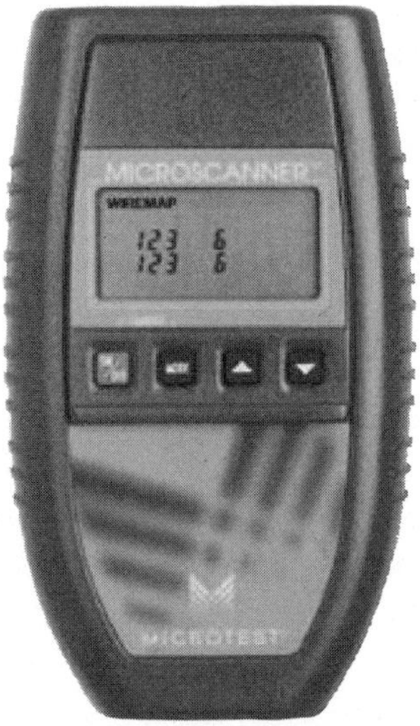

FIGURE 9.32
Microtest Microscanner.

FIGURE 9.33
Microtest Pentascanner.

These advanced testers are more than most network techs need. Unless you have some very deep pockets or find yourself doing very serious cable testing, stick to the medium-priced testers.

When do you need to pull out a cable tester? First of all, a good-quality, professionally installed cable rarely goes bad—unless there is a serious hamster problem! Always assume software problems first. The most important clue that you may have a bad cable is when a user tells you "I can't see the network!" An error reveals that "No server is found" or in Network Neighborhood no systems other than theirs are visible. Double check the NIC driver to make sure that it hasn't magically decided to die, and run the NIC's internal diagnostic and hardware loopback if possible. If the NIC passes the tests, it might be a cable problem.

Check the link lights on the NIC and hub first. If they are not lit, you know the cable is not connected somewhere. Try another patch cable to the outlet. Still no good? Then check to see if other people can access the network; make sure other systems can see the shared resource (server) that the problem system is trying to access. Use the same logon name and password (if possible) on other systems to make sure they can access the shared resource. Make a quick visual inspection of the cable from the back of the PC to the outlet. Last, if you can, plug the system into another outlet and see if it works. If none of these works, you should begin to suspect the structured cabling. In most cases, assuming the cable was installed properly and was working previously, a simple continuity test will confirm your suspicion.

Be warned that a bad NIC may generate the same "I can't see the network" problem. This problem worsens because it is usually due to a failure of the port on the NIC, making the NIC's diagnostics useless. Knowing this, most NIC diagnostics include a "test the network" diagnostic. This makes the NIC send or receive packets. You usually need an identical NIC in another system running the same diagnostic to do this test. On occasion, you can insert a hardware loopback plug into the NIC to perform the test.

If only broken cables were the worst problem! The rarity of that problem, combined with the relative ease of diagnostics, makes bad cables an uncommon and simple-to-fix issue. Another problem, far more common than broken cables, takes place in every network installation—tracking cable.

Toners

It would be nice to say that all cable installations are perfect; that over the years, they do not grow into horrific morasses of piled up, unlabeled messes. In reality, you will find yourself having to locate ("trace," as we say) cables. Even in the best of networks, labels fall off ports and outlets, mystery cables disappear behind walls, and new cable runs are added. Most networks require you to be able to pick out one particular cable or port from a stack.

When the time comes to trace cables, all network techs turn to a toner for help. "Toner" is a generic term for two separate devices that are used together: a tone generator and a tone probe. These two devices are often referred to as "Fox and Hound," the brand name of a popular toner made by Triplett Corporation. The tone generator connects to a cable with alligator clips, tiny hooks, or a network jack, and sends an electrical signal on the wire at a certain frequency. A tone probe emits a sound if it comes close to the cable the tone generator is connected to (Figure 9.34).

FIGURE 9.34
Tone probe at work.

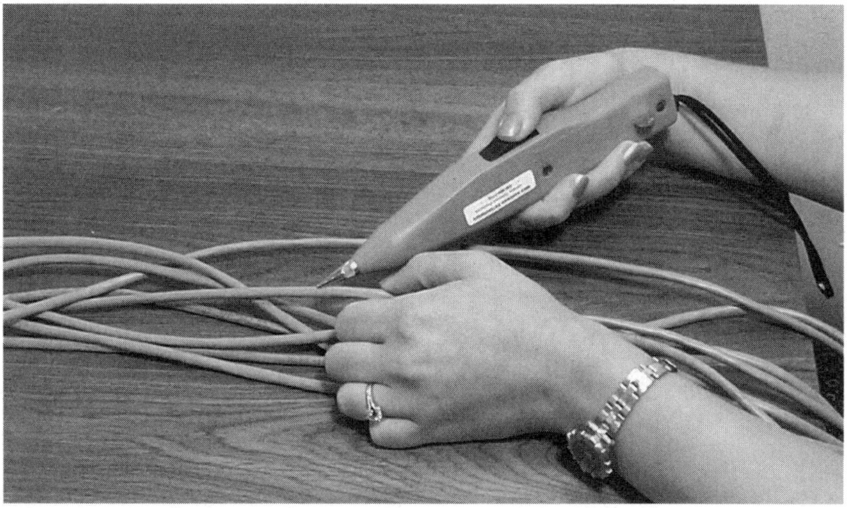

To trace a cable, the tone generator is connected to the cable and the tone probe is moved next to all the possible cables. The tone probe then makes a sound when it is next to the right cable. More advanced toners will include phone jacks, enabling the person manipulating the tone generator to communicate with the person manipulating the tone probe. Some toners have one probe working with multiple generators. Each generator emits a different frequency and the probe emits a different sound. Good toners are inexpensive (~$75). Bad toners can cost less than $25, but usually do not work very well. If you want to support a network, you'll own a toner.

Together, a good, medium-priced cable tester and a good toner are the most important tools used by those who support, but don't install networks. Be sure to add a few extra batteries—there's nothing worse than sitting on the top of a ladder holding a cable tester or toner that has just run out of juice.

Installer? No. Informed Consumer? Yes!

Cable types, connectors, fire ratings, racks, and tools: how much of this do you need to know? You are just going to get your Network+ and then work in some network somewhere by just sitting at a keyboard all day, right? Wrong. CompTIA created the Network+ exam to test for knowledge that anyone working on a network should have. Those who work on a network will find themselves needing to expand the network and being the first line of defense for problems that come up. This chapter covers what you need to know to pass the Network+ exam. It barely touches the vast amount of knowledge and training needed to become a cable installer. Understanding the components of structured cabling, combined with a few basic tools and techniques, won't make you a professional cable installer, but it most certainly will make you comfortable with the workings of network cabling. Such knowledge enables you to make basic fixes and to communicate with the pros!

Review Questions

1) Which of the following cables should *never* be used in a structured cabling installation?
- a) UTP
- b) STP
- c) Fiber optic
- d) Coax

2) Which type of fire rating should be used in horizontal cabling?
- a) Mil Spec
- b) Plenum
- c) PVC
- d) UTP

3) The CAT 5 level defines how many pairs of wires in the cable?
- a) 2
- b) 4
- c) 8
- d) It doesn't

4) The best type of inter-building cabling is:
- a) UTP
- b) Coax
- c) Fiber optic
- d) STP

5) A __________ protects the horizontal cabling from unnecessary movement and organizes the incoming horizontal cables in the equipment room.
- a) Rack
- b) Patch panel
- c) Outlet
- d) 110 Jack

6) Which of the following would never be seen in an equipment rack?

a) Patch panel
b) UPS or SPS
c) PC
d) All of the above can be seen in an equipment rack

7) Where are patch cables used? (Choose all that apply.)

a) Connecting different equipment rooms
b) Connecting the patch panel to the hub
c) As crossover cables
d) Connecting PCs to outlet boxes

8) A user complains of an inability to log into the network on a Windows 95 system that has worked perfectly for months. The user can successfully log in using the same username and password from any other system. The NIC passes all diagnostics. What should you do next?

a) Check the link light.
b) Replace the patch cables.
c) Replace the NIC.
d) Verify the network address.

9) Jane needs to increase network throughput on a 10BaseT network that consists of one hub and 30 users. Which of the following hardware solutions would most inexpensively achieve this?

a) Add a fiber backbone.
b) Upgrade the network to 100BaseT.
c) Replace the hub with a switch.
d) Add a router.

10) What type of cable tester is used to determine the length of a cable?

a) Time Domain Reflectometer (TDR)
b) Continuity tester
c) Tone probe
d) Toner generator

Review Answers

1) **D.** Coax cable should not be used in structured cabling networks.

2) **B.** Plenum-rated cabling should be used in horizontal cabling.

3) **D.** The CAT 5 level does not define the number of pairs in UTP.

4) **C.** EIA/TIA specifies fiber optic cabling as the preferred inter-building cabling.

5) **D.** The patch panel organizes and protects the horizontal cabling in the equipment room.

6) **D.** All are seen in equipment racks.

7) **B and D.** Patch cables connect the hub to the patch panel and the PCs to the outlet boxes.

8) **A.** Check the link light.

9) **D.** Upgrading to 100BaseT will work, but replacing the hub with a switch is much cheaper.

10) **A.** A TDR is used to determine the length of a cable.

CHAPTER 10

Remote Connectivity

Local Area Networks (LANs) provide organizations with abilities essential for today's business needs. A LAN gives access to important databases, e-mail, printers, fax machines—all the things needed to get a job done. In the vast majority of organizations, if employees want to get work done, they need to have access to the LAN (Figure 10.1).

FIGURE 10.1
I need my LAN.

A LAN is a static item. Organizations and the people that populate them, on the other hand, are not static. People need to fly to a sales meeting in Topeka, they need to train new employees in Austin, and they need to open a new office in Smyrna. Most organizations start as a single entity—with a single LAN—but inevitably grow in such a way that people end up being far away from the precious LAN (Figure 10.2).

The people in your organization need access to the LAN, no matter where they are working. In particular, they need access to the company's data. Other network resources such as printing take on much less importance to a person who is 500 miles away from the printer. While there are many methods to access this information from far away, most people want to be able to access the network exactly as though they were sitting at a local system on the LAN. The secret to appreciating these many methods requires understanding two very basic and very abused terms: "Local" and "Remote."

FIGURE 10.2
I need my LAN!

Local vs. Remote

The "L" in LAN stands for "Local." In the classic LAN, all the systems are local. All the systems are connected together via some type of *dedicated* connection, usually a cable. In essence, the system links permanently with the network—when the computer starts, it logs onto the network. As long as the machine runs, it stays connected to the network. The user simply walks up to the machine and can access the network's shared resources. Even if the system has not logged on, a user can connect to the network simply by logging back on. It is unusual for the system NOT to be connected to the network. Physically disconnecting the system creates an error scenario (Figure 10.3).

A remote system, in contrast, accesses the LAN via a connection that the organization does not own, often through some type of telephone line. Remote access requires two devices, a server and a client. The remote access server has a dedicated connection to a LAN and some type of modem or modem equivalent. It has special software that works with the modem to listen for rings, authenticate the user, and provide network access. The remote access client has a modem or equivalent plus software to enable it to link into the server (Figure 10.4).

FIGURE 10.3
Oops!

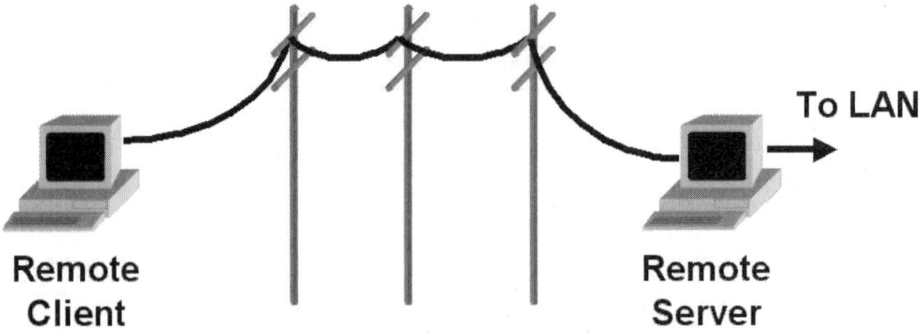

FIGURE 10.4
Remote client and server.

If there is a remote access server and a remote access client, which is local and which is remote? Two different definitions exist. First, many people look at the terms remote and local in a relative way. The local system is the system that physically exists with you—the system where you are. The remote system is the far-away one. Imagine a salesman with a laptop in North Zulch, TX trying to access a server in Intercourse, PA. From the salesman's standpoint, his laptop is the local system and the server is the remote system. From the server's point of view, the server is the local system and the laptop is the remote system. The second, and preferred way to define local and remote is not relative at all—the remote access server is always the "local" system and the remote access client is always the "remote" system. This more absolute definition makes understanding remote access easier. Just be prepared for Network+ to throw questions at you that use either definition (Figure 10.5).

FIGURE 10.5
Relative local and remote.

Remote access uses telephone lines. If you want to understand remote access, you need to understand telephony, another badly abused word. *Telephony* is technically the science of converting sound into electrical signals, moving those signals from one location to another, and converting those signals back into sounds. This includes modems, telephone lines, the telephone system, and the many products used to create a remote access link between a remote access client and a server. Unfortunately, many people use the word telephony the way they use "thing-a-ma-bob"—they can't think of the right word so they throw in telephony. Be careful with the way other people use the term.

The Links

Becoming an expert on how one computer can use telephone lines to link to another is a totally separate career path. Once again, Network+ does not want to turn you into a telephony expert, just an informed consumer. You need to know the different types of telephone lines: in particular the amount of data they can carry. Also, you need to know the hardware that goes with those lines and how they work together to get the PC connected to the telephone line.

Certainly, the first and most important decision in creating a remote connection is the choice of line that will connect the two systems. The most basic types of telephone lines are cheap and require little effort to install. More advanced types of lines are very expensive to install and have high monthly costs. You don't want to put in a telephone line that is too expensive or will not be fast enough for your remote connectivity needs.

There are many different types of telephone lines available, but all the choices break down into either dedicated or dial-up access. Dedicated telephone lines are always "off the hook." They never end, or hang up, on each other. A true dedicated connection does not have a phone number. In essence, the telephone company creates a permanent, hard-wired connection between the two locations, rendering a phone number superfluous. Dial-up lines, in contrast, have phone numbers and dial each other up to make a connection. When they finish, they hang up. Many locations use dial-up lines in a dedicated manner (telephone companies hate this). If a dial-up connection is made and the two ends never disconnect, this is basically the same function as a dedicated connection. But it is still a dial-up connection, even if the two sides rarely disconnect. In this section we look at the most common dial-up lines used—PSTN and ISDN—and offer a brief discussion of two new high-speed consumer Internet access technologies, ADSL and Cable Modems. Most of the expensive, dedicated types of phone lines are of no interest to Network+ (including ADSL and Cable), but are included here for completeness.

Public Switched Telephone Network (PSTN)

The oldest, slowest, and most common phone connection is the Public Switched Telephone Network (PSTN). PSTN is also known as Plain Old

Telephone Service (POTS). PSTN is just a regular phone line, the same line that runs into everyone's home telephone. It was designed long before computers were common and was designed to work with only one type of data—sound. PSTN takes the sound you transmit—usually your voice translated into an electrical "analog" waveform by the microphone—and transmits it to another phone that then translates that signal into sound via a speaker. The important word to note here is **analog**. The telephone microphone converts the sounds into electronic waveforms that cycle 2400 times a second. An individual cycle is known as a *baud*. The number of bauds per second is called the *baud rate*. Almost all phone company PSTN lines have 2400 baud rate.

PSTN uses a connector called RJ-11. This is the classic connector you see on all telephones. (See Figure 10.6.)

FIGURE 10.6
Standard RJ-11 PSTN wall outlet.

The device that takes the analog signals from the PSTN wall jack and converts it into a signal is called a modem (MOdulator DEModulator). Modems connect to serial ports to provide the interface to the PC. Refer to Chapter 8 for a discussion of modems and serial ports (Figure 10.7).

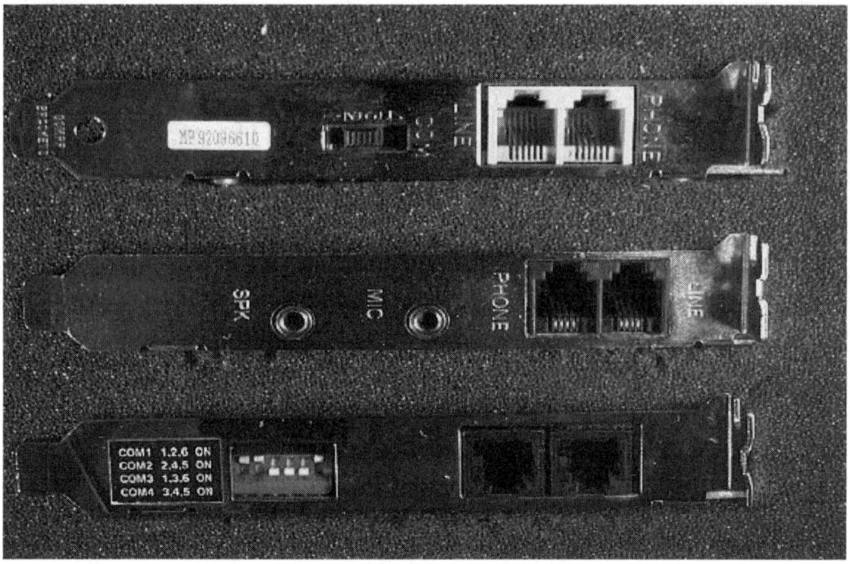

FIGURE 10.7
Typical modems.

V Standards

Modems utilize phone lines to transmit data, not just voice, at various speeds. These speeds cause a world of confusion and problems for computer people. This is where a little knowledge becomes dangerous. Most of us have dealt with modems to some degree. Today's modems have speeds up to 56Kbps. That's Kilobits per second—not baud. The problem here stems from the fact that most of us confuse the terms baud and bits per second. This confusion comes from the fact that for modems, the baud rate and the BPS are the same until the data transfer between the modems surpasses 2400 baud. Basically, a phone line can make analog samples of the sound 2400 times a second. This standard was determined a long time ago as an acceptable rate for sending voice over the phone lines. While 2400-baud analog signals are great for voice communication, they are a big problem for computers sending data. Computers hate analog signals and in fact, work only with digital signals. In order for two computers to communicate over PSTN, one computer must have its digital (ones and zeros) signal changed into an analog signal that can be transferred over the telephone. Then the other computer must take the analog signals and transform them into digital signals. This is the job of the modem. Modems take incoming digital signals from the computer and then send these signals in an analog form using the baud cycles from the phone system. The earliest modem used four analog bauds just to send one bit of data—those we often erroneously called 300-baud modems. They weren't 300-baud modems, they were 300bps modems, but the name "baud" stuck for describing modem speeds. As technology progressed, modems became faster and faster. To get past the 2400-baud limit, modems would modulate the 2400 baud signal twice in each cycle, making 4800 bits per second. To get 9600, the signal would be modulated four times. That's why all PSTN modem speeds are always a multiple of 2400. Look at the following speeds and see how many look like classic modem speeds:

2400 baud/sec x 1 bit/baud = 2400 bits/sec
2400 x 2 = 4800
2400 x 4 = 9600
2400 x 6 = 14400
2400 x 8 = 19200
2400 x 12 = 28800
2400 x 24 = 57600 (56K)

If someone says to you "Is that a 56K baud modem?", look them straight in the eye and say, "No, it's a 2400-baud modem. But its bits per second is 57,600!" You will be technically correct, although you will have no friends.

In order for two modems to run at their fastest, it is critical that they modulate signals in the same fashion. The two modems must also query, or negotiate with, each other in order to determine the fastest speed of each modem. The modem manufacturers themselves originally standardized these processes under what were known as "proprietary protocols." The downside to these protocols was that unless you had two modems from the same manufacturer, the two modems often would not work together. Very quickly, the European standards body, the CCITT, established standards for modems. These standards are known generically as the "V" standards and define the speeds at which modems can modulate. The most common speed standards are:

V.22	1200 BPS
V.22bis	2400 BPS
V.32	9600 BPS
V.32bis	14400 BPS
V.34	28000 BPS
V.90	57600 BPS

In addition to speed standards, the CCITT, now simply the ITT, has established standards that enable two modems to compress data and to perform error checking. These standards are:

V.42	Error Checking
V.42bis	Data Compression
MNP5	Both

The beauty of these standards is that there is no special work involved to enjoy their benefits. If you want 56K data transfers, for example, simply ensure that the modem in the local system and the modem in the remote system are both V.90 standard. Assuming good line quality, etc., the connections will run at (close to) 56K.

NOTE

Many people get a little confused on the concept of port speed and modem speed. All versions of Windows make it possible to set the port speed. This is the speed of the data between the serial port (really the UART) and the modem, not between the modems. As a rule, always set this speed to the highest rating of 115,200bps, assuming your UART is a 16500 or better.

ISDN

There are many pieces to a PSTN telephone connection. First is the phone line that runs from your phone out to the network interface box (the box on the side of your house), and into a central switch. (In some cases, there are intermediary steps.) Standard metropolitan areas have a large number of central offices, each with a central switch. Houston, Texas, for example, has nearly 100 offices in the general area. These central switches connect to each other through high-capacity "trunk" lines. Before 1970, the entire phone system, from your phone to the other phone, was analog. Over time, phone companies began to upgrade their trunk lines to digital systems. The entire telephone system by now, with the exception of the line from your phone to the central office, has become digital.

During this same upgrade period, customers have continued to demand higher throughput from their phone lines. The old PSTN was not expected to be able to produce more than 28.8 Kbps (the 56K modems were a big surprise to the phone companies and didn't come out until 1995) so the phone companies were very motivated to come up with a way to generate higher capacities. The answer was fairly simple—make the entire phone system digital. Using the same copper wires used by PSTN, adding special equipment at the central office and the user's location, the phone companies can achieve a throughput of up to 64K per line (see below). This process of sending fully digital lines "end-to-end" is known as *Integrated Services Digital Network (ISDN)*.

ISDN service consists of two types of channels known as *bearer* or *B* channels and *delta* or *D* channels. B channels carry data and voice information at 64Kbps. D channels carry setup and configuration information. Most providers of ISDN allow the user to choose between one or two B channels. The more common setup is the two B–one D, usually called a BRI (Basic Rate Interface). A BRI setup still only has one physical line, but each B channel sends 64K each, making a total of 128K throughput. ISDN also connects much faster than PSTN, alleviating the nasty, long, "mating call" of PSTN. The monthly cost of each B channel is slightly more expensive than PSTN, and it usually has a fairly steep initial cost for the installation and equipment. Not everyone can get ISDN. You usually need to be within about 18,000 feet of a central office to use ISDN.

The physical connections of ISDN bear some similarity to PSTN modems. An ISDN wall socket is usually nothing more than what looks like a standard RJ-45 network jack. The most common interface is a device called a Terminal Adapter (TA). TAs look very much like regular modems and come in external and internal variations. You can even get TAs that are also hubs, allowing a direct LAN connection (Figure 10.8).

NOTE

There is another type of ISDN, called PRI (Primary Rate Interface), composed of 24 B channels and 1 D channel, giving it a total throughput of 1.5 megabits per second. PRI uses a special type of telephone line called a "T1" and is very expensive. PRI ISDN lines are rarely used as dial-up connections–they are far more common on dedicated lines.

There are a number of telephony options with remote access. The most common by far are PSTN (POTS) and ISDN. While this chapter concentrates on these two types of connections, keep in mind that there are options for remote access. Two other technologies, ADSL and cable modems, deserve a few quick words. Keep in mind that Network+ does not list either of these technologies in the objective list. The fast-growing popularity of these technologies, however, will certainly compel the CompTIA people to update the Network+ exams to reflect these powerful new methods of remote connectivity.

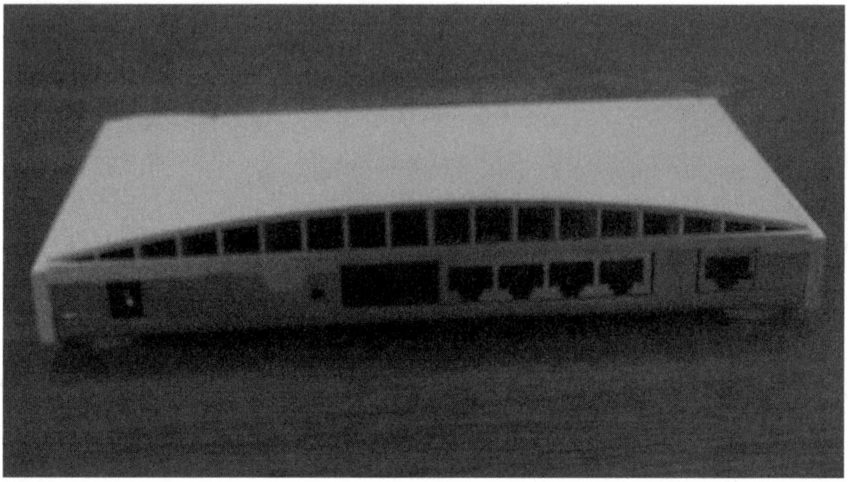

FIGURE 10.8
Combination Hub/ ISDN terminal adapter.

ADSL

Asymmetric Digital Subscriber Line (ADSL) is the next "great leap forward" for telephone lines. It is a fully digital, dedicated (no phone number) connection to the telephone system that provides download speeds up to 9 Mbps and upload speeds up to 1 Mbps over PSTN lines. The phone company can take your PSTN line and make it go at speeds approaching that of 10BaseT. To make it even more attractive, the same ADSL line you use for data can also work with your telephone, allowing simultaneous data and voice over the same line. The only downside to ADSL is that your ISP must also support ADSL. As of this writing, there is a mad scramble by ISPs to provide that support.

ADSL is actually only one type of a group of similar technologies known as xDSL. The fact that the upload and download speeds are different is the "asymmetric" part of ADSL. Other xDSL technologies provide equal upload and download speeds. ADSL seems to be the xDSL that has become by far the most common, however, due in part to its support by big ISPs such as the Baby Bells, GTE, and Sprint. ADSL has roughly the same distance restrictions as ISDN—around

18,000 feet. ADSL has many variations in upload/download speed, depending on the telephone company that provides the ADSL service. Southwestern Bell, for example, provides two levels of ADSL. The more basic service gives a download of 1.5 Mbps maximum with a guarantee of 384Kbps and an upload of 128Kbps. The faster—and a lot more expensive—service gives a download of 9Mbps maximum, with a guarantee of 1.5Mbps and a upload of 384Kbps. Different providers will give different rates.

The most common installation for ADSL consists of an "ADSL modem" that connects to the wall jack. This device is not a modem; it is more like an ISDN terminal adapter but the term has stuck and even the manufacturers of the devices call them ADSL modems. The ADSL modem connects to a standard NIC, providing the ADSL service. If you want to use the ADSL line for your regular telephone service, a "POTS splitter" is added to the line between the ADSL modem and the wall outlet (Figure 10.9). Of course, there are ADSL cards that connect to the PC, combined ADSL/hubs, and ADSL capable routers. It becomes simply a question of money.

FIGURE 10.9
Typical ADSL configuration.

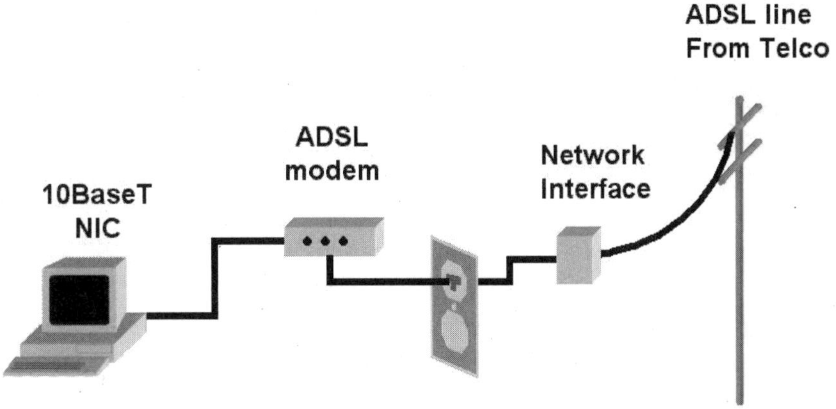

The basic ADSL service described usually costs about the same as (or a little less than) ISDN for installation, equipment, and monthly service. This, combined with the fact that you can use the same line for your phone (ISDN requires a special ISDN telephone or adapter) makes ADSL a cheaper and very attractive option for the future.

NOTE

The one place where ADSL might "bite you" in cost is the ISP link. Most ISPs add a significant surcharge to use ADSL. Before you choose ADSL, make sure that your ISP provides ADSL links at a reasonable price. Most telephone companies bundle ISP services with their ADSL service for a very low price.

Cable Modems

The big competition to ADSL comes from the cable companies. Almost every house in America has a big chunk of coax cable running into it. In a moment of genius, the cable industry came to the realization that if they could put the Home Shopping Network and the History Channel into every home, why couldn't they provide Internet access? The entire infrastructure of the cabling industry needed some major changes to support issues like two-way communication, but most large cities now provide cable modem service. By the time you read this, cable modems will be as common as the cable box on the television.

The single most impressive aspect of cable modems is their phenomenal top speeds. These speeds vary from cable company to cable company, but most advertise speeds in the 10 to 27 Mbits/sec range. That massive throughput must be shared with all those who have cable modems. As more people in the neighborhood connect, the throughput will drop. How significant will this drop be? The technology is so new that no one wants to give a clear answer. Some early installations show that a heavily used cable line's throughput can drop to under 100Kbits/sec. Only more experience with the technology will determine what you can expect for a realistic cable modem speed.

A cable modem installation consists of a cable modem connected to a cable outlet. In most cases, the cable modem gets its own cable outlet separate from the one that goes to the television. This is the same cable line—it is just split from the main line just as though you were adding a second cable outlet for another television. As with ADSL, the cable modem connects to a PC via a standard NIC (Figure 10.10).

Take your time when choosing the type of remote connection you need. Be sure to consider the upload/download speeds, the cost of equipment and installation, the monthly cost, and the availability. When studying for the Network+, be sure to watch for these same criteria. Remember, Network+ wants informed consumers, not telephone/cable experts!

FIGURE 10.10
Typical cable modem configuration.

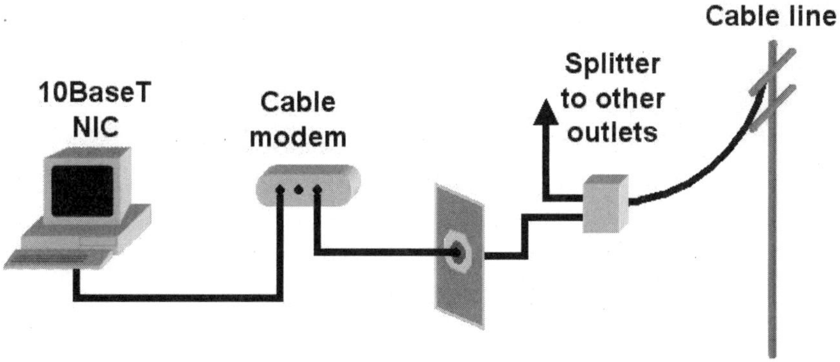

The Protocols

Telephone lines need a data link layer protocol to handle the non-voice data sent between computers. The existing data link protocols, like Ethernet and Token Ring, simply will not work on a phone line. They are designed to run too quickly and they do not address a multitude of telephone-only issues. For many years, every type of data link protocol was proprietary. There was no way to make one system talk to another brand's system. This was fine in the days of mainframe computers, but the world of generic PCs, especially PCs trying to connect to the Internet, required a generic data link protocol that could work over telephone lines. The first Internet-supported data link protocol for telephone was known as SLIP (Serial Line Internet Protocol).

SLIP

SLIP was the first effort to make a data link protocol for telephony and it shows. About the only thing good you can say about SLIP is that it worked. SLIP had a couple of major limitations: first, it only supported IP. If you had a NetBEUI or IPX network, you were out of luck. Second, any system that used SLIP required a static IP address. This was not a big issue in the early days of the Internet, but today's shortage of IP addresses makes SLIP unacceptable. SLIP continues to be supported by most remote access programs, primarily as a backward-compatibility option. Don't use SLIP.

PPP

SLIP's many shortcomings fostered the need to create an improved data link protocol called Point-to-Point Protocol (PPP). PPP fixed all of the shortcomings of SLIP and has totally replaced SLIP in all but the oldest connections. While PPP has many powerful features, its two strongest are the ability to support IPX and NetBEUI as well as IP, and the ability to support dynamic IP addresses. All remote access software comes with the PPP protocol. PPP is the one to use.

PPTP

An offshoot of PPP is Microsoft's Point-to-Point Tunneling Protocol (PPTP). Buying ISDN or T1 lines is an expensive proposition compared to PSTN. If the remote location is fixed, like a satellite office, the extra cost of ISDN or T1 often makes good sense. But what does the person who needs to access the company network in New York do from a hotel room in Chicago? There are two choices. First the company can set up its own remote access server and the person can dial in over a long distance line. This works well but can be very expensive. All the bigger ISPs have accounts that allow a person to dial into the Internet using local access numbers. Enabling the user to dial into the Internet using a local phone number and access the company's network through the Internet is PPTP's job.

NOTE PPTP is currently supported only by Microsoft products and the UNIX clone Linux.

PPTP does not replace PPP. It works with PPP to create an encrypted tunnel—a direct link through the Internet between the remote system and the PPTP server. Both the remote access server and the remote access client will need special PPTP software to accomplish this connection. Once the PPTP connection is made, the Internet becomes nothing more than the cable linking the client with the server.

The only downside to using the Internet, or even directly dialing into a remote server, is that your login, password, and data must travel over public telephone lines. These data can be tapped and intercepted. With PPTP, the data are also moving through routers that can be easily intercepted by the wrong people. To prevent the data from falling into the wrong hands, remote access usually includes some type of encryption options that scramble the data. Depending on the type of encryption used, you can encrypt the login name, the password, and even the data before they are sent on the network. The server and the client set up the encryption before any important data are set, even before the client has the opportunity to log in, making encryption an important part of remote access. One benefit of PPTP is its powerful, automatic encryption. Other remote access software usually requires that the user set whether or not to use any level of encryption.

A Few Tips on Remote Access

While there are a number of remote access software options, they all contain similar configuration options. On the server software, you first have to select the device that receives the incoming call and add the PPP protocol. Figure 10.1 shows a Windows 98 system's remote access client, Dial-up Networking, with PPP installed.

FIGURE 10.11

Setting PPP on remote client.

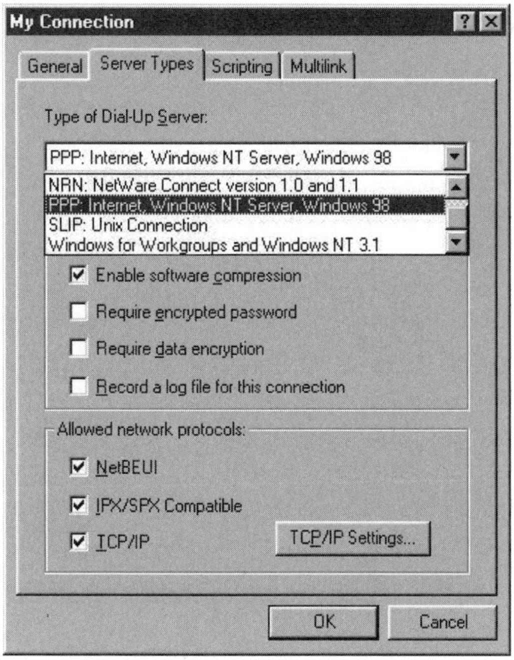

You then need to configure the server to accept calls, provide the necessary passwords, (many RAS servers have a separate logon password just to allow the user to access the remote access server), and set the dial-up user's rights/permissions on the server. If there are any encryption requirements, you set them up now. Figure 10.12 shows the popular Microsoft Remote Access Server being configured.

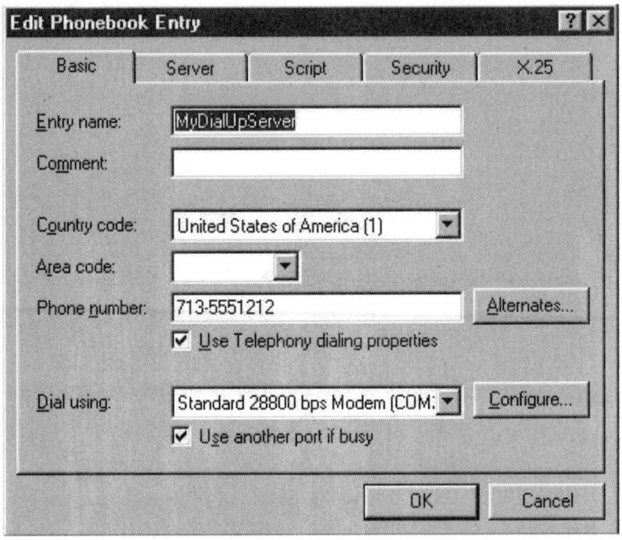

FIGURE 10.12

Configuring remote server.

On the client side, the giant of all remote access clients is Microsoft's Dial-up Networking (DUN). Like all remote access clients, DUN will need a device to use, a phone number to dial, and, depending on the network protocol used, special settings like IP address, gateway, etc. (Figure 10.13).

The secret to succeeding on the remote access question on Network+ is to keep it simple. What do you need to make remote access work? You need a telephone link, hardware, a data link protocol, and the correct software. Make sure that you know the difference between PSTN and ISDN. Know that you want to use PPP instead of SLIP. Last, know that encryption exists and that the type of remote access software will determine the amount of encryption you can have. Remember these and you will do fine!

FIGURE 10.13
Configuring TCP/IP settings on remote client.

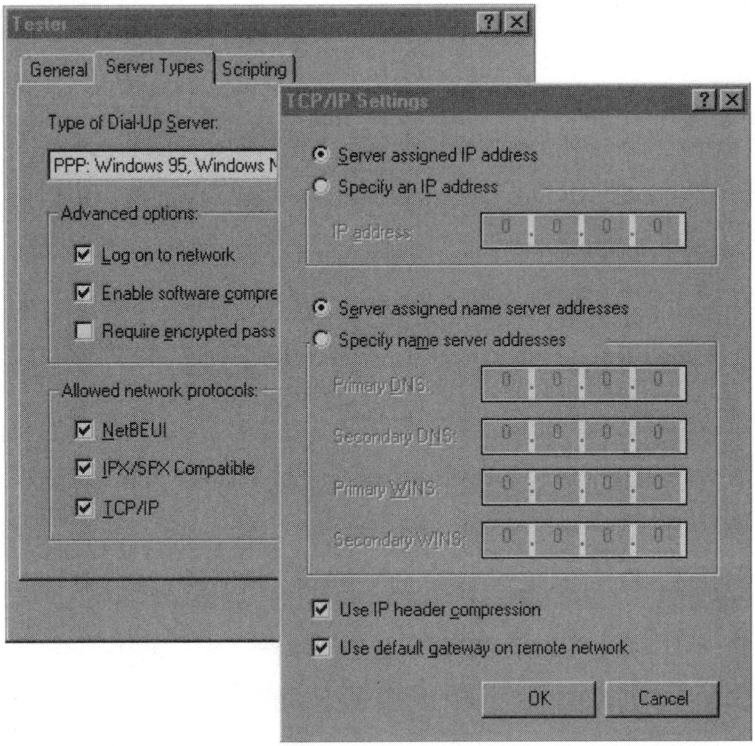

Review Questions

(Select the best answer)

1) Which of the following is *not* a data link protocol for telephone lines? (Select all that apply)

a) SLIP
b) IP
c) PPP
d) PPTP

2) Which of the following provides the fastest throughput?

a) PSTN
b) ISDN BRI
c) ISDN PRI
d) POTS

3) The popular Microsoft remote access client is called __________ .

a) RAS
b) Dial-up Networking
c) Dial-up Server
d) Microsoft Client for Networks

4) Pepe is concerned that e-mail sent from his laptop to the RAS system in the home office could be read by others. He needs to use:

a) A password.
b) Encryption.
c) A login name.
d) SMTP.

5) BRI ISDN uses:

a) One B channel and 24 D channels.
b) 24 B channels and one D channel.
c) One B channel and two D channels.
d) Two B channels and one D channel.

6) The V.90 standard defines a modem speed of:

a) 56K bps.
b) 33.6K Baud.
c) 28.8K bps.
d) 2400 Baud.

7) Which of the following V standards defines error checking?

a) V.42
b) V.42bis
c) V.34
d) MNP 8

8) The ISDN equivalent of a modem is called:

a) A terminal point.
b) A network interface device.
c) A terminal adapter.
d) A network adapter.

9) Which of the following are benefits of ISDN over PSTN? (Select all that apply)

a) ISDN is more available.
b) ISDN is faster.
c) ISDN connects more quickly.
d) ISDN is cheaper.

10) Generally, how close do you need to be to a central office to use ISDN?

a) 1800 feet
b) 1800 meters
c) 18000 feet
d) 18000 meters

Review Answers

1. **B** and **D.** SLIP and PPP are data link protocols for telephone lines.
2. **C.** ISDN PRI has a throughput of 1.5 megabits per second. The next closest is ISDN BRI at 128 kilobits per second.
3. **C.** Dial-up Networking. RAS is a remote access server software.
4. **B.** He needs to use some form of encryption.
5. **D.** BRI ISDN uses two B channels and one D channel.
6. **A.** The V.90 standard defines a 56K bps modem speed.
7. **A.** The V.42 standard defines modem error checking.
8. **C.** The ISDN equivalent of a modem is called a terminal adapter.
9. **B** and **C.** ISDN is faster than PSTN and connects more quickly.
10. **C.** You need to be within 18000 ft of a central office to take advantage of ISDN.

CHAPTER 11

Maintain and Troubleshoot the Network

Even if you are just starting into the life of a network technician, you probably already know the disappointing fact that networks, like the machines and cables on which they are based, break. Your job is to do as much as possible to prevent the breaks and to fix the breaks as quickly as possible when they do occur. Preventing the breaks, and making the fixes are as easily as possible, is based on a set of preventive measures: obtaining and creating documentation, creating baselines, preventing viruses, and planning for recoverability. Once the inevitable happens, however, and something does break, you should follow a troubleshooting model for fixing the problem: determine the problem by eliminating impossibilities and focusing on the clues and indicators you're given, and document the steps you take to try to fix the problem (especially that one sneaky step that finally does fix the problem).

Before It Breaks

The best time to get your network's ducks in a row is when it is working correctly. During those blissful moments, you should obtain the manufacturers' documentation and create your own documentation for all the elements of your network. You should also determine what is normal for your network—that is, create a *baseline*—so that when users complain that something is slower or different from normal, you can tell if they are correct. Next, you should work to prevent one of the biggest network villains—viruses. Finally, you should plan how to recover the data that makes your company money in the unlikely event that all your preventive measures were not enough to save the patient.

Documentation

The cornerstone of a healthy network is the documentation you have on the elements of your network. *Documentation* is a broad category that encompasses not only the manuals and read-me files from manufacturers, but also your own documentation, such as network maps, change logs, and network history. You need to get and create this documentation, and then you need to find a way to store, manage, and update it as necessary.

What You Get from the Manufacturers

The first category of documentation to hoard in your network library is the information you can get from the manufacturers. Examples of the types of documentation you want to obtain and keep from a software or hardware manufacturer are listed below:

- Read-me files (often called README.TXT or README.DOC) on the installation CD/Diskette can often give information about known bugs or incompatibilities. These files also give notes about installation procedures.
- Official software and hardware documentation, such as users' manuals, usually come with both the hardware and software that you install. These manuals often give in-depth installation instructions, frequently asked questions, and troubleshooting suggestions. These manuals also provide direction to more updated information, patches, or additional drivers, in the form of FTP sites, Web URLs, BBS lines, or help lines to call.
- Manufacturers' Web sites are veritable fonts of useful knowledge. On Web sites you can find searchable troubleshooting databases (often called "knowledge bases") that are compiled based on the questions and problems that other customers have brought to the attention of the manufacturer. When the issue is resolved, it gets added to the database for your benefit. Also available on manufacturers' Web sites are downloadable patches, to fix bugs in software, and updated drivers.
- The Usenet has many newsgroups that discuss specific types of hardware and software, as well as general hardware and networking topics. These groups are a good place to visit regularly, just to keep an eye on the current topics. They are also a good place to go when you have a problem—someone else may already have solved a similar one.

When you get new hardware and software, the manufacturer probably sends you a mass of manuals, licenses, read-me files, and warranties that you immediately put aside so you can install the software. It would be more to your network's advantage if you looked over this documentation before you ran into problems or errors. How often have you skipped reading the instructions, only to get halfway through installing some widget under your sink and suddenly realize that you won't be able to turn your water back on until you get to the local hardware store and buy two other widgets that you thought came in the package? It is the same situation, but perhaps a more dire fate for your network if you are in the midst of installing a new NIC, only to realize that there is a known incompatibility between this brand of NIC and your machine's video card. In general, it is better at least to skim the documentation before installing any new hardware or software—look specifically for installation instructions and known bugs or incompatibilities.

After glancing through this provided documentation, many network administrators stick it in a pile and assume they can sort it out later. Unfortunately, when later comes, that same administrator is probably running around because his main e-mail server is down and he cannot find the documentation for that server's NIC. It is best to organize your documentation by machine, or class of machine. If all your servers, for example, are built to the exact same specification, with the exact same components, you should keep a file for all the documentation for the server-class machines. When any server has even one piece of hardware that is not standard, that server should have its own file, with all the documentation for all its components. This allows you, when you are preparing for upgrades or doing troubleshooting, to take one binder or file folder and have all the information for that machine at your fingertips.

What You Create Yourself

The list of documentation about your network that you should create yourself is even longer and more far-reaching than the documentation you obtain from other sources. This documentation must accurately reflect the configuration of the hardware and software installed, as well as any changes that get made to it. Your documentation should have the following elements:

- Each piece of hardware and software has a variety of numbers associated with it, such as serial numbers, part numbers, and license numbers. It is important to keep a list of all the numbers associated with the hardware and software installed in each machine.
- Each of the machines in your environment was built at some point by somebody who put certain pieces of hardware and software into it. You should know what pieces of hardware and software are in the machines, when they were installed and configured, and by whom. This allows you to check back with that person for more information or

assistance, if it becomes necessary. Look at Figure 11.1 for a sample of a log that might give all the necessary details on a particular machine.

FIGURE 11.1

Sample log.

Function and software	Location/Phone	TCP/IP Settings	Hardware
PDC; Houston_WRT domain	Houston Server Room	IP=223.190.190.1	Standard Compaq Proliant 7000
OS = NT 4 Service Pack 3	713-999-9999	subnet = 255.255.255.0	inventory number SRVC7x01
Added SP 4 3/99		Gateway = 223.190.100.1	Video Card=S3 Virge DX
Added SP5 6/99			inventory number VCS301
			NIC=Intel 10/100
			inventory number NICI01

- The folder for each machine should also reflect each time one of the machines is changed in any way, including hardware and software upgrades, upgrades to BIOS or drivers, or changes of location.
- A network map, created with a program such as Visio, is often useful. Figure 11.2 shows an example of a network map created with Visio. This map would include the servers, workstations, printers and other peripherals, cables and cable closets, patch panels, hubs, routers, and any other elements of your network. This enables you to find the connections between problems as well as locate specific pieces of your hardware.

FIGURE 11.2

Sample Visio network diagram.

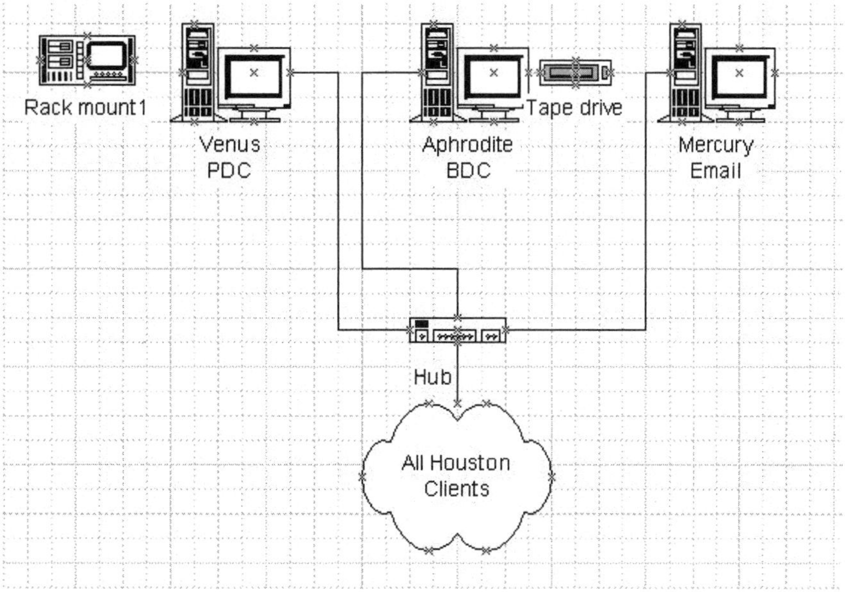

- Each time a new procedure is created for installing, fixing, or configuring an element of your network, it must be documented and made available to anyone in your organization who might perform that task.
- Each time a new policy is set—for issues such as password length, login times, available storage space, or other issues—it must be documented.
- All domains, servers, or accounts that require an administrator's account should have a super-administrator account created and documented. This account information and password should not be available to most administrators. You might store it with the network manager or with the other sensitive network documentation.
- Most network operating systems have the ability to configure groups and permissions or rights. You should document what users are members of which groups. Then document which groups and users have which level of permissions or rights to which resources.
- Each network has mapped drives, servers that contain special data or have special functions, and other "details." These details are important to document. New employees or consultants need this information when familiarizing themselves with your network.
- As you begin to create special configurations or batch files, or collect special drivers, these should be documented and backed up—what does that strange JOEBOB.BAT do on the primary domain controller machine? Is it necessary? If you were a new network administrator just coming into an environment that had no documentation, you might be tempted either to run the batch file or to delete it. In one case, it might be a destructive Trojan horse (a type of virus) left by a disgruntled former administrator to delete your most important configuration files; in the other case, it might be the file that runs the nightly backup. Neither scenario bodes well for your stress levels. If all the batch files were documented, however, you would know when each one could be run.

This list of suggested documentation for your network, while long, is just the tip of the iceberg. Each organization has elements of its network configuration that are unique—these are the elements that must be documented and available to the administrators, contractors, or consultants working on your systems.

How to Manage the Documentation

All the hours spent on documentation will be wasted if you allow elements of the network to be changed without updating the documentation. Similarly, no amount of documentation can help if the server that stores it all is the one machine that is irrevocably fried. Managing your documentation is as important as creating it. Managing documentation consists of ensuring that changes made to the systems or networks are reflected in the documentation and that all the documentation is available when it is necessary.

First, you should ensure that all changes to machines get logged. Similarly to the original log of how the machine was configured, the change log should include the who, when, what, and why information, as shown in Figure 11.3. This enables you not only to keep track of how your machines are currently configured, but also to ensure that you can return to the original configuration if necessary.

FIGURE 11.3

Sample change log.

Change Log				
Name	**Added Software**	**Date/Who**	**Added Hardware**	**Date/Who**
Venus	NT Service Pack 4	3/1/99		
		John X. Tech		
	NT Service Pack 5	6/1/99		
		John X. Tech		
			Additional 10/100 NIC	John X. Tech
			inventory number NICI07	6/2/99

Next, you need to ensure that the documentation you have created and organized and updated is available when you need it. While it makes a great deal of sense to use a software-based knowledge management system for your documentation, make sure you can immediately put your hands on at least one hard copy and a software backup of the documentation. This ensures that even if your network or the server that stores the information is unavailable, you have the information you need to troubleshoot that problem.

Baseline

A *baseline* is a static picture of your network and servers when they are working correctly. This enables you to compare your static picture to new readings, especially useful when your systems or network are not working. One of the common tools used to create a baseline is the Performance Monitor utility that comes with Windows NT. You can also create baselines using most network sniffer and systems management utilities. We should run through an example baseline with NT's Performance Monitor.

Administrators use Performance Monitor (PerfMon) to view the behavior of hardware and other resources on NT machines, either locally or remotely. PerfMon can monitor both real-time and historical data about the performance of your systems. To access the Performance Monitor applet, choose Start...Programs...Administrative Tools...Performance Monitor from any Windows NT machine.

Once you access Performance Monitor, you need to configure it to display data. The process of configuring Performance Monitor requires you to understand the concept of objects, counters, and views. An *object* in Performance Monitor relates directly to the component of your system that you want to monitor, such as the processor or memory. Each object has different measurable aspects, called *counters*. These are the portions of an object that you want to track. As you decide which object(s) to monitor in your system, select one or multiple counters for each object. Add these counters to whichever view you need to use. Performance Monitor can display selected counter information in a variety of views, with each view imparting different types of information. The Log view, for example, lets you store data about your systems to be reviewed later. This is the view used to create a baseline, and is the only one discussed here, although the other views (Chart, Alert, and Report) are useful for troubleshooting problems as they arise.

To access the Log view, either click the Log view button or choose View...Log. To add objects to the Log view, either click the Add To button (the plus sign) or choose Edit...Add to Log. In the Add to Log dialog box, first select the computer to monitor. Choose either the local machine (the default), or a remote machine. To monitor a remote machine, type in the computer name using Universal Naming Convention (UNC). To monitor a machine named HOUBDC1, for example, you would type \\HOUBDC1 in the "Computer" field. You can also use the Select Computer button (at the right end of the Computer field) to view the available machines and select the one you want to monitor, as shown in Figure 11.4.

FIGURE 11.4

Select computer in Performance Monitor.

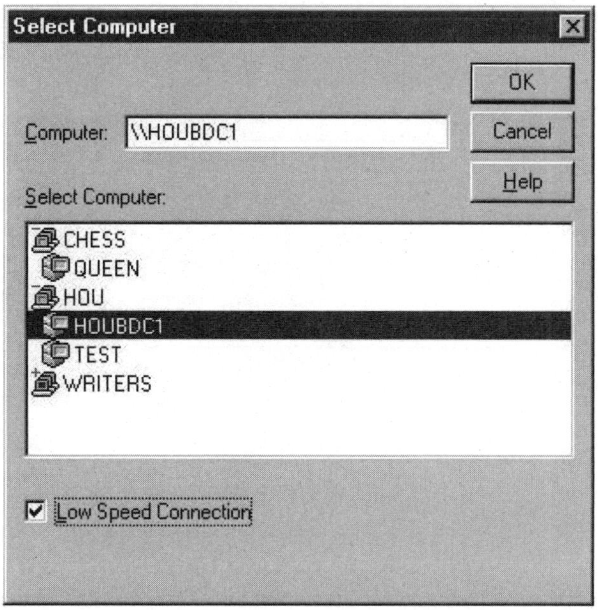

NOTE

While it is often easiest to monitor a machine locally, it is often more accurate to monitor the machines remotely. Performance Monitor running on a machine uses a certain amount of resources to take the measurements and to display the data graphically. Especially when you troubleshoot issues with disk performance, memory and paging, or processor use, you should not corrupt your results by monitoring locally. There are some cases where monitoring locally is preferred or required. If you are monitoring network access or networking protocol objects, for example, monitoring locally will affect the readings less than monitoring remotely. Similarly, you must monitor a system locally if you cannot access that system over the network. Finally, when you monitor objects created by a specific application, such as Exchange, you should monitor locally, as the objects related to this application are only created locally and will not be available from another system.

Once you have selected a system to monitor, either locally or remotely, you must select the object to monitor. Select one or more objects to monitor from the list in the Object field. Note that the Log view is somewhat different from the other views in that you only add objects to the view, not the specific counters for the objects, as shown in the Add To Log dialog box in Figure 11.5.

FIGURE 11.5

Add To Log in Performance Monitor.

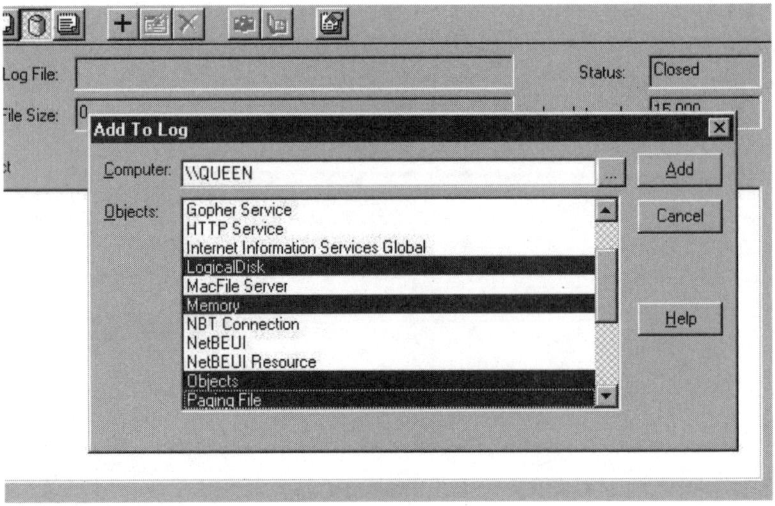

After you select the objects for Performance Monitor to track and log, select Options...Log Options to save the data to a log file and to start the logging by clicking the Start Log button, as shown in Figure 11.6. This dialog box also gives you the opportunity select the update method and time.

FIGURE 11.6

Start Log in Performance Monitor.

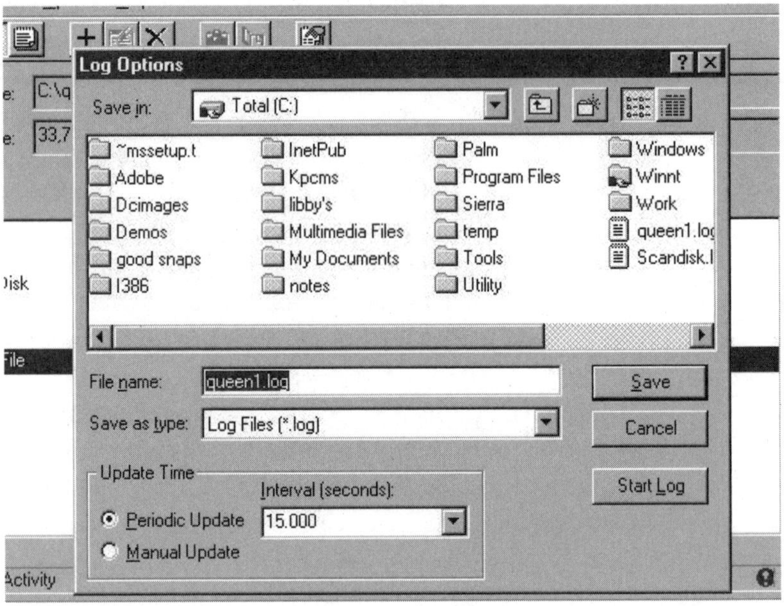

After you have configured the log to save to a particular file, you can see the log file name, status of the logging process, log interval, and file size of the log in the Performance Monitor dialog box. To stop collecting data in a log, open the Log Options dialog box again and click Stop Log. You can then choose to create a new log file and begin logging again, if necessary. You will also have the ability to view data from one of these saved log files by selecting Options...Data From. In the Data From dialog box, shown in Figure 11.7, you can choose to continue obtaining data from the current activity or to obtain data from a particular log file.

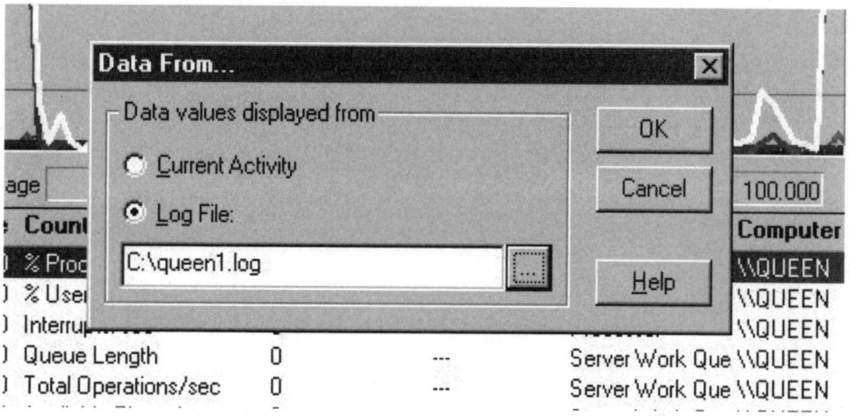

FIGURE 11.7 *Data From dialog box in Performance Monitor.*

When you choose to obtain data from a saved log, you go back to that frozen moment in time and add counters to the other views for the objects you chose to save in the log. In our Log options, we selected to store data for the Logical Disk object, for example. After we have loaded that particular log file, we can change to the Chart view, add counters for the Logical Disk object, and view a static chart for that moment in time, as shown in Figure 11.8. You may want to select a wide variety of objects, so that when you open the log to display in any of the other views (chart, alert, and report), you can add any counters necessary.

The Performance Monitor utility described here is specific to Windows NT systems, but you should create a baseline on whatever types of systems you have and for all aspects of your network. Be certain to create multiple baselines, to show both the systems at rest and in use, using Performance Monitor as well as other systems management or network sniffer tools.

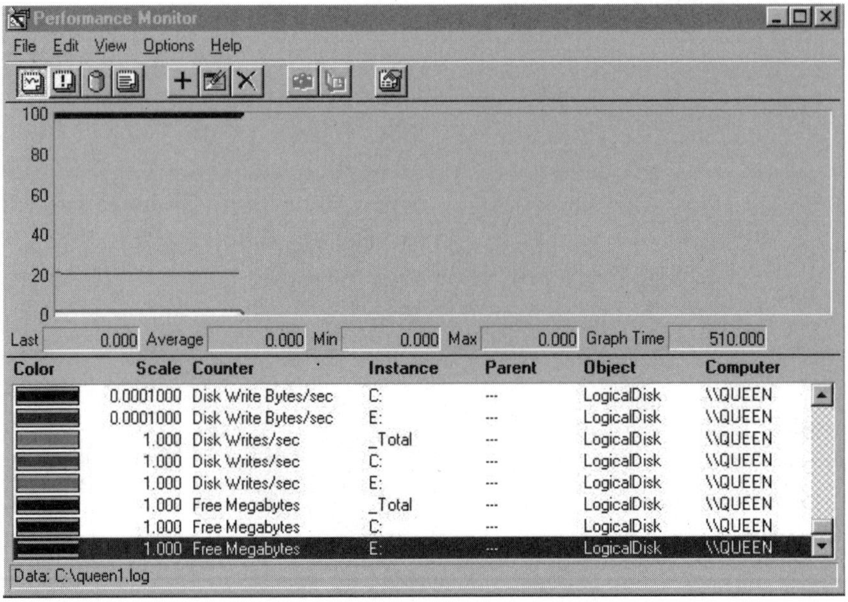

FIGURE 11.8 *Viewing a static chart in Performance Monitor.*

Virus Issues

The greatest villain in today's sharing, networked computer society is the virus. Viruses today can be executable files, Java or JavaScript applications, and macros that run in other applications. These viruses can be transmitted in a variety of ways, including downloading documents from the Web, receiving viruses or infected documents via e-mail, or through more traditional means, such as accidentally booting from an infected disk or running a Trojan horse. The first step toward protecting your network from these unwanted viruses is buying good network-based virus protection software. For protection from downloaded viruses, you might also invest in a firewall that has the ability to screen out unwanted hangers-on.

A variety of companies, among them Network Associates and Symantec, offer virus protection suites to help protect your network. These software suites enable scanning and cleaning of viruses on the servers and workstations in your network. You have two important tasks to make this work. First, buy and install the virus protection software. Second, make sure you keep it updated. Most virus protection software depends on often-updated files, usually called data, definition, or signature files, that search for and clean particular viruses. If you have good virus software but an out-of-date definition file, the newer viruses can have a field day in your systems. It is best to check for new data files on a regular basis (once per week, for example) and have a predetermined method for making sure all the proper locations get updated. This is the only way to protect your machines from infestation. The virus protection suite is the best all-around method of protection for your network. It enables you to scan not only your servers, but also your workstations, and in some cases, specific downloaded files and e-mail. The more complete a suite you are able to buy, the more protected your network can be.

TIP

EXAM TIP:

You must remember how important it is to update the virus definitions regularly—just having virus protection software will not protect you if your resident Web addict just downloaded the newest virus created only two days ago.

An additional way that systems can get infected with viruses is by attacks from hackers or other unwanted users. These users often gain access to your systems or networks through accidentally open ports or other back doors. One precaution you can take is to purchase firewall software that can block unwanted users. These users often attack networks by infecting them with viruses. If you do not allow these users to sneak into your system, they cannot infect you with viruses. Firewalls can also be configured to block certain files or types of files from being downloaded. While you probably would not want to block the download of all .DOC or .EXE files, you might block specific, known virus files.

Planning for Recoverability

Think about how much work you have done to create your nice, stable servers, workstations, and network. Imagine how many hours your users have spent creating data and storing it on those servers. Now imagine a virus that deletes critical data or configuration files. As you can also imagine, this situation is not good for either your blood pressure or your job security. What common sense dictates is that you create backups of your data. Backups are useless, however, if you only make them once. It is no good to restore a file that has been changed for three weeks since the last time it was backed up. You should therefore create a scheduled backup that ensures that your data are backed up regularly and can be restored easily. The best way to start is to make sure that you have a backup plan in place. The backup plan should include the following details:

- When the backups will occur and what the tape rotation schedule will be
- What types of backups will be done at each time
- Where the backups will be stored.

Perhaps the most important details are the types of backups and the schedule, or strategy, of backups.

What Are the Types of Backups?

The goal of backing up is to ensure that whenever a system dies, there will be an available, recent backup to restore the system. At first thought, you might simply back up the complete system at the end of each day—or whatever interval you feel is prudent to keep the backups "fresh." But complete backups can be a tremendous waste of time and materials. Most files don't change that often—so why back them up? Instead of backing up the entire system, take advantage of the fact that files don't always get changed; most backup software solutions have a series of backup options available other than the old complete (usually called full or normal) backup.

The cornerstone to understanding backups other than the full backup is something called the Archive attribute. All files have little one-bit storage areas called attributes. The most common attributes are Hidden (don't show it when DIR is typed), System (shows that it is a critical file for the system), Read-Only (can't erase it), and the Archive bit. These attributes were first used in FAT formatted drives (DOS) but are still completely supported today by all file formats. The archive bit basically works like this: whenever a file is saved, the archive bit is turned on. Opening a file will affect the current state of the archive bit. A backup program will usually turn off the file's archive bit when it is backed up. In theory, if a file's archive bit is turned off, there is a good backup of that file on some tape. If the archive bit is turned on, that means that the file has been changed since the last backup (Figure 11.9).

FIGURE 11.9

Archive bit.

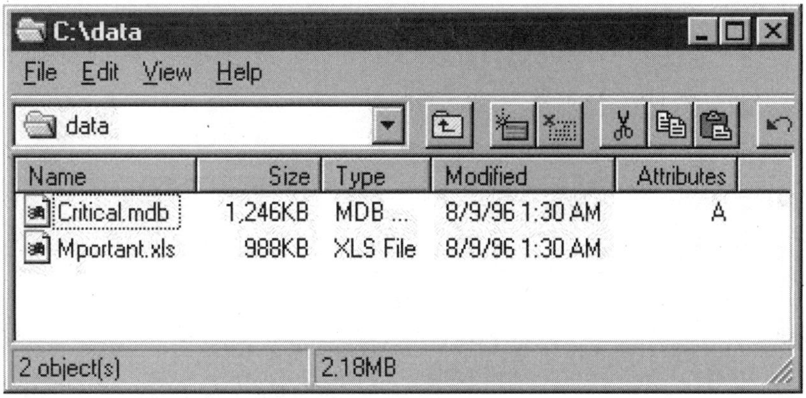

Archive bits are the tool we use to perform backups that are not full backups. The following backups are most often supported:

- *Normal* is a full backup. Every file selected will be backed up. The archive bit will be turned off for every file backed up. This is the standard "back it all up" option.
- *Copy* is identical to Normal with one exception. The archive bits are not changed. This is used (although not often) for making extra copies of a previously completed backup.
- *Incremental* backups only back up the files that have the archive bit turned on. An incremental backup only copies the files that have been changed since the last backup. It then turns off the archive bits.
- *Differential* backups are identical to incremental backups, but don't turn off the archive bits.
- *Daily*, better known as *Daily Copy*, makes a backup of all of the files that have been changed that day. It does not change the archive bits.

NOTE

EXAM TIP:

You really need to know the different types of backups, including which ones change the archive bits and which ones do not.

The motivation for having both the incremental and differential backups is not always clear. They seem—at first glance—to accomplish the same thing. Incremental might appear the better option at first. If a file is backed up, you probably want the archive bit turned off, right? There is one common scenario where that might not be very attractive. Most backups do a big weekly Normal backup, followed by daily incremental or differential backups at the end of every business day. Let's look at the difference in Figure 11.10.

FIGURE 11.10 *Incremental vs. differential.*

Incremental

MON	TUE	WED	THU	FRI
Full Backup	All Tuesday Changes	All Wednesday Changes	All Thursday Changes	All Friday Changes

Differential

MON	TUE	WED	THU	FRI
Full Backup	All Changes Through Tuesday	All Changes Through Wednesday	All Changes Through Thursday	All Changes Through Friday

Notice that a differential backup is cumulative. Since the archive bits are not set, it keeps backing up all changes since the last normal backup. Clearly, the backups will get progressively larger through the week as more files are changed. The incremental backup, in contrast, only backs up the changes since the last backup. Each incremental backup will be small and also totally different from the previous backup. Let's assume that the system is wiped out during the day on Thursday. How will you restore the system? Well, with an incremental backup, you need first to restore the weekly backup, then the Tuesday backup, and then the Wednesday backup before the system is restored. If you use a differential backup, on the other hand, you only need the weekly backup and then the Wednesday backup to restore the system. The greater the distance between normal backups, the more incremental backups you need to restore. A differential will always be only two backups to restore (Figure 11.11). Suddenly, the differential backup looks better than the incremental!

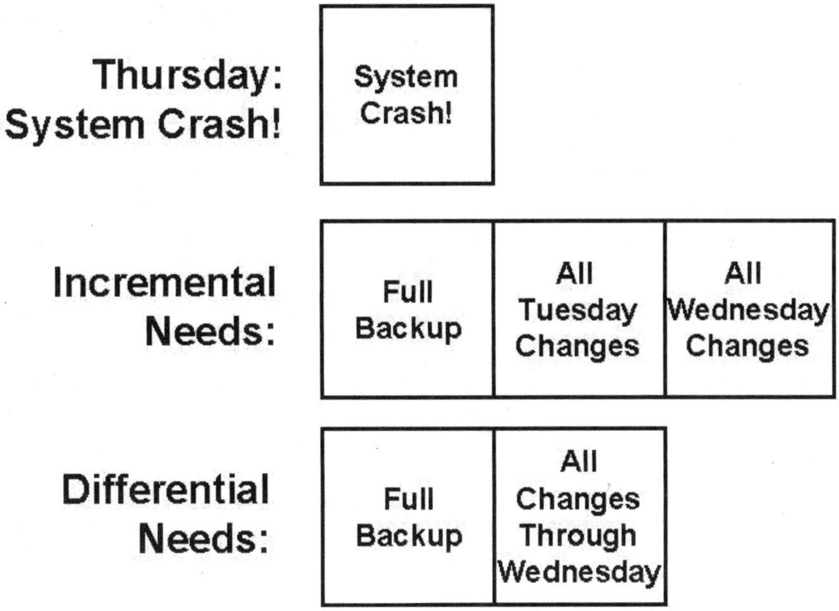

FIGURE 11.11
Restoring from backups.

There are a number of backup strategies to use, each one making incremental or differential backups more attractive. One big benefit of incremental over differential is backup size. Differential backups will be massive compared to incremental. The type of backup you perform will determine the type of backups system you use.

Backup Strategies

In order to answer questions on backups and recoverability successfully, you need a specific strategy for your network environment. First, ensure that you can back up and easily restore all the important information from each indispensable machine. Second, you have to do something with the tapes themselves. Backups to protect against a hacker or virus will mean little, after all, if your tapes get washed away in a flood!

There is no hard and fast rule for minimum hardware requirements when doing backups. As mentioned in Chapter 8, tape backup devices are the most common hardware used in backups. What you may notice in larger environments, however, is that backups begin taking too long, as you add data, servers, and workstations to the backup mix. You may have backups scheduled to begin at 11pm to ensure that all your users are gone and have closed their files. When you arrive at 8 am, however, you may notice that your backups are still running, or have just finished. This could hinder the network and server performance for users just arriving. In this case, you should begin adding tape devices to other machines until your backups are taking an acceptable amount of time, or consider other, non-tape devices for backup storage. After you have backed up all your data, you should give some thought to data integrity on the backup tapes as well as to the safekeeping of those tapes. To verify data integrity, test the restore procedures on a regular basis. All that entails is doing a restore on some of the files from a tape to an alternate location and then comparing the data to make sure they are usable and correct. In addition, tapes do wear out. If you have used the same tapes for a long period of time, splurge on some new ones. Set a schedule for taking tapes out of production and either archiving them or destroying them, and replacing them with new tapes.

Speaking of archiving tapes, have you given any thought to where you will store the tapes? If you said "At my desk," or "In the server room," think again. You should always store backups off site, in a secure location. Imagine that your building has had a fire. You want the backup tapes as far from the servers they are backing up as possible. Similarly, you do not want to store all your backups on a single tape. You should rotate tapes so that you always have the tapes necessary to do a full restore procedure back to your last full backup. Depending on the type of backup you have chosen to do, this may entail having a full week's worth of tapes that you rotate, or even a month's worth of tapes that you rotate.

Ok, It Broke—Now What?

All your planning and documenting is about to come in handy, because your network or system is about to do something that causes one of your end-users to call you up, crying or sputtering or yelling—or all of the above! You now need to go from planning and prevention mode to troubleshooting mode. When you move into troubleshooting mode, your purpose is to figure out what the problem really is. This can be challenging, as you can imagine when a user calls you complaining that he cannot log on to the server. This symptom could be traced to a variety of causes, including (but not limited to) user error, broken or unplugged cable, server crash, or incorrect protocol configuration. The trick is to figure out which one. This requires a troubleshooting model or method that helps you keep your mind open while ruling out things that are obviously not causing your problem. With this troubleshooting model, it also helps to know which tools to use to diagnose problems. There are a variety of both software and hardware tools that can aid in ruling out your wild guesses.

Troubleshooting Model

No matter how complex and fancy we decide to make it, any troubleshooting model can be broken down into three simple steps: figure out what's wrong, fix it, and write it down so that it doesn't happen again. While each of these steps is more complex than this, the step that really holds the key (and is most tested on the Network+ exam) is the first step: figure out what's wrong. This step carries so much weight because when you figure out what's wrong, you've probably also figured out how to fix the problem and how to prevent it from happening in the future. To complete this step, it helps to break it down into a variety of component parts:

- Determine the extent of the problem
- Try to isolate the causes of the problem
- Try to recreate the problem.

The process begins when someone or something brings a problem to your attention. This can occur with a phone call, frantic visit, page, or stumbling across the problem yourself. Usually the problem described to you is merely a symptom, such as "I can't get to the Internet" or "I can't log in to the server." These symptoms can be traced to a variety of causes, and it is your job to figure out this cause. One of the first steps in trying to determine the cause of a problem is to understand the extent of the problem. Find out if the problem is specific to one user or if the problem is network-wide. Sometimes, this entails trying the task yourself—from that user's machine and from your own machine. If the user tried to log in to the network, for example, you need to go to that user's machine and try to use his username to log in. This lets you determine if the problem is user error of some kind, as well as enabling you to see the symptoms of the problem yourself. Write down what happens—what you tried and which error message you received. Next, you probably want to try logging in with your own username from that machine or try having the user log in from another machine. In some cases, you can ask other users in the area if they are experiencing the same problems—this helps you determine if the problem is larger than one user. Depending on the size of your network, find out if the problem is occurring in only one part of your company, or across the entire network. What does all of this tell you? Essentially, it tells you how big the problem is. If nobody in an entire remote office can log in, you may be able to assume that the problem is the network link or router connecting that office to the server. If nobody in any office can log in, you may be able to assume that the server is down or not accepting logins. If only that one user in that one location cannot log in, it may be a problem with that user, that machine, or that user's account.

Eliminating variables is one of the first tools in your arsenal of diagnostic techniques. Imagine you're back in high school and studying the scientific method—the first thing that you were taught was that you can only do an experiment on one variable at a time; this holds true in troubleshooting technical problems as well. After determining the extent of a problem, the next step requires eliminating all the extra variables—all the *other* possible causes of the problem. If you have determined that the problem is specific to that user on that machine, you have already learned a great deal. First, you have learned that it is not a user account problem, because you tested that user's ability to log in from another machine. You have also determined that it isn't user error, because you've tried it yourself. By having other users try the task, you have also eliminated the possibility that the server is down. Now that you have eliminated some possibilities, it is time to eliminate others. It is a good idea to try to figure out if the problem is hardware or software. You might start by checking to make sure that the network cable is plugged into the network card (NIC) and the patch panel, jack, or hub. If it is connected, make sure the lights on the NIC and hub are lighting—if you do not see a light, you may have a bad cable, for example. On the other hand, if you can access something else on the network, such as another server, you may have a software configuration problem with the protocol or other element. In this step, use any tools you have to eliminate possibilities. Some of these tools are physical and easy to quantify, such as the hardware tools described in Chapter 9 and the software tools described in Chapter 6 (and below). Other tools are less easy to describe, such as the questions you can ask the users, the knowledge you bring with you about how the network should function, and the baselining and planning work you have performed earlier. Regardless of what tools or techniques you use to accomplish it, the goal of this step is to isolate the problem.

Another useful step is to try to recreate the problem. Sometimes, if a problem cannot be recreated, this will tell you that it was user error, or that it was due to a network slowdown or other event that has been corrected. If you cannot recreate a problem, it may be useful to check the user's operating procedure. If you are able to recreate a problem, you may discover the steps that were taken that caused the problem. When trying to recreate a problem, you should write down each step you take, both to enable you to back out of the steps as well as to enable you to remember all the steps that you took. If you recreate the problem, but then cannot remember what you did, you will have gained nothing and lost time.

While no single book can tell you how to fix all the network problems you will eventually face, the steps of determining the extent of the problem, eliminating variables to isolate the cause of the problem, and recreating the problem give you a method that will enable you to track down any network problem.

What Tools Can You Use to Determine the Problem?

While working through the process of determining the cause of a problem, you will need to use many tools. Some of these tools, as mentioned above, are difficult to quantify—such as asking questions, referring to your network baselines and documentation, and synthesizing all your network knowledge. Other tools are easier to describe—these are software and hardware tools that enable you to gain more information about your network. Many of the tools that fall into this category have been described already, such as hardware or software loopback testing devices, utilities such as PING and TRACERT, and hardware tools such as tone locators. The trick is in knowing how to apply these tools to solve your network problems.

"Touchy Tools"

The tools that are most difficult to quantify because they are mostly within you are those "touchy tools." An example of a "touchy tool" is the questions that you ask the person who has the problem. This is touchy because there are no set questions to ask—you have to use your background knowledge and intuition to tell you which questions are the right ones. The types of questions you need to ask fall into several categories:

- Questions designed to find out exactly what steps the user took that caused the symptom are important so that you know how to try to recreate the problem. In addition, these types of questions can give you some insight into whether the problem was caused by user error or improper procedures. Be careful with how you phrase these sorts of questions. "What did you do, you idiot!" generally causes users to clam up. The goal, remember, is to extract information.
- Questions designed to find out the exact error messages can help you when you try to search manufacturers' knowledge bases and support lines.
- Questions designed to find out what the user has tried to do to fix the problem can help you determine when you are dealing with many layers of problems. Many users try to fix things, but forget to write down what they do. Suddenly they cannot back out of their "fixes" and come crying for help. Be gentle! If you can determine most of the things the user tried, you can get back to the original problem instead of having a layered problem.

Another "touchy tool" is the comparisons you should make to the baselines and documentation you created for your network. When users complain of slow connections or downloads, for example, you should compare the bandwidth and connection speeds from your baseline to what you are able to test while the "problem" exists. You may find that the "problem" lies more with the user's expectations than in any real network problem. You are then left to decide whether you can upgrade your systems and connectivity or whether the users just need to understand the limitations.

The most complicated "touchy tool" to describe and quantify is the network knowledge you have that can be applied to your network's problems. You will find many network troubleshooting questions on the Network+ exam, for example, which you should be able to answer not from reading this chapter, but from reading the rest of the book. Troubleshooting is often just the application of other knowledge in a different way. You know, for example, that an IP address, a subnet mask, and a default gateway are all required to communicate with the Internet using the TCP/IP protocol. Edgar complains that he cannot connect his Windows 95 client to the Internet. His hardware seems to be functioning correctly (link lights are on and his NetBEUI connection to the NT Server is working) and the proxy server is up. At that point you might check his TCP/IP configuration by using the WINIPCFG utility. If you notice that he has no default gateway, you have solved the problem. The knowledge to solve this problem came partially from understanding how to troubleshoot by eliminating possibilities, but also from your knowledge of all the elements required to connect a machine to the Internet. As you prepare for the exam, and for administering your company's network, ask yourself how each thing you learn about networking could be applied toward troubleshooting the network. This prepares you for the time when you have to make that leap.

Hardware

In Chapter 9, you read about a few hardware tools used when configuring your network. These included cable testers, protocol analyzers, hardware loopback devices, and toners. Each can be applied to troubleshooting to help you eliminate or narrow down the possible causes of certain problems. In addition, other pieces of hardware, although they cannot actively be used for troubleshooting, can provide clues to the problems you face.

A cable tester enables you to determine if a particular cable is "bad." Bad can be defined in a variety of ways, but essentially means that the cable is not delivering the data for whatever reason—the cable is broken, crimped badly, or sits too close to a heat or electrical source. In most troubleshooting situations, you will use other clues to determine if you have a hardware or software problem. Then, if you have narrowed down the problem to a hardware connectivity issue, a cable tester can help you determine if the cable is good or bad. Another option, if you are without one of these tools, is to replace the cables (one at a time) and test the connectivity. In the "I can't log on" scenario, for example, if you have determined that everyone else in the area can log on, and that this user can log on from another location, you have narrowed the problem to either a configuration or a hardware issue. If all network activity is broken (i.e., nothing is available in Network Neighborhood or you cannot PING the default gateway), you may choose to test cables connecting the PC to the server. This is not the only option, but it is one variable that can be tested and eliminated.

Protocol analyzers come in both hardware and software flavors. Most of the hardware analyzers have an additional software component. These tools enable administrators to determine what types of traffic are flowing through their networks. Most analyzers translate the packets flowing over the network to provide destination, source, protocol, and some information about content. In a situation where you have a network slowdown, you might use a protocol analyzer to determine what types of packets are passing over your network, and where they are originating. In some cases, a dying network card can produce large numbers of packets, often called a *broadcast storm*, which can be detected by using a protocol analyzer and noticing that all the packets are coming from one location. Once you have narrowed your problem down to a particular machine, you can concentrate on that rather than blaming your servers, bandwidth, or other elements.

Another device often used to confirm that a NIC is functioning correctly is a hardware loopback device. This device usually plugs into the NIC directly, allowing you to test that it is functional. Tone generators and tone locators, described in Chapter 9, round out the network tech's troubleshooting toolbox. These devices enable you to determine which cable is which when the labels that you so carefully attached are accidentally ripped off or become outdated.

Other pieces of hardware, although they are not directly related to testing or troubleshooting a problem, can often give clues to the cause of a problem, just by your observing them. Lights on hubs or NICs, for example, should be illuminated when the device is functioning and sending or receiving data. If the lights are not lit on a NIC in a machine that cannot connect to the network, testing or replacing the NIC may help solve the problem. The lights might also be off because of a bad cable, which would be another thing to test in that scenario. The temperature of servers and workstations can also be an issue. If you notice that a particular machine is very hot to the touch, or that the room a server is in is very warm, those environmental issues might be affecting the hardware. A broken A/C unit on a hot, humid summer day at the Bayland Widget Corporation's Houston office, for example, could completely disable their network.

Other problems can be caused by the proximity of your network hardware to other pieces of hardware or machinery. If your network experiences problems every time you turn on a particular light or other device in the area of the cables or hubs, there might be an electrical problem. Be aware of the times you can use pieces of hardware directly to troubleshoot problems or eliminate possible causes of a problem, but also be observant of clues that other, non-troubleshooting hardware provides.

Software

Throughout the book, you have read about software tools that can be used when configuring your network and can also be applied to troubleshooting. Since most of these have been described elsewhere in the book, this is just a review of the basic purpose of these tools. Software troubleshooting tools include the following:

- *Software-based protocol or network analyzers* include applications such as the Network Monitor (NETMON) provided with Windows NT. Also called packet sniffers, these tools collect and analyze individual packets on a network to determine bottlenecks or security breaches. Use these tools when you have unexplained slowdowns on your network, to help determine which machines are sending packets. This enables you to determine if there is a broadcast storm (or just too much broadcasting in general), or if you are the victim of a hacker attack, for example.
- *System logs*, such as Windows NT's Event Viewer, display any errors or problems that have occurred in your system. If a user repeatedly failed at log in, for example, this might be recorded in the appropriate view in the Event Viewer tool. That information could be the clue you need to determine that a user is locked out, either because he forgot his password or because someone has been trying to hack into that account. Logs also provide information on services or components of the operating system that do not start or are receiv-

ing errors. This is a good way to troubleshoot system crashes on a particular machine.

- *Performance monitors*, such as the Performance Monitor tool described earlier in this chapter, provide a clue to the utilization of a particular machine. When users complain of slowdowns or logon problems that can be traced to a specific system or server, this tool can often give you a clue about what is happening on the system to cause the problems. If a system is going to 100% memory utilization when a particular application is started, for example, it may mean that you need more RAM or should put that application on a dedicated server. Use this tool for troubleshooting when the problem has been tracked to a particular machine, but you need to determine where in that machine the bottleneck exists.
- *Systems management software suites*, such as Microsoft's SMS server or the Tivoli management tools, combine all the above applications with other elements, including user registration, security auditing, software installation. These suites give large environments a centralized tool for managing and monitoring their network. These suites usually also include pager or e-mail notification of certain events, such as system outages or network slowdowns.
- *Network card utilities* are usually included with any new NIC and its drivers. These utilities provide a way to determine if the network card is functioning properly and if it is installed correctly. If you have installed a NIC and it does not seem to be working, network card utilities will enable you to troubleshoot the card itself.
- *PING* is a TCP/IP utility used to determine if a remote machine can be reached using the TCP/IP protocol. The command is PING [IP address] or [hostname]. If you use the hostname option, you are also testing DNS or host file name resolution. To limit the variables, first try the command with the IP address. Then, if necessary, try the command with the hostname. The results of a PING show whether the destination host is reachable and how long the packet takes to reach it. You can also use PING with the loopback address (127.0.0.1) or with the host name *localhost* to determine if the local machine's TCP/IP stack is configured correctly. PING can be used in a variety of troubleshooting scenarios. Any time you need to verify connectivity, the PING utility is a quick and easy option to try. Be aware that if your machine uses a proxy or other non-standard con-

nection to the destination machine, PING may not work. A sample PING output is shown in Figure 11.12.

FIGURE 11.12

PING output.

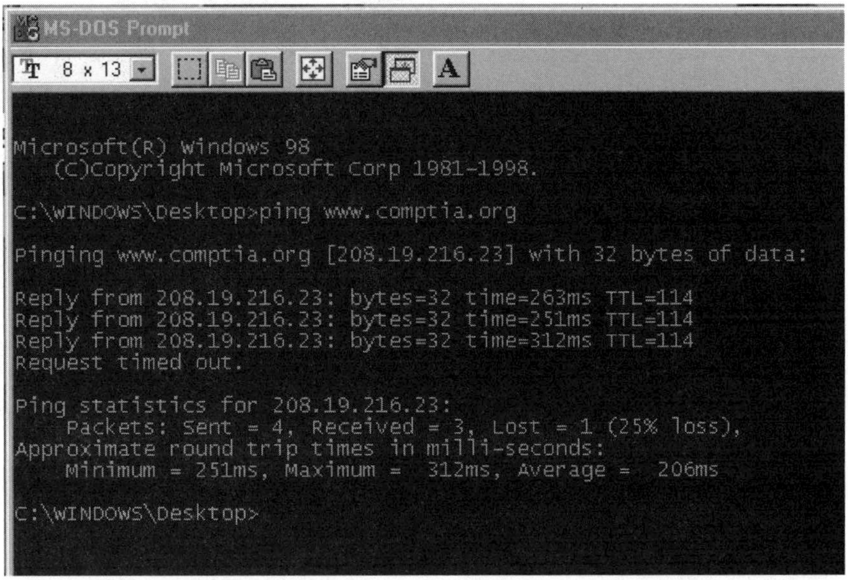

- *TRACERT* is a TCP/IP utility used to show the route a packet takes to get to its destination. The command is TRACERT [IP address] or [hostname]. If you use the hostname option, you are also testing DNS or host file name resolution. To limit the variables, first try the command with the IP address. After trying this, then try the command with the hostname. The output describes the route from your machine to the destination machine, including all devices it passes through and how long each hop takes. Use this utility to troubleshoot bottlenecks. When users complain that it is difficult to reach a particular destination using TCP/IP, this utility enables you to determine if the problem exists on a machine or connection over which you have control, or if it is a problem on another machine or router. Similarly, if a destination is completely unreachable, TRACERT can again determine if the problem is on a machine or router over which you have control. A sample output of TRACERT is shown in Figure 11.13.

TRACERT
8 x 13
A
C:\WINDOWS\Desktop>tracert www.comptia.org
Tracing route to www.comptia.org [208.19.216.23]
over a maximum of 30 hops:
1 155 ms 152 ms 153 ms hou-tx-pm94.netcom.net [163.179.40.138]
2 164 ms 163 ms 140 ms hou-tx-gw1.netcom.net [163.179.40.33]
3 142 ms 156 ms 147 ms h5-0-2.dfw-tx-gw1.netcom.net [163.179.233.69]
4 211 ms 232 ms 203 ms h1-0-30.was-dc-gw1.netcom.net [163.179.232.246]
5 200 ms 201 ms 230 ms h1-0.mae-east.netcom.net [163.179.220.182]
6 271 ms 251 ms 282 ms sl-mae-e-f0-0.sprintlink.net [192.41.177.241]
7 261 ms 299 ms 258 ms sl-bb4-dc-1-1-0-T3.sprintlink.net [144.228.10.93
]
8 274 ms * 235 ms sl-bb12-rly-3-3.sprintlink.net [144.232.7.157]
9 266 ms 244 ms 270 ms sl-bb11-rly-8-0.sprintlink.net [144.232.7.213]
10 288 ms 278 ms 230 ms sl-bb11-pen-7-0.sprintlink.net [144.232.8.154]
11 262 ms 233 ms 241 ms sl-bb10-nyc-6-0-622M.sprintlink.net [144.232.9.1
01]
12 324 ms 281 ms 274 ms sl-bb10-chi-6-0.sprintlink.net [144.232.9.150]
13 294 ms * 243 ms sl-gw15-chi-5-0.sprintlink.net [144.232.0.226]
14 284 ms 259 ms 253 ms sl-aquila-1-0-T1.sprintlink.net [144.228.55.42]
15 312 ms 241 ms 285 ms s43.aquila.com [204.95.88.43]
16 * 277 ms 248 ms s30.worknetinc.com [207.40.37.30]
17 280 ms 316 ms 288 ms www.comptia.org [208.19.216.23]
Trace complete.
C:\WINDOWS\Desktop>

FIGURE 11.13
TRACERT output.

- *NBTSTAT* is a command-line utility to determine the connections open on a machine using NetBIOS over IP. The command is NBTSTAT with various switches, such as –r (to display names resolved by broadcast or by WINS) or –R (to purge and reload the name cache for the local machine). An example of the NBTSTAT –r command, intended to show which names the current machine knows and how it knows those names, is shown in Figure 11.14. Note that NBTSTAT is case sensitive—using a lowercase switch when you meant to use an uppercase switch (or vice versa) can cause some spectacularly unexpected results!
- *NETSTAT* is a command-line utility for determining which TCP/IP connections a machine currently has open. The command is NETSTAT, with a variety of switches available, to show statistics and port information. This command enables you to determine if your machine is connecting over a particular port, for example. Use this utility to troubleshoot TCP/IP connectivity problems. A sample output is shown in Figure 11.15.

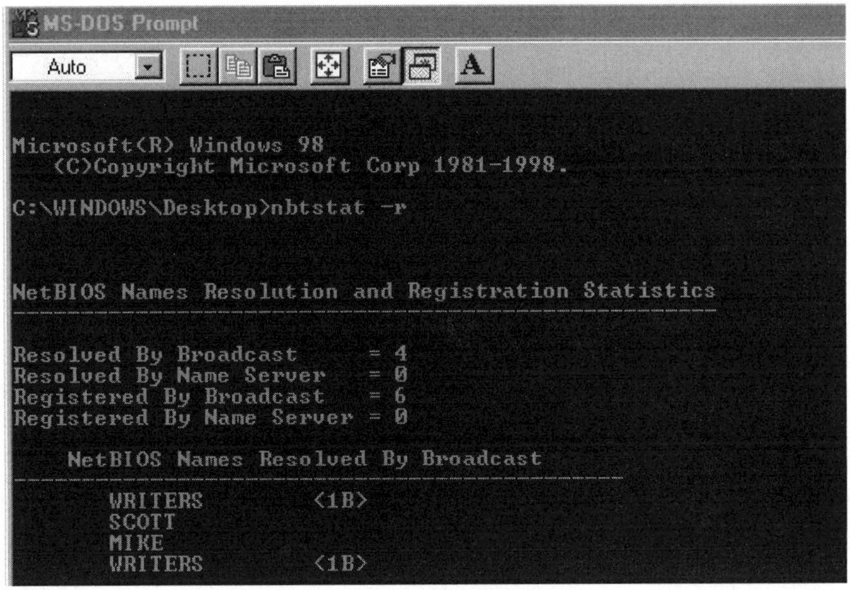
MS-DOS Prompt
Auto
Microsoft(R) Windows 98
(C)Copyright Microsoft Corp 1981-1998.
C:\WINDOWS\Desktop>nbtstat -r
NetBIOS Names Resolution and Registration Statistics
Resolved By Broadcast = 4
Resolved By Name Server = 0
Registered By Broadcast = 6
Registered By Name Server = 0
NetBIOS Names Resolved By Broadcast
WRITERS <1B>
SCOTT
MIKE
WRITERS <1B>

FIGURE 11.14

NBTSTAT -r output.

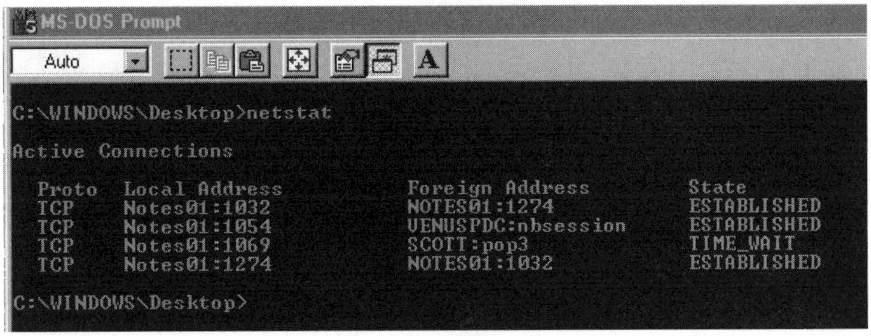
MS-DOS Prompt
Auto
C:\WINDOWS\Desktop>netstat
Active Connections
Proto Local Address Foreign Address State
TCP Notes01:1032 NOTES01:1274 ESTABLISHED
TCP Notes01:1054 VENUSPDC:nbsession ESTABLISHED
TCP Notes01:1069 SCOTT:pop3 TIME_WAIT
TCP Notes01:1274 NOTES01:1032 ESTABLISHED
C:\WINDOWS\Desktop>

FIGURE 11.15

NETSTAT output.

- *IPCONFIG* is the Windows NT utility for determining your TCP/IP settings. Use this utility to verify IP address, default gateway, subnet mask, DNS, and other IP-related settings. The output is similar to the WINIPCFG output shown below.
- *WINIPCFG* is the Windows 95/98 utility for determining your TCP/IP settings. Use this utility to verify IP address, default gateway, subnet mask, DNS, and other IP-related settings. A sample output is shown in Figure 11.16.

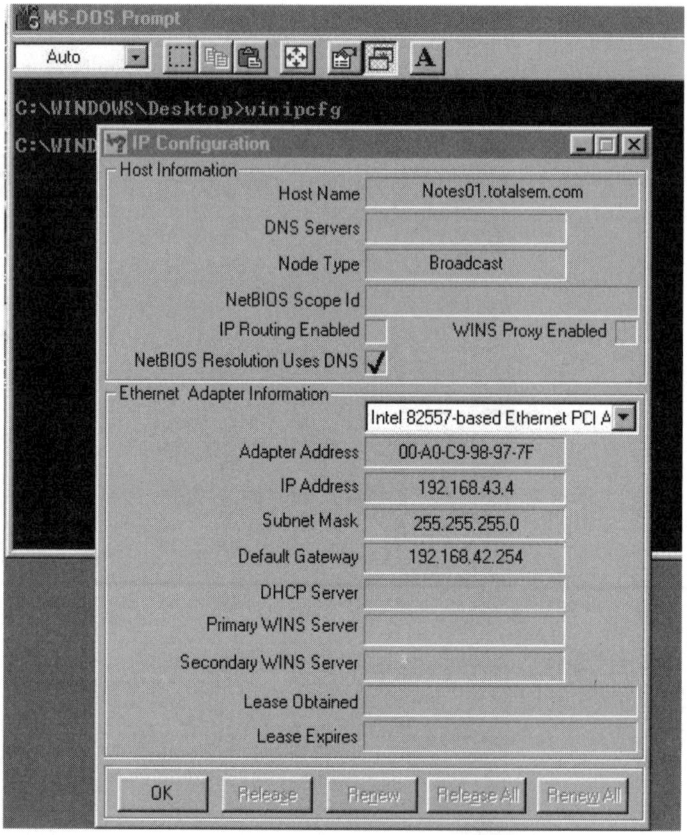

FIGURE 11.16
WINIPCFG output.

- *IFCONFIG* is the Linux (UNIX) utility for determining and changing your TCP/IP settings. Use this utility to verify IP address, default gateway, subnet mask, DNS, and other IP-related settings.

Another set of software tools for troubleshooting is the patches, bug fixes, and knowledge bases that most manufacturers provide for their hardware or software. When you are troubleshooting a problem, it is often wise to access the manufacturers' Web sites and search for information about your particular problem. Many hardware and software manufacturers offer searchable support sites that help you find lists of other people's problems. When you find one that is similar to yours, you can then use the site to download a fix or patch, update the software or drivers, or find lists of steps to take to correct the problem.

Troubleshooting as Art

Troubleshooting is not something that can be easily described in a neat list of ten easy steps. It is more of an art—an ability to be "one with the network" and intuit where the problems are hiding. The best troubleshooters are those who have a huge amount of knowledge about each of the elements of the network—hardware, software, connections, etc. These people can then synthesize all that knowledge into some good guesses about where to start looking for the problems. All the steps above should serve to give you a theoretical idea of where to look and how to proceed with troubleshooting your own network. The theory, however, is easier to implement in real life if you have some examples to give you the feel of the art of troubleshooting. The scenarios below describe the art of tracking down where the problem is by a variety of methods. These scenarios by no means cover all the trouble spots you will encounter in your own networking adventures, but they should begin to give you the feel for where to look and what tools to use.

"I Can't Log In!"

One of the most complex issues surrounding troubleshooting is that the same symptoms, in this case a user's inability to log in, can have many causes. Woody has called complaining that he cannot log in to the company's intranet. When Suzy Tech tries to complete the log in from her workstation, using Woody's ID and password, she is able to access the intranet site. Suzy might also want to have other users try to log in, or confirm that other users are not having the same problem. Next, Suzy should have Woody try the log in from another machine. This will help Suzy determine whether the problem is related to the user's ability to perform a log in or related to Woody's Windows 98 workstation or connectivity.

If Woody is unable to log in from any other machine, Suzy should probably take steps to ensure that Woody is using the correct login ID, password, and procedure to perform the log in. On the other hand, if Woody is able to log in when trying from another user's workstation, Suzy should probably start trying to determine if Woody's workstation is working and connecting to the network. Steps to try here include PINGing Woody's workstation. If Suzy is able to PING Woody's machine successfully, she knows that the machine is up, the TCP/IP protocol is configured correctly, and that it is connected to the network. Suzy might then look at the configuration of the network client on Woody's workstation. If Suzy had not been able to PING the workstation, however, she might need to test the cables and NIC using cable testers or loopback devices and to verify that TCP/IP was correctly configured using WINIPCFG.

"I Can't Get to this Web Site!"

Reaching external Web sites requires a variety of components to be configured correctly. Some of these components are within your company's internal control; many of them are not. When Fatima calls and tells Suzy Tech that she cannot reach **http://www.comptia.org**, Suzy's first step is to try to reach that site herself. In this case, Suzy was also unable to get a response from the site. One of her next steps is to try to PING the site—first by name and then by IP address. She gets no response by name, but she does get a normal response when she tries to PING the site by IP address. This immediately indicates to her that the problem lies with name resolution—in this case DNS.

On the other hand, if she had been unable to PING with either IP or host name, she might consider two things. First, if her company uses a firewall or proxy server to reach the Internet, she would want to PING that machine. This is usually the same IP address as the default gateway TCP/IP setting. If Suzy can successfully PING her default gateway, it is almost certain that the problem is not something she or her company has any control over. To verify this, Suzy should attempt to reach some other external sites—both by PINGing and with a browser. If she can reach other sites successfully, the problem is most likely with the site or gateway.

"Our Web Server is Sluggish!"

When response from a server is slow, it can be related to a variety of things. Usually, however, it comes down to a connection to the server or to the server itself. When Wanda calls in from working at home and tells Suzy Tech that she is having very slow response from their company's Web site, Suzy Tech tries to reach the offending server and is immediately connected, which indicates that it may be a connectivity problem for that user. She asks Wanda to try a TRACERT from her workstation to the slow server. This reveals to Suzy that the slowdown is from one of the intermediate steps that Wanda connects through. This problem is out of Suzy's hands, unless she can offer a direct dial-up option for Wanda.

If Suzy finds that she cannot reach the offending server quickly when she tries from her workstation, however, then the problem may lie with the server itself. Suzy checks the Change Log for the Web server, to see if anyone has changed anything recently. She finds that a new anti-virus component was recently added, so she checks the vendor's Web site to make sure that there are no known problems or patches for that piece of software. She also uses Performance Monitor to compare the server's current responses to the baseline that she has. This helps her note that the bottleneck is related to excessive paging, indicating that the server may need more physical memory, or RAM.

"I Can't See Anything in Network Neighborhood!"

When a user is completely cut off from the network, the problem is usually limited to that user's workstation or network connection. When Suzy gets a call from Johnny saying that his Windows 98 machine is on, but he can't log in and he can't see any other machines on the company's TCP/IP network, Suzy goes to Johnny's office to run some tests. The first test that Suzy runs is a PING to an external machine. She doesn't expect it to work, but tests just to be certain. Next, she tries a PING of Johnny's machine by using either PING Localhost or PING 127.0.0.1. When the PING of the local machine does not work, Suzy guesses that the problem is in the TCP/IP configuration. To view the machine's TCP/IP configuration, Suzy uses WINIPCFG. She notices that the IP address is blank. After checking her network documentation to verify what IP address Johnny's machine should have, she adds an IP address and is able to connect to the network.

If Suzy's PING 127.0.0.1 had worked, she would have had to assume that the TCP/IP and networking configuration of Johnny's machine was correct. She now moves to checking hardware—she uses a network card utility to verify that the NIC itself is working correctly. She uses a cable tester to verify that the cable from Johnny's workstation is working correctly. When the cable tester shows that the cable is bad, she replaces the cable between Johnny's workstation and the patch panel and is able to connect.

The art of network troubleshooting can be a fun, frolicsome, and usually frustrating skill to gain. By applying a good troubleshooting methodology and constantly increasing your knowledge of networks, you can develop into a troubleshooting artist. This takes time, naturally, but stick with it. Learn new material, document problems and fixes, talk to other network techs about similar problems. All these factors can make your life much easier when crunch time comes and a network disaster occurs—and it will, even in the most robust network.

Review Questions

1) Which of the following should be included in your network documentation? Select all that apply.

a) Patches
b) Drivers
c) Network map
d) Change log

2) Which of the following could be used to create a baseline for your server?

a) README.TXT
b) Performance Monitor
c) TRACERT
d) WINIPCFG

3) The most important thing(s) to consider with virus software is (are):
(Choose all that apply.)

a) Update the virus definition files often.
b) Run the virus scan on all incoming attachments, documents, and e-mail.
c) All servers and workstations should have virus-scanning software.
d) All virus software requires a firewall server.

4) Which of the following will help protect your systems/network from viruses if your users download new files every day?
a) Firewall
b) Proxy
c) Virus scanning software
d) Updated virus definition files

5) Which of the following backup types change the archive bit?
a) Daily
b) Differential
c) Incremental
d) Copy

6) Polly is creating a backup plan for her network's servers. She wants to have a backup of all her data that will allow her to restore very quickly when needed. This is even more important than how long the backup takes to perform. Which of these is a good backup plan?
a) Full backup on Sundays; daily for each day of the week
b) Full backup on Sunday; incremental for each day of the week
c) Full backup on Sunday; differential for each day of the week
d) Full Backup on Sunday; copy backup for each day of the week

7) If Joe in Accounting cannot log in to his company's TCP/IP network, what should Suzy do first to determine the scope of the problem?
a) PING Joe's workstation
b) Have users in Joe's office/segment try to log in
c) Have users in other offices/segments try to log in
d) Run WINIPCFG at Joe's workstation

8) Hannah calls Suzy saying she can't see any other machines in the network. Suzy wants to confirm that Hannah's Windows NT workstation has been configured correctly for her TCP/IP segment. What should she try?

a) IPCONFIG
b) WINIPCFG
c) IFCONFIG
d) Use a protocol analyzer to verify that TCP/IP is configured correctly on the machine

9) If Julieana needs to verify that her IP configuration is working, which of the following PING commands can she use?

a) PING 255.255.255.0
b) PING 127.0.0.1
c) PING LOCALHOST
d) PING HOST 127.0.0.1

10) Which tool(s) should Basil use to find the bottleneck on his company's Web server when it suddenly begins running slowly?

a) Performance Monitor
b) Protocol analyzer
c) Change log
d) Hardware loopback adapter

Review Answers

1) C and **D.** Your network documentation should include a Network map and Change log. Patches and drivers should be updated regularly from the vendor.

2) **B.** The log view of Performance Monitor is one way to create a baseline. README.TXT files contain installation and configuration information. TRACERT is a TCP/IP utility to determine the route packets take to their destination. WINIPCFG is a Windows 95/98 utility used to determine the TCP/IP configuration.

3) **A, B,** and **C** are all correct. It is very important to update the virus definition files regularly, as new viruses are being discovered all the time. It is also important to make sure that the virus scanning software is available on all machines in the network and that it is scanning all data that come into the environment.

4) **A, C,** and **D** are correct. A firewall can help determine what files can be downloaded and which should be kept out. Virus scanning software with up-to-date definition files is necessary to ensure that all downloaded files get checked for viruses.

5) **C** and **D** are correct. Incremental and copy backups change the archive bit.

6) **C** is the best answer. A differential backup would only require two tapes to restore the data—the first, full backup and the differential from the appropriate day.

7) **B.** Have users in the same segment try to connect first. Then have users in other segments try to log in.

8) **A.** IPCONFIG is used for Windows NT; WINIPCFG is used for Windows 95/98 machines; IFCONFIG is used in UNIX.

9) **B** and **C** can both be used to verify the functioning of the local TCP/IP interface.

10) **A** and **C.** Performance Monitor helps determine what elements of the server are causing the slowdown. A Change log could tell you if anything has been added to the machine recently that might be causing the problem.

APPENDIX A

Network+ Exam Quick Reference Section

The following are some key study points to remember when going in to take the exams, even if you don't remember anything else. If you look at a note and it doesn't automatically make sense to you—and suggest about 10 other, related facts—go back and review. These notes should be the last things you run through before you go in to take your exam. While this list is not the only information necessary to pass, it gives you some basic points to memorize.

Chapter 1: Bus Topologies and Ethernet

- Review the star, bus, ring, and mesh topology diagrams in Chapter 1.
- IEEE 802.2 describes Logical Link Control; 802.3 describes Ethernet (a.k.a. CSMA/CD); 802.5 describes Token Ring.
- Ethernet packets contain the following: the data, the MAC address of the sender, the MAC address of the recipient, and a CRC for data checking.
- MAC addresses are unique 48-bit addresses given to each NIC. Use WINIPCFG to see a MAC address on a Windows 9x machine.
- 10Base5, or Thick Ethernet, transmits at 10 megabits/second, uses baseband signaling, and its segments can be a maximum of 500 meters long. 10Base5 NICs use a 15-pin AUI connector and an external transceiver. There can be a maximum of 100 nodes, which must be spaced at 2.5-meter intervals. The ends of the cable must have terminating resistors.
- 10Base2, or Thin Ethernet, transmits at 10 megabits/second, uses baseband signaling, and its segments can be a maximum of 185 meters long. 10Base2 uses BNC connectors and thin coaxial cable (RG-58). 10Base2 requires T-connectors to connect to the NICs and to allow for a terminating resistor.
- Repeaters recreate packets across segments, allowing greater distances between machines and more nodes on the network.

Chapter 2: Ethernet: Bigger, Faster, Stronger than Before

- 10BaseT, using a star bus topology, runs at 10 megabits/second, uses baseband signaling, and its segments can be a maximum of 100 meters. 10BaseT uses 4-pair UTP cabling (CAT 3 or better) with RJ-45 connectors.
- Hubs provide the bus part of the topology. They act like repeaters.
- 5-4-3 rule: 5 repeaters, 4 segments, and 3 populated segments between nodes in a collision domain.
- Bridges (operating at the data-link layer of OSI) filter and forward traffic based on MAC addresses.
- Routers (operating at the network layer of OSI) filter and forward traffic based on network addresses. Routers can choose among multiple paths.
- 100BaseTX and 100BaseT4 run at 100 megabits/second over Category 5 UTP cabling. 100BaseT4 can also run over CAT 3 cabling. TX uses 2 pairs; T4 uses 4 pairs. Maximum segment length is 100 meters.
- 100BaseFX runs at 100 megabits/second over fiber optic cable; maximum length is 400 meters.
- Half-duplex cards cannot send and receive at the same time, but full duplex can.

Chapter 3: Ring Topologies and Token Ring

- Token Ring (802.5) machines can only talk when they have the token. The token is regenerated at the original sending machine after a message is passed.
- Token Ring hubs are MAUs or MSAUs. When connecting multiple MAUs, the Ring In port goes to the Ring Out port.
- Token Ring can use UTP or STP.

Chapter 4: The OSI Model

- OSI seven layers = 1) Physical, 2) Data Link, 3) Network, 4) Transport, 5) Session, 6) Presentation, and 7) Application.
- The physical layer turns binary into physical pulses (electrical or light). Repeaters and hubs operate at the physical layer.
- The data link layer identifies devices on the physical layer. MAC addresses are part of the data link layer. Bridges operate at the data link layer.
- The network layer moves packets between computers on different networks. Routers operate at the network layer. IP and IPX operate at the network layer.
- The transport layer breaks data down into manageable chunks. TCP, UDP, SPX, and NetBEUI operate at the transport layer.
- The session layer manages connections between machines. NetBIOS and Sockets operate at the session layer.
- The presentation layer, which can also manage data encryption, hides the differences between various types of computer systems.
- The application layer provides tools for programs to use to access the network (and the lower layers). HTTP, FTP, SMTP, and POP3 are all examples of protocols that operate at the application layer.

Chapter 5: The Protocol Suites

- NetBEUI is not routable.
- NetBIOS manages connections based on 15-character maximum computer names.
- IPX/SPX is routable. SAP is part of the IPX protocol suite and sends broadcasts to create connections.
- NWLink is Microsoft's implementation of IPX/SPX.

Chapter 6: TCP/IP

- An IP address has a host ID that describes the particular machine and a network ID that describes the network on which the machine lives.

- Class A addresses start with 1-127, allow 16.7 million hosts, and have a default subnet mask of 255.0.0.0.
- Class B addresses start with 128-191, allow 65,546 hosts, and have a default subnet mask of 255.255.0.0.
- Class C addresses start with 192-223, allow 254 hosts, and have a default subnet mask of 255.255.255.0.
- 127.0.0.1 is the loopback address reserved for testing the local machine's TCP/IP configuration.
- TCP/IP requires an IP address and a subnet mask. To be routable, it also requires a default gateway.
- TCP is connection-oriented. UDP is connectionless.
- HTTP uses port 80; SMTP uses port 25; FTP uses port 20; POP3 uses port 110; HTTPS uses port 443; Telnet uses port 23; SNMP uses port 161.
- Proxy servers can cache copies of pages that have been requested by users on their network. Proxy servers can act as firewalls. Firewalls can filter traffic in or out of a network.
- DNS and HOSTS files resolve host names to IP addresses.
- WINS and LMHOSTS files resolve NetBIOS names to IP addresses.
- DHCP automates all the TCP/IP settings, including IP address, subnet mask, default gateway, and DNS server.
- WINIPCFG is a Windows 95/98 utility to show the IP configuration. IPCONFIG is the Windows NT version.
- Know the PING, TRACERT, ARP, NETSTAT, and NBTSTAT commands and what their output looks like.

Chapter 7: Network Operating Systems

- Client-server.
- Peer-to-peer—all machines act as both servers and clients.
- User profiles allow for specific configurations for each user.
- NT uses domains and the SAM.
- Novell NetWare 3.x uses the Bindery and IPX/SPX. Novell NetWare 4.x uses the NDS tree and IPX/SPX. Novell NetWare 5.x uses NDS and native TCP/IP.
- UNIX uses FTP and NFS.

Chapter 8: The Complete Network PC

- 10Base5 uses female DB-15 connectors (also called DIX connectors)—these connectors go to the AUI, or external transceiver.
- 10Base2 uses BNC connectors.
- 10BaseT, 100BaseTX, 100BaseT4, and 100BaseVGAnyLAN use RJ-45 connectors.
- 10BaseFL and 100BaseFX use SC or ST connections.
- Token Ring NICs use either female DB-9 connectors or RJ-45 connectors.
- Modems use RJ-11 connectors.
- Parallel ports use female DB-25 connectors. Serial ports use male DB-9 or male DB-25 connectors.
- Printers use 36-pin Centronix connectors.
- External SCSI devices use 50-pin Centronix connectors or high-density 50- and 68-pin DB connectors.
- The connection light on a NIC or a hub should be solid on; the activity light on a NIC or a hub should flicker.
- Most devices on a PC need a unique IRQ to talk to the CPU. Review the IRQ table in Chapter 8.
- Almost all devices also need an I/O address and some need a DMA channel and a memory address. Review these addresses from Chapter 8.
- RAID 0 is disk striping and provides no redundancy. RAID 1 is disk mirroring and disk duplexing. RAID 3, 4, and 5 are all disk striping with parity. RAID 5 is most common.

Chapter 9: Connectivity Hardware

- Star topology using UTP is the most common.
- To connect 10Base5 to UTP, add a transceiver; to connect 10Base2 to UTP, get a hub that has an extra 10Base2 port.
- Electrical devices can cause interference and failure with cables that are too close or not properly protected.
- Use PVC cabling from the wall to the PC; use plenum-grade cabling inside the walls and crawl spaces for fire safety.

- EIA/TIA specification for maximum distance is 90 meters; the extra 10 meters available for all the other technologies is reserved for the patch cables.
- Fiber optic cabling provides longer distances and immunity to electrical interference.
- CAT5—'nuff said.
- Use a cable tester to determine if a cable is good.
- Use a toner (tone generator and tone locator combination) to find specific cables (if you forgot to label them, that is).
- An SPS provides power only during an outage; a UPS always provides power.

Chapter 10: Remote Connectivity

- PSTN usually has a 2400-baud rate. It is analog and uses an RJ-11 connector.
- A modem converts analog signals into digital signals, and vice versa.
- Baud is an analog measurement; a bit per second (bps, Kbps) is a digital measurement.
- A V.90 standard is for 57,600 bps (a.k.a., 56 Kbps).
- ISDN is a telephone line that uses a digital connection. It has B (64K) channels and D channels, usually in a 2-B 1-D configuration—allowing a 128K throughput.
- A T1 line is ISDN that uses 24 channels for a 1.5Mbps throughput.
- ADSL supports download speeds of up to 9 Mbps over dedicated PSTN lines.
- SLIP only supports IP with a static IP address.
- PPP supports IP, IPX, and NetBEUI, as well as dynamic IP addresses.
- PPTP works with PPP to create a secure tunnel using encryption.

Chapter 11: Maintain and Troubleshoot the Network

- Look for updated drivers, README.TXT files, patches, and other installation or configuration instructions on the installation disks that come with any new hardware or software.

- Look for similar information on manufacturers' Web sites, BBSs, and from phone support.
- Document everything in your network, including parts and manufacturers, addresses, and who installed what when.
- Document changes to your network when they are made.
- A baseline is a static picture made when your systems and network are working correctly. Make one. Performance Monitor is one tool that can help.
- Get virus protection software and update its definition files regularly.
- Do tape backups regularly and then store some of them offsite.
- Normal and incremental backups turn off or change the archive bits. Copy, differential, and daily copy do not change the archive bits.
- To troubleshoot a problem, find out the scope by trying the same procedures elsewhere in the network.
- Use utilities like WINIPCFG, PING, and TRACERT to verify IP configuration and connectivity.
- Servers should be kept in cool, dry environments.
- Other electrical devices can affect your network because of voltage and interference.
- Look for link lights (solid) and activity lights (blinking) to see if a NIC or hub is connected or receiving data.
- Use cable testers and toners to verify that cables are working and which cables are which.

APPENDIX B

Glossary

5-4-3 Rule A rule of thumb for approximating the correct size of a collision domain. In a collision domain, no two nodes may be separated by more than 5 repeaters, 4 segments, and 3 populated segments.

10Base2 An Ethernet LAN designed to run on common coax RG-58 cabling, almost exactly like the coax for cable television. It runs at 10 megabits per second and has a maximum segment length of 185 meters. Also known as Thinnet or Thin Ethernet, it uses baseband signaling and BNC connectors.

10Base5 The original Ethernet LAN, designed to run on specialized coax cabling. It runs at 10 megabits per second and has a maximum segment length of 500 meters. Also know as Thicknet or Thick Ethernet, it uses baseband signaling. It uses DIX or AUI connectors and external transceivers.

10BaseT An Ethernet LAN designed to run on UTP cabling. 10BaseT runs at 10 megabits per second. The maximum length for the cabling between the NIC and the hub (or switch, repeater, etc.) is 100 meters. It uses baseband signaling.

100BaseFX Fiber optic implementation of Ethernet that runs at 100 megabits per second. It uses baseband signaling. Maximum length of the cable is 400 meters.

100BaseT A generic term for any Ethernet cabling system that is designed to run at 100 megabits per second on UTP cabling. It uses baseband signaling.

100BaseT4 An Ethernet LAN designed to run on UTP cabling. It runs at 100 megabits per second and uses 4 pairs of wires on CAT3 or better cabling.

100BaseTX An Ethernet LAN designed to run on UTP cabling. It runs at 100 megabits per second and uses 2 pairs of wires on CAT5 cabling. It uses baseband signaling.

100BaseVG Also called 100BaseVGAnyLAN. This uses CAT 3 cabling and an access method called demand priority.

100BaseFX An Ethernet LAN designed to run on fiber optic cabling. It runs at 100 megabits per second and uses baseband signaling.

1000BaseX Gigabit Ethernet

16450, 16550, 16550A, 16550AF, 16550AFN Incremental improvements in UARTs. The 16550AFN is considered the most sophisticated UART available today. Note: the 16450 should not be used with any modem faster than a 14.4Kbps modem.

16-bit To be able to process 16 bits of data at a time.

24-bit color Referred to as 24 bit or true color, using 3 bytes per pixel to represent a color image in a PC. The 24 bits enable up to 16,777,216 colors to be stored and displayed.

286 Also called 80286—Intel's second-generation processor. The 286 has a 16-bit external data bus and a 24-bit address bus. It was the first Intel processor to achieve protected mode.

386 Also called 80386DX—Intel's third-generation processor. The 386 DX has a 32-bit external data bus and 32-bit address bus. It was Intel's first true 32-bit processor and could run in both protected mode and enhanced mode.

386SX Also called 80386SX. This was a hybrid chip that combined the 32-bit functions and modes of the 80386DX with the 16-bit external data bus and 24-bit address bus of the 80286.

486DX Intel's fourth-generation CPU. Essentially an 80386DX with a built-in cache and math coprocessor.

486DX/2–486DX/3–486DX/4 486 CPUs that operate externally at one speed and internally at a speed which is two, three, or four times faster. Although the internal speed can be more than two times as fast as the external speed, these CPUs are known collectively as "clock doublers."

486SX A 486DX without the built-in math coprocessor.

586 An unofficial, generic term, that describes the Intel Pentium processor or Pentium family of CPUs.

8086/8088 The first generation of Intel processor to be used in IBM PCs. The 8086 and 8088 were identical with the exception of the external data bus—the 8086 had a 16-bit bus while the 8088 had an 8-bit bus.

8086 Mode See Real Mode

8237 The part number for the original DMA controller. Although long obsolete, the name is still often used in reference to DMA usage.

8259 The part number for the original IRQ controller. Although long obsolete, the name is still often used in reference to IRQ usage.

Access The reading or writing of data; as a verb, to gain entry to data. Most commonly used in connection with information access, via a user ID, and qualified by an indication about the kinds of access permitted. For example, "read-only access" means that the contents of the file may be read but not altered or erased.

Access Time The time interval measured from the moment that data is requested to the moment it is received. Most commonly used in measuring the speed of storage devices.

Account A registered set of rights and/or permissions to an individual computer or to a network of computers.

Address Bus The wires leading from the CPU to the memory controller chip that enable the CPU to address RAM. Also used by the CPU for I/O addressing. An internal electronic channel from the microprocessor to RAM, along which the addresses of memory storage locations are transmitted. Like a post office box, each memory location has a distinct number or address; the address bus provides the means by which the microprocessor can access every location in memory.

Address Space The total amount of memory addresses that an address bus can contain.

ADSL *Asymmetric Digital Subscriber Line.* A fully digital, dedicated connection to the telephone system that provides download speeds up to 9 Mbps and upload speeds up to 1Mbps.

AGP *Accelerated Graphics Port.* A 32-bit expansion slot designed by Intel specifically for video; it runs at 66 MHz and yields a throughput of 254 megabytes per second, at least. Later versions (2X, 3X, 4X) give substantially higher throughput.

AIX *Advanced Interactive Executive.* IBM's version of UNIX, which runs on 386 or better PCs.

Algorithm A set of rules for solving a problem in a given number of steps.

ALU *Arithmetic Logic Unit.* The circuit that performs CPU math calculations and logic operations.

Amplifier A device that strengthens electrical signals, enabling them to travel further.

Analog An analog device uses a physical quantity, such as length or voltage, to represent the value of a number. By contrast, digital storage relies on a coding system of numeric units.

Analog Video Picture signals represented by a number of smooth transitions between video levels. Television signals are analog compared to digital video signals which assign a finite set of levels. Because computer signals are digital, analog video must be converted into a digital form before it can be shown on a computer screen.

ANSI *American National Standards Institute.* The body responsible for standards like ASCII.

ANSI Character Set The ANSI-standard character set defines 256 characters. The first 128 are ASCII, and the second group of 128 contains math and language symbols.

Anti-Aliasing In computer imaging, a blending effect that smoothes sharp contrasts between two regions—i.e. jagged lines or different colors. This reduces the jagged edges of text or objects. In voice signal processing, it refers to the process of removing or smoothing out spurious frequencies from waveforms produced by converting digital signals back to analog.

API *Application Programming Interface.* A software definition that describes operating system calls for application software; conventions defining how a service is invoked.

APM *Automated Power Management.* The BIOS routines that enable the CPU selectively to turn on and off selected peripherals.

Application A program designed to perform a job for the user of a PC. A word processor and a spreadsheet program are typical applications.

Application Servers Servers that provide clients access to software or other applications that run on the server only. Examples include Web servers, e-mail servers, and database servers.

Archive To copy programs and data onto an relatively inexpensive storage medium (disk, tape, etc.) for long-term retention.

Archive Bit An attribute of a file that shows whether the file has been backed up since the last change. Each time a file is opened, changed, or saved, the archive bit is turned on. Some types of backups will turn off this archive bit to indicate that a good backup of the file exists on tape.

Argument A value supplied to a procedure, macro, subroutine, or command that is required in order to evaluate that procedure, macro, subroutine, or command; synonymous with parameter.

ARP *Address Resolution Protocol.* A protocol in the TCP/IP suite used with the command-line utility of the same name to determine the MAC address that corresponds to a particular IP address.

ASCII *American Standard Code for Information Interchange.* The industry standard 8-bit characters used to define text characters, consisting of 96 upper- and lowercase letters, plus 32 non-printing control characters, each of which is numbered. These numbers were designed to achieve uniformity among different computer devices for printing and the exchange of simple text documents.

Aspect Ratio The ratio of width to height of an object. In TV it is 4:3.

Assembler A program that converts symbolically-coded programs into object-level, machine code. In an assembler program, unlike a compiler, there is a one-to-one correspondence between human-readable instructions and the machine-language code.

Asynchronous Communication The receiving devices must send an acknowledgement or "ACK" to the sending unit to verify that data have been sent.

ASPI *Advanced SCSI Programmable Interface.* A series of very tight standards that enable SCSI devices to share a set of highly compatible drivers.

AT *Advanced Technology*. The model name of the second generation, 80286-based IBM computer. Many aspects of the AT such as the BIOS, CMOS, and expansion bus have become de facto standards in the PC industry.

AT Bus The 16-bit expansion bus used in the IBM personal computer and the 32-bit bus of computers using the Intel 386 and 486 microprocessors.

ATA–AT Attachment A type of hard drive and controller. ATA was designed to replace the earlier ST506 and ESDI drives without requiring replacing the AT BIOS, hence AT attachment. These drives are more popularly known as IDE drives. (See ST506, ESDI, and IDE).

ATAPI *ATA Programmable Interface.* A series of standards that enable mass storage devices other than hard drives to use the IDE/ATA controllers. They are extremely popular with CD-ROMs and removable media drives like the Iomega ZIP drive. (See EIDE)

AUI *Attachment Unit Interface.* The standard connector used with 10Base5 Ethernet, it is a 15-pin female DB connector. It is also known as DIX.

AUTOEXEC.BAT A batch file that DOS executes when the system is started or restarted. AUTOEXEC.BAT is not necessary, but in running a computer to which several devices and several different software applications have been attached, the file is essential for efficient operation. AUTOEXEC.BAT files commonly include PATH statements that tell DOS where to find application programs, and commands to install a mouse or operate your printer.

Backbone A generalized term defining a primary cable or system that connects networks together.

Background Processing Users may use a terminal for one project and concurrently submit a job that is placed in a background queue the computer will run, as resources become available. This also refers to any processing in which a job runs without being connected to a terminal.

Backside Bus The set of wires that connect the CPU to Level 2 cache. They first appeared in the Pentium Pro and most modern CPUs have a special backside bus.

Some busses, such as that in the later Celeron processors (300A and beyond), run at the full speed of the CPU, whereas others run at a fraction of that speed. Earlier Pentium IIs, for example, had backside busses running at half the speed of the processor. See also Frontside Bus and External Data Bus.

Back up To save important data in a secondary location as a safety against loss of the primary data.

Backward Compatible Compatible with earlier versions of a program or earlier models of a computer.

Bandwidth A piece of the spectrum occupied by some form of signal, whether it is television, voice, fax data, etc. Signals require a certain size and location of bandwidth in order to be transmitted. The higher the bandwidth, the faster the signal transmission, thus allowing for a more complex signal such as audio or video. Because bandwidth is a limited space, when one user is occupying it, others must wait their turn. Bandwidth is also the capacity of a network to transmit a given amount of data during a given period.

Bank The total number of SIMMs that can be simultaneously accessed by the MCC; the "width" of the external data bus divided by the "width" of the SIMM sticks.

Baseband Digital signaling that has only one signal (a single signal) on the cable at a time. The signals are only in three states: one, zero, or idle.

Baseline Static image of a system's (or network's) performance when all elements are known to be working properly.

BASIC *Beginners All-purpose Symbolic Instruction Code.* A commonly used personal-computer language first developed at Dartmouth during the 1960s and popularized by Microsoft.

Baud One analog cycle on a telephone line. In the early days of telephone data transmission, the baud rate was often analogous to bits-per-second. Due to advanced modulation of baud cycles as well as data compression, this is no longer true.

BBS *Bulletin Board System.* A term for dial-up online systems from which users can download software and graphics, send and receive e-mail, and exchange information; usually run by individuals from their homes. Although once very popular, BBS sites are rapidly diminishing in number due to the popularity of the Internet.

Binary Numbers A number system with a base of 2, unlike the number systems most of us use which have bases of 10 (decimal numbers), 12 (measurement in feet and inches), and 60 (time). Binary numbers are preferred for computers for precision and economy. Building an electronic circuit that can detect the difference between two states (on–off, 1–0) is easier and more inexpensive than building one that could detect the differences among 10 states (0–9).

Bindery Security and account database used by default on Novell NetWare 3.x servers and available to NetWare 4.x and 5.x servers.

BIOS *Basic Input/Output Services.* Classically, the software routines burned onto the system ROM of a PC. More commonly seen as any software that directly controls a particular piece of hardware. A set of programs encoded in Read-Only Memory (ROM) on computers. These programs handle startup operations and the low-level control for hardware such as disk drives, the keyboard, and monitor.

Bit *Binary Digit.* A single binary digit; any device which can be in an on or off state.

BNC Connector A connector used for 10Base2 coaxial cable. All BNC connectors have to be locked into place by turning the locking ring 90 degrees.

Boot To initiate an automatic routine that clears the memory, loads the operating system, and prepares the computer for use. The term boot is derived from "pull yourself up by your bootstraps." PCs must do that because RAM doesn't retain program instructions when power is turned off. A "cold boot" occurs when the PC is physically switched on, while a "warm boot" enables the system to reset itself without putting a strain on the electronic circuitry by pressing CTRL+ALT+DELETE keys at the same time.

Boot Sector The first sector on an IBM PC hard drive or floppy disk; track 0. The bootup software in ROM tells the computer to load whatever program is found there. If a system disk is read, the program in the boot record directs the computer to the root directory to load MS-DOS (or other operating system).

BPS *Bits Per Second.* A measurement of how fast data is moved from one place to another. A 28.8 modem can move 28,800 bits per second.

Bridge A device that connects two networks and passes traffic between them based only on the node address, so that traffic between nodes on one network does not appear on the other network. For example, an Ethernet bridge only looks at the Ethernet address. Bridges filter and forward packets based on MAC addresses and operate at Level 2 (data link layer) of the OSI seven-layer model.

Broadband Analog signaling that sends multiple signals over the cable at the same time. The best example of broadband signaling is cable television. The zero, one, and idle states (see Baseband) exist on multiple channels on the same cable.

Broadcast A packet addressed to all machines. In TCP/IP, the general broadcast address is 255.255.255.255.

BTW *By The Way*. Common abbreviation used by BBS, Usenet, and IRC users.

Buffer Electronic storage, usually DRAM, that holds data moving between two devices. Buffers are used anywhere there is a situation where one device may send or receive data faster or slower than the other device with which it is in communication. For example, the BUFFERS statement in DOS is used to set aside RAM for communication with hard drives.

Bug A programming error that causes a program or a computer system to perform erratically, produce incorrect results, or crash. The term bug was coined when a real bug was found in one of the circuits of one of the first ENIAC computers.

Bus A series of wires connecting two or more separate electronic devices, the bus enables those devices to communicate.

Bus Topology All computers connect to the network via a central bus cable.

Byte Eight contiguous bits, the fundamental data unit of personal computers. Storing the equivalent of one character, the byte is also the basic unit of measurement for computer storage. Bytes are counted in powers of two.

Cable Tester Device that tests the continuity of cables. Some testers also test for electrical shorts, crossed wires, or other electrical characteristics.

Cache A special area of RAM that stores the data most frequently accessed from the hard drive. Cache memory can optimize the use of your systems.

Cache Memory A special section of fast memory chips set aside to store the information most frequently accessed from RAM.

Card Generic term for anything that can be snapped into an expansion slot.

CAT3 Category 3 wire is an EIA/TIA standard for UTP wiring that can operate up to 20 megabits per second.

CAT5 Category 5 wire is an EIA/TIA standard for UTP wiring that can operate up to 100 megabits per second.

CD-I CD interactive "green disk" format by Philips; designed to play compressed movies.

CD-ROM *Compact Disk/Read Only Memory*. A read-only compact storage disk for audio or video data. Recordable disks, such as CD-Rs, are updated versions of the older CD-ROM disks.

Chat A multi-party, real-time text conversation. The Internet's most popular version is known as Internet Relay Chat, which many groups use to converse in real time with each other, moving toward true point-to-point voice communications.

Chipset Electronic chips that handle all of the low level functions of a PC, which in the original PC were handled by close to 30 different chips. Chipsets usually consist of one, two, or three separate chips to handle all these functions. The most common chipsets in use today are the Intel family of chipsets (BX, ZX, etc.).

CHS *Cylinder/Heads/Sectors*. The acronym for the combination of the three critical geometries used to determine the size of a hard drive—Cylinders, Heads, and Sectors per Track.

CISC *Complex Instruction-Set Computing*. CISC is a CPU design that enables the processor to handle more complex instructions from the software at the expense of speed. The Intel x86 series (386, 486, Pentium) for PCs are CISC processors.

Client A computer program that uses the services of another computer program. Software that extracts information from a server; an auto-dial phone is a client, and the phone company is its server. Also a machine that accesses shared resources on a server.

Client/Server A relationship in which client software obtains services from a server on behalf of a person.

Client/Server Application An application that performs some or all of its processing on an application server rather than on the client. The client usually receives only the result of the processing.

Client/Server Network A network that has dedicated server machines and client machines.

Clipboard A temporary storage space where captured data (print-screen selected) can be copied or pasted into other documents.

Clock An electronic circuit utilizing a quartz crystal that generates evenly spaced pulses at speeds of millions of cycles per second. The pulses are used to synchronize the flow of information through the computer's internal communication channels. Some computers also contain a circuit that tracks hours, minutes, and seconds.

Cluster The basic unit of storage on a floppy or hard disk. Two or more sectors are contained in a cluster. When DOS stores a file on disk, it writes those files into dozens or even hundreds of contiguous clusters. If there aren't enough contiguous open clusters available, DOS finds the next open cluster and writes there, continuing this process until the entire file is saved. The FAT tracks how the files are distributed among the clusters on the disk.

CMOS *Complimentary Metal-Oxide Semiconductor*. Originally, the type of non-volatile RAM that held information about the most basic parts of your PC such as hard drives, floppies and amount of DRAM. Today, actual CMOS chips have been replaced by "Flash" type non-volatile RAM. The information is the same, however, and is still called CMOS—even though it is now almost always stored on Flash RAM.

Coax (Short for coaxial). Cabling in which an internal conductor is surrounded by another, outer conductor, thus sharing the same axis.

Code A language for expressing operations to be performed by a computer.

Collision The result of two nodes transmitting at the same time on a multiple-access network such as Ethernet. Both packets may be lost or partial packets may result.

Collision Domain A set of Ethernet segments that receive all traffic generated by any node within those segments. Repeaters, amplifiers, and hubs do not create separate collision domains, but bridges, routers, and switches do.

COM In DOS, a device name that refers to the serial communications ports available on your computer. When used as a program extension, .COM indicates an executable program file limited to 64K.

COMMAND.COM In DOS, a file that contains the command processor. This must be present on the startup disk for DOS to run. COMMAND.COM is usually located in the root directory of the hard drive.

Command A request, typed from a terminal or embedded in a file, to perform an operation or to execute a particular program.

Command Processor The part of the operating system that accepts input from the user and displays any messages, such as confirmation and error messages.

Communications Program A program that makes a computer act as a terminal to another computer. Communications programs usually provide for file transfer between microcomputers and mainframes.

Compiler A program that translates human-readable programs into a form the computer understands. The input (source code) to the compiler is a description of an algorithm in a problem-oriented language; its output (object code) is an equivalent description of the algorithm in a machine-oriented language.

Compression The process of squeezing data to eliminate redundancies, allowing files to be stored or transmitted using less space.

Computer A device or system capable of carrying out a sequence of operations in a distinctly and explicitly defined manner. The operations are frequently numeric computations or data manipulations, but also include data input and output. The ability to branch within sequences is its key feature.

Concentrator A device that brings together at a common center connections to a particular kind of network (such as Ethernet), and implements that network internally.

CONFIG.SYS An ASCII text file in the root directory that contains configuration commands. CONFIG.SYS enables the system to be set up to configure high, expanded, and extended memories by the loading of HIMEM.SYS and EMM386.EXE drivers, as well as drivers for non-standard peripheral components.

Connectionless Protocol A protocol that does not establish and verify a connection between the hosts before sending data—it just sends it and hopes for the bests. This is faster than connection-oriented protocols. UDP is an example of a connectionless protocol.

Connection-oriented Protocol A protocol that establishes a connection between two hosts before transmitting data, and verifies receipt before closing the connection between the hosts. TCP is an example of a connection-oriented protocol.

Contiguous Adjacent; placed one next to the other.

Controller Card A card adapter that connects devices, like a disk drive, to the main computer bus/motherboard.

Conventional Memory In any IBM PC-compatible computer, the first 640K of the computer's RAM. 640K has proven to be insufficient because of programs that demand more memory and for users who want to run more than one program at a time. Many users equip their systems with extended or expanded memory and the memory management programs needed to access this memory.

Copy Backup A type of backup similar to normal or full, in that all selected files on a system are backed up. This type of backup *does not* change the archive bit of the files being backed up.

Cross-linked Files In DOS, a file-storage error that occurs when the FAT indicates that two files claim the same disk cluster. These occur when the system is abnormally halted. To repair, run SCANDISK or Norton Disk Doctor.

Crossover Cable Special UTP cable used to connect hubs or to connect network cards without a hub. Crossover cables reverse the sending and receiving wire pairs from one end to the other.

Crossover Port Special port in a hub that crosses the sending and receiving wires, thus removing the need for a crossover cable to connect the hubs.

CSMA/CD *Carrier Sense Multiple Access with Collision Detection.* The access method Ethernet systems use in local area networking technologies; enables packets of data information to flow through the network to reach address locations.

CPU *Central Processing Unit*. The "brain" of the computer. The microprocessor that handles the primary calculations for the computer. They are known by names like 486 and Pentium.

CRC *Cyclical Redundancy Check*. A mathematical method that is used to check for errors in long streams of transmitted data with very high accuracy. Before data is sent, the main computer uses the data to calculate a CRC value from the data's contents. If the receiver calculates a different CRC value from the received data, the data was corrupted during transmission and is resent. Ethernet packets have a CRC code.

CRT *Cathode Ray Tube*. The CRT is the tube of a monitor in which rays of electrons are beamed onto a phosphorescent screen to produce images.

Cursor A symbol on a display screen that indicates the position at which the next character entered will be displayed. The symbol often blinks so that it can be easily noticed.

Cyrix Company that makes CPUs in direct competition with Intel.

Daily Backup Also called a daily copy backup, this backup type makes a copy of all files that have been changed on that day without changing the archive bits of those files.

Daisy Chain A method of connecting several devices along a bus and managing the signals for each device.

DAT *Digital Audio Tape*. Higher storage capacity tape recording system that uses digital recording methods; used for digital audio and video as well as data backups.

Database A collection of interrelated data values that may be integrated permanently into a single connected structure or integrated temporarily for each interrogation, known as a query. In its most technical sense, database implies that any of the data may be used as a key for specific queries. In more common usage it means any accessible collection of information, and that only a limited set of data values may be used to specify queries.

DB Connectors D-shaped connectors used for a variety of different connections in the PC and networking world. Can be male or female with a varying number of pins or sockets.

DB-15 DB connector (female) used in 10Base5 networks. See also DIX and AUI.

DBMS *Database Management System*. A systematic approach to storing, updating, securing and retrieving information stored as data items, usually in the form of records in one or more files.

Debug To detect, trace, and eliminate errors in computer programs.

Dedicated Circuit Circuit that runs from a breaker box to specific outlets.

Dedicated Server A machine that uses no client functions, only server functions.

Dedicated Telephone Line A telephone line that is an always open, or connected, circuit. Dedicated telephone lines usually do not have numbers.

Default A software function or operation which occurs automatically unless the user specifies something else.

Defrag Defragmentation. A procedure in which all the files on a hard disk are rewritten on disk so that all parts of each file are written in contiguous clusters. The result is an improvement of up to 75% of the disk's speed during retrieval operations.

Default Gateway In a TCP/IP network, the nearest router to a particular host. This router's IP address is part of the necessary TCP/IP configuration for communicating with multiple networks using IP.

Device Driver A subprogram to control communications between the computer and peripherals.

DHCP *Dynamic Host Configuration Protocol*. A protocol that allows a DHCP server to set TCP/IP settings automatically for a DHCP client.

Differential Backup Similar to an incremental backup in that it backs up the files that have been changed since the last backup. This type of backup does not change the state of the archive bit.

DIMM *Dual In-line Memory Module*. A type of DRAM packaging, similar to SIMMs with the distinction that each side of each tab inserted into the system performs a separate function; comes in 72-pin "SO," 144- and 168-pin versions.

Directory A logical container of files and other directories; synonymous with folder. Typically implemented as a file that contains pointers (directions) to files or other directories.

Disk Drive Controller The circuitry that controls the physical operations of the floppy disks and/or hard disks connected to the computer.

Disk Striping Process by which data are spread among multiple (at least two)drives. It increases speed for both reads and writes of data. Considered RAID level 0, because it does *not* provide fault tolerance.

Disk Striping with Parity Provides fault tolerance by writing data across multiple drives and then including an additional drive, called a parity drive, that stores information to rebuild the data contained on the other drives. Disk striping with parity requires at least three physical disks: two for the data and a third for the parity drive. It provides data redundancy at RAID levels 3–5 with different options.

Display A device that enables information, either textual or pictorial, to be seen but not permanently recorded. The most widely used kind is the cathode ray tube.

Dithering A technique for smoothing out digitized images; using alternating colors in a pattern to produce perceived color detail.

DIX Connector (Digital, Intel, Xerox) The original implementation of Ethernet. The DIX connector is the standard connector used with 10Base5 Ethernet, also known as the AUI.

DLT *Digital Linear Tape*. Huge data capacity tapes used for tape backups.

DMA *Direct Memory Access*. A technique that some PC hardware devices use to transfer data to and from the memory without requiring the use of the CPU.

DNS *Dynamic Name System*. A TCP/IP name resolution system that resolves host name to IP address.

DNS Domain A specific branch of the DNS name space. First-level DNS domains include .COM, .GOV, and .EDU.

Document A medium and the data recorded on it for human use; for example, a report sheet or book. By extension, any record that has permanence and that can be read by a human or machine.

Documentation A collection of organized documents or the information recorded in documents. Instructional material specifying the inputs, operations, and outputs of a computer program or system.

Domain Term used to describe groupings of users, computers, or networks. In Microsoft networking, a domain is a group of computers and users that share a common account database, called a SAM, and a common security policy. For the Internet, a domain is a group of computers that share a common element in their hierarchical name. Other types of domains exist—e.g. collision domain, etc.

Domain Controller A Microsoft Windows NT machine that stores the user and server account information for its domain in a database called a SAM (security accounts manager) database.

DOS *Disk Operating System*. The set of programming that allows a program to interact with the computer. Examples of disk operating systems include Microsoft's MS-DOS, IBM's PC-DOS and OS/2, and Apple's MacOS System 7. Microsoft's Windows 3.1 is not technically an operating system, since it still requires MS-DOS to work, but it is often referred to as one. Windows 95/98 and Windows NT are true disk operating systems.

DOSKEY A DOS utility that makes it possible to type more than one command on a line, store and retrieve previously used DOS commands, create stored macros, and customize all DOS commands.

DOS Prompt A letter representing the disk drive, followed by the greater-than sign (>), which together indicate that the operating system is ready to receive a command.

Dot-Matrix Printer A printer that creates each character from an array of dots. Pins striking a ribbon against the paper, one pin for each dot position, form the dots. The printer may be a serial printer (printing one character at a time) or a line printer.

Download The transfer of information from a remote computer system to the user's system. Opposite of upload.

DPI *Dots per Inch*. A measure of printer resolution that counts the dots the device can produce per linear inch.

DRAM *Dynamic Random Access Memory*. The memory used to store data in most personal computers. DRAM stores each bit in a "cell" composed of a transistor and a capacitor. Because the capacitor in a DRAM cell can only hold a charge for a few milliseconds, DRAM must be continually refreshed, or rewritten, to retain its data.

DSP *Digital Signal Processor*. A specialized microprocessor-like device that processes digital signals at the expense of other abilities, much as the FPU is optimized for math functions. DSPs are used in such specialized hardware as high-speed modems, multimedia sound cards, MIDI equipment, and real-time video capture and compression.

Double Word A group of 32 binary digits. Four bytes.

Duplexing Also called disk duplexing or drive duplexing. Similar to mirroring, in that data are written to and read from two physical drives for fault tolerance; in addition, separate controllers are used for each drive, for both additional fault tolerance and additional speed. Considered RAID level 1.

Dynamic Link A method of linking data so that they are shared by two or more programs. When data are changed in one program, they are likewise changed in the other.

Dynamic Routing Process by which routers in an internetwork automatically exchange information with all other routers, enabling them to build their own list of routes to various networks, called a routing table. Dynamic routing requires a dynamic routing protocol, such as OSPF or RIP.

Dynamic Routing Protocol A protocol that supports the building of automatic routing tables, such as OSPF (Open Shortest Path First) or RIP (Routing Information Protocol).

EDB *External Data Bus.* The primary data highway of all computers. Everything in a computer is tied either directly or indirectly to the external data bus. See also Frontside Bus and Backside Bus.

EDO *Extended Data Output.* An improvement on FPM DRAM in that more data can be read before the RAM must be refreshed.

EEPROM *Electrically Erasable Programmable Read-Only Memory.* A type of ROM chip which can be erased and reprogrammed electrically. EEPROMs were the most common storage device for BIOSs until the advent of Flash ROM.

EIA/TIA *Electronics Industry Association/Telecommunications Industry Association.* The standards body that defines most of the standards for computer network cabling. Most of these are defined under the EIA/TIA 568 standard.

EIDE *Enhanced IDE.* A marketing concept by Western Digital that consolidated four improvements for IDE drives. These improvements included >528MB drives, four devices, increase in drive throughput, and non-hard drive devices. (See ATAPI, PIO, Secondary controller).

EISA *Enhanced ISA.* An improved expansion bus, based on the ISA bus, with a top speed of 8.33MHz, a 32-bit data path, and a high degree of self-configuration. Backwardly compatible with legacy ISA cards.

E-mail *Electronic Mail.* Messages, usually text, sent from one person to another via computer. E-mail can also be sent automatically to a large number of addresses (mailing list).

EMM386.EXE An expanded memory emulator that enables DOS applications to use the extended memory as if it were expanded memory. EMM386.EXE also allows the user to load device drivers and programs into the upper memory area.

EMS *Expanded Memory Specification.* A method of memory management developed by Intel, Lotus, and Microsoft that enabled MS-DOS computers to use memory exceeding the 640K limit imposed by MS-DOS. Memory that conforms to this standard is called expanded memory. Originally, this standard required that a special hardware device be added to the computer, but that was quickly supplanted by a less efficient but much cheaper software solution. Expanded memory has been made almost obsolete by the Windows environment, which is not limited by the "640K barrier." EMS is now required almost solely by DOS-based games.

EMI *Electromagnetic Interference*. EMI is an electrical interference from one device to another, resulting in poor performance in the device capabilities. This is similar to having static on a TV while running a blow dryer, or placing two monitors too close together and getting a "shaky" screen.

Encapsulation The process of putting the packets from one protocol inside the packets of another protocol. An example of this is TCP/IP encapsulation in NetWare servers, which places IPX/SPX packets inside TCP/IP packets, enabling Novell NetWare to use TCP/IP for transport while still allowing the network operating system to gain the data it needs from IPX/SPX.

EPROM *Erasable Programmable Read-Only Memory*. A special form of ROM that can be erased by high-intensity ultraviolet light and then rewritten (reprogrammed).

Equipment Room A central location for computer or telephone equipment and, most important, centralized cabling. All cables will usually run to the equipment room from the rest of the installation.

ESD *Electrostatic Discharge*. The movement of electrons from one body to another. ESD is a real menace to PCs as it can cause permanent damage to semiconductors.

ESDI *Enhanced Small Device Interface*. Second-generation hard drives, distinct from their predecessors (ST506) by greater data density and lack of dependence on CMOS settings. Completely obsolete.

Ethernet Name coined by Xerox for the first standard of network cabling and protocols. Ethernet is based on a bus topology.

Expansion Bus Set of wires going to the CPU, governed by the expansion bus crystal, directly connected to expansion slots of varying types (ISA, PCI, AGP, etc.). Depending on the type of slots, the expansion bus runs at a percentage of the main system speed (8.33—66 MHz).

Expansion Slot A receptacle connected to the computer's expansion bus, designed to accept adapters.

External Data Bus (EDB) The primary data highway of all computers. Everything in the computer is tied either directly or indirectly to the external data bus. See also Frontside Bus and Backside Bus.

FAQ *Frequently Asked Questions*. Common abbreviation coined by BBS users and spread to Usenet. This is a list of questions and answers that pertain to a particular topic and are maintained so that users new to the group do not all bombard the group with similar questions. Examples are "What is the name of the actor who plays X on this show, and was he in anything else?" or "Can anyone list all of the books by this author in the order that they were published so that I can read them in that order?" The common answer to this question is "Read the FAQ!"

Fast Ethernet Any of several flavors of Ethernet that operate at 100 megabits/second.

FAT *File Allocation Table*. A hidden table of every cluster on a hard disk. The FAT records how files are stored in distinct clusters. The address of the first cluster of the file is stored in the directory file. In the FAT entry for the first cluster is the address of the second cluster used to store that file. In the entry for the second cluster for that file is the address for the third cluster, etc. This table is the only way for DOS to know where to access files. There are two FATs created, mirror images of themselves, in case one is destroyed or damaged.

FDDI *Fiber Distributed Data Interface*. A standard for transmitting data on optical fiber cables at a rate of around 100 million bps.

Fault Tolerance The ability of any system to continue functioning after some part of the system has failed. RAID is an example of a hardware device that provides fault tolerance.

Fiber Optics A high-speed channel for transmitting data, made of high-purity glass sealed within an opaque tube. Much faster than conventional copper wire such as coaxial cable.

File A collection of any form of data stored beyond the time of execution of a single job. A file may contain program instructions or data, which may be numerical, textual, or graphical information.

File Format The type of file, such as picture or text; represented as a suffix at the end of the filename (text = TXT or .txt, etc.).

File Fragmentation The allocation of a file in a non-contiguous sector on a disk. Fragmentation occurs because of multiple deletions and write operations.

File Name A name assigned to a file when the file is first written on a disk. Every file on a disk within the same folder must have a unique name. Since Windows 95, it is possible to use up to 32 characters for file names, and file names can contain any character (including spaces), except the following: \ / : * ? " < > |.

File Server A computer designated to store software, courseware, administrative tools, and other data on a local- or wide-area network. It "serves" this information to other computers via the network when users enter personal access codes.

Firewall A device that restricts traffic between a local network and the Internet.

Firewire An IEEE 1394 standard to send wideband signals over a thin connector system that plugs into TVs, VCRs, TV cameras, PCs, etc. This serial bus developed by

Apple and Texas Instruments enables connection of 60 devices at speeds ranging from 100 to 400 megabits per second.

Flash ROM A type of ROM technology which can be electrically reprogrammed while still in the PC. Flash is the overwhelmingly most common storage medium of BIOS in PCs today, as it can be upgraded without even having to open the computer on most systems.

Flat Name Space A naming convention that gives each device only one name, that must be unique. NetBIOS uses a flat name space. TCP/IP's DNS uses a hierarchical name space.

Floppy Disk A removable and widely used data storage medium that uses a magnetically coated flexible disk of Mylar enclosed in a plastic envelope or case.

Folder A place where a user's e-mail messages may be stored. Every user has a folder for new messages, and on most systems may create other folders for specific purposes.

Font A set of consistent size, shape or style of printer characters, including alphabetic and numeric characters and other signs and symbols.

FPM *Fast Page Mode.* DRAM that uses a "paging" function to increase access speed and to lower production costs. Virtually all DRAMS are FPM DRAM. The name FPM is also used to describe older style, non-EDO DRAM.

FPU *Floating Point Unit.* A formal term for the math coprocessor (also called a numeric processor). This is a specialized processor that handles certain calculations faster than the CPU. A math coprocessor calculates using floating point math (which allows for decimals), whereas the CPU can only deal with integers. Intel's 486 and Pentium chips and Motorola's PowerPC have FPUs built into the CPU chips, whereas earlier designs (for example Intel's 80387) needed a separate chip to be installed.

Freeware Software that is distributed free, with no license fee.

Frontside Bus Name for the wires that connect the CPU to the main system RAM. Generally running at speeds of 66-133 MHz. Distinct from the Expansion Bus and Backside Bus, even though sharing wires with the former.

FRU *Field Replaceable Unit.* Any part of a PC that is considered to be replaceable "in the field," i.e. a customer location. There is no official list of FRUs—it is usually a matter of policy for the repair center.

FTP *File Transfer Protocol.* A set of rules that allows two computers to talk to one another as a file transfer is carried out. This is the protocol used when a file is transferred from one computer to another across the Internet.

FUBAR Fouled Up Beyond All Recognition.

Full-Duplex Describes any device that can send and receive data simultaneously.

Function Key A keyboard key that gives an instruction to a computer, as opposed to keys that produce letters, numbers, marks of punctuation, etc.

Gateway The technical meaning is a hardware or software setup that translates between two dissimilar protocols. For example, Prodigy has a gateway that translates between its internal, proprietary e-mail format and Internet e-mail format. Another, sloppier meaning of gateway is any mechanism for providing access to another system; AOL might be called a gateway to the Internet. See Default Gateway.

GIF *Graphics Interchange Format*. A method of storing graphics developed for CompuServe in the early 80s. GIF is a compressed format—it takes up much less disk space than conventional file formats, and therefore can be transmitted faster over phone lines. GIF is a non-lossy format (meaning that no data is lost when an image is converted to GIF), but the format is limited to 8-bit graphics, or 256 colors. Because GIF is based on a copyrighted compression algorithm, CompuServe recently decided to charge a licensing fee for software developers who wish to incorporate the GIF standard in their products. For these reasons, GIF was rapidly being supplanted by JPEG as the format for transferring images. The introduction of GIF version 89, which allowed for transparent portions of an image and animated GIF images, has made the format more popular.

Giga- The prefix for the quantity 1,073,741,824. One gigabyte would be 1,073,741,824 bytes. One gigahertz would be 1,073,741,824 hertz.

Gigabyte 1024 megabytes

Gopher A widely successful method of making menus of material available over the Internet. Gopher is a client- and server-style program, which requires that the user have a Gopher client program. Although Gopher spread rapidly across the globe in only a couple of years, it has been largely supplanted by Hypertext, also known as WWW (World Wide Web). There are still thousands of Gopher servers on the Internet and we can expect they will remain for a while.

Graphic A computer-generated picture produced on a computer screen or paper, ranging from simple line or bar graphs to colorful and detailed images.

Green PC A computer system designed to operate in an energy-efficient manner.

Groupware Software that serves the group and makes the group as a whole more productive and efficient in group tasks. Example: group scheduling.

GUI *Graphical User Interface.* The method by which a computer and a user interact. Early interfaces were text-based; that is, the user "talked" to the computer by typing and the computer responded with text on a CRT. A GUI, on the other hand, enables the user to interact with the computer graphically, by manipulating with a mouse or other pointing device icons that represent programs or documents.

Half-Duplex Any device that can only send or receive data at any given moment. Most Ethernet transmissions are half-duplex.

Handshaking A procedure performed by modems, terminals, and computers to verify that communication has been correctly established.

Hang When a computer freezes, so that it does not respond to keyboard commands, it is said to "hang" or to have "hung."

Hang Time The amount of seconds a too-often-hung computer is airborne after it has been thrown it out a second-story window.

Hard Drive A data-recording system using solid disks of magnetic material turning at high speeds.

Hardware Physical computer equipment such as electrical, electronic, magnetic, and mechanical devices. Anything in the computer world that you can hold in your hand. A floppy drive is hardware, Microsoft Word is not.

Hayes Command Set A standardized set of instructions used to control modems. Examples are:

AT	Attention (used to start commands)
ATDT	Attention Dial Tone
ATDP	Attention Dial Pulse
ATH	Attention Hang Up

Heap In Microsoft Windows, a special storage area used for critical resources. These heaps are limited to 64K in size, and the "NOT ENOUGH MEMORY" message results.

Hex *Hexadecimal.* Symbols based on a numbering system of 16, (computer shorthand for binary numbers) using 10 digits and six letters to condense 0s and 1s to binary numbers. Hex is represented by digits 0 through 9 and letters A through F. 09h has a value of 9, for example, and 0Ah has a value of 10.

Hierarchical Name Space A naming scheme where the full name of each object includes its position within the hierarchy. An example of a hierarchical name is www.totalseminars.com, which includes not only the host name, but also the domain names.

High Resolution Using a sufficient number of pixels in display monitors or dots per inch when printing to produce well-defined text characters as well as smoothly defined curves in graphic images.

HIMEM.SYS A DOS device driver that configures extended memory and high memory so that programs conforming to XMS can access it.

HMA *High Memory Area.* The first 64K of memory above 1 megabyte is known as the HMA. Programs that conform to XMS can use HMA as a direct extension of conventional memory. Most of the portions of DOS that usually load into conventional memory can be loaded into the HMA.

Homepage The Web page that a browser is set to use when it starts up; the main Web page for a business, organization, person; or simply the main page out of a collection of Web pages.

Horizontal Cabling Cabling that connects the equipment room to the work area.

Host A single device (usually a computer) on a TCP/IP network that has an IP address—any device that can be the source or destination of a data packet. Also, in the mainframe world, a computer that is made available for use by multiple people simultaneously.

Host ID The portion of an IP address that defines a specific machine.

HOSTS File A static text file that is used to resolve host names to IP addresses.

HTML *Hypertext Markup Language.* An ASCII-based script-like language for creating hypertext documents like those on the World Wide Web.

HTTP *Hypertext Transfer Protocol.* Extremely fast protocol used for network file transfers in the WWW environment.

Hub A device that is a center of network activity because it connects multiple networks together.

Hypertext A document which has been marked up to allow a user to select words or pictures within the document, click on them, and connect to further information. The basis of the World Wide Web.

IDE *Intelligent (or Integrated) Drive Electronics.* A PC specification for small to medium-sized hard drives in which the controlling electronics for the drive are part of the drive itself, speeding up transfer rates and leaving only a simple adapter (or "paddle"). IDE only supported two drives per system of no more than 504 megabytes each, and has been completely supplanted by Enhanced IDE. EIDE supports four drives of over 8 gigabytes each and more than doubles the transfer rate. The more common name for ATA drives. See ATA.

IEEE *Institute of Electronic and Electrical Engineers.* IEEE is the leading standards-setting group in the United States.

IEEE 802.1 IEEE subcommittee that defined the standards for Higher-layer LAN Protocols.

IEEE 802.2 IEEE subcommittee that defined the standards for Logical Link Control.

IEEE 802.3 IEEE subcommittee that defined the standards for CSMA/CD (a.k.a. Ethernet.

IEEE 802.4 IEEE subcommittee that defined the standards for Token Bus.

IEEE 802.5 IEEE subcommittee that defined the standards for Token Ring.

IEEE 802.6 IEEE subcommittee that defined the standards for MAN (Metropolitan Area Network).

IEEE 802.7 IEEE subcommittee that defined the standards for Broadband.

IEEE 802.8 IEEE subcommittee that defined the standards for Fiber Optic.

IEEE 802.9 IEEE subcommittee that defined the standards for Isochronous LAN.

IEEE 802.10 IEEE subcommittee that defined the standards for Security.

IEEE 802.11 IEEE subcommittee that defined the standards for Wireless.

IEEE 802.12 IEEE subcommittee that defined the standards for Demand Priority/100BaseVG.

IEEE 802.14 IEEE subcommittee that defined the standards for cable modems.

IFCONFIG A command-line utility for Linux servers and workstations that displays the current TCP/IP configuration of the machine, similar to IPCONFIG and WINIPCFG.

IMO, IMHO *In My Opinion, In My Humble Opinion.* Common abbreviation coined by BBS users and spread to Usenet. Used in e-mail messages and real-time chat sessions. IMHO is often used when the speaker wants to convey that this is not an area of expertise, but it also can be used sarcastically.

Impedance The amount of resistance to an electrical signal on a wire. It is used as a relative measure of the amount of data a cable can handle.

Incremental Backup A type of backup that backs up all files that have their archive bits turned on, meaning that they have been changed since the last backup. This type of backup turns the archive bits off after the files have been backed up.

Interrupt A suspension of a process, such as the execution of a computer program, caused by an event external to the computer and performed in such a way that the process can be resumed. Events of this kind include sensors monitoring laboratory equipment or a user pressing an interrupt key.

Intranet A private network inside a company or organization that uses the same kinds of software found on the public Internet, but that is only for internal use.

Interlaced The TV/video systems in which the electron beam writes every other line; then retraces itself to a second pass to complete the final framed image. Originally this reduced magnetic line paring, but took twice as long to paint, which added some flicker in graphic images.

InterNIC The I-net; Info Center; maintains the DNS services, registrations, etc. run by Network Solutions, General Atomics, and AT&T.

IPCONFIG A command-line utility for Windows NT servers and workstations that displays the current TCP/IP configuration of the machine, similar to WINIPCFG and IFCONFIG.

I/O *Input/Output*. A general term for reading and writing data to a computer. The term input includes data from a keyboard, pointing device (such as a mouse), or loading a file from a disk. Output includes writing information to a disk, viewing it on a CRT, or printing it to a printer.

IP *Internet Protocol*. The Internet standard protocol that provides a common layer over dissimilar networks used to move packets among host computers and through gateways if necessary. Part of the TCP/IP protocol suite.

IP Address The numeric address of a computer connected to the Internet; also called Internet address. The IP address is made up of octets of 8-bit binary numbers that are translated into their shorthand numeric values. The IP address can be broken down into a network ID and a host ID.

IPX/SPX *Internetwork Packet Exchange/Sequence Packet Exchange*. Protocol suite developed by Novell, primarily for supporting Novell NetWare-based networks.

IRC *Internet Relay Chat or Chat*. An on-line group discussion.

IRQ *Interrupt Request*. A signal from a hardware device, such as a modem or a mouse, indicating that it needs the CPU's attention. In PCs, IRQs are sent along specific IRQ channels associated with a particular device. It is therefore important to ensure that two devices do not share a common IRQ channel.

ISA *Industry Standard Architecture*. The Industry Standard Architecture design is found in the original IBM PC for the sockets on the motherboard that allowed additional hardware to be connected to the computer's motherboard. An 8-bit, 8.33MHz expansion bus that was designed by IBM for its AT computer and released to the public domain. An improved 16-bit bus was also released to the public domain. Various other designs such as IBM's MicroChannel and EISA bus tried to improve on the design without much popularity. ISA only supports 8- and 16-bit data paths, so 32-bit alternatives such as PCI and AGP have become popular. Although ISA slots linger on most motherboards, they are on the way out, replaced by the newer 32-bit slots. The Intel-sponsored PC99 specification, in fact, calls for the elimination of the ISA slot from motherboards by the end of 1999.

ISDN *Integrated Services Digital Network*. The CCITT (Comité Consutatif Internationale de Télégraphie et Téléphonie) standard that defines a digital method for communications to replace the current analog telephone system. ISDN is superior to telephone lines because it supports up to 128Kbps transfer rate for sending information from computer to computer. It also allows data and voice to share a common phone line.

ISP *Internet Service Provider*. An institution that provides access to the Internet in some form, usually for money.

ISV *Independent Software Vendor*. A firm that develops and markets software.

IT *Information Technology*. The business of computers, electronic communications, and electronic commerce.

Java A network-oriented programming language invented by Sun Microsystems that is specifically designed for writing programs that can be safely downloaded to a computer through the Internet and immediately run without fear of viruses or other harm to computer or files. Using small Java programs (called "Applets"), Web pages can include functions such as animations, calculators, and other fancy tricks.

JPEG *Joint Photographic Experts Group*. A method of formatting images for efficient storage and transfer across phone lines; JPEG files are often a factor of 10 or more times smaller than non-compressed files. JPEG is a lossy format, meaning that some data are lost when an image is converted. Most JPEG conversion software allows the user to decide between more or less compression at the cost of image quality. JPEG supports 24-bit images (up to 16.8 million colors). Because computers running MS-DOS are limited in their file names, this format is also referred to as JPG.

Jumper A series of pairs of small pins that can be shorted with a "shunt" to configure many different aspects of PCs. Usually used in configurations that are rarely changed such as MASTER/SLAVE settings on IDE drives.

K- Most commonly used as the suffix for the binary quantity 1024. 640K means 640 x 1024 or 655,360. Just to add some extra confusion to the IT industry, K is often misspoken as "kilo," the metric value for 1000. 10 KB, for example, spoken as "10 kilobytes," actually means 10240 bytes rather than 10000 bytes.

Kbps *Kilobits per second.* Data transfer rate.

Kermit A communications protocol that enables transferral of files between a computer and on-line network systems. Kermit has built-in error correction and can handle binary (non-text) files.

Kern The amount of distance between characters in a particular font.

Kernel The core portion of the program that resides in memory and performs the most essential operating system tasks.

LAN *Local Area Network.* A group of PCs connected via cabling, radio, or infrared; that use this connectivity is used to share resources such as printers and mass storage.

Laser Printer An electrophotographic printer in which a laser is used as the light source.

Layer A grouping of related tasks involving the transfer of information. Also, a level of the OSI reference model.

Layer 2 Switch Also known as a Bridge. Filters and forwards data packets based on the MAC addresses of the sending and receiving machines.

Layer 3 Switch Also known as a Router. Filters and forwards data packets based on the network addresses of the sending and receiving machines.

LBA *Logical Block Addressing.* A translation (algorithm) of IDE drives promoted by Western Digital as a standardized method for breaking the 504-megabyte limit in IDE drives. Subsequently universally adopted by the PC industry and is standard on all EIDE drives. Allows drives up to 8.4 gigabytes.

LCD *Liquid Crystal Display.* A display technology that relies on polarized light passing through a liquid medium rather than on electron beams striking a phosphorescent surface.

LED *Light Emitting Diodes.* Solid state devices that vibrate at luminous frequencies when current is applied.

Link Segments Segments that link other segments together but are unpopulated, or have no computers directly attached to them.

Linux Open source UNIX-clone operating system.

LMHOSTS File A static text file used to resolve NetBIOS names to IP addresses.

Local Bus A high-speed data path that directly links the computer's CPU with one or more slots on the expansion bus. This direct link means signals from an adapter do not have to travel through the computer expansion bus, which is significantly slower.

Localhost An alias for the loopback address of 127.0.0.1, referring to the current machine.

Logical Address An address that describes both a specific network and a specific machine on that network.

Logical Drives Sections of a hard drive that are formatted and assigned a drive letter, each of which is presented to the user as if it is a separate drive.

Loopback Address A reserved IP address for internal testing: 127.0.0.1.

Low-Level Format Defining the physical location of magnetic tracks and sectors on a disk.

Luminescence The part of the video signal that controls the luminance/brightness of the picture. Also known as the "Y" portion of the component signal.

MAC *Media Access Control.* Unique 48-bit address assigned to each network card. IEEE assigns blocks of possible addresses to various NIC manufacturers to help ensure each address is always unique. The data-link layer of the OSI model uses MAC addresses for locating machines.

MAN *Metropolitan Area Network.* A group of computers connected via cabling, radio, leased phone lines, or infrared; this connectivity is used to share resources such as printers and mass storage. Usually the distance is between that of a LAN and a WAN—different buildings, but within the same city. An typical example of a MAN is a college campus. There is no firm dividing line among a WAN, MAN, and LAN.

Mass Storage Hard drives, CD-ROMs, removable media drives, etc.

Math Coprocessor Also called math unit, floating point unit or FPU. A secondary microprocessor whose function is the handling of floating point arithmetic. Although originally a physically separate chip, math coprocessors are now built into CPUs.

Machine Language A programming language or instruction code immediately interpretable by the hardware of the machine concerned.

Mainframe The cabinet that houses the central processing unit and main memory of a computer system, separate from peripheral devices such as card readers, printers, disk drives, etc. and device controllers. The term has come to be applied to the computer itself in the case of large systems.

MAU *Multistation Access Unit.* A hub used in Token Ring networks. Also abbreviated as MSAU.

MB *Megabyte.* 1,048,576 bytes. Often abbreviated as a Meg.

MCA *MicroChannel.* Expansion bus architecture developed by IBM as the (unsuccessful) successor to ISA. MCA had a full 32-bit design as well as being self-configuring.

MCC *Memory Controller Chip*. The chip that handles memory requests from the CPU. Although once a special chip, it has been integrated into the chipset on all PCs today.

Mega- A prefix that usually stands for the binary quantity 1,048,576. One megabyte is 1,048,576 bytes. One megahertz, however, is a million hertz. Sometimes shortened to Meg, as in "a 286 has an address space of 16 Megs."

Memory A device or medium that serves for temporary storage of programs and data during program execution. The term is synonymous with storage, although it is most frequently used for referring to the internal storage of a computer that can be directly addressed by operating instructions. A computer's temporary storage capacity is measured in kilobytes (KB) or megabytes (MB) of RAM (random-access memory). Long-term data storage on disks is also measured in kilobytes, megabytes, gigabytes, and terabytes.

Mesh Topology Each computer has a dedicated connection to every other computer in a network.

MHz *Megahertz*. A unit of measure that equals a frequency of 1 million cycles per sec.

Microcomputer A computer system in which the central processing unit is built as a single tiny semiconductor chip or as a small number of chips.

Microprocessor Main computer chip that provides speed and capabilities of the computer. Also called CPU.

MIDI *Musical Instrument Digital Interface*. The interface between a computer and a device for simulating musical instruments. Rather than sending large sound samples, a computer can simply send "instructions" to the instrument describing pitch, tone, and duration of a sound. MIDI files are therefore much more efficient. Because a MIDI file is made up of a set of instructions rather than a copy of the sound, it is easy to modify each component of the file. Additionally, it is possible to program many channels, or "voices" of music to be played simultaneously, creating symphonic sound.

MIME *Multipurpose Internet Mail Extensions*. A standard for attaching binary files (such as executables and images) to the Internet's text-based mail (24 kbps-packet size). The first packet of information received contains information about the file, audio, postscript, and word, etc.

MIPS *Millions of Instructions per Second*. Used for processor benchmarks.

Mirroring Also called Drive Mirroring. Reading and writing data at the same time to two drives for fault tolerance purposes. Considered RAID level 1.

MLA *Multi Lettered Acronym.* The abbreviation for any object or thought that can be condensed to an abbreviation.

MMU *Memory-Management Unit.* A chip or circuit that translates virtual memory addresses to physical addresses and may implement memory protection.

Modem *MOdulator/DEModulator.* A device that converts a digital bit stream into an analog signal (modulation) and converts incoming analog signals back into digital signals (demodulation). The analog communications channel is typically a telephone line and the analog signals are typically sounds.

Monitor A television-like screen that shows text, graphics, and other functions performed by the computer.

Mouse A device moved by hand to move a pointer to indicate a precise position on a display screen. The device has one or more buttons and a cable connected to a computer; it may use wheels and be friction-driven or it may use light reflected from a special pad.

MPEG *Motion Picture Experts Group.* A sophisticated video standard that enables digital video to be compressed using a form of JPEG image compression and a technique called "differencing"—in which only the differences between frames are recorded, rather than the frame itself.

MP3 *MPEG-1 audio layer 3.* An audio compression scheme used extensively on the Internet.

MSAU *Multistation Access Unit.* A hub used in Token Ring networks. Also abbreviated as MAU.

Multimedia Assembled using elements from more than one medium, such as high-resolution color images, sounds, video, and text that contains characters in multiple fonts and styles.

Multiplexer A device that merges information from multiple input channels to a single output channel.

Multitasking The process of running multiple programs or tasks on the same computer at the same time.

Motherboard The primary circuit board that holds all of the core components of the computer.

NBTSTAT A command-line utility used to check the current NetBIOS name cache on a particular machine. The utility compares NetBIOS names to their corresponding IP addresses.

NDS *Novell Directory Services.* The default security and directory system for Novell NetWare 4.x and 5.x. Organizes users, servers, and groups into a hierarchical tree.

NetBEUI *NetBIOS Extended User Interface.* A protocol supplied with all Microsoft networking products that operates at the transport layer. Also a protocol suite that includes NetBIOS. NetBEUI does not support routing.

NetBIOS *Network Basic Input/Output System.* A protocol that operates at the session layer of the OSI 7-layer model. This protocol creates and manages connections based on the names of the computers involved.

NetBIOS Name A computer name that identifies both the specific machine and the functions that machine performs. A NetBIOS name consists of 16 characters: 15 characters of a name, with a 16th character that is a special suffix that identifies the role the machine plays.

NETSTAT A command-line utility used to examine the sockets-based connections open on a given host.

Network A collection of two or more computers interconnected by telephone lines, coaxial cables, satellite links, radio, and/or some other communication technique. A computer network is a group of computers connected together and communicate with one another for a common purpose. Computer networks support "people and organization" networks, users who also share a common purpose for communicating.

Network ID A number that identifies the network on which a device or machine exists. This number exists in both IP and IPX protocol suites.

Newsgroup The name for discussion groups on Usenet.

NFS *Network File System.* Enables UNIX systems to treat files on a remote UNIX machine as though they were local files.

NIC *Network Interface Card.* An expansion card that enables a PC to physically link to a network.

Nickname A name that can be used in place of an e-mail address.

Node A member of a network or a point where one or more functional units interconnect transmission lines.

Noise Undesirable signals bearing no desired information and frequently capable of introducing errors into the communication process.

Normal Backup A full backup of every selected file on a system. This type of backup turns off the archive bit after the backup.

NOS *Network Operating System.* An operating system that provides basic file and supervisory services over a network. While each computer attached to the network will have its own OS, the NOS describes which actions are allowed by each user and coordinates distribution of networked files to the user who requests them.

Ns *Nanosecond.* A billionth of a second. Light travels 11 inches in one nanosecond.

NWLink Also known as IPX/SPX-compatible protocol, this is Microsoft's implementation of IPX/SPX. See also IPX/SPX.

OCR *Optical Character Recognition.* The process of converting characters represented in a graphical format into ASCII. This is usually done in conjunction with a scanner to allow for editing of printed material.

OEM *Original Equipment Manufacturer.* Contrary to the name, an OEM does not necessarily manufacture all the parts of a computer. Most OEMs design the reference boards and components and then either outsource the manufacturing or manufacture the parts themselves. OEMs put their own stamp on the finished product. Apple Computers is the archetypical OEM with their Macintosh-branded personal computers. Companies that put together systems based on generic parts designed and manufactured by third parties are in contrast called Value Added Resellers (VARs). These terms are often erroneously used synonymously.

Ohm Electronic measurement of a cable's impedance.

OLE *Object Linking and Embedding.* The Microsoft Windows specification that enables objects created within one application to be placed (embedded) in another application. The two applications are "linked," meaning that when the original object is modified, the copy is updated automatically.

Open Source Applications and operating systems that offer access to their source code; enables developers to modify applications and operating systems easily to meet their specific needs.

OS *Operating System.* The set of programming that enables a program to interact with the computer. Examples of PC operating systems include Microsoft's MS-DOS, IBM's PC-DOS and OS/2, and Apple's MacOS System 8. Most computers on the Internet use a variant of the UNIX operating system. Microsoft's Windows 3.1 is not technically an operating system, since it still requires MS-DOS to work, but it is often referred to as one. Windows 95/98 and Windows NT are true operating systems.

OSI *Open Systems Interconnect.* An international standard suite of protocols defined by the International Organization for Standardization (ISO) that implements the OSI reference model for network communications between computers.

OSI Seven-Layer Model An architecture model based on the OSI protocol suite that defines and standardizes the flow of data between computers. The seven layers are listed below:

Layer 1—The physical layer defines hardware connections and turns binary into physical pulses (electrical or light). Repeaters and hubs operate at the physical layer.

Layer 2—The data link layer identifies devices on the physical layer. MAC addresses are part of the data link layer. Bridges operate at the data link layer.

Layer 3—The network layer moves packets between computers on different networks. Routers, IP and IPX operate at the network layer.

Layer 4—The transport layer breaks data down into manageable chunks. TCP, UDP, SPX, and NetBEUI operate at the transport layer.

Layer 5—The session layer manages connections between machines. NetBIOS and Sockets operate at the session layer.

Layer 6—The presentation layer, which can also manage data encryption, hides the differences between various types of computer systems.

Layer 7—The application layer provides tools for programs to use to access the network (and the lower layers). HTTP, FTP, SMTP, and POP3 are all examples of protocols that operate at the application layer.

Overclocking Running a CPU or video processor faster than its rated speed.

Overdrive Generic name given to processors designed as aftermarket upgrades to computer systems.

Overscanning Displaying less that the complete area of an image to the viewer. Most monitors may slightly overscan. Also of value when using a Twain scanner to capture 2K x 2K images, and allowing playback in a smaller window, but moving beyond the normal borders to view close-up detail of portions of the image controlled by the mouse pointer.

Packet Basic component of communication over a network. A group of bits of fixed maximum size and well-defined format that is switched and transmitted as a complete whole through a network. It contains source and destination address, data and control information. See also Frame.

Parallel Port A connection for the synchronous, high-speed flow of data along parallel lines to a device, usually a printer.

Parameter A variable, or quantity, that can assume any of a given set of values, of which there are two kinds: formal and actual.

Parity A method of error detection in which a small group of bits being transferred is compared to a single "parity" bit which is set to make the total bits odd or even. The receiving device reads the parity bit and determines if the data are valid based on the oddness or evenness of the parity bit.

Partition A section of the storage area of a hard disk. A partition is created during initial preparation of the hard disk, before the disk is formatted.

Patch Cables Short (2–5 foot) UTP cables that connect patch panels to hubs.

Patch Panel A panel containing a row of female connectors (ports) that terminate the horizontal cabling in the equipment room. Patch panels facilitate cabling organization and provide protection to horizontal cabling.

Path The route the operating system must follow to find an executable program stored in a subdirectory.

PBX *Private Branch Exchange*. A private phone system used within an organization.

PC *Personal Computer*. A more popular phrase than the more correct term microcomputer, PC means a small computer with its own processor and hard drive, as opposed to a dumb terminal connected to a central mainframe computer. Used in this fashion, the term PC indicates computers of many different manufacturers, using a variety of processors and operating systems. Although the term PC was around long before the original IBM PC was released, it has come to be almost synonymous with IBM-compatible computers, hence the incorrect but common question "Are you a Mac or a PC person?"

PCI *Peripheral Component Interconnect*. PCI is a design architecture for the sockets on the computer motherboard that enable system components to be added to the computer. PCI is a "local bus" standard, meaning that devices added to a computer through this port will use the processor at the motherboard's full speed (up to 33MHz), rather than at the slower 8 megahertz speed of the regular bus. In addition to moving data at a faster rate, PCI moves data 32 or 64 bits at a time, rather than the 8 or 16 bits that the older ISA busses supported.

PCMCIA *Personal Computer Memory Card International Association*. A consortium of computer manufacturers who devised the standard for credit card-sized adapter cards that add functionality in many notebook computers, PDAs, and other computer devices. The simpler term PC card has become more common in referring to these cards.

PDA *Personal Digital Assistant*. A handheld computer that blurs the line between the calculator and computer. Earlier PDAs were calculators that enabled the user to program in such information as addresses and appointments. Newer machines, such as the Palm Pilot, are fully programmable computers. Most PDAs use a pen/stylus for input rather than a keyboard. A few of the larger PDAs have a tiny keyboard in addition to the stylus.

Peer-to-Peer Networks A network in which each machine can act as either a client or a server.

Pentium Name given to the fifth generation of Intel microprocessors—distinct with 32-bit address bus, 64-bit external data bus, and dual pipelining. Also used for subsequent generations of Intel processors—the Pentium Pro, Pentium II, Pentium II Xeon, Pentium III, and Pentium III Xeon.

Peripheral Any device other than the motherboard components of the computer. The CPU is not a peripheral; the floppy drive is a peripheral.

Phosphor An electrofluorescent material used to coat the inside face of a cathode ray tube (CRT). After being hit with an electron, phosphors glow for a fraction of a second.

Physical Address A physical address defines a specific machine without any reference to its location or network. A MAC address is an example of a physical address.

PIM *Personal Information Manager*. A software application designed to hold and manage personal information such as phone numbers, contact notes, schedules, and to-do lists.

PING *Packet Internet Groper*. Slang term for a small network message (ICMP ECHO) sent by a computer to check for the presence and aliveness of another. Also used to verify the presence of another system.

PIO *Programmable Input/Output*. Using the address bus to send communication to a peripheral. The most common way for the CPU to communicate with peripherals.

PIO Mode A series of speed standards created by the Small Form Factor committee for the use of PIO by hard drives. The PIO modes range 0 to 4.

Pixel *Picture Element*. In computer graphics, the smallest element of a display space that can be independently assigned color or intensity.

Platen The cylinder that guides paper through an impact printer and provides a backing surface for the paper when images are impressed onto the page.

Platform Hardware environment that supports the running of a computer system.

Plenum Usually a space between a building's false ceiling and the floor above it. Most of the wiring for networks is located in this space. Plenum is also the fire rating of the grade of cable allowed to be installed in this location.

Plug-and-Play Also known as PnP. A combination of smart PCs, smart devices, and smart operating systems that automatically configure all the necessary system resources and ports.

POP *Post Office Protocol.* Also known as Point Of Presence. Refers to the way e-mail software such as Eudora gets mail from a mail server. When you obtain a SLIP, PPP, or shell account you almost always get a POP account with it; and it is this POP account that you tell your e-mail software to use to get your mail.

Populated Segment A segment that has one or more nodes directly attached to it.

Port That portion of a computer through which a peripheral device may communicate. Often identified with the various plug-in jacks on the back of your computer. On a network hub, it is the connector that receives the wire link from a node.

Port Number Number used to identify the requested service (such as SMTP or FTP) when connecting to a TCP/IP host. Some example port numbers include 80 (HTTP), 20 (FTP), 69 (TFTP), 25 (SMTP), and 110 (POP3).

PostScript A language defined by Adobe Systems, Inc. for describing how to create an image on a page. The description is independent of the resolution of the device that will actually create the image. It includes a technology for defining the shape of a font and creating a raster image at many different resolutions and sizes.

PPP *Point-to-Point Protocol.* A protocol that enables a computer to connect to the Internet through a dial-in connection and enjoy most of the benefits of a direct connection. PPP is considered to be superior to SLIP because of its error detection and data compression features, which SLIP lacks, and the ability to use dynamic IP addresses.

PPTP *Point-to-Point Tunneling Protocol.* Protocol that works with PPP to provide a secure data link between computers using encryption.

Program A set of actions or instructions that a machine is capable of interpreting and executing. Used as a verb, to design, write and test such instructions.

Promiscuous Mode A mode of operation for a network interface card where the NIC processes all packets that it sees on the cable.

Prompt A character or message provided by an operating system or program to indicate that it is ready to accept input.

Protected Mode The operating mode of a CPU to allow more than one program to be run while ensuring that no program can corrupt another program currently running.

Protocol An agreement that governs the procedures used to exchange information between cooperating entities; usually includes how much information is to be sent, how often it is sent, how to recover from transmission errors, and who is to receive the information.

Protocol Stack The actual software that implements the protocol suite on a particular operating system.

Protocol Suite A set of protocols commonly used together and operating at different levels of the OSI 7-layer model.

Proprietary Technology unique to a particular vendor is proprietary.

Proxy Server A device that fetches Internet resources for a client without exposing that client directly to the Internet. Most proxy servers accept requests for HTTP, FTP, POP3, and SMTP resources. The proxy server will often cache, or store, a copy of the requested resource for later use.

PSTN *Public Switched Telephone Network*. Also known as POTS (Plain Old Telephone Service). Most common type of phone connection that takes sounds—translated into an analog waveform by the microphone—and transmits them to the other phone.

PVC *Poly-Vinyl Chloride*. A material used for the outside insulation and jacketing of most cables. Also a fire rating for a type of cable that has no significant fire protection.

QIC *Quarter Inch Tape (or Cartridge)*. Tape backup cartridges that use quarter-inch tape.

Queue The waiting area for things to happen. Example: the printer queue, where print jobs wait until it is their turn to be printed.

RAID *Redundant Array of Inexpensive Devices (or Disks)*. A way of creating a fault-tolerant storage system. There are 6 levels. Level 0 uses byte-level striping and provides no fault tolerance. Level 1 uses mirroring or duplexing. Level 2 uses bit-level striping. Level 3 stores error correcting information (such as parity) on a separate disk, and uses data striping on the remaining drives. Level 4 is level 3 with block-level striping. Level 5 uses block-level and parity data striping.

RAM *Random Access Memory*. Memory in which any address can be written to or read from as easily as any other address.

Raster The horizontal pattern of lines that form an image on the monitor screen.

Real Mode The original 64K segmented memory, single-tasking operating mode of the Intel 8086 and 8088 CPUs.

Real-Time Processing of transactions as they occur rather than batching them. Pertains to an application in which response to input is fast enough to affect subsequent inputs and guide the process and in which records are updated immediately. The lag from input time to output time must be sufficiently small for acceptable timeliness. Timeliness is a function of the total system: missile guidance requires output within a few milliseconds of input, scheduling of steamships requires response time in days. Real-time systems are those with response time of milliseconds, interactive systems in seconds and batch systems in hours or days.

Refresh Repaint the CRT screen, causing the phosphors to remain lit (or change).

Remote Access The ability to access a computer from outside a building in which it is housed. Remote access requires communications hardware, software, and actual physical links.

Repeater A device that takes all the data packets it receives on one Ethernet segment and recreates them on another Ethernet segment. This allows for longer cables or more computers on a segment. Repeaters operate at Level 1 (physical) of the OSI 7-layer model.

Resolution A measurement expressed in horizontal and vertical dots or pixels for CRTs and/or printers. Higher resolutions provide sharper details and thus display better-looking images.

Resource Anything that exists on another computer that a person wants to use without going to that computer. Also an online information set or an online interactive option. An online library catalog and the local school lunch menu are examples of information sets. Online menus or graphical user interfaces, Internet e-mail, online conferences, telnet, FTP, and Gopher are examples of interactive options.

Ring Topology All the computers on a network attach to a central ring of cable.

RISC *Reduced Instruction-Set Computing.* A CPU design that requires that the processor handle very simple instructions. This allows the processor to execute these instructions at a very high speed. Motorola's PowerPC, used on both Mac and PC platforms, is an example of RISC design.

RJ *Registered Jack.* Connectors used for UTP cable for both telephone and network connections.

RJ-11 Type of connector with 4-wire UTP connections; usually found in telephone connections

RJ-45 Type of connector with 8-wire UTP connections; usually found in network connections and used for 10BaseT networking.

ROM *Read Only Memory*. The generic term for non-volatile memory that can be read from but not written to. This means that code and data stored in ROM cannot be corrupted by accidental erasure. Additionally, ROM retains its data when power is removed, which makes it the perfect medium for storing BIOS data or storing information such as scientific constants.

Root Directory The directory that contains all other directories.

Router A device connecting separate networks that forwards a packet from one network to another based only on the network address for the protocol being used. For example, an IP router looks only at the IP network number. Routers operate at Layer 3 (network) of the OSI 7-layer model.

Routing Table List of paths to various networks required by routers. This can be built either manually or automatically.

RS-232C A standard port recommended by the Electronics Industry Association for serial devices.

RTM Read The Manual.

RTFM Read The "Fine" Manual.

RTS Read The Screen.

RTFS Read The "Fine" Screen.

SAMBA An application that enables UNIX systems to communicate using SMBs (Server Message Blocks); which in turn enables them to act as Microsoft clients and servers on the network.

Scalability The ability to support network growth.

Scanner A device that senses alterations of light and dark. It gives you the ability to import photographs and other physical images and text into the computer in digital form.

SCSI *Small Computer System Interface*. A powerful and flexible peripheral interface popularized on the Macintosh and used to connect hard drives, CD-ROM drives, tape drives, scanners, and other devices to PCs of all kinds. Because SCSI is less efficient at handling small drives than IDE, it did not become popular on IBM-compatible computers until price reductions made these large drives affordable. Normal SCSI enables up to seven devices to be connected through a single bus connection, whereas Wide SCSI can handle 15 devices attached to a single controller.

Sector A segment of one of the concentric tracks encoded on the disk during a low-level format. Sectors hold 512 bytes of data.

Segment The bus cable to which the computers on an Ethernet network connect.

Sequential A method of storing and retrieving information that requires data to be written and read sequentially. Accessing any portion of the data requires reading all the preceding data.

Server A computer that shares its resources, such as printers and files, with other computers on the network. An example of this is a Network File System Server that shares its disk space with a workstation that does not have a disk drive of its own.

Server-Based Network A network in which one or more systems function as dedicated file, print, or application servers, but do not function as clients.

Session Networking term used to refer to the logical stream of data flowing between two programs and being communicated over a network. There may be many different sessions emanating from any one node on a network.

SDRAM *Synchronous DRAM.* DRAM that is tied to the system clock and thus runs much faster than traditional FPM and EDO RAM.

Share Level Security Security system in which each resource has a password assigned to it; access to the resource is based on knowing the password.

Shareware Protected by copyright; holder allows (encourages!) you to make and distribute copies under the condition that those who adopt the software after preview pay a fee to the holder of the copyright; derivative works are not allowed; you may make an archival copy.

Shell Generally refers to the user interface of an operating system. A shell is the command processor that is the actual interface between the kernel and the user.

Shunt A tiny connector of metal enclosed in plastic that creates an electrical connection between two posts of a jumper.

SIMM *Single In-line Memory Module.* A type of DRAM packaging distinguished by a number of small tabs which install into a special connector. Each side of each tab is the same signal. SIMMs come in two common sizes: 30-pin and 72-pin.

SL Enhanced A CPU that has the ability to turn off selected peripherals as well as run on low (3.3v or less) power. See also SMM.

SLIP *Serial Line Interface Protocol*. A protocol that enables a computer to connect to the Internet through a dial-in connection and enjoy most of the benefits of a direct connection. SLIP has been nearly completely replaced by PPP, which is considered superior to SLIP because of its error detection and data compression, features that SLIP lacks, and the ability to use dynamic IP addresses.

SMB *Server Message Blocks*. Protocol used by Microsoft clients and servers to share file and print resources.

SMM *System Management Mode*. A special CPU mode that enables the CPU to reduce power consumption via the selective shutdown of peripherals.

SMTP *Simple Mail Transport Protocol*. The main protocol used to send electronic mail on the Internet.

SNAFU Situation Normal, All Fouled Up.

SNMP *Simple Network Management Protocol*. A set of standards for communication with devices connected to a TCP/IP network. Examples of these devices include routers, hubs, and switches.

Socket A combination of a port number and an IP address that uniquely identifies a connection.

Software Programming instructions or data stored on some type of binary storage device.

Source Code The program in a language prepared by the programmer. This code cannot be directly executed by the computer and must first be translated into object code. Also the building blocks of an operating system or application.

Spool A scheme that enables multiple devices to write output simultaneously to the same device, such as multiple computers printing to the same printer at the same time. The data are actually written to temporary files while a program called a spooler sends the files to the device one at a time.

Spreadsheet Software program that enables users to perform mathematical calculations, such as budgeting, keeping track of investments, or tracking grades.

SPS *Stand-by Power Supply (or System)*. A device that supplies continuous clean power to a computer system immediately following a power failure. See also UPS.

SQL *Structured Query Language*. A language created by IBM that relies on simple English statements to perform database queries. SQL enables databases from different manufacturers to be queried using a standard syntax.

SRAM *Static RAM*. A type of RAM that uses a flip-flop circuit rather than the typical transistor/capacitor of DRAM to hold a bit of information. SRAM does not need to be refreshed and is faster than regular DRAM. It is used primarily for cache.

ST506 A model of hard drive developed by Seagate. This drive, as well as the WD1003 controller, developed by Western Digital, created the standard for the first generation of hard drives and controllers. As a result, any drive that copied the connections and BIOS commands of the ST506 is known as an ST506 drive.

Star Topology The computers on a network connect to a central wiring point.

Star Bus Topology A hybrid of the star and bus topologies. This topology uses a physical star, where all nodes connect to a single wiring point such as a hub, and a logical bus that maintains the Ethernet standards. One benefit of a star bus topology is fault tolerance.

Static Routing The process by which routers in an internetwork obtain information about paths to other routers. This information must be supplied manually.

Storage A device or medium that can retain data for subsequent retrieval.

STP *Shielded Twisted Pair*. A popular cabling for networks composed of pairs of wires twisted around each other at specific intervals. The twists serve to reduce interference (also called crosstalk); the more twists, the less interference. The cable has metallic shielding to protect the wires from external interference. A Token Ring network is the only common network technology that uses STP, although Token Ring more often now uses UTP.

Subnet In a TCP/IP internetwork, each independent network is referred to as a subnet.

Subnet Mask The value used in TCP/IP settings to divide the IP address of a host into its component parts: network ID and host ID.

Switch A device that filters and forwards traffic based on some criteria. A bridge and a router are examples of switches.

Synchronous Describes a connection between two electronic devices where neither must acknowledge ("ACK") when receiving data.

System BIOS The primary set of BIOS stored on an EPROM or Flash chip on the motherboard. Defines the BIOS for all the assumed hardware on the motherboard, such as keyboard controller, floppy drive, basic video, RAM, etc.

Sysop *System Operator*. A sysop is anyone responsible for the physical operations of a computer system or network resource. A system administrator decides how often backups and maintenance should be performed and the system operator performs those tasks.

T-1 A leased-line connection capable of carrying data at 1,544,000 bits per second.

T-3 A leased-line connection capable of carrying data at 44,736,000 bits per second.

TARFU Things Are Really Fouled Up.

TCP *Transmission Control Protocol.* Part of the TCP/IP protocol suite, TCP operates at Layer 4 (the transport layer) of the OSI 7-layer model. TCP is a connection-oriented protocol.

TCP/IP *Transmission Control Protocol/Internet Protocol.* A set of communication protocols developed by the U.S. Department of Defense that enables dissimilar computers to share information over a network.

TDR *Time Domain Reflectometer.* Advanced cable tester that tests the length of cables in addition to their continuity.

Telephony The science of converting sound into electrical signals, moving those signals from one location to another, and then converting those signals back into sounds. This includes modems, telephone lines, the telephone system, and any products used to create a remote access link between a remote access client and server.

Telnet A program that enables users on the Internet to log in to remote systems from their own host system.

Tera- A prefix that usually stands for the binary number 1,099,511,627,776; 2 to the 40th power. When used for mass storage, often shorthand for a trillion bytes.

Terminal A "dumb" device connected to a computer network that acts as a point for entry or retrieval of information.

Terminal Emulation Software that enables a PC to communicate with another computer or network as if it were a specific type of hardware terminal.

Terminating Resistor Any device that absorbs excess electrical signals off a wire. Examples include the device used at each end of a coaxial cable to absorb excess electrical signals—this helps avoid signal bounce or reflection. The level of resistance in an RG-58 coaxial cable requires these resistors to have 50 ohm impedance. Another device with the same name is used to terminate the ends of the SCSI chain.

Terabyte 1,099,551,627,776 bytes

TIFF *Tagged Image File Format.* A graphical file format in which images are divided into discrete blocks or strips called tags. Each tag contains formatting information—such as width, number of colors, etc.—for the entire image. The TIFF format is useful because it can describe many different types of images, but is also complex and difficult to write software for.

TLA *Three Letter Acronym.* Any acronym of three letters, such as FAT (File Allocation Table) and GIF (Graphics Interchange Format).

Token Ring A LAN and protocol in which nodes are connected together in a ring; a special packet called a token passed from node to node around the ring controls communication. A node can send data only when it receives the token and the token is not in use. This avoids the collision problems endemic in Ethernet networks.

Toners Generic term for two devices used together—a tone generator and a tone locator (probe)—to trace cable by sending an electrical signal along a wire at a particular frequency. The tone locator then emits a sound when it distinguishes that frequency. Also referred to as Fox and Hound.

Topology The pattern of interconnections in a communications system between devices, nodes, and associated input and output stations. Also describes how computers connect to each other without regard to how they actually communicate.

TRACERT Also TRACEROUTE. A command-line utility used to follow the path a packet takes between two hosts.

TSR *Terminate and Stay Resident*. A DOS program that mostly closes immediately after starting up, but leaves a tiny piece of itself in memory. TSRs are used to handle a broad cross-section of DOS-level system needs, such as running hardware (MOUSE.COM) or applying higher-level functionality to hardware already under the control of device drivers. MSCDEX.EXE, for example, assigns a drive letter to a CD-ROM drive after the CD-ROM driver has loaded in CONFIG.SYS.

TWAIN *Technology Without An Interesting Name*. A programming interface that enables a graphics application, such as a desktop publishing program, to activate a scanner, frame grabber, or other image-capturing device.

UART *Universal Asynchronous Receiver/Transmitter*. A device that turns serial data into parallel data. The cornerstone of serial ports and modems.

UDP *User Datagram Protocol*. Part of the TCP/IP protocol suite; an alternative to TCP. UDP is a connectionless protocol.

UMA *Upper Memory Area*. The memory area between the first 640K and 1024K reserved for system use and device drivers.

UMB *Upper Memory Block*. The open areas of the Reserved Memory (the 384K block above conventional memory) loading adapter ROM and device drivers.

UNIX A popular computer software operating system used on many Internet host systems.

UPS *Uninterruptible Power Supply*. A device that supplies continuous clean power to a computer system the whole time the computer is on. Protects against power outages and sags. The term UPS is often used mistakenly when people mean SPS.

Usenet The network of UNIX users, generally perceived as informal and made up of loosely coupled nodes, that exchanges mail and messages. Started by Duke University and UNC-Chapel Hill. An information cooperative linking around 16,000 computer sites and millions of people. Usenet provides a series of "news groups" analogous to online conferences.

User Anyone who uses a computer.

User Account A container that identifies a user to the application, operating system, or network, including name, password, user name, groups to which the user belongs, and other information based on the user and the OS or NOS being used. Usually defines the rights and roles a user plays on a system.

User-Level Security A Security system in which each user has an account; access to resources is based on user identity

User Profiles A collection of settings that correspond to a specific user account and may follow the user regardless of the computer at which he or she logs on. These settings enable the user to have customized environment and security settings.

URL *Uniform Resource Locator.* An address that defines the location of a resource on the Internet. URLs are used most often in conjunction with HTML and the World Wide Web.

USB *Universal Serial Bus.* A 12Mbps serial interconnect for keyboards, printers, joysticks, and many other devices. Enables hot-swapping and daisy-chaining devices.

UTP *Unshielded Twisted Pair.* A popular cabling for telephone and networks composed of pairs of wires twisted around each other at specific intervals. The twists serve to reduce interference (also called crosstalk). The more twists, the less interference. The cable has no metallic shielding to protect the wires from external interference, unlike its cousin, STP. 10BaseT uses UTP, as do many other networking technologies. UTP is available in a variety of grades, called categories, as defined below:

Category 1—UTP Regular analog phone lines—not used for data communications

Category 2—UTP Supports speeds up to 4 megabits per second

Category 3—UTP Supports speeds up to 16 megabits per second

Category 4—UTP Supports speeds up to 20 megabits per second.

Category 5—UTP Supports speeds up to 100 megabits per second.

VESA *Video Electronics Standards Association.* The Video Electronics Standards Association is a consortium of computer manufacturers that standardized improvements to common IBM PC components. VESA is responsible for the Super VGA video standard and the VLB bus architecture.

VGA *Video Graphics Array.* The standard for the video graphics adapter built into IBM's PS/2 computer. It supported 16 colors in a 640x480 pixel video display, and quickly replaced the older CGA (Color Graphics Adapter) and EGA (Extended Graphics Adapter) standards.

Virtual Pertaining to a device or facility that does not physically exist, yet behaves as if it does. For example, a system with 4 megabytes of virtual memory may have only one megabyte of physical memory plus additional (slower and cheaper) auxiliary memory. Yet programs written as if 4 megabytes of physical memory were available will run correctly.

Virus A program that can make a copy of itself without users necessarily being aware of it; some viruses can destroy or damage files, and generally the best protection is always to maintain backups of files.

Virus Definition or Data File Also called signature files depending on the virus protection software in use. These files enable the virus protection software to recognize the viruses on a system and clean them. These files should be updated often.

VLB *VESA Local Bus.* VESA local bus is a design architecture for the sockets on the computer motherboard that enable system components to be added to the computer. VLB was the first "local bus" standard, meaning that devices added to a computer through this port would use the processor at its full speed, rather than at the slower 8 megahertz speed of the regular bus. In addition to moving data at a faster rate, VLB moves data 32 bits at a time, rather than the 8 or 16 bits that the older ISA busses supported. Although it was common on machines using Intel's 486 CPU, modern computers now use PCI busses instead.

Volatile Memory that must have constant electricity in order to retain data.

Volume A physical unit of a storage medium, such as tape reel or disk pack that is capable of having data recorded on it and subsequently read. Also refers to a contiguous collection of cylinders or blocks on a disk that are treated as a separate unit.

VRAM *Video RAM.* A type of memory in a video display adapter that is used to create the image appearing on the CRT screen. VRAM uses dual-ported memory, which enables simultaneous reads and writes, making it much quicker than DRAM.

WAN *Wide Area Network.* A geographically dispersed network created by linking various computers and local area networks over long distances, generally using leased phone lines. There is no firm dividing line between a WAN and a LAN.

Warm Boot A system restart performed after the system has been powered and operating. This clears and resets the memory, but does not stop and start the hard drive.

WAV *Windows Audio Format.* The default sound format for Windows.

WB *Write Back.* Defines a certain type of SRAM cache where instructions from the CPU to write changes are held in the cache until there is time available to write the changes to main memory.

WIN32 A programming interface or API for an early PC 32-bit mode fully supported by Windows NT. Many functions are supported in Windows 3.x, and written to the Win32 subset to gain improved performance on a 386. Windows 3.x translates the 32-bit calls in an application into its native 16-bit calls.

Window A rectangular area on a display screen in which part of an image or file is displayed. The window can be any size up to that of the screen and more than one window can be displayed at once.

Windows A set of graphical operating systems produced by Microsoft, including Windows 95, Windows 98, and Windows NT. Also, in the case of Windows 3.x, a graphical shell for DOS.

WINIPCFG A command-line utility for Windows 95 and 98 machines that displays the current TCP/IP configuration of the machine; similar to IPCONFIG and IFCONFIG.

WINS *Windows Internet Name Service.* A name resolution service that resolves NetBIOS names to IP addresses.

Winsock *WINdows SOCKets.* Microsoft Windows implementation of the TCP/IP Sockets interface.

Word A group of 16 binary digits or two bytes.

Word Processor A program used to enter or edit text information in personal computers, often used to create a file before it is uploaded to a network; may also be used to process text after it has been downloaded.

Word-Wrap An editor feature that causes a word that will not fit on a line to be moved in its entirety to the next line rather than be split at the right margin.

Workstation A general-purpose computer small enough and inexpensive enough to reside at a person's work area for his or her exclusive use. It includes microcomputers such as Macintosh, and PCs running DOS, as well as high-performance desktop and tower computers.

WS *Wait State*. A microprocessor clock cycle in which nothing happens.

WT *Write Through*. Defines a certain type of SRAM cache where instructions from the CPU to write changes are pushed through the cache immediately, writing to the cache and the main memory at the same time.

WWW *World Wide Web*. The (graphical) Internet that can be accessed using Gopher, FTP, HTTP, telnet, USENET, WAIS, and some other tools.

XGA *Extended Graphics Array*. IBM video display to bring 1,024x768 resolution to monitors. Can display 65,536 colors at low resolution, and 256 at high resolution.

XMS *Extended Memory Services*. The RAM above 1 megabyte that is installed directly on the motherboard, and is directly accessible to the microprocessor. Usually shortened to simply "Extended" memory.

Xmodem A file transfer protocol (FTP) that provides error free asynchronous communications through telephone lines.

Ymodem A file transfer protocol (FTP) that is more robust than Xmodem; it features a time and date stamp transfer, as well as batch file transfers.

ZIF Socket *Zero Insertion Force Socket*. A socket for CPUs that enables insertion of a chip without much pressure. Intel promoted the ZIF socket with its overdrive upgrades. The chip is dropped into the socket's holes and a small lever is turned to lock them in. Somewhat replaced in modern motherboards by Slot 1 and Slot A architecture, but still in style in Super Socket 7 and Socket 370 motherboards.

Zmodem Streaming synchronous file transfer protocol (FTP) used by communication software. Very popular for downloading.

Index

Note: Boldface numbers indicate illustrations.

A

B

C

D

E

F

G

H

I

J

K

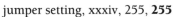

L

M

N

O

P

Q

R

S

T

U

V

W

X

About the Authors

MIKE MEYERS is the President and Head Computer Nerd of Total Seminars. Mike's idea of fun is to configure the latest NT Server beta while simultaneously kicking Brian's butt at Half-Life [Editor's Note—Mike wishes! Brian kicks HIS butt!]. He's one of those people you want around when something goes wrong with a computer or a network. With fifteen years experience in the computing industry, Mike recognized a need for good quality, easy to understand training materials for IT professionals. Thus came Total Seminars. His folksy manner, good humor, and clever teaching methods have attracted thousands to his videos, seminars, and books. Mike is the author of the popular McGraw-Hill's *A+ Certification Exam Guide*. E-mail Mike at **michaelm@totalseminars.com**.

BRIAN SCHWARZ realized sometime in the early '90s that playing with computers was more fun than his real job, and leapt into the computer training and course development field with both feet. Fortunately, he wasn't wearing his rollerblades at the time. As a member of the Total Seminars team, Brian has taught classes all over the United States for clients ranging from Lucent Technologies to the United States Army. Practicing what he teaches, Brian is a Microsoft Certified Systems Engineer (MCSE) and an A+ and Network+ Certified Technician. E-mail Brian at **brian@totalseminars.com**.

LIBBY INGRASSIA SCHWARZ has been in the computer industry doing technical writing, training, course development, and consulting in Lotus Notes, Windows NT, and other technologies since 1994. Although she would rather be writing poetry for a living, little things like food and a roof over her head have turned her into a Jill of All Trades—and mistress of several—in the industry. She has planned and implemented installations, taught classes, developed applications, and even slung cable through the bowels of major office buildings. E-mail Libby at **libbys@totalseminars.com** and maybe she will send you some Domino haiku.

Libby has so many certifications that she needs a higher ceiling on her office walls. She is a Microsoft Certified Systems Engineer, a Certified Lotus Professional in both Application Development and System Administration for R4 and R5, a Network+ Certified Technician, a Microsoft Certified Trainer, a Certified Lotus Instructor, and a Certified Technical Trainer.

SCOTT JERNIGAN wields a mighty red pen as Chief Technical Editor for Total Seminars. With a Master of Arts in Medieval History, Scott feels as much at home in the musty archives of London as he does in the warm CRT glow of Total Seminars' Houston headquarters. After fleeing a purely academic life, Scott has spent the last few years teaching computer hardware seminars around the United States, including stints at the FBI Academy and the United Nations, among others. E-mail Scott at **SCOTTJ@TOTALSEMINARS.COM**.

TOTAL SEMINARS is a unique group of teachers, authors, and presenters, who all share one common trait: we love computers. *Total* has many venues that enable us to display that love of computers, including seminars, videos, CD-ROMs, and books, such as the one you are reading right now. We have trained thousands of people from every level, including individuals as well as corporate, federal, state, and local government employees. Visit our Web site at **www.totalseminars.com**.

What's on the CD?

Your CD contains the **Total Seminars' Network+ Practice Examinations**. The practice exams on this CD are designed to give you *the closest experience to the actual Network+ exams possible*! There are a total of eight exams, each with 65 questions: two free exams plus six more exams that can be purchased online for only US$49! Just click on one of the extra exams for details.

All exams can be run in "Practice Mode" or "Exam Mode." The practice mode gives you hints and chapter references. The exam mode simulates the actual Network+ exam.

To install the test program, simply load the CD and the installation will start automatically. If the program fails to start automatically, just click the SETUP.EXE program.

For problems with installation, check the **Installation FAQ at <u>www.totalsem.com</u>** or call 800-446-6004.